Community Organization and Development

Community Organization and Development

from its history towards a model for the future

Steve Clarke

UNIVERSITY OF WALES PRESS
2017

www.uwp.co.uk

British Library CIP Data
A catalogue record for this book is available from the British Library

ISBN: 978-1-78683-0500
eISBN: 978-1-78683-0517

The right of Steve Clarke to be identified as author of this work has been asserted in accordance with sections 77 and 79 of the Copyright, Designs and Patents Act 1988.

Typeset by Marie Doherty

Printed by CPI Antony Rowe, Chippenham

Contents

Dedication

I learned my community development under rather harsh circumstances, under the apartheid regime in South Africa. Working with disadvantaged and displaced communities was politically risky as well as a challenging task in highly pressured social circumstances. Dr Harvey Cohen was the inspiration for the student charity, and development agency (WITSCO), which I ran for some four years. In addition to providing a 'womb to tomb' health and welfare service to a large Black community, this organisation gave rise to the foundations of political structures for Black South Africans. It also gave me my first six years in community development, both as fieldworker and manager. Names linked to Dr Cohen in this activity are Mary Edgington, Ronny Rosenbaum, Sheila Barsel, Paul Davies, Rodney Waldeck and Brian McKendrick. To them I owe my capability to begin this publication.

From South Africa, I came to London, where the late June Bell introduced me to poverty, disaffected youth, and the possibility to build healthy lives and vibrant communities out of the dispossessed in London. I was privileged, also, to be taught by Sugata Dasgupta, the Gandhian disciple, at the LSE in 1970/71. From being a 'white African', and all that brought with it, I was transformed into a listening, non-assertive, and capable community development worker. I was now much better equipped for working in the field.

Community development came to the social disarray of de-industrialising South Wales through the Young Volunteer Force Foundation project *Polypill*. Here, a community of about 7,000 people made me welcome, and we worked for 12 years to bring coherence and cohesion to a community blighted by 'planning' and officialdom. The team, over the years, comprised: Rose Hughes, Pat Charters, Joan Stacey, Steve Dowrick, Mike Fleetwood, Iona Gordon, Jane Hutt, Martin Notcutt and Martin Cumella. From each of them I was able to glean fresh insights into what was to become my burning passion – to bring community development to a wider audience, and to develop further its capacity to assist community life.

Swansea University sheltered me from the real world for the next 25 years, but the post-grad students in the Social Work and Health Science presented a fresh challenge every day. The (almost) truism that field workers do not read was brought home to me, and fresh insights into my trade were forthcoming in Swansea in abundance. Getting the chance to share in the acquisition of new knowledge with so many is a rare privilege.

To Terrie, who had to endure this long, drawn-out process for many years, and was a constant source of support and inspiration, I owe the greatest debt — Many thanks, indeed!

Foreword

Community development has been a prominent component of Welsh Government strategic thinking, not only in urban regeneration but across a wide range of Public Health issues as well. Since 1999, the devolved Welsh government has incorporated community development in all of its community-oriented social policy and through its *Communities First* programme, brought community capacity development and engagement into social planning as a priority. The Welsh Voluntary Sector, also, has produced vital results in the field of raising community awareness and capabilities. Community Development Cymru was funded by the Welsh Government to promote standards and support for community development across Wales.

This volume provides an important perspective on the pedigree of community development across the United Kingdom. It provides a theoretical platform on which today's practitioners can build their work. It also provides powerful insights into the history of professional practice in this field and links it convincingly with its other British connections. The research that has gone into this work shows how much community work in Wales, and in the UK generally, owes to the wider international scene, with the United States featuring prominently in this.

Steve Clarke is an experienced worker in this field, in Wales and across a variety of international settings. He has also demonstrated how engaging this subject can be at the level of educating future practitioners and managers in Public Health and for those planning social change. His book shows how challenging this activity can be and how a sound base of theory and discipline underpins success.

Mark Drakeford AM
Cabinet Secretary for Finance and Local Government
Welsh Government
Cardiff
June 2016

Acknowledgements

Acknowledgements are made to the following sources of figures used in the text:

Figure 1. Institute for Futures Studies, Stockholm, for: Dahlgren, Goran, and Whitehead, Margaret. (1991) *Policies and strategies to promote social equity in health*, Figure 1, p. 11.

Figure 5. Taylor & Francis, Abingdon, for: Plummer, J. (1999) *Municipalities and Community Participation: a sourcebook for capacity building*, Box 2.1, p. 8

Figure 8. Ashgate Publishing, Farnham, for: Clarke, S. J. G. (2000) *Social Work as Community Development: a management model for social change*, Figure 7, p. 265.

List of Figures

Abbreviations

ACW	Association of Community Workers
CCETSW	Central Council for Education and Training in Social Work
CDF	Community Development Foundation
CDJ	Community Development Journal
CDP	Community Development Project
CDP IIU	CDP Information and Intelligence Unit
CDWW	Community Development Workforce Wales
CPF	Community Projects Foundation
CtC	Communities that Care
CYC	Company of Young Canadians
DCLG	Department for Communities and Local Government
DETRs	Department of the Environment, Transport and Regions
EU	European Union
FCDL	Federation of Community Development Learning
HMSO	Her Majesty's Stationery Office
IASSW	International Association of Schools of Social Work
ICSSW	Independent Commission on Social Services in Wales
IDA	Improvement and Development Agency
IDS	Institute of Development Studies Sussex University
IIU	[CDP] Information and Intelligence Unit
IMF	International Monetary Fund
LDDC	London Docklands Development Corporation
LSE	London School of Economics
MSC	Manpower Services Commission
NAforW	National Assembly for Wales
NCSS	National Council of Social Service
NDC	New Deal for Communities
NHS	National Health Service [UK]
NISW	National Council for Social Work
NICE	National Institute for Health and Clinical Excellence
OCS	Office for Civic Responsibility
OECD	Organization for Economic Co-operation and Development

OFMDFM	Office of the First Minister and the Deputy First Minister (Northern Ireland)
ONS	Office of National Statistics
OPCforW	Older People's Commissioner for Wales
PSSRU	Personal Social Service Research Unit
QUANGO	Quasi-Autonomous Non-Governmental Organisation
SCDC	Scottish Community Development Centre
SCP	Southwark Community Project
SEU	Social Exclusion Unit
SIP	Single Integrated Plan
SRB	Single Regeneration Budget
TSO	The Stationery Office
UK	United Kingdom
UN	United Nations Organization
UNICEF	UN International Children's Emergency Fund
USA	United States of America
VISTA	Volunteers in Service to America
VSO	Voluntary Service Overseas
WAG	Welsh Assembly Government
WEFO	Welsh European Funding Office
WG	Welsh Government
WI	Women's Institute
WLGA	Welsh Local Government Association
WHO	World Health Organization
WHOEurope	WHO Regional Office for Europe
YVFF	Young Volunteer Force Foundation
YMCA	Young Men's Christian Association
YWCA	Young Women's Christian Association

Introduction

This book has been written because that there has never been a comprehensive history of community development. It attempts to trace that history and to link it, analytically, with the pressing social and economic issues that accompanied its evolution. The intention is to draw as much from this history such that lessons can be learned as to the nature and purpose of community development and how these can be applied to contemporary issues.

From this starting point, three factors emerge. The first is the unfulfilled role for community development in the delivery of the welfare needs of the community, particularly in its inability to promote itself successfully in the market place of professionalism.

Secondly, the many and mixed messages in the literature about the nature and objectives of community development have sowed confusion as to its real nature and purpose.

Thirdly and historically, many initiatives to introduce consistency into the social planning and locality development areas of public policy have failed due to the anomalies and disparities in social, material, physical and environmental development between peoples and geographical areas (Gilbert and Specht, 1977a).

Over the latter decades of the twentieth century, tackling these anomalies and disparities became the pressing agenda for the World's major agencies for social change – the United Nations and World Health Organization (WHO). One agenda heading on which international agreement could be reached with unusual facility was 'Health' – in particular 'Public Health'. This study focuses hard on health as broadly defined by the WHO, as a justification for community development intervention. It is the intention of this volume to clarify these issues and to provide an answer to them.

Lessons from America?

One of the most interesting aspects in the history of community development is that the paths it has taken in the USA and the UK are running in parallel with each other, with little practical contact between them. This is a great pity as each has a great deal to offer the other. Additionally, the tradition in the UK is that the practice models for 'internal', British consumption and for 'external' delivery to others, i.e. foreign beneficiaries, are separated by seemingly impermeable membranes. This phenomenon appears to extend throughout the textbook literature and the two seem to co-exist, separate but in parallel, within the journals. In the world of accountability, there is a much closer scrutiny of the British 'export model' due to the fact that it is mostly evaluated by government agencies. For the domestic 'internal model', however, the administration of programmes is fragmented across the many local authorities, driven by local priorities and politics. Thus, an overall analysis of what is going on, and why, is dominated more by political expediency or ideological posturing rather than on a collective approach. Consequently, an agreed measurement of outcomes is usually lacking. There are, therefore, a number of bridges to be crossed before a coherent message from community development can be understood – What are the messages, theory, practice models most often used in the USA, and in the UK? Why are there differences between the British model of community development used in the domestic British context and that which is exported as part of an international AID package? One earlier attempt to break down some of these barriers was firmly rejected by the reviewers back in 1998 (Oakley, 1998).

This is not so in the USA, where the 'export model', at least in part, learns from and feeds into the 'internal model' (Ohmer and DeMasi, 2009). We have a definite view on the American practice models that we analyse later. We will use it to assist us in putting right the deficit in the British approach. The reader will discover here that there are no insuperable barriers to achieving this. The synthesising of philosophies, principles and models from widely differing contexts into one thorough-going framework for application in the field is not just possible, but it is an imperative for progress.

The most interesting aspect of the American scene is the co-existence of two distinct models of social intervention by professional community development workers. One of these models is based upon consensus outcomes but the second is predicated upon the professional interventions being focused upon conflict between interest groups – namely between the more powerless elements of society and their more powerful and, usually, institutional opponents. Conflict modelling is not an option for most British community development interventions, largely because of the lack of independence in funding. The pervading philosophy of the Welfare State paying for most social change initiatives permeates the thinking of the citizen at large, and this produces a stricture on thinking about ownership and control of objectives.

The need for change in Britain

There is great pressure on governments to find effective and yet financially viable ways of providing health and welfare support for its vulnerable citizens. In Britain, with its Welfare State, there is constant tension between the expanding needs and expectations of the population and the ability to provide the services to them. This is because the health and welfare services are still, mostly, paid for by general taxation, and, in principle, universally available and for the most part free at the point of delivery. In parallel to the debate about the quantities and priorities for service delivery and the incessant pressure on funding, runs the constant examination of outcome choices and quality objectives. The well-being and even 'happiness' of the beneficiaries is now firmly on the official agenda (Layard, 2011). There have been calls for major restructuring of the way in which the services are paid for and provided (e.g. Wanless, 2002), but no clear direction has emerged. Apart from increasing strictures on finance, reform from within the system is slow in coming. Consequently, the funding crisis persists without any real reduction in the financial liability of the public purse. The question remains: can a cheap and sustainable remedy be found to bridge these difficulties, given that there is considerable political and social resistance to the raising of tax levels? The spiralling costs of social care in particular, and the inability of the state and the individual citizen to meet them may force politicians and citizens to contemplate a new form of social contract. Were this to be the case, this volume hopes to provide a template for its application.

Given that the available fiscal resources are committed to maintaining what can be preserved within the existing Welfare State, one of the few openings that might be available to government is the exploitation of the community itself to engage in the support of the welfare system. The direct engagement of the citizen in the support for its vulnerable and needy members has to be imagined if the core Health Service is to be sustained. Given that it is the taxes of the community that already provide for the running costs of the 'universal' welfare state, this might be a tall order. In Britain, expectations are already long-established that the State supports the vulnerable and the sick. Can a mechanism be found that would get around this seeming contradiction – of persuading the community to pay twice, once through taxation, and secondly in kind, through structured and administered voluntary work, for the non-clinical aspects of health and well-being? This would be a workable process to achieve the freeing up of mainstream taxation to pay for the acute services.

Of foremost importance, any such structuring would have to be reliable and sustainable. A completely fresh model of welfare delivery would have to be developed for this purpose and a dynamic tension around the question of ownership – by the State or by the community doing the work – would have to be resolved. The political risks would be considerable as it involves supporting vulnerable people and the solving of social issues that arise. The vested interests built up over sixty years of public investment in physical structure, demarcation protocols and funding patterns within the Welfare State will have to be co-opted or overcome. There is now an imperative for new thinking and deployment of scarce resources. Revised objectives and priorities are urgently needed. Indeed, universality could not be aspired to nor significant coverage be attained for some years whilst the new approach was bedded in. Moreover, the community itself urgently needs to be engaged in defining its needs and setting its priorities. The survival of the whole system is at stake.

It can be demonstrated that community development, backed by the resolve of state policy, together with compliant and focused public administrators, can be the most appropriate vehicle for starting this process. Nevertheless, it is recognised that there are considerable difficulties in promoting a model for social reform, within or across international boundaries. Some of these can be explained by the differences in cultural perceptions and established institutional practices. These might constitute barriers to their being adopted and for their significance being fully understood or prioritised. Consequently, compromises might have to be made in defining what is offered, and in describing some of the consequences and outcomes that might emerge. One of the questions that will be addressed is: can and should a firm model be identified, applied and justified in the cause of planned social change?

Special reference to Wales and the WHO

Since the hand-over of the reins of power from the Welsh Office to the devolved National Assembly for Wales in 1999, and even before that, all policies pertaining to Wales have contained the core philosophies developed by the World Health Organization (WHO), viz.:

> the promotion of social responsibility for health; increased investment for health development; consolidation and expansion of partnerships; increasing community capacity and individual empowerment; securing an infrastructure for health promotion (WHO Jakarta Declaration, 1997a).

Welsh Government policy documents have upheld this framework, but it has not been easy to obtain the necessary progress at the point of service management or, more pertinently, at the point of service delivery. The strengths and weaknesses of the Welsh situation will be reviewed in detail as it attempts to keep pace with the WHO and also to provide leadership for the other nations of the UK. As will be shown, policy advances in the field of the elderly have led the way, but limitations of government have seen these positives fall short in terms of a thorough-going model for problem-solving where Wales's elderly population needs it most – in social care. We will explore the varied routes adopted in England in the search for similar outcomes – 'beacon' authorities, the *Big Society* concept for volunteering, etc. The Care Act 2014 (for social care in England) shows that the Westminster Government is anxious to catch up with Wales. Thus, many of the concepts of the pioneering Welsh policies are now embedded in this legislation.

Providing a perspective

The reasoning behind the claim that a structured and sustainable model can be delivered will be developed. This entails both a history of community development and an analysis of previous approaches to harnessing the public towards problem-solving activities for common cause. The outcome is a model for a public intervention programme that engages the community and the public administrative resources on agreed and focused objectives. The community development process is the catalytic and enabling function that knits the whole process together.

The history of community development within the UK really begins in the 1970s with the Government's search for a way to head off potential urban unrest around housing and racial issues. But the pedigree of community development stretches back over more than a century and a half before that. Additionally, whereas the germ of the idea may have emerged initially in Britain, the hard work of analysing, implementing and refining its methodology and underlying philosophy was done in the United States. This is a factor scarcely acknowledged in Britain. Some of the reasons for this lie in the British fear of embracing ideological or messianic tendencies that come with the emergence of distinct 'schools of thought' on this matter. In the United States, there is now an established 'sector' for localised development that embraces the private, not-for-profit and academic interest groups. There, a combination of 'market forces', opportunism, pragmatism and localised political preferences all compete in a scramble for acceptability. These all appear to contradict and oppose the philosophy of 'universalism' inherent in the British 'Welfare State' and may explain why Britain lags so far behind. In Britain, it appears to be almost taboo to invoke the American experience or thinking on the matter. As there is so much to learn from the American practice models, this book will attempt to challenge the taboo and rectify the deficit.

Chapter 1 outlines the broad approach to thinking on this subject, together with providing some definitions. Lewis Carroll's famous example of dogmatism will be gently applied here. Thus spake Humpty Dumpty in *Through the Looking Glass* (Carroll, 1939, p. 181): 'When I use a word, ... it means just what I choose it to mean – neither more nor less.' Communication is dependent on the acceptance of a common language, at least for the duration of any meaningful discussion and it is necessary here as some words in common usage need to be identified and defined. A connection will be made with international policy attitudes towards the engagement of the community in taking responsibility for, the planning of and the delivery health services, as seen through the prism of WHO initiatives since the late 1940s. Reference will be made to the evolution of a transparent policy towards the development and regeneration of communities in Wales. Here, all social policy since 1998 has been defined by its requirement for social development, partnership and community participation. The reasoning for its only partial success in this regard will be examined. Examples and shifts in trend from England, Scotland and Northern Ireland will also be included.

Chapter 2 outlines the development of thinking, social intervention and problem solving both in Britain and the United States, from the middle of the eighteenth century to 1940. The date 1940 is significant in the progression of thinking in the United States as it marks a milestone in the acceptance of community development in institutional behaviour. It will be shown how, in the United States but not in the United Kingdom, the thinking behind the Settlement movement was carried into creative forms that allowed the boundaries of institutional control to be reversed in favour of the population at large.

Chapter 3 continues with the analysis of social planning, neighbourhood intervention and social action in the United States. It identifies the major ideological differences between 'schools of thought' on these approaches to planned social change and identifies the major players in the field.

Chapter 4 returns to the history of community development in the United Kingdom. In addition to describing the thinking that shapes community development intervention, it outlines the attempts by the government of harnessing this discipline with the intention of social engineering. An explanation will be provided of why this failed within an ethos of ambivalence and indecision and how a fresh approach might be more successful.

Chapter 5 provides a thorough analysis of all the strands that have emerged and will conclude with the development of a sustainable and measurable model that might successfully be applied for tackling the severe social issues that have emerged from the weakness of the Welfare State described above. Systems theory will be the vehicle for creating the final model. In the final analysis, some of the clearest thinking on the subject comes not from the United States but from the analysis obtained from British and International agencies' work in developing countries. If the American models are extended to include this, then a firm grasp can be taken of the challenge of applying a model that might have universal application.

This study has been informed by 50 years of fieldwork within many ethnic, cultural and political settings. Some of these experiences have been positive for all concerned, for others not so much so. Community development is a mixture of vision, mission, application and good fortune. It has to be supported by the idea that its ends are attainable, but that the costs of failure have to be minimised. Community development, however transparent it may be designed to be, is a vehicle of unequal power relations. At the very least, community development is a political intervention and so there is no real escape from the incursion of ideological motives, influences and covert agendas. It is hoped that the model that is developed here will reduce the influence of these forces and enable all participants, through high levels of engagement, to sustain their motivation to carry on.

As a reference point for the development of this analysis and model, the area targeted for reference has been the aging sector of society. It is a topical area: culturally, economically, and policy-wise. In all these dimensions of policy interest, it presents critical and unresolved boundaries between the general concern of the public at large and official policy. In any area of social intervention, the application of community development principles and practice models demands a high degree of flexibility, at all levels: conceptualisation, planning, management, recruitment and application. Our ageing population presents many complex issues demanding resolution and, therefore, presents an engaging target for this analysis.

1

Background to community development and its relevance to sustainable planning

Methodology issues, definitions and the challenges facing an ageing society

The underlying questions

Around the globe, community development is practised in many settings — rural, urban, developed economies, developing economies, long-term, short-term — with diverse forms and value systems. Nevertheless, the claims are that it actually conforms to a basic vision across this wide terrain (Midgley, 1995). Weil puts it thus: 'the essential purpose of strengthening communities and services and pressing for access, equality, empowerment and social justice ...' (Weil, 2013, p. xi). The difficulty with development of any kind is that, for it to be relevant and effective, it is dependent on the local context and situation for its priorities and methods. Consequently, the language used to describe and explain what is going on can be extremely localised to a culture or geography. The different ways in which it has developed, therefore, may now act as much as barriers to meaningful communication between those practising the same 'art' in different locations and/ or from within different cultures. In the United States, for example, creating a *'consensus'* means something completely different for disciples of the late Saul Alinsky than it does for graduates of Michael Eichler's *Consensus Organizing Center* at San Diego State University (Alinsky, 1972; Eichler, 2007). For the one it means *'we agree amongst ourselves against "them"'*, whereas for the other it means *'we all agree, inclusively'*. One person's *'conflict'* is another person's *'consensus'*. In the UK, these words are hardly ever used, perhaps because there is a certain coyness about being explicit about the role of professional organisers. In the British approach, *'process'* is more important than defining the concrete objectives (Ledwith and Springett, 2010). Social engineering is held to be a taboo role for this kind of 'social worker' and it is now rare to find a 'social worker' who has even heard of community development. In the parlance of international development agencies, however, the targeted funding of intervention in local cultures and environments is taken as for granted in order to accomplish 'beneficial' outcomes for the local population and for society as a whole (Islam, 2015; Department of Social and Economic Affairs, 2014).

Can the gulf between these idealistic and pragmatic differences be bridged? In the face of the social and economic problems facing all societies and the need for there to be agreement, common purpose and understanding between like-minded professionals, there is an urgent need for consensus around the way thinking and practice might progress. This volume will undertake to come to grips with where and why some of these differences occurred, how a synthesis of thinking might be forged and how consistency over time and place might be regulated.

One of the practical reasons that this might be needed is encapsulated in the situation facing older people in developed societies. Vulnerable older people need sustainable support. This can be variable over time and also intimate in nature. So, can we design a model of community development that will provide a viable framework for this? Can such a model be applied across geographical and cultural boundaries through the use of universally recognised frameworks and measurements? This is a reasonably straightforward question, but it disguises many complex issues. These issues and the questions they raise will be expanded and discussed in the subsequent Chapters. In this section, the aim is to set out a framework, through which this task might be pursued, and to describe, as well as define, many of the basic terms and frames of reference that have to be used in getting into the subject. Unfortunately, the terminology in this subject area is an arena where fashion, ideology and practice usage change continuously. This makes a time-line analysis of the material a task requiring continuous adjustment and redefinition of terminology.

Example: President Obama was a Community Organizer before he became a Member of the US Senate. In America, *Community Organization* is a generic term, within which *community development* is a specific practice sector. In America, to be a *community organizer* is to be contracted into a paid, leadership role that has to deliver a consensus outcome, or, alternatively, to create organised strategies for conflict (see below). In any event, the role is one of paid, organisational leadership that enables the community to achieve any of the social, political, or economic objectives that they, the community, might agree (Ganz, and Hilton, 2010). Did the fact that Barack Obama worked for a *'faith-based'* organisation have any effect on the way he worked or the sort of objectives that were prioritised while he was there? It is this sort of question that needs some transparency through the application of a framework analysis.

In the US, the 'theory', and creation of practice models is expressed through the generic portal of *community organization*. In the UK, the generic term is '*community development*', where, to make matters more difficult, the term *community organisation* (with an 's') means 'working developmentally with a number of established organisations'. In the U.S., this is called *social planning*. Whereas, in the UK, *community organization* means working through a <u>conflict</u> model of development, it can sometimes be called *community action*, or *social action*. As the dictionary is ambivalent about the usage of a 'z' or an 's' in the word 'organisation/organization', the definition of terms and location of usage is going to have to be specified carefully. In this work, <u>*community development*</u> will be used as the generic term, unless otherwise specified.

Resource materials for the research

This analysis has been greatly aided by the new transparency and availability of source materials from government agencies. In the case of the UK Government, the Scottish Government and the (regional) Welsh Government, a great depth of material is readily available through their websites, as all official documentation is in the public domain. This feature also applies to most official sources in the UK (NHS, for example), and also to many of the prominent Voluntary Organisations. The latter material is especially important for it is on the Internet that much of the ongoing commentary and analysis of state policy is posted by the not-for-profit sector, and, in some instances, by the for-profit sector as well. All public policy in this field of study is heavily analysed and scrutinised by the independent, non-state sectors, and thus state policies receive highly critical, public appraisal.

The same approach exists towards communication with the public across the technologically developed world with whom the British are accustomed to communicate (basically, the 'Old' Commonwealth). Additionally, there is a wealth of material in the United States of America, where every policy and service option appears to have been attempted and evaluated across the decades by many States and institutions. Of even greater significance to us, however, is the archive of historical material on *community organization*. From the very earliest days of experimentation with community organization, Americans have been writing books about their experience, and much of the earliest material is now available on the Internet through: www.archive.org. This archive covers government-sponsored work as well as voluntary sector activities, particularly religious organisations. Significant documents have emerged providing detailed insights into the efforts of American institutions, using problem-solving approaches, to deal with the most pressing problems of their times. These include: poverty (Residents and Associates, 1903); agricultural and rural communities (Lever/US Dept of Agriculture, 1913); the work of Edward Devine (1904; 1916); the first organised texts on the methods and objectives of community organization (Hanifan, 1914; Clarke, 1918; State Council for Defense, 1918; Follett, 1919; Hart, 1920). Wilson demonstrated how this organizing had by now assumed professional status (Wilson, 1919), and in the 1920s, McMechen pointed us in the direction of what we now call *community social work* (McMechen, 1920). McClenahan described how complex the role might be when real leadership had to be disguised in the name of carving a consensus out of confusion. Tactics and strategies had to be varied according to the setting of the work (McClenahan, 1922). Thus, when the Lane Committee (1940) was set up by the US National Conference of Social Work to formalise *community organization* within American Social Work, it was armed with a wealth of texts and practice examples. This Committee set out formal definitions and instructions for community organization. It attempted to highlight the theoretical progress that has been made to date and to draw a line under the development in the field up to the beginning of the Second World War. This was an opportune moment because the ensuing economic and social change the War brought about were to have profound influences on the future of community organization. Nevertheless, we can discern from these early works some of the symptoms of lax definition and omission, which continue to bedevil communication and understanding within social policy concerning community development today.

Despite the fact that contemporary American community development/organization workers contribute regularly to the (British) *Community Development Journal* (CDJ) about current practice in the United States, there is scant mention of American approaches, theories, models or practice in the British literature. This may signify that some of the salient themes found in current social policy in the UK, and as is reflected in practice analysis in the literature, displays little cross-fertilisation across national boundaries. Community development practice, as reflected in current policy, is focused upon issues such as partnership, inter-organisational practice, etc. Consequently, the absence of American experience from the internal British discussion on these subjects shows that the essential values purported by the occupation do not extend as far as international co-operation and/or the mutual recognition of much intellectual exchange.

This discrepancy arises historically, because American (and other foreign) material passes more or less without comment in the annals of community development in the UK and the Commonwealth. The first, and, in reality, the only significant mention in the UK literature of the early American experience appears in the Colonial Office booklet/Report on British plans to develop democratic institutions in the (mainly African) Colonies and Empire holdings (Colonial Office: Advisory Committee, 1943). It is explained that (p. 54, paraphrased) in the southern states of the USA, there is work going on in the 'extension' field among disadvantaged Afro-Americans. Black and White live alongside each other but with insurmountable economic and social barriers between them. Health and other specialised workers (agriculture, education, for example) worked alongside each other as a Field Service Unit. They demonstrate how a local school can become a focus for joint action and how the general community can move forward together. They 'awaken the people to a sense of their needs'... and how to meet them.

This publication marks the dawn of British literature on community development, spawning the *Community Development Bulletin*, the forerunner of the CDJ. The *'Bulletin'* was specifically designed to act as a communication vehicle for British Colonial development administrators, District Commissioners, and the like, as they pushed their respective colonial dependants towards Independence. Based at London University, the *Bulletin* was edited for most of its life by Professor T. R. Batten, who wrote the earliest texts for British overseas development workers (see Batten, 1957; etc.). These texts attempt to translate policy into a framework that is somehow an 'approved practice methodology'. In investigating the heirs to these early works, we shall see that, in many respects, things have not moved on very far. Luckily, these texts are readily available (the exception being the CD Bulletin).

England and Wales: the role of the state and the development of social policy

Of critical importance today is the question of the role of the State in the process of financial and social support for communities, particularly the situation of older people. In light of the build-up of excessive demand for social, residential and community support for an increasingly ageing population, a mechanism is required to ensure that the necessary support can be generated (Acheson, 1998; HM Government, 1999; National Assembly for Wales (NAforW), 2001; Welsh Assembly Government (WAG), 2003c; Ministry of Health, 2014a, b). Both within and outwith government circles, there is general agreement that the continued reliance by the state on a network of benefits and social services to provide social and financial support for the vulnerable members of society is costly, variable in benefit and difficult to manage successfully. Specifically, for those trying to reduce the influence of, and burden on, the state in these matters, it has not proved malleable or responsive enough (Auditor General, 2006; WAG, 2003a). Thus, the possibility of a fresh approach to this question might be welcomed by those planning future social policy. Part of the way forward is to engage the client groups themselves in the exercise of planning and delivering services. The WAG Strategy for Older people put it thus: 'To enhance the engagement with and participation of older people in society and at all levels of government' (WAG, 2003c, p. 14). It is interesting to note the direction from which this initiative is coming – from the top down, and not vice versa (Bury, 2008).

For well over a decade, there has been a continuing crisis in public finances (Wanless, 2002). This has been generated by a steadily increasing public expenditure on health and welfare services, a general lack of growth in the tax base in a sluggish economy, a legacy of fiscal confusion and increased national debt. In the UK as a whole, net government debt has risen from 38% of Gross National Product to just over 60% in 2010 (Office for National Statistics (ONS), 2010) and to 86.2% by January, 2015 (ONS, 2015a, b). This process continues to worsen despite budget control over public spending. Figures for Regional Governments are distorted due to the Barnet Formula funding structure and the responsibility for debt interest by the UK Treasury (Twigger/House of Commons Library, 1998). The Government is now obligated nationally and internationally to reduce public expenditure drastically in order to create a more viable economy for the future prosperity of the nation. These internal austerity policies and its dependence on stagnant international markets for exports, consign the economy to slow progress for some time to come.

In light of this, in the welfare sector, consequent upon a demographic shift towards an older population, together with a measurable and predictable increase in the number of these people living at the margins of financial sustainability, pressure on public services is likely to become more intense than ever (WAG, 2007a; Independent Commission for Social Services, 2010). This question is dealt with in detail below, in Chapter 5. From the study of the policies, both national and international, it will be seen that there are some, albeit not many, explicit references and exhortations to administrations that they should seek alternative and expanded approaches to providing support for their vulnerable populations (Centers for Disease Control, 2007; Chief Medical Officer, 2004; Dahlgren and Whitehead, 2006; Whitehead and Dahlgren, 2006; Department of Health, 2009; Norman, 2010; Welsh Assembly Government, 2003a; WHO 1986; 1997 b, c). Where explicit direction is given, however, there is also guidance as to how and when it should be administered. According to the National Institute for Health and Clinical Excellence (NICE), this should start with the engagement of the community in the planning, initiation and evaluation of any community-based activities in the name of transparency, relevance and sustainability (NICE, 2015). This is in support of the Department of Health's holistic policy for the 'New' Public Health in England, where the responsibility for health is shifted towards the engagement of the local community and away from the clinical services (Dept of Health, 2011). Health and Well-being Boards will have the responsibility for this process of community engagement (Dept. of Health, 2011, p. 2). The National Health Service requires the same shift in thinking and service delivery at the community level if its forward planning is to make any headway. Fresh and creative initiatives, which cut across the previously demarcated boundaries in Primary Care, have to be brought in. A good example of this is the *Dementia Friendly Communities* being built locally by the Alzheimer's Society (National Health Service, 2014, p. 15; Green and Lakey, 2013).

A limiting force in this process is that the State, from the national level, has certain limits to its powers to intervene at the local level. These powers have been delegated to local government across centuries of struggle, negotiation and as a consequence of the advance of democracy and active citizenship at all levels. In the case for the 'New Public Health' in England, however, the Department of Health will retain a strong direct linkage with the new Local Authority Health and Well-being Boards (Dept of Health, 2011, p. 4). The creation of the Scottish

Government (Scotland Act 1998) and the NAforW (Government of Wales Act 1998) opened up a fresh approach to transparency in the relationship between regional government and the local civil administrations.

(Note: the NAforW recognised in 2000 that it needed to distinguish between actions and policies of the Welsh Government Executive from the overall instrument of governance in Wales. NAforW became the legal term for the instrument of governance, while WAG became the name of the Executive, its policies and administrative processes. In 2011, the WAG was re-named the 'Welsh Government' (WG).)

One of the earliest of such policy documents, prepared as a foundation framework for the new NAforW (Welsh Office, 1998c), set out the stall of 'central' government (NAforW) in its role of influence over local authority activities, in public health in particular. *Better Health Better Wales* (Welsh Office, 1998a, 4–5) made explicit the form of local administration that it wanted to see implemented: the cornerstone of the NAforW's policy for sustainable health 'is to put in place new partnerships and real collaboration aimed at sustainable health and well-being'. At the local level, each of the determinants of health affected by public policy – environment, employment, housing, access to leisure, health and social care, education and other services – should be considered together rather than as separate policies, taking into account their potential impact on health (Welsh Office, 1998a, p. 4, *et seq*.). In this, the Welsh take-off point for national government incorporated a holistic definition of 'health' and introduced the concept of 'well-being' within its core principles. In Scotland, 'well-being' only became a key strategic goal from 2007 onwards (Scottish Government, 2007), but for England, this did not take place until 2010 (Cabinet Office, 2013a). From 1999, in Wales, at least, the new structure for government was going to aim at ensuring that wasteful and outdated methods of administration were jettisoned in favour of those which might bring more immediate benefit, better value for money, and more efficient working practices into being.

Britain's Thatcher Government, in 1985, instigated considerable limitations of local authority spending powers through its 'Rate Capping' policy and intrusive audits into Local Government financial expenditure (Local Government Finance Act 1982). When fresh financial strictures became inevitable in 2003, as the considerable government deficit first became a publicly stated fact (Wanless, 2002; WAG, 2003a), WAG clearly reflected the dilemmas in spending options. This brought to the surface the knock-on consequences of the planned restrictions for local government, as WAG debated the ring fencing of spending for the National Health Service in Wales (Williamson, 2010). There will be more references to the attempts by WAG to adhere to a consistency of emphasis on public health as it develops public policies over its first sixteen years of existence.

There is a need, also, to consider the stance that the State takes on the question of community development. Care has been taken to consider various terms associated with planned social change, sustainability, and development. The State has at certain times faced in contradictory directions regarding the values, the models and the means for obtaining social change through this medium. In many respects, community development represents the essential contradiction of: 'government of the people, by the people'.

As will be shown, across the UK, community development, at both the national and at the local level of government, has become a contrivance for the manipulation of people, communities, and agencies of government, themselves, for the creation of social change. The direction of this change has (mostly) been, at the very least, mapped in advance by an agency empowered and primed for that role. In other words, community development, at the level of government, can represent central or regional governmental interference in local affairs. At the local level, community development can (usually, must) represent local governmental interference in the democratic processes (Addams, 1912; State Council of Defense, 1918; McClenahan, 1922; Loney, 1983; Rothman, 2001; Clarke, et al., 2002a). It will be shown that in different countries the State may adopt a different attitude towards social change. In fact, the British State may affect different standards and plan different outcomes, depending on where this investment is made. In Scotland, national policies prevail over local government, whereas in Wales central government exerts less influence over local priorities. More glaring anomalies arise elsewhere. As a proportion of UK Overseas AID is devoted to community development objectives, the literature may reflect this in a variety of ways. At the very least, it represents a decided UK influence in the domestic affairs of another sovereign state to which AID is given. This study will endeavour to determine what the differences are in this regard. For these reasons, it is necessary to determine just what is meant by the term 'community development'.

We must also distinguish between spontaneous, and even continuous, organised, citizen action and those activities that are the outcome of a focused intervention by an agent of some kind, who has the specific intent of promoting development. This distinction also extends to the creation and sustaining of local institutional activity: for example, religious organisations, local campaigns around 'political' issues such as traffic congestion.

Community development

There are a number of terms currently in use to describe this activity: community development (Barr, et al., 1996; Clarke, 1996a; Craig, et al., 2004), community organization (Ross, 1955; Brager and Specht, 1973; Rothman, 2001a), community organisation (Henderson and Salmon, 1995), community regeneration (Adamson, et al., 2001), community empowerment (Craig, G. and Mayo, M., 1995); social action (Cannan, C. and Warren, C., 1997), social development (Midgley, 1995), social planning (Marris, 1982; Plummer, 1999), community health development

16

(Thomas, 1995a; Labonté, 1999); rural development, (Chambers, 1983); social work (Lane, 1940; Clarke, 2000), neighbourhood work (Henderson and Thomas, 1987), participatory practice (Ledwith and Springett, 2010), communitarianism (Etzioni, 1993), ... even, under exceptional circumstances, community work (Calouste Gulbenkian, 1968, 1973; Popple, 1995; Twelvetrees, 2008).

A definition I have used myself in teaching has evolved over thirty years into one that provides the broadest canopy to cover the greatest number of possible scenarios for this kind of intervention – viz.:

> Community Development is a professional intervention strategy, aimed at producing a programme of planned social change. This involves the mobilisation and integration of the maximum amount of social and other resources at all levels for the achievement and sustaining of that change.

Within this process, the professional community development worker assumes the responsibility of preparing and organising the social and institutional forces available, notably the local and greater community, its organisations at every level, and the setting up of the appropriate planning structures and implementation programmes. This involves: liaison with established institutions and organisations, the recruitment, identification and training of leaders and other support personnel, the creation of new organisations and organisational structures, and the development of learning processes which help to sustain existing activities and nurture fresh initiatives. The recording, monitoring and evaluating of these processes and their effects is of critical importance.

There are a number of distinct schools of thought involved in this terminology, and it will be a task of this study to separate them. What we do know now is that there is a more-or-less complete divide between American literature and British (including the Commonwealth) literature. Also, there is virtually no cross-over between the literature describing 'developed economies community development' and that describing 'developing economies community development'. It will be necessary to interpret this terminology, and to establish themes from the philosophical strands that emerge from the literature and to examine the action frameworks across and within these schools of thinking. The question of just what constitutes 'professionalism' within the definition is another moot point. Does the 'professional', working for an agency, and as a person with training, personal ethical and moral outlooks, take direction, and, if so, from whom – the 'client population', if identifiable, or the employer? Is there such a thing as professional independence and autonomy in these matters? Who is managing the planning, and for whom? Although there are National Occupational Standards for qualification in community development, there is ample room for argument about the value approach of workers in defining their actual client group, deciding how ethical boundaries are to be drawn, and how priorities are established in setting objectives. The role of *social planning* (see below) within community development is of special significance in this discussion (PAULO, 2003; Barr, 1996; Clarke, 2000; Clarke, 2004a; Communities Scotland, 2005). Defining these undercurrents intensifies the complexity of this study.

Various themes are going to emerge from the literature concerning the fundamental value base of the activity (and stated ethical/moral stance). The essential differences in this spread of forms concern the questions of *Building Consensus v. Building Conflict v. Managed Change.* A poignant question for theoreticians and for practitioners is: '*Within which of the above categories is the analysis made in a particular planning/practice situation?*' For trainers, theoreticians and practice managers the question might also be: '*Can the three approaches be combined, and, if they are not, what are the consequences for the community/system involved?*' The following discussion will unpick the complexities and show how the source materials for this thesis must be examined if they are to bring some systematic sense to the ongoing discussion about the nature of community development.

At this point, it is worth noting that almost all community development practiced in the UK since the Second World War has been directly or indirectly sponsored by the State. As the State in the UK generally lacks the power to intervene directly in the local situation (see Local Government Act 1868, *et seq.*), funding for local community development emanating from central government policy often takes the form of direct grants to the Local Authority or to the Voluntary Sector (see Hansard, HL Deb, 11 June 1968, vol 293, cols 3–4, regarding the establishment of the Young Volunteer Force Foundation, in 1969). More recently, after being badly stung by the experience of the national state-sponsored *Community Development Project* in the 1970s (Loney, 1983), local and central governments have begun, tentatively, to enter the field again. A good example of this in Wales is the *Communities First* programme of social and economic regeneration (NAforW, 2000; WAG, 2002b; WG, 2014).

In the United States, a similar statutory situation exists, but the Federal Government does have certain powers to over-ride 'States' Rights' when a situation of National urgency arises – the AmeriCorps VISTA (Volunteers in Service of America – from 1965, until today, founded under Lyndon Johnson's *Economic Opportunity Act* of 1964), and War on Poverty schemes (Cox, 1970). At the launch of the *War on Poverty*, President Johnson stated that the Act would: '... give every American community the opportunity to develop a comprehensive plan to fight its own poverty – and help them to carry out their plans.' (Johnson, 1964). However, although this central intervention was/is still managed at the local level by local Boards, this central government initiative did not gain universal approval (Marris and Rein, 1967).

Beyond the role of the State, in the USA, there are other major forces at work in the community. These are the huge philanthropic Foundations, such as the Ford Foundation, or the Bill and Melinda Gates Foundation (Bill and Melinda

Gates Foundation, 2007), which endow community effort in many situations. There are other major institutions, such as the Churches (especially the Roman Catholic Church), which make funds available to local communities for social programmes and local regeneration issues. In the United States, most 'charities', non-profit organisations, operate in a manner similar to corporations. They see themselves much like normal businesses, and have no qualms about entering into associations with finance institutions, 'leveraging' loans with their own fundraising resources, etc. (Twelvetrees, 1996; Orozco, et al., 2008). Community Chest organisations in America often combined with national initiatives to tackle local issues (United Way, 2008).

Consensus

Consensus is most often the unspoken agenda theme for that form of community development that is described, promoted, sponsored, staffed, (sometimes) evaluated, and (most often, unfortunately) under-funded and under-managed and prematurely cut off, by the State. From this concept, immediately, emerges the difficulty that stems from power relations. These arise when problem-solving initiatives come face to face with the underlying nature of the problem that has to be solved. At this point, vested interests and formal protocols resist change and seek to sustain the status quo. Friction between the practice element of the programme and its managers/sponsors is the usual outcome, which at times can become virulent (Inter-Project Editorial Team, 1977). An investigation will be made of whether or not consensus can be built up, contrived, and, if this is possible, can it, or how should it best be, sustained? What form of consensus can be established that is not merely a conduit for the opinions and objectives of the sponsors, especially should these sponsors be powerful and coercive?

Almost every book published in the UK on community development in the 1960s held to the principle of consensus, or social-management-without-conflict by the instigators of this form of planned social change (Batten, 1957, 1962; Batten, T. and Batten, M., 1967; Kuenstler, 1961; du Sautoy, 1962, 1966; Littlejohn and Hodge, 1965; Leaper, 1968). The most prominent forms of this, written specifically for the UK, set the scene for the coming decade in establishment thinking. This was, first, the *group work and neighbourhood development* framework (Kuenstler, 1955; Goetschius, 1969; Barr, et al., 1996; Henderson, P. and Thomas, D., 2000), where (for example) Goetschius highlights the opening up of positive communication, and resolving any conflicts that may arise (1969). Following this, the government-initiated, but privately sponsored Calouste Gulbenkian Study Groups drew attention to the possibility of a rift between interest groups, but decided firmly that there are three forms of community development: *grass-roots work with community groups; inter-agency co-ordination;* and *social planning* (Calouste Gulbenkian, 1968, 1973) – all consensus models. The vehicle for delivery of this method of social change would be mainly in the Youth Work or Social Work sectors of professionalism (Seebohm, 1968; Min. of Education/Albemarle, 1960). Later on, when the political atmosphere surrounding social intervention of this kind had changed (see 'conflict', below), Barr set out his claim that to organise along conflict lines would have been dysfunctional (Barr, 1977, p. 17). Subsequently, this outlook made a heavy impact on official British community development thinking, and this view still pervades the policy documents on the subject published in England and Wales (Dept of the Environment, etc., 1998; WAG, 2000). A whole new tranche of terms have been introduced, almost without examination or criticism – participation, social capital, capacity-building, empowerment (Social Exclusion Unit, 1998; NAforW, 2000; Dasgupta, and Serageldin, 2000; Field, 2003; WAG, 2003b; Dept of Communities and Local Government, 2006a, b; WAG, 2006a; Dept of Communities and Local Government, 2009; WAG, 2009a), and these are in need of critical examination.

At every level, careful examination of the texts is going to be important to discern the nuances of meaning and intent in this body of literature. In the United States, similar difficulties were being experienced, but there was already an expanding body of literature, which gave substance to a much wider range of approach and values than that emerging in the UK (Ross, 1955; Dunham, 1958; Biddle, W. and Biddle, L., 1965; Rothman, 1970). It is evident that there, too, there is confusion over the problem of non-cross-over between sectors/approaches. For example, Rubin and Rubin (2001) make no mention of Rothman (1970, etc.) in their influential text on *Community Organizing*, which appears, to an outsider, like professional jealousy, as Rothman is a towering figure in the annuls of US community organization literature and teaching.

Returning to the UK, another class of literature exhorts professional workers that their true calling stems from the organic spirit of certain classes of people, who need to recognise their potential in order best to resist the State and all its policies (Corrigan, 1975; Cockburn, 1977; Bolger, et al., 1981). Consensus-building, in this instance, is different from that promoted by straightforward problem-solving of a more general nature. There are two forces at work: 'them' and 'us', and we must work towards internal consensus in order that we can unite against 'them'. In the 1960s and 1970s, there was a whole lexicon devoted to class-based analysis within community development. Today, this has been somewhat diluted into a standard proclamation about 'working for social justice', and 'basic human rights' (Ledwith, and Springett, 2010).

Conflict

Conflict is the essence of the adversarial nature of our political and judicial systems, and so it must be inevitable that, where civic engagement is systematically developed, the potential for conflict within the parameters of democracy must exist. Problems arise when those drawn into the processes of social change of this nature are not also prepared in advance for the rules of the game. Community development has played around the edges of this process since it was first formulated. From the 1940s onward, in the United States, one particular framework for practice was being developed that focused on the generation of conflict within society as a legitimate professional goal for community organizers. It was demonstrated in some communities that only through applying this method would marginalised peoples be empowered to work towards the achievement of the 'American Dream' (Alinsky, 1957, 1969, 1972; Fisher, 1993; Walls, 2014). This approach did not preclude the founder of the method from being vilified as a 'communist', a 'Jew', a 'fascist', etc. (Alinsky, 1957).

In 1970, O'Malley recorded the frustration and exhilaration of confronting the local Council on planning decisions that worked against the perceived community interest. The tone of this was two dimensional, however, as opposed to the American conflict model. O'Malley was adamant that it was the class interests, as well as the material interests, of the people that were being oppressed. The social value of this class of poor, working people was being denigrated by the administration in a move to deprive them of their small-value homes. This, in turn, was Class oppression (O'Malley, 1970). Like so many similar confrontations of this nature in Britain at that time, the outcomes were not positive for the 'oppressed class'.

In this study, we have not considered *spontaneous citizen* action, however well organised in its own right it might be. Spontaneous action should not be confused with *community development* – which is agent-enhanced citizen activity. In the case of O'Malley's Golborne (a district of Notting Hill, London) situation, the issue is considerably confused. Notting Hill was seething with community action at this time, led by activists and pamphleteering: *Oz Magazine*, Michael X and Black Power, Darcus Howe and the Black Panthers, *Release* (with Caroline Coon, Richard Branson), (see Notting Hill *Timeline*, Chapters 11 and 12 on www.housemans.com) – years of unrest following the anti-fascist and anti-Rachman riots of the 1960s, and then the London *West Way* controversy, homelessness and total disenchantment with organised democracy (O'Malley, 1977). In fact, in Golborne throughout the whole of the Neighbourhood Council episode, a community development worker, Pat Healy was in post (I know this as I was on professional placement with him *in situ* during this episode). Healy supported the community leader, George Clark, in his work to establish a legally recognised form of community representation, a Neighbourhood Council, in Golborne. Whereas, Darcus Howe was an organizer for the *Black Panthers*, but in the role of an *activist*, rather than as an agent, the lines are often hard to draw in practice.

In the Alinsky (USA) approach, all citizens needed to be reminded of the fundamental traditions of American political organisation – power goes to the best organised, and ordinary people possessed the means, if organised properly, to grasp this power for themselves. The overthrow of the American State was never the question there, nevertheless, in the case of San Antonio, Texas, a social movement organised along Alinsky lines has successfully taken over the administration of the city (Fisher, 1994; Chambers, 2004). In this case, the boundaries that have to be examined are those between *social movements* and targeted community development initiatives (Burdick, 1992; Foweraker, 1995).

In Britain, however, the pretensions of the activist writers saw a different agenda. Social tensions gave rise to more militant social resistance to change (immigration, urban redevelopment, homelessness, etc.). In 1968, the UK Government was planning a major investment within the Local Government Act 1966 grant-funding mechanism – the Community Development Project (CDP). This would provide a network of experimental community development projects, covering a wide geographical spread, from urban London (Southwark, Waltham Forest) to rural Cumbria (Butcher, et al., 1979), and the Afan Valley (Penn and Alden, 1977). By as early as 1970, however, Hodge commented that, in this initiative, community development had been applied without proper consideration or insight (Hodge, 1970) and, by 1972, he seemed to be right. The lack of proper planning elicited the following: the Royal College of Health discussed the problems of urban discontent, how participation and civic empowerment could be enhanced, and how social conflict (including civic disobedience) could be diverted (Blair, 1972). '*Community development officers should be appointed to secure the involvement of those people who do not join organizations*' (Blair, 1972, p. 159 – my emphasis). This programme of community development projects, together with a parallel investment in local authorities' own schemes (the Urban Programme), costing a total of £27 million, between 1968 and 1974 (Batley and Edwards, 1975), started to become unstuck from the very beginning. Tensions rose rapidly in the CDP areas, and, within three years, local authorities were demanding the removal of these projects due to the civic resistance they generated (Loney, 1983). The programme was denounced as being 'naïve' and without proper monitoring mechanisms that might, at best, produce 'anecdotal' accounts of progress (Rossi, quoted in Loney, 1983, p. 26). The literature emanating from these sources called for the overthrow of the economic order, the formation of alliances with forces dedicated to that cause (the Trades Union, apparently), and the adoption of a strict Marxist orthodoxy (Corrigan, 1975; Smith and Anderson, 1972; Bolger, 1981; Leonard, 1975a, b; 1979).

The task here (see Chapter 4) is to delve deeply into the aims, methods and outcomes of the interventions, to discover the boundaries and to try and trace the actions of the instigators of the social change process. In this way, the relationship between 'development' and planned social change can be identified and ways of minimising risk, wastage and the arousing of social tension can be enhanced.

Social planning

Social planning is an action framework at the macro-level, which maximises resource inputs. It defines strategic objectives and provides for the implementation of subsequent development decisions through the creation of appropriate structures for their successful administration, including accountability and evaluation.

Most government documents, in addition to the outline of policy, with its hopes and ambitions for the responsible Department of State as to the intended outcomes, usually contain instructions on how these objectives are to be achieved. Additionally, they will contain something of the administrative structure that will be used, through which to achieve it. This explicit approach announces that there has been considerable deliberation, and that, as a consequence of that deliberation, certain action priorities have been decided. At the level of implementation, therefore, we will have to decide whether or not social planning, in the community development sense, is the way forward. A good example of this is the (WHO) World Health Organization Europe Strategic initiative: the *Healthy Cities Programme*, within which the UK is still a very active player (Tsouros, 1990; WHO Europe, 1996; Boonekamp, 1999; National Public Health Service Wales, 2009). In 2009, the Welsh Assembly Government put it thus:

> On top of individuals taking responsibility for their own health, all our partners have a significant role to play. This includes the Welsh Assembly Government, the NHS, Local Government, the third sector and the private sector (WAG, 2009a, p. 2).

The NHS will mainly be responsible for the discharge of this role, and partnerships will provide the framework for implementation. '*Health and well-being for all*' would be the objective, and the most deprived groups would be targeted strategically. Other strategies targeting poverty, especially child poverty, and community cohesion will be introduced (WAG, 2009b, p. 13; WAG, 2009f). Spelling out the precise processes of policy-implementation is more difficult. The Local Strategic Partnership (LSP) is the preferred vehicle for ongoing strategic development in Wales (and in the rest of the UK) under the Local Government Act 2000 (see also DETR *White Paper*, 1998). The difficulties in achieving the aims of this strategy are spelled out in *People, Plans and Partnership* (WAG, 2006b).

The exploration of how the community development approach to strategic planning can fit into this framework will be the function of Chapters 4 and 5, below. Certainly, the model has been tried in many cases, with varying degrees of success (Marris and Rein, 1967; Marris, 1974; Rein, 1977; Morris, 1970; Swedner, 1983a; Midgley, 1995; Clarke, 2006). There is evidence of much advance in thinking between the earlier introduction of the strategic approach to local planning and today's practice, but what is evident is that central government, because of its statutory limitations for acting locally, has not been able to impose much coherence in approach (WAG, 2006c). In 1998, the DETR had anticipated:

'Clause 3.25 The Government recognises that under any model it will be vital to have clarity about roles, and in particular about where powers to act will reside and the degree of veto or control' (DETR, 1998). In 2006, WAG reported that there were: 'problems in defining who the community is and how to engage them. Community councils are seen as out of touch and unrepresentative so existing structures are not seen to be working' (WAG, 2006b, p. 220).

There is considerable controversy around this role from a values and ideological standpoint. Sanders (1975) highlights the dilemmas of the professional organiser engaged in steering a change of policy through in this developmental mode. The complexity of the role, as outlined in these three sections, when all dimensions of the community development spread of focus have to be adopted, is described. The main task here is to consider the literature, and to discover what consequences for interventions have emerged due to the assumption of more or less ambitious roles in this regard. Rein (1977) considers that the process of social planning usually boils down to a conspiracy of elites, which is justified to the world by citing the breadth of spread across the elite stratum within the planning structure. Grosser claimed that many of the planning processes are aimed at alleviating the lot of the poor, but, as the disadvantaged are not fully engaged in the planning and delivery process, it is hard to claim that it is being done for their benefit at all (Grosser, 1975). Slavin describes how the inevitable frictions that emerge out of differing perceptions of the course and direction of planned change can and should be managed (Slavin, 1975). Many of those who advocate conflict (see above) would stress that submerging parochial interests in joint and co-operative action through a planning implementation process is a betrayal of parochial interests, and should be challenged and avoided.

The above three frames (consensus, conflict, social planning) through which community development can be analysed may, or may not, be sufficient to the task. Certainly Thomas, (1983) would go further, and would attach more significance to the form of intervention regarding target groups. Rothman selected a structural approach when he chose 'locality development', 'social planning' and 'social action' as the core 'Modes' for his classic framework (Rothman, 2001, p. 27). Rothman recognises that values are often pluralistic and conflicting, 'and may well come in pairs of divergent commitments' (p. 60). As community development has to be applied across a wide variety of settings and scales, the specification of structure may be a limiting factor. Structural systems lend themselves better to evaluation and measurements of effectiveness than do attestations of value. Nevertheless, it is possible to use both approaches for analytical purposes. This will be analysed in Chapter 5. Walton (1975) stresses that if problems are to be solved through this process of planned social change, then differences have to be recognised, and this boils down, finally, to identifying value differences and working on points of mutual interest in order to find a solution (Walton, 1975, p. 383).

Social capital

Personal growth, alongside institutional development, within the community context is a basic objective behind organising a community. The building of well-being, alongside the consolidation of community leadership reflects the width and depth of the community development challenge. One indicator of this process is called social capital. Social capital eludes precise definition as it is dependent upon the degree of presence of a number of factors, namely the level of connectivity between the members of a community (networks, social groupings, business connections), the sharing and understanding of common or parallel cultures, the feeling of personal identity within this nexus of social forces, etc. (OECD, 2007; Campbell, et al., 2010; Dale and Newman, 2010; Foxton and Jones, 2011). Social capital has to be quantified through the assessment of its component indicators that can be measured. Essentially, social capital can be understood as the level of mutual trust that can be assumed between citizens sharing an environment and this trust is measured by the level of well-being experienced by these citizens (Cabinet Office, 2013a).

The challenges raised by an ageing population

One of the challenging areas facing modern society is the issue of the impact that an ageing population has on the social structure, the cultural mores, and the ways in which the changing needs of this sector of the population impact on the economic and welfare resources. The fight to provide equality of health opportunity, together with the emergence of universal provisions of education, economic opportunity and primary care within developed societies has produced societies with ageing populations. This has resulted in social pressures that combine the expectations of independence and economic self-sufficiency with an ongoing social role for these older people that is both personally fulfilling and respected as such in society at large (WHO, 1947; Newell, 1975; WHO Europe, 1981; Welsh Office, 1983; Kirckbusch, et al., 1988; Tsouros, 1990; Dahlgren and Whitehead, 1991; Wallerstein, 1993; Singer and Manton, 1998; Welsh Office, 1998a, b; WAG, 2003a, b; Cracknell, 2007; Age Cymru, 2011; OPCforW, 2012a; WG, 2012a, b; WLGA, 2012; AgeUK, 2013; Randall and Corp, 2014).

In 1958, Jensen reflected the need for the reform of attitudes towards older people in society when he called for a radical change in outlook towards older people, whose status had been eroded by changes in family living patterns, economic and social forces, and technology (Jensen, 1958). In a society driven by materialism and science, social role validation had usually to be achieved personally, rather than having status ascribed to individuals. Role validation was now being determined by the capacity of the individual to perform the functions now being required by the new value system. Older people were being pushed aside if they failed to function at the level required, and their perceived social worth declined. This was emphasised by Townsend, who considered the rise of the 'new retirement culture'. Within this were absorbed many or most of the culturally displaced older people, and their defined roles as 'retired' became a euphemism for unemployment. The replacement of wages by pensions then reinforced a slide into dependency and poverty for many older people (Townsend, 1981).

Where increased longevity also saw a rise in infirmity, demands on the health and welfare systems increased, and pressure on services, coupled with material dependency and loss of family status, saw older people become stigmatised as a group (Andersson and Karlberg, 2000). This was resented by older people and their supporters. Nevertheless, despite their reluctance, they were often under pressure to adapt their lifestyles to residential situations that reinforced the stigmatisation of wider society (Bland, 1999; Lloyd, et al., 2014).

In a seminal document in 2002, the United Nations recorded the desire of nations to recognise the new situation: the changing demography and lengthening life expectancy across the globe, the development of rights and responsibilities within and between nations in their cultural attitudes and statutory policies regarding older people, and the severe consequences that were incurred when the potential and contribution of older people were ignored (United Nations, 2002). Their contribution across the economy and social structures of society must be recognised (United Nations, 2002, p. 10), and the active participation of older people at all levels, as participants and as decision-makers, must actively be promoted (United Nations, 2002, p. 3 and 10 *et seq.*). Older people must be considered to be full members of society in all aspects of public life, and their needs within their private lives must also be given heightened priority (United Nations, 2002, p. 36 *et seq.*). Older people are an asset, and not a burden. The immediate upshot of this Report was the convening of an international meeting in Vienna in 1983 to verify these findings and to decide on an Action Plan for nations in their search for their policy framework for older people (United Nations, 1983). From this Action Plan, nations were able to develop consistency in their approach to planning, implementing and analysing progress towards attaining the objectives of their domestic strategies.

An international perspective on planned social change

In the 1950s, the United Nations began to come to grips with the need for focused and planned development for the poorest communities on Earth. While the 'Cold War' of politics began to heat up, the war on poverty and disease was engaged across a wide political landscape of ethnicity, culture and economic sophistication. The United Nations (UN) and its related health organisation, the World Health Organization (WHO) mounted a two-pronged attack on the real scourges of humankind – epidemics and starvation. This linked, directly, economic with health objectives. It must be remembered that, whereas the UN has some coercive power over its member states through its Security Council Resolutions, which have standing in the International Court of Justice (ICJ – Article 36 of the ICJ Statute), the WHO has no such privilege. WHO 'policies' and programmes depend totally on voluntary, individual adoption by its signatory nations. Within these limitations, the WHO can be seen as an extremely persuasive and successful international agency.

Between the 1960s and 1970s, WHO was busy defining its terms and preparing to shift the World dramatically in its cultural perceptions of the realities of a new Public Health. The costs of conventional treatments were escalating and their application onto newly emergent causes of ill health was proving ineffective. Because epidemics of communicable diseases had all but been eliminated in the industrialised economies, it could now be predicted that they could also be successfully treated, contained or controlled *pharmaceutically* in the developing economies. But new, non-communicable diseases and social conditions had emerged that defied conventional, therapeutic and public health treatment measures. These had emerged, partly, through the effects of economic progress itself (a widening poverty gap between rich and poor), and also through the forces of urbanisation (stress and mental conditions), demographic changes (ageing, non-productive populations), and from an increasingly wealthy and sedentary culture (consumption patterns, heart disease, organ failure). These conditions had emerged as a consequence of the very successes of earlier, preventive public health interventions. Now, fresh methods altogether had to be found to tackle them. They required a complete shift in thinking and called for the application away from interventionist, curative solutions towards public engagement and culturally preventative measures – a *holistic* view of human development (WHO, 2008, p. 137). To a large extent, they required a focus on lifestyle causes of inequality and ill health (WHO, 1968, p. 365 *et seq.*; Newell, 1975). Thus, WHO began to focus its resources on individualised, personal health issues, how they manifested themselves at the community level and how they might be dealt with through community engagement.

In 1991, two papers provided substance to WHO's efforts to focus World attention on some of the most pressing issues it faced: societal inequality and community-based solutions to health issues. In the first (Dahlgren and Whitehead, 1991), an analysis was provided for describing a holistic/ecological appraisal of individual needs, based upon the scenario outlined by Bronfenbrenner (Bronfenbrenner, 1979). The specific targeting of an individual's personal health symptoms was completely inadequate for providing a successful remedial intervention. The whole situation of the person, within a family, neighbourhood, economic

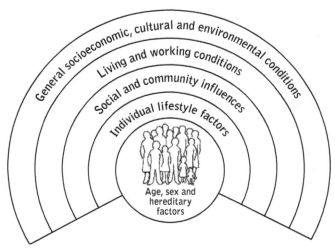

Figure 1: Inequalities in health – a holistic framework for action

environment and the society's value system had to be considered. Only with this insight could a meaningful assessment be made and a strategic approach to planning change be developed. The second paper (WHO Study Group, 1991; see also WHO 1985), laid down the priorities for strengthening communities in their quest to overcome inequalities and their mission to become engaged in solving their own health issues. The responsible agency (local health administration) was responsible for the active promotion of this approach and for the strengthening of the local communities for this purpose (WHO Study Group, 1991, p. 13).

Since 1992, the UN had defined *'sustainability'* as development that meets current needs without prejudicing those of future generations, and it concentrated very much on channelling international AID funding into national programmes for creating resources: infrastructure and localised initiatives to uplift the very poor (UN General Assembly, 2014, p. 6). Generally, these objectives were to become known as the *Millennium Objectives* (UN, 2000). In the early days, the efficacy of community development was not recognised as a panacea for uplifting *'80% of the World's population'* (UN Bureau of Social Affairs, 1955, pp. 5–6). Nevertheless, over the decades through the 1980s to the 2000s, a progression in thinking had taken place within the UN. It moved from prioritising catch-up development to a broader focus upon *'sustainable development'*. This centred on individuals, community groups and non-governmental organisations being *'empowered'* to move forward the agenda of economic and social development themselves (UN, 1992). It embraced the need to strengthen human capacity to solve its own problems and to obtain national and international support for social and cultural minorities (UN, 1992, pp. 271, *et seq.*). Both the UN and the World Bank took up the issue of human resource potential and the way the social environment had to be enhanced to provide whole communities with the stability to sustain itself over time and through change processes (UN Research Institute, 2011; World Bank, 2011; United Nations, 2014).

During this period, WHO's thinking also progressed through several key stages of development: from moving towards holistic care at the community level (Alma Ata Declaration, WHO, 1978), through identifying Health Promotion as the most effective function for preventive intervention, the Ottawa Charter (WHO, 1986), to the Jakarta Declaration (WHO,1997a) where the twin pillars of good health – personal responsibility for health and public engagement in Health planning – were identified as vital stages in attaining sustainable '*Health for All*' by the year 2000. This strategy was first developed by the WHO Regional Office for Europe (WHO Europe, 1999; Kenzer, 1999). Since 1978 (Alma Ata, above, Clause VII), WHO was concerned to introduce community development into its strategies. By 1985, WHO Europe was actively talking of strengthening neighbourhoods and improving public and general health through community development methods (WHO Europe) and, by 1996, this was codified into international agreement (Price and Tsouros, 1996). The Ljubljana Charter of 1996 provided a concrete framework for definitions and objectives for a new regime in Public Health (WHO, 1996; Michael, 2008), but there were already warnings that not enough community development staff members were being trained in constituent countries (WHO Europe, 1996).

Since its inauguration in 1984 at its Toronto Conference, and to date, the WHO *Healthy Cities* movement moved from strength to strength. It expanded from eleven participating cities in Europe, to a point where all nations are now represented. In the UK, four of the first twenty-four to sign up represented all of the Home UK nations, except Wales (Cardiff did not attain full status until 2009). All these cities adopted a clearly defined stance on the need for professional agents operating at the community level for the attainment of change objectives towards the health priority goals required (Aston, 1988; WHO Europe, 1997). This was firmed up considerably in 2008, when the follow-up Report on '*Our Cities Our Future*' went into great detail as to how this was to be achieved (Kjellstrom et al., 2008). Three key components were identified for successful intervention at the community level: 1. community development; 2. a Public Health agenda; and 3. healthy Public policy (p. 95). These criteria have, of course, considerable implications for those framing public policy, and for those trying to implement them.

In this way, WHO, especially under the leadership of the European Office, became a pathfinder in providing practical and ideological support for the *New Public Health* agenda (Lalonde, 1974; Baum, 1990). What is significant about this shift in thinking within the New Public Health agenda is (a) a holistic analysis, and (b) it requires active intervention at the community level if changes are to be affected. However, remedies cannot merely be prescribed. They must be dealt with through instrumental and institutional methods, but WHO lacks the means for this, outside emergency relief operations (Newell, 1975; WHO Europe, 1994). Communities have to be actively empowered so that they can take care of their own destinies and, particularly, their relations with authority (Marmot, 2010). This remains the responsibility of national governments and local administrations. Health Promotion was seen as the key ingredient of an integrated approach for health planning and the delivery of services (WHO Europe, 2012). The WHO's initiative into the *New Public Health* and *Health Promotion* was endorsed by the new journal *Health Promotion*, which was launched in 1986. In its first edition, community development was given strong impetus (Kickbusch, 1986).

The WHO, health and the community in the UK

Immediately after the WHO Europe launched its *Healthy Cities* programme in 1986 (Ashton, et al., 1986), a network of participating cities was established to consolidate progress towards its goals and to facilitate communication (Tsouros, 1992). The newly launched, UK-based journal, *Health Promotion*, echoed the message of the 1986, WHO *Ottawa Charter* for communities to be strengthened (Health Promotion, 1986) and the progressive and expanding *Healthy Cities* programme appeared to be the logical place for this to start. There was a long way to go, however, as the UK, proud of its comprehensive National Health Service, was still firm in the belief that public services could direct and deliver a nation's health from the centre. Despite all the Conferences and policy outlines, there was still a fair distance to go, ideologically, before it might seriously be envisaged that the British people, themselves, might have an active role in delivering on their own health status (WHO Europe, 1986). As we shall see in Chapter 5 below, the British Government had been deeply stung by the traumatic political impact of the experimental Community Development Project in the early 1970s. The notion that community development and the National Health Service might be more closely connected never really became a policy option. Consequently, community development and the Health agenda never really connected in England. In any event, most active community development workers saw their role more as political activists than ministering to the actual health or welfare needs of the population (Stevenson, 1978; Baldock, 1982).

Wales

Had there been any governmental interest in this direction, there was no shortage of evidence to support an active initiative. As a strong participant and contributor to the WHO work programme, the administration of Health in Wales, particularly, was to play a significant role in this purpose. Even before the *Healthy Cities* programme, Wales began to experiment in the accommodation of people with Learning Disabilities (defined as Mental Handicap, in those days). The *All Wales Strategy for Services for People with a Mental Handicap* and the *NIMROD* resettlement and social support network in Cardiff provided pathfinder models for community-based service provision (Welsh Office, 1983; Lowe, 1992). Unfortunately, whereas from 1981, community development was to play a key role in the development of thinking in WHO and the UN, this was not to be the case in Wales, or in the UK.at large (WHO Europe, 1994, 1999, 2000a, 2002, 2008; Dahlgren and Whitehead, 2006; Whitehead and Dahlgren, 2006; WHO, 2008). It was not until the establishment of the National Assembly for Wales in 1999 that community development became a term with some currency at the administrative level. Even then, opportunities were lost to take a firm hold on what was being made available through clear policy guidelines and enabling legislation. The WHO Europe offered Wales a project in the ground-breaking *Verona Initiative*, to establish a health-focused, local government planning and implementation scheme in 1999. This was launched in Caerphilly (Watson, 2000; WHO Europe, 2000a, c), but it was allowed to fade away without publicity or any learning taking place (Clarke, 2001). Beyond a health agenda per se, policy implementations in Wales will be examined below (Chapter 5).

Scotland

From the beginning, Scotland led the way in a concerted effort to provide some unity of thinking and action in this area. In social work training programmes, community development was taken up with enthusiasm after the publication of their Secretary of State investigation into social development needs in the community (Scottish Education, 1966). Community development was seen as an essential ingredient to state intervention to engage with the persistent social issues of the day – poverty and social disorganisation (Brodie, et al., 2008). This was not only developed strongly in Strathclyde, the most populous Scottish Region, but the remote Highland areas were also provided with their own state-driven development agency that had specific responsibility for promoting the '*social and cultural values of the area*' (Highlands and Islands Development Board, 1978, 1982; Lloyd and Black, 1993). It was in Scotland, too, that there was a positive learning experience from the (UK) Home Office experiment in community development called the *Community Development Programme* (CDP – see Chapter 4, below). Scotland was able to benefit from the expanding range of WHO initiatives through the strong working relationships between government administrations and the Scottish Community Development Centre (SCDC – see below).

Additionally, in Scotland, collaboration between Social Work and Education Departments at the Regional level after 1975 enabled a thriving community sector to emerge in the most deprived areas of social and economic need (Kirkwood, 1975; Bryant, 1975; English, 1998). Community development was seen as a fully fledged element in the social work training curriculum, and grant-aid for youth workers and for community organisations underpinned professional support for these initiatives (Shaw, 1964; Scottish Education Department, 1966; Twelvetrees,

1976; McConnell, 1983). All these policy restructurings enabled the Scottish administration address Health issues at the community level in line with WHO expectations.

England

In England, *'inspiration'* for a renewed Public Health strategy for combating inequality was 'found in the World Health Organization's *Health for All'* (Acheson, 1998, p. ii; WHO Europe, 1981, 1985, 1986). This, in turn, drew heavily on the four-year review of *Inequalities in Health* carried out by the Black Committee from 1977 to 1980, ordered by the Dept of Social Services (Dept of Social Services, 1980). Earlier, Townsend had emphasised the importance of *'lifestyle'* in determining a person's life-chances. His reasoning dwelt on the fact that, when an individual was pressed upon by the surrounding culture and economic structure, freedom of expression was made very difficult. Further, when a person's dire economic circumstances limited their scope even to conform to the simplest of cultural norms, then lifestyle choices became haphazard (Townsend, 1979, pp. 54 and 369 *et seq.*).

The Black Report embraced this view, while stressing that under-spending on prevention would rack up knock-on costs in the future and that there was generally a complete lack of useable data on the nature and extent of social inequalities in health (Dept of Social Service, 1980, clause 4.42, clauses 7.85–7.87). In the face of this, it is easy to see why these policy pronouncements carried little weight at the local level. The Black Report (clause 1.7) acknowledges that 'once a conception of disease finds embodiment in a structure of service major changes become difficult to introduce'. Seedhouse demonstrates this: activities, in the Speke district of Liverpool, at the community level and within the spirit of the *New Public Health*, as promoted by the WHO, met considerable resistance within the corridors of officialdom. This went so far as the Authority applying direct pressure to desist from the new approach, such that the only way forward was to disengage altogether. Thus, quite a sophisticated local initiative, aiming to influence lifestyle and attitudes towards health, was passed up. A totally top-down approach was favoured by the District Health Authority (Seedhouse and Cribb, 1989, pp. 108–9). Eventually, Liverpool did come around to adopting the WHO's agenda for *Healthy Cities*. They adopted a historical import from London, the *Health and Recreation Team* approach from Peckham (Ashton, 1989, p. 123). Between 1926 and 1939, a team of medical practitioners established a Health Centre in Peckham, London. It was funded through voluntary charitable contributions and community fund-raising. Through this concentrated and focused approach to medical practice, they evolved an ecological approach to diagnosis and treatment – health, not disease, was their target. Early on in their work, they recognised the value and positive effects of well-being within the family and in the surrounding community. They then built their approach around this process, engaging the community members in a range of social and educational experiences to enhance their feelings of mutuality and to raise awareness of the benefits of good health (Pearse, I. and Crocker, L., 1941). In many respects, the *Peckham Experiment* foreshadowed the WHOs *New Public Health*. Unfortunately, from the point of view of establishing an ecological and developmental approach to Public Health, it was to take another 40-plus years for the message to get through to the Health Authorities that centralised Services could only go so far in the establishment of a healthy population. Commenting from the side lines, in Wales, Townsend recorded that, despite the fact that the UK had signed up to the WHO *Health for All by the Year 2000* convention and target objectives in 1981 and again in 1985, inequalities in health had widened by 2001 (Townsend, 2001, p. 1; WHO, 1981; WHO Europe, 1985).

It was not until the election of a Labour Government in 1997 that England began to come to grips with the full implications of WHO policies. But, by 2005, as Hills and Stewart report, policy was still a long way ahead of implementation. The focus of Health expenditure was still focused upon the centralised and service-oriented National Health Service (Hills, J. and Stewart, K., 2005, p. 6). This was, in part, because the Office of the Deputy Prime Minister, the Ministry of Communities and Local Government and the Labour-created Social Exclusion Unit were more concerned with Housing, economic regeneration, etc., and had not taken on a holistic, health-embracing view of Public Health (Office of the Deputy Prime Minister, 2005a, b; Social Exclusion Unit, 2001). It was not until 2006 that the Government published its White Paper on *Strong and Prosperous Communities*, where the holistic model was prioritised (Department of Communities and Local Government, 2006a, p. 26 *et seq.*).

In 2004, the Audit Commission compiled a series of Reports on servicing an ageing population. A complete breakdown of openings and good practice measures were outlined (Audit Commission, 2004a, b and c). In 2008 and 2009, the National Audit Office and the Audit Commission revisited the area of inter-agency co-operation and collaboration (National Audit Office, 2008; Audit Commission, 2009). They found that they still had to urge government Departments and the agencies of local government to develop ways of working together, to overcome *'compartmentalisation'* (National Audit Office, 2008, p. 14). Whereas partnership working had now become more or less *'compulsory'* (Audit Commission 2009, p. 7), there was still a great deal of evidence that these partnerships across sectors and Departments were costly, un-monitored, and managed with a lack of due diligence (Audit Commission, 2005; Audit Commission, 2009).

The UK's government at National, local and Regional/National levels had gone some way towards realising the WHO's aims towards a holistic approach, but there was still a long way to go in the face of confused local resolve, misinterpretation and lack of focus. In 2010, Eric Pickles, Secretary of State for Communities and Local Government, announced that he was scrapping the *Comprehensive Area Assessment* reporting requirement of local government, thus making the whole system of governance more *'transparent'* (UKGov website, https://www.gov.uk/government/news/pickles-strips-away-pointless -town-hall-red-tape-targets, accessed 1 June 2015). It is not believed that calling on agencies of government to become more *transparent* through cancelling an in-depth progress and monitoring mechanism is going to work.

When we consider the pressing need for change from an international per-spective, the rate of adoption of policies has been exceedingly slow. As community development methods have to be employed to implement the community engage-ment elements of this policy, it is not surprising that champions of community development were kept on hold. As the Department of Communities and Local Government was abolished in 2010, and the Office of Deputy Prime Minister in 2015, a lot of reorganisation will now stand between the declaration of integrated Health policies and their implementation. Since the Cabinet Office took over responsibility for this work, the emphasis has been on voluntary and unregulated activity, rather than policy being implemented by a statutory agency (Cabinet Office, 2013b; Cameron, et al., 2015).

We can see from an overall view of the UK's attitude towards integrated and inter-service co-operation towards Health objectives that there is a very frag-mented and tardy approach at work. The Audit Commission had produced an early guide to effective, inter-agency partnership, but this did not really take hold (Audit Commission, 1998a, b; Audit Commission, 2002). It seemed that statutory agencies faced too many administrative, financial and status difficulties to imple-ment solutions that might bring them money, produce efficiencies and enable them to solve collective problems. One ingredient was missing, we contend ... Community Development.

Older people in this scenario

Since the emergence of fresh appraisals of the place of older people in society, role changes have been profound in many cases, and these changes, mainly from dependence to independence for older people, present an infinite range of aspir-ations, requirements and social adjustments as they are also accompanied with the development of individual patterns of need as old age progresses. 'One-size-fits-all' remedies are no longer considered to be appropriate (Wanless, 2006; ICSSW, 2010).

The theme of 'Planning with Communities' (Illsley, 2002, pp. 1–5; Tsouros, 1995) for those providing services to the public now resonates powerfully within policy documents, and the role and needs of older people feature prominently within them (WAG, 2002a, c; WAG, 2004a; WAG, 2006b; WAG, 2007b; Wales Centre for Health, 2007; WAG, 2008a, b, c; Wellbeing Wales Network, 2010; WAG, 2011; AgeUK, 2013). This study, here, sets out the task facing those seeking fully to take up this challenge (Green, et al., 1996; Harding, 1999; ICSSW, 2010).

It explores the policy framework as it has developed, both nationally and internationally, and seeks a holistic approach that is consistent within this framework. Whereas specific policies that target the needs of older people may be necessary in order to remedy perceived shortfalls in support and engagement processes, social and governmental attitudes towards inclusion and engagement require that society as a whole is considered as the focus for sustainable change and development (Dahlgren, G. and Whitehead, M., 1991; Dahlgren, G. and Whitehead, M., 1992; Whitehead, M. and Dahlgren, G., 2006; WAG, 2010a, b, c; AgeUK, 2013). In Sweden, reform of the health and welfare service systems sought to reverse regressive trends through the adoption of a fully integrated model of supportive social care and full recognition of older people by the community. This needed to be flexible and adaptive for the accommodation of changing needs through the ageing process (Andersson, G. and Karlberg, I., 2000; IASSW, et al., 2010). This theme has been taken up by Payne (2012) in the search for a more holistic and supportive model for British social work and by Warburton, et al., 2013, within the question of social inclusion. Loneliness and isolation for the ageing population are suggested to be two of the main factors causing distress and reliance on acute services, especially in rural areas (AgeUK, 2013). It will be suggested that community development is a mechanism that can go a long way to meet this challenge.

Later in the text (Chapter 5) we describe the efforts that the Welsh Government has made to promote a policy climate that is amenable towards and beneficial to the needs of an ageing population. In 2003, three documents heralded a departure from the traditional approach to the provision of universal welfare benefits. In its publication of its Health, Social Care and Wellbeing Strategy (WAG, 2003a), WAG underlined the holistic approach it wished to follow in the achievement of welfare objectives — 'social, environmental and economic factors' were to be taken as a whole, and 'community development' was to be one of the vehicles for achieving this (WAG, 2003a, p. 49). This was followed by its *Strategy for Older People in Wales* (WAG, 2003b), where the overarching philosophy was to remove as many barriers to participation by older people in all aspects of society, whilst gearing up services to provide support where and when it was most needed (WAG, 2003b, pp. 11–13). The then Minister for Health and Social Services, Jane Hutt, emphasised that 'Older people play a vital role in society and we must ensure this is recognised and that their contribution is both valued and further enhanced' (Hutt, 1999, p. 5). This policy document launched a defined phase in the Welsh Government's adoption of the framework originally delivered by the Welsh Office in its handover of administrative guidance in 1998 (Welsh Office, 1998b). It was a purposeful step towards achieving the objectives of the earlier '*A Good Old Age: an initiative on care of the aged in Wales*' (Welsh Office, 1985), where 'self-help and self-care' should be the essence of any approach to the support of the older section of the population (Welsh Office 1985, p. 8). As we shall see, however, there was to be a long and unfulfilled attempt by government in Wales to achieve the 'pooling of local authority and National Health Service funds ... (and the) removal of the structural obstacles' in the way of attainment of common goals as envisaged by the Welsh Planning Forum in 1994 (Welsh Health Planning Forum, 1994, p. 18).

In this study, guidance has been taken from the United Nations/WHO leadership in focusing on holistic analyses and sustainable objectives. The Welsh Government has taken steps to realise this scenario, including the first, within Europe, Commissioner for Older People, in 2008. The work of this agency will be examined below (Chapters 5), but suffice it to say that in the latest statement by the Commissioner, only in one of the 12-point statement of priorities can any inference be drawn that a community-wide, developmental and proactive plan of action will be possible (OPCforW, 2013). Since 2008, there has been very little deviation from the original framework, laid out by the first Commissioner, and there is little evidence from successive Annual Reports, etc., that might indicate that the Commission might envisage a developmental approach (OPCforW, 2010b; 2011a, b; 2012b; 2013). In 2010, the Welsh Government inaugurated the *Welsh Senate for Older People*, but no moves have been made there to enhance the empowerment of older people per se through this route (see Chapter 5 below). If this trend continues without a change of heart and direction, there will not be much scope for a holistic model to be implemented (see Chapter 5 below). The aim of a holistic change model, which we explore in this study, is to discover a mechanism for independence for all through inclusion in economic, social and political life, and sensitive and sustainable support as needs change over time. Such a mechanism has to be sufficiently flexible to account for the varied circumstances of each individual, be they geographical (urban/rural) or cultural. One-size-fits-all solutions cannot meet these criteria.

Personal experience – the bridge between practice and theory

Community development can be a high-profile political activity, which sits uncomfortably within government programme-delivery boundaries. Planned social change rarely is able to deliver its own declared planned outcomes, and political and administrative protocols are bruised by this. They usually lack the flexibility to cope with uncertainty. Problem-solving, the essence of the community development approach, runs counter to the actual processes and expectations of politics, politicians and senior administrators in secure and established employment positions. Nowhere is this situation shown more clearly than in my experience working as the director of a community development organisation under the Apartheid regime of the White South African Government between 1964 and 1970.

The *raison d'être* of this organisation was the bringing together of *White* and *Non-White* people for the purposes of problem-solving, development and serious learning about social issues, problems, and their alleviation. This was actually **against the law** in South Africa at that time, and had to be carried out with the collusion of some people in authority. It was, at all times, under constant surveil-lance from those who were not in collusion with us. Those who were charged with the protection of the established political regime of *'separate development'* had another agenda. Despite the fact that a high public profile ensured that the South African Government officially recognised the legitimacy of the organisa-tion (Charity Registration was a highly political hurdle to be overcome – which it was, successfully, on my watch), other agents of that same Government actively undermined the work, impugned the motives, threatened the participants, and sought at every turn to halt or severely limit the organisation's effectiveness (see Alinsky, 1957, above).

I had, for four-and-a-half years, complete managerial responsibility for the deployment of up to 3,000 volunteer professionals-in-training, and their highly qualified professional supervisors. In addition, the organisation employed three University lecturers, who were seconded by the organisation to the University for the training and supervision of students in training (who were also the actual employers). The organisation aimed at providing a womb-to-tomb health and welfare service to 12,000 people of *mixed race* near Johannesburg. Community development work, in this instance, required a sophisticated management style, public relations and diplomatic activity of great sensitivity, and intense attention to detail for every action. Community development might well prove to be easier in a political (more democratic) environment less prone to oppression, but it is evident that the climate is not really more optimistic, even in Britain in 2016.

Across the World, sound practice and programme management has demon-strated that the essentials of community development are effective, that they can be replicated, and can produce planned and positive outcomes for all concerned – **provided that** certain conditions are met:

- that the processes of community development are understood by all involved: funders, planners, management, field workers and community participants;
- that the staff are properly prepared for their work; and
- that the political climate is conducive to risk-taking and the discovery of problematic information about its own social environment, and is prepared to deal positively with the solutions that present themselves.

If these conditions are not found, then the professionals, themselves, must be personally confident and able to take personal responsibility for their actions – to act as autonomous, free-standing professionals.

Conclusion

Community development, public health and the administration of public policy for the achievement of better social conditions for all is tied in with the social and economic circumstances that pertain at the time. This study will attempt to isolate the themes as they emerge, and as they change over the time period. It is important to study the whole range of material, especially within the corpus of community development literature. Despite the radical and sweeping changes in social outlook over the past 150 years, certain values and approaches have remained constant, whereas others have changed. Are there cycles involved here? Can we discern certain constants within the overall approach to social intervention and change that hold good despite the changing circumstances of the workers, target populations/clientele, economic and/or social conditions?

Some of the research theories expounded here have proved to be attractive, particularly thematic analysis, critical analysis, and the overall historical method. Findlay entitled her contribution (Findlay, 2002) 'Negotiating the Swamp' when it comes to researchers determining how 'inter-subjective elements transform their research' (p. 209). Including the need to ensure that pragmatic solutions be found to accommodate an intended audience, etc., room must also be found to explore the imperfections in the research approach, and to be aware that knowledge may well be *imperfect*, or *partial* (Findlay, 2002, p. 227). Alvesson and Sköldberg explore the complexity of interpretation (hermeneutics) in all of this, but because there is no real satisfactory way of resolving the problems of abstract dialectics, '*empathy*' in the researcher is a prominent factor in shaping the outcome of an investigation (Alvesson, M. and Sköldberg, K., 2000, p. 54). The closer that the researcher comes to adopting a *post-modernistic* analysis, the more that '*pluralism*' has to be accepted. This compounds the problem of clarifying understanding (p. 187). As the outcomes of community development and policy implementation is community change, the more that '*analysis*' hinges upon the eventual '*evaluation*'. This renders contemporaneous dissection and micro-analysis somewhat redundant, but this discussion must take place at some level in order to ensure that nothing important is omitted in the final analysis.

The wide range of resource material, notably in community development, presents the need to ensure that the major traits of national and professional 'schools' of thought are identified and their meaning and influence is plotted. The scale of the American contribution is enormous, and thoroughly under-rated in the UK. Attention will be paid to this element, and also an attempt will be made to discover why the documentation of community development and its potential role in the creation of a preventive and supportive welfare state in the UK has been under-reported. Many of the problems identified in this sector of analysis were identified by Harry Specht in 1976, when he was invited to provide an initial appraisal of the British, State-directed Community Development Project (CDP) by the National Institute for Social Work (Specht, 1976). In his private capacity, Specht castigated British community development workers for their naïve socialism in the face of dramatic social problems in the country, and the urgent need for strict professional intervention approaches to tackling them (ref. personal recording, 1978, made under auspices of Young Volunteer Force Foundation).

In the case of policy material, there has been a flood of material from the Welsh Assembly Government/NAforW since 1999. Differentiating this in the body of this study is going to be an exercise in itself. At the present time, four documents will provide a platform, points of reference for the other documentation: *Better Health Better Wales* (Welsh Office, 1998a), The *Review of Health and Social Care in Wales, 2003* (WAG, 2003a); *Strategy for Older People in Wales* (WAG, 2003b), and the *Beecham Report* (WAG, 2006c). Further analysis of the WAG policies will reveal whether or not it is feasible, desirable and/or sustainable for the institution of government to integrate diverse and pressing interests (the vulnerable, the financial realities, and the agents of governance) in common cause. The State has a direct role in this, and it also produces the framework through which the work has to be achieved. The main questions will arise around the content of: *Making the Connections – Delivering Beyond Boundaries: Transforming Public Services in Wales* (WAG, 2006d), its response to the *Beecham Report*, and how WAG has responded since. With regard to the emergent policy and practices following the WAG *Strategy for Older People in Wales*, the focus of the following analyses will be firmly on the identification of opportunities for the development of a model capable of implementation within the parameters of that Strategy.

Community development can be seen as a fairly straightforward approach to social change, but it has never realised its potential. Can the literature reveal why this is so? Within its diversity, it must be possible to identify the most salient traits, criteria that define its role, value and most opportune opening for interventions. The PAULO '*Occupational Standards*' for practice in community development do not go nearly far enough to satisfy my own criticisms, nor those of Harry Specht (above) (PAULO, 2003; Clarke, 2001). In light of my own considerations about the nature and direction for community development, the works of Chambers (1983), Ledwith, M. and Springett, J. (2010), and Plummer (1999) are of importance in taking this discussion forward.

Theoretically, the boundaries and formations of community development and social policy do not lend themselves to modernistic theorising, but the purposes and outcomes of both are up for scrutiny. As has been shown above, there are many 'theoretical' approaches to theorising about research methods where indeterminate inputs and outcomes might be discussed, correlated, analysed and pronounced upon. This is not an empirical study, and falls within the boundaries of analysis of a more '*post-modernist*' or '*reflexive*' nature (Beck, 1994; Hughes, 2006). Nevertheless, the outcomes of the implementation of social policy and the actions of community development interventions are pragmatic, as much as they may be bounded by principle, governed by statute, or subject to professional guidelines. The logical extension of the reflexive and analytical research methodologies leads to insights and speculations well beyond their usefulness to this study

(Strauss, A. and Corbin, J., 1998; Peräkylä, 2005). As a consequence, this study will concentrate on thematic analysis, and will incorporate as much of the other methodologies as possible, signifying this process as it arises.

The theorists of sociology, the researchers of social formations and change and those that formulate strands of philosophical thought are all on one side of the equation. Those that practise planned social intervention and change on the ground, in the community, within the systems of administration and governance are on the other. We are interested in the practical, economic, social and political outcomes of intervention. We are informed by the theories and the values of researchers and the like, but we are bound by the dynamics of change themselves, and by the endurance of those participating in the process. This produces a dynamic far removed from the protestations of the textbook and the treatise. The trick here is to find the space for reflection and introspection. Do the numbers add up to support the outcomes sought in the first place? In the end, there is no 'right' way of doing this. As well as being instrumental in so many immediate and practical ways, community development is strategic, long-term, incremental and preventive if it is implemented correctly, on the locally grounded agenda for change (Clarke, 2014).

Summary

1. In Britain, the adoption of community development approaches to community problem-solving occurred much later than in America.
2. The terminology used within community development requires clarification when interpreting different people's usage.
3. There is little cross-Atlantic collaboration over the nature of community development.
4. Terminology such as 'social capital', 'consensus', etc. needs careful scrutiny.
5. Discernible models of community development exist and should be used in programme planning.
6. British, especially Welsh, Public Health policy closely follows UN/WHO/EU-led changes in priority.
7. The social, economic and political positions of older people constitute important areas for the application of community development interventions.

2

The historical development of community development to 1940

It took one hundred years to establish and settle the path of those who wanted to present problem-solving approaches to social problems into what we know today as community development. Even then, after yet another sixty years, although the issues are now clear, the received wisdom on the subject is still subject to some confusion and lack of agreement. At least, most of the terms used are now recognised and the general purposes are agreed, but the struggles go on. There is still no agreement over the ethics, the values, and the most expedient pathway towards the objectives. This chapter plots one identifiable course – from charity work to official recognition, across the first one hundred years.

Within this phase, there is some considerable continuity in this progress. We will show how the emergence of charity work in the poorest communities by outside organisations made way for the establishment of community-based organisations (Settlements). This process then developed into the founding of social work as a profession, which, in turn, divided to provide a distinctive branch of social intervention targeting part of or the whole community (community development). How this distinctive form of providing support for the community evolves in the first four decades of the twentieth century will be described in detail, and it will be shown how clarity of purpose and the acceptance of a strong value base for this activity assisted in its becoming formally accepted within the emergent institution of social work. The ramifications of this process might be recognised at national as well as the local level. It will also be seen that this is largely a development that takes place in the United States.

Introduction

From the beginning of the nineteenth century, community development emerged from a melange of competing institutions, movements and social interventions as a response to the failure of more structured methods to, ultimately, solve the problems or resolve the issues that troubled society. In the mid-nineteenth century, the need to create a formal mechanism for engaging poverty, solving chronic unemployment, and arresting the decline in public morality saw the birth of the philanthropic, charitable organisation and, later, the (University) Settlement movement. Both of these mechanisms worked in their own way for a period, and then they, too, mostly, gave way to formal social work. Latterly, this function was subsumed by the State, and social case work assumed an almost hegemonic control over the official practice and value frameworks (Richmond, 1917; 1922). But still the social problems persisted, despite the proliferation of State and non-governmental institutions designed to overcome them. Within this regime of progress, increasing professionalisation, and the institutionalisation of welfare solutions, community development became recognised, but it continued developing on a low key (Steiner, 1925). Gradually it refined its theoretical philosophy, practice models and contextual competencies, until, the mid-1900s. It then began to crystallise into a format that could be understood and integrated into the formal practice and training structures of social work (Lane, 1940). In between these periods of rising popularity and inclusion, community development sometimes became the vehicle for visionary change initiatives in society, or was the accredited agency of the State, or even, sometimes, the mechanism for faith organisations to harvest souls from within the disadvantaged classes. This chapter traces that path, providing insight into the major threads of inspiration and value, and the changes in emphasis that have endured as public and historic pressure paved the road. We are also going to trace the development of the tensions that develop when a *functional* view of social welfare intervention begins to clash with more philosophical concepts, in particular the hiatus arising out of the debate about the nature of *social justice*, and *human rights*.

From alms to self-help

Since the early nineteenth century, in the industrialising and urbanising nations, various approaches emerged for dealing with poverty, marginalisation, and social dysfunction. In the UK, these often conflicted with the orthodoxy enshrined in the culture through the Poor Laws, and those of the traditional moral positions created by religious organisations. The Poor Laws dictated the social and administrative framework for the alleviation and treatment of those in poverty and indigence. They defined the relations between local government and alms-giving. Whereas there had always been a tradition of giving support to those in need through Christian charitable work, the Poor Laws formalized this relationship. They sought to regulate the scale and direction of public giving and the consequential rights that a community held in relation to the expected behaviour of the destitute. The Workhouse was to become the main expression of 'relief' (Poor Law Amendment

Act, 1834, Clause XXIII), and churches and local charities continued to provide alms and material support as well as they chose.

As the century progressed, considerable debate arose about the relative merits of *indoor* and *outdoor* relief. The Poor Law Amendment Act 1834 was never fully implemented, and so the system of giving relief to the poor was fragmented (Bosanquet, 1874). Many Workhouses, the location for *indoor relief*, were never built, or delayed for decades, and during this time the level of poverty rose inexorably. These conditions were to persist until well into the twentieth century (Carpenter, 1861; Hopkins, 1878; Hill, 1877; London Congregational Union, 1883; Engels, 1892; Rowntree, 1901; Booth, 1902). In their *Bitter Cry of Outcast London*, of 1883, as the London Congregational Union put it – while they had been building churches, solacing themselves with religious practice and dreaming about the coming millennium – 'the poor have been growing poorer, the wretched more miserable, and the immoral more corrupt', and the gulf between the poor and the respectable classes was ever-widening. This 'separates the lowest classes of the community from our churches and chapels, and from all decency and civilization' (London Congregational Union, 1883, p. 2).

For civil society, even limited and patchy compliance with the reformed Poor Law was not cheap, as, by 1868, the cost of relief had risen to £1.3 million and 'Thirteen per cent of the whole population of London were relieved as paupers in 1851, and in 1868 the percentage had increased to 16' (Greenwood, 1869, p. 311).

The giving of Relief to the poor, those who were neither elderly, infirm or handicapped, was borne by the Parishes and charitable organisations. The conditions of relief were varied and harsh, as a claimant had to prove that they were *able-bodied* and deserving of support. On the subject of *outdoor relief* (at home, and not in the Workhouse), Octavia Hill saw structural problems: 'You can never make a system of relief good without perfect administration, far-sighted watchfulness in each individual case; and this is specially true in an age in which bad systems of relief have trained the people to improvidence' (Hill, 1877, p. 20).

The effects of the Poor Law were to break up families and increase wretchedness for all that came under its control (Greenwood, 1869). It was because of this persistent situation, and through direct experience with it, that modern social work developed. The industrial revolution brought social dislocation and ravaged the lives of the newly urbanising population (Ashton, 1962; Southgate, 1958). The prevailing philosophy of those in charge of industrial investment all pointed in one direction, and the stability required for the implementation of the Poor Laws pointed in another. Class consciousness became divided at the place of work as the new *Working Class* emerged in the 1830s (Engels, 1892; Thompson, 1968). In an attempt to deal with the reality of poor workers, the destitution and the vices of the urban situation that emerged, Thomas Chalmers, a community-based clergyman, began, in the 1820s, to minister to his flock through creating self-help groups and mutual interest formations in his parish. This is one of the earliest records of community development as a purposeful activity (Chalmers, 1832; also cited in Richmond, 1917, pp. 29–30). Philanthropy began to flourish (Southgate, 1958) and charitable work in the community around the major issues of the day – godlessness, illiteracy, alcohol addiction – drew many highly motivated, better-off people into the poorer communities where they offered assistance and leadership.

This was also a time of radical thinking, and people like Adam Smith, Wilfred Owen and Jeremy Bentham were making their mark on the thinking of people about their relations with government (Bentham, 1914; Ashton, 1962; Thompson, 1968; Payne, 2005). Additionally, gender relations in society, particularly in middle- and upper-class society, were undergoing change, particularly in terms of expectations and the realisation of human potential among women (Bennett, 1919; Hirsch, 1998; Schafer, 2006; Simey, 2005; Darley, 2007).

From the beginnings of missionary work amongst the needy masses, there has been a tension between the need to proselytise, thus to control the process of transferring wisdom and enlightenment, and to develop self-sustaining mechanisms in the community itself (Hopkins, 1878; Schaeffer, 1914). Carpenter explains how, originally, Christian responsibility for the souls of the wretched led to the establishment of community facilities, especially for the young, so that their energies (and, subsequently, their souls) might be drawn towards more fulfilling and beneficial goals (Carpenter, 1861). Sunday Schools led on to 'Ragged Schools' for the indigent, which led to more Christian activists being drawn into these communities for the service of the greater good. Some of their motives were mixed, as they looked to provide a service for the poor and to provide for the freedom and happiness for all. Nevertheless, there was also the intention to safeguard against civil unrest through providing basic education and socialization in their schools: 'The Dangerous Classes in England, no less than in France, consist of those whom vice or poverty, or ignorance, generally all three, have placed in a state of warfare with social order' (Cornwallis, 1851, pp. 22–3).

Generally, there was a degree of uncertainty about the process, and about the right way forward, especially as new ideas were heavily contested by those who believed in the essential worthlessness of the poor and the criminal. Octavia Hill cautions against over-zealousness, saying that: 'The uninitiated speak fervently, but ignorantly, about the need to spend full-time lives with the poor – there is considerable sacrifice involved' (Hill, 1877, p. 24), then goes on to say that (p. 25): 'The poor should be treated and considered as normal people, and not a separate class.' These are ideas that do not go down well, from either a conservative standpoint (Smiles, 1873): 'Heaven helps those who help themselves' (p. 1); and then: 'perseverance and diligence are needed to serve to combat the species of moral weakness which is the disease of the present generation', (p. 224), or a radical one (Engels, 1892): 'What is true of London, is true of Manchester, Birmingham, Leeds, is true of all great towns. Everywhere barbarous indifference, hard egotism on one hand, and nameless misery on the other, everywhere social warfare, ...' (p. 24).

In their *Handbook of Settlements*, Woods and Kennedy trace the pattern of thinking that allowed parochial ministers of religion, and otherwise pious laity, to open up their perspectives on society, and towards the poor in particular; this to allow 'unsectarian' thinking to advise their work (Woods and Kennedy, 1911, p. i; see also Woods and Kennedy, 1922). As Octavia Hill put it: 'It is necessary to believe that in thus setting in order certain spots on God's earth, still more in presenting to a few of His children a somewhat higher standard of right, ... and that he will not permit us to lose sight of His large laws, but will rather make them evident to us through the small details' (Hill, 1875, p. 25).

Hill was drawn to the thinking of Ruskin, Robert Owen and Thomas Chalmers, all of whom believed firmly in the ability of the common person to become self-determining, if given the right leadership and conditions (Hill, 1877; Henderson, 1899; Woods and Kennedy, 1911). Christian Socialism became a popular and acceptable vehicle for their outlook and activities (Woods and Kennedy, 1911, p. 8). This diverted activists from the revolutionary thoughts of the likes of Marx and Engels (1848).

A great expansion of charity and philanthropy took place after the passing of the Poor Law Reform Act of 1834. This saw the emergence of organisations specialising in the welfare of specific sources of distress in the community: mental illness; illiteracy, drunkenness and intemperate behaviour; moral wretchedness. It also saw a rise in the incidence of concerned citizens around issues of public order and public health. It is from these origins that the emergence of substantial structures and regulation developed, which can be shown to be the direct forbears of community development theory and practice. In pursuit of their varied objectives, charitable societies and religious missionaries probed deeply into the areas of poverty, bad housing and moral decay (London Congregational Union, 1883).

The notion of ascribing responsibility for a discrete area to one particular welfare worker appears to have originated in Elberfeld, Germany in 1852, where their programme of *outdoor relief* involved social support from volunteer 'visitors' (Davy, 1888). A combination of local government planning and investment in institutions, plus a consistent 'ecclesiastical' input, provided a solid base for relief (p. 52). This thesis was taken up by the prominent British parliamentarian, William Rathbone, who wrote, in 1867: 'Where good is to be done to individual men, it should come from the free-will of fellow-men ... with the trappings of any welfare institution away from the picture, and on face-to-face terms' (William Rathbone, 1867, quoted in Rathbone, 1905, p. 368).

William Rathbone was a solid supporter of the charitable work done in Liverpool by the *Select Vestry* (a Liverpool Board of Guardians) and also, and in particular, of the Liverpool Central Relief Society (formed in 1846, and a forerunner of the Charity Organisation Society's (COS) town-wide approach to co-ordination of charity – see below). He prevailed upon the Liverpool Central Relief Society to study the approach of Elberfeld, Germany, and which: 'is now the only Society working over the whole town which investigates claims on the charitable and gives systematic relief in cases of distress.' Up until 1887, the Elberfeld Society had done its charitable relief work almost entirely by means of paid agents, although in two districts of the town it had a few years before begun making some use of the services of independent committees of volunteers (Rathbone, 1905, p. 375; Davy, 1888). This latter system seems to have taken over by 1905, as the success of the scheme considerably reduced the number of welfare beneficiaries (Gilman, et al., 1905, p. 735).

An early example of individual creativity and drive in the welfare field is the work of Mary Carpenter, who devoted her life to the treatment of offenders, and the engagement of disaffected young people (Carpenter, 1861). Her inspiration drew in others to assist her, and a prototype for the later *Settlement* movement approach was formed in this way. There can be little doubt that the influence of her dedicated, residential, volunteer helpers at *Red Lodge School* (for girls) became the forerunners for the 'residents' of the welfare Settlements established later in the nineteenth century (Browne, 1887). One of these, who was a resident for five years at the '*Lodge*', recollected: 'The work at Red Lodge was full of interest, but it required a great deal of patience; indeed no one who has not actually laboured amongst the depraved and criminal can imagine how discouragements and disappointments were every-day affairs' (p. 104). Carpenter's influence spread beyond the shores of Britain, and Bruno (1957, p. 63) traces this through the annals of the National Conference of Social Work in America, where the idea of 'treatment' itself replaced punitive punishments as a general philosophy for those delivering welfare support to offenders, and their communities.

In America, another reformer in the community sphere was Josephine Shaw Lowell, who championed abused women in the home, and actively sought ways of enhancing the effectiveness of charitable intervention. She was a person of her times, and some of her reasoning is certainly dubious by today's standards and values: (on indigence) '... we find that he does not work for exactly the same reason that keeps the black man and the pauper from working. He gets all he wants without working.' (Lowell, 1911, p. 201; see also: Lowell, 1884, pp. 96 *et seq.*) Nevertheless, Lowell's input into the National Conference of Charities and Corrections towards the end of the nineteenth century ensured that the foundations of today's social work considered charity and welfare intervention from new perspectives: '[The] rule is that the best help of all is to help people to help themselves', and that no amount of thought or time or money could be considered wasted if it is spent on this effort. 'The best way forward was to encourage thrift, and to start provident schemes that, in turn, encourage, providence, skill training, and self-control, for the poor. This activity reflects the best of society's charitable values' (p. 109). It was this idea of people helping themselves, rather than being consigned as burdens in perpetuity on the alms of their neighbours that drove all her efforts at reform. Lowell saw the best line that charity could take was for those with the means and charitable intent to encourage self-help through intervention and organizing within the impoverished community (pp. 98–9).

During the American Civil War and in contradiction of the predominant, white, cultural view of that history, it must be remembered that Black (*Negro*) community leaders had emerged to organise the *Underground Railway*, the only effective way for Black slaves to win their freedom. Henry Bibb became a formidable organiser, among many Black Americans of the period for the freed slave cause in Canada. In Detroit, Bibb began and inspired the '*Colonizer Movement*' to resettle escapee slaves in a free environment (Bibb, 1849; Landon, 1920).

During the days up to and after the Civil War (1838–65), Black Americans and Canadians (mostly escaped slaves) set up a thriving network in the Northern States of the USA, and in Canada, with or without co-operation from other anti-slavery members of their communities. Here they received and settled escapees (Ward, 1855), and thus began a long tradition within the American Black community of public service. Local, Black self-help organizations flourished after the Reconstruction era (1863–77) in the Southern States of the USA. The local Church became a magnet for self-help, education as well as spiritual upliftment. Du Bois documents the capacity of these organisations to produce coherence for communities, which underwent severe pressures during the imposition of the segregationist *Jim Crow* legislation that followed (du Bois, 1907; Ball, 2013). As the '*Reconstruction*' period had such a devastating effect on the Black community in the American South, self-help and public service paled into virtual obscurity (Pike, 1874). One exception was the rise of the Black business and self-help institution, *True Reformers*, which flourished between 1891 and 1910. Eventually engulfed in scandals in their financial arm, *True Reformers* nevertheless contributed greatly to the capacity of the post-reconstruction Black community to enter mainstream economic life (Hollie, 2012). This aspect of American history is skimmed over in the history of American community organizing and in social work literature. Something of a revival followed the outbreak of the First World War, in April, 1917, for Americans – see below.

As the movement for social reform progressed, many, like Josephine Lowell, found themselves in direct contact with powerful people in government, and the role of the welfare lobbyist became firmly established. They also tackled, head on, the establishment approach to *charity*, which admonished against *careless giving*, for fear of causing more physical suffering and more poverty: 'it does so by undermining the independence, self-reliance, and energy of persons whose only capital consists in those invaluable qualities' (Lowell, 1911, p. 215). Nevertheless, there was an inexorable expansion of the Charity Organization

Society form across most major cities and towns both in Britain, and in the USA (McLean, 1910).

Fifty years on, in England and Wales, the 'new' Poor Laws were still not being implemented as planned, and the rising tide of charity and philanthropic endeavour was producing duplication, variable standards of relief, and, apparently, a rising tide of dependence upon charitable handouts (London Congregational Union, 1883). Bailward (1895, pp. 155–7) claims that the syndrome of the: 'revolving door' of giving as charity occurred again and again, and multi-generational pauperism was all around. They saw the contradictions of giving creating unfair economic advantage – i.e. giving a 'capital' item then used as a trade good or business facility, for example, a mangle (p. 155).

He cites Gibbon, and *The Decline and Fall of Rome*, in the creation of dependency amongst the plebeians, and how demanding they became. 'There are misguided poor, and those that have had poverty thrust in them' – i.e. rent arrears in economic downturn times (p. 157). As time went on, the Poor Law relief system began to fail altogether, and a concerted effort had to be made to rectify the system, overall. For example, in Whitechapel, a poor district in the East of London, outdoor relief had been practically abolished, because: 'In 1869–70 there was a hard winter ... The figures in the sixth week of the first quarter of the year were: in-door paupers relieved, 1,419 ; out-door paupers relieved, 5,339; and the cost of out-door relief was £168 17s. 4d. per week.' The Poor Law Commissioners' money began to run out (Loch, 1890, pp. 26–7). As Greenwood expressed it in 1869, moneys being levied are being wasted as well: 'The very heart and core of the poor-law difficulty is to discriminate between poverty deserving of help, and only requiring it just to tide over an ugly crisis, and those male and female pests of every civilized community whose natural complexion is dirt, whose brow would sweat at the bare idea of earning their bread, and whose stock-in-trade is rags and impudence' (Greenwood, 1869, p. 315).

Many became dissatisfied with the outcome of the 'reforms' of 1834, as the system did not appear to become any more effective than it had been before (Greenwood, 1869). 'Professor Fawcett's dictum that "you may have as many paupers as you choose to pay for" is no less true to-day than it was seventy years ago' (cited by Bailward, 1920). It seemed that the public purse had to be infinitely elastic, without a proper solution to the problem being found. Many of the misgivings had been pointed out in the past by those actively engaged in the community: 'public charity, so far from harrowing the territory of human wretchedness, has widened and extended it; and thus left a greater field than it at first entered on, for the exercise of that private charity, which it has at the same time weakened, both in its means and in its motives' (Chalmers, 1832, p. 290).

After 1834, discontent, especially among activists, but also among taxpayers and business leaders, led to ideas for reform (MacKay, 1896). Eventually, these were to lead to the charity *Visitor* system, and, more specific to our interests, the *Settlement Movement*. As the *Settlement* idea began to establish itself, first in England, and then in the United States, a fundamental change began in the way that alms and charity were perceived and then delivered.

These questions were not fully answered for some time, certainly not before the new social science of social enquiry began to place before a concerned public some of the facts of the case (Engels, 1892; Booth, 1902; Rowntree and Sherwell, 1899; Rowntree and Lasker, 1911; Rowntree and Pigou, 1914). Social conditions became a source of tension and dismay for anyone with a social conscience, or a keen eye on public health issues (Hemenway, 1916). As Engels had described a generation earlier, concerning the creation of the English Working Class (in 1844), and urban conditions: 'The brutal indifference, the unfeeling isolation of each in his private interest becomes the more repellent and offensive, the more these individuals are crowded together, within a limited space.' (Engels, 1892, p. 24). 'Society in such districts has sunk to a level indescribably low and hope-less' (p. 36). The tensions for charity workers in these areas are described by the London Congregational Union tract on the subject, of 1883 (p. 9): 'The poverty, we mean, of those who try to live honestly; for notwithstanding the sickening revelations of immorality which have been disclosed to us, those who endeavour to earn their bread by honest work far outnumber the dishonest'. They go on to describe the inhabitants as: 'costermongers, bird catchers, street singers, liberated convicts, thieves, and prostitutes ...' It continues that, should one turn out of one of these streets and enter a narrow passage, about ten yards long and three feet wide, to a court eighteen yards long and nine yards wide: 'Here are twelve houses of three rooms each, and containing altogether 36 families. The sanitary condition of the place is indescribable. A large dust-bin charged with all manner of filth and putrid matter stands at one end of the court, and four water-closets at the other. In this confined area all the washing of these 36 families is done, and the smell of the place is intolerable.' (London Congregational Union, 1883, p. 18).

Because of the sheer scale of these problems, and the increasing and contin-uing engagement with the social issues involved, and as the Poor Law models of relief (indoor and outdoor) failed to stem the tide of poverty and social wretch-edness (Bailward, 1895; Jackson, 1895; Residents and Associates, etc., 1898b; Addams, 1902), charity workers began to seek a more systematic approach to their work. Barnett observed that those in contact with the problems of the poor began to 'distrust the machinery for doing good' (Barnett, 1898, p. 12), and this sparked a lively debate. Bailward called for the essential dignity of the working class to be recognised and developed as an asset in the fight against poverty (Bailward, 1895, p. 168). There was no stigma and everything to gain, from befriending the poor and seeking out the evils of squalor and inhumane conditions (such as child labour), which held the poor captive (Gorst, 1895). 'How can we arouse the people to a realization of their selfish interest in efficient public health administration?' (Hemenway, 1916, p. iii) summed up the mood of the time, and was accompanied by a call for the recognition for professional services to be at the disposal of local government for direct intervention in this arena. He goes on that one result of the rapid strides made by science has been a greatly increased workload for local government, which is stuck without properly trained staff: 'Incompetence and ignorance on the part of the field force must necessarily result in unsatisfactory work. It is therefore of importance to the people of the nation that provision be made to remedy the present deficiency' (p. 254).

Arising out of these social forces, between 1870 and 1940, in Britain and the USA, a sea change took place in the relations between those with the means to provide support for those marginalised by society, and those on the receiving end of their efforts (Gorst, 1895). Taking the lead from, perhaps, Elberfeld (above), and William Rathbone, in 1870, *The Society for the Organisation of Charitable Relief and Repressing Mendacity* was formed in London (later to be known as The London Charity Organisation Society – COS) (Hill, 1877; Addams, 1902; Payne, 2005). Reviewing the situation historically, Devine puts it thus:

> A new unity has been discovered underlying various charitable activities which centre in the homes of the poor. It has become apparent that relief societies, charity organization societies, religious, educational, and social agencies, and public departments charged with the care of dependents, form practically a single group with many common interests, methods, difficulties, and dangers (Devine, 1904, pp. 10–11).

While still clinging to the principle that there were *deserving* and *undeserving poor*, the new COS began to co-ordinate charitable and philanthropic efforts, and to arbitrate over standards of practice on a more detached, less statutory and less moralistic basis (Bailward, 1895). A strong moralistic ideology still pertained in many establishments (Smiles, 1873; Richmond, 1907; Plater, 1914; Potter, 1929), and missionary work remained as the essence of many institutions in marginal areas. In the 'Popular Edition' of Smiles' *Self Help* (1873), this 'best seller' thinking of the time was well-reflected in phrases such as: 'perseverance and diligence (are needed) ... to serve to combat the species of moral weakness which is the disease of our present generation' (p. 336), and 'Good rules may do much, but good morals far more' (p. 368).

Nevertheless, there was considerable disagreement with this approach that differentiated between '*deserving*' and '*undeserving*' poor people, but legislative reform was not feasible in the Victorian era (Richmond, 1907; Jenks, 1910). Richmond, sustaining a strong Christian outlook, appealed not only for more Good Samaritans, but also 'more innkeepers, each one doing their special work' to sustain the stability of society for all (Richmond, 1907, p. 14).

The charity societies began to respond to the considerable effects of public health issues. Octavia Hill called for the consolidation of the considerable knowledge gleaned by the local branches of the Charitable Organisation Society and the Church in determining the best way forward in dealing with these issues (including the spiritual lives of the poor) (Hill, 1877). She was caught between the need to retain the goodwill of the middle-class donors of charitable gifts for the war chests of the field-based charities, and the need to inform this same public about the severe limitations of this form of support. 'Money', she wrote, '... is perhaps the most difficult thing to give without doing harm' (Hill, 1877, p. 93). 'Our ideal must be to promote the happy natural intercourse of neighbours' mutual knowledge, mutual help', she wrote in the same presentation (p. 23).

Some acceptable mechanism had to be found to bring clarity to the system, and to reassure both government and the philanthropists alike that wastage and duplication welfare was being minimised, and that some coherence was being drawn into the institutions of public welfare and relief. The formation of the Charities Organisation Society (COS – and its off-shoot, the University Settlement Movement, see below) began this process. This saw the purposeful institutionalisation of service provision, and a fresh approach to the alleviation of social suffering induced by poverty, waywardness, and those receiving aid of this kind. The first major change was the emergence of a less judgmental, and a more *professional* approach to the provision of social and economic support to those in special circumstances (of rehabilitative work). In essence, in tandem with the fresh thinking and the application of the new social sciences to the problems arising from poor public health (e.g. Chadwick, 1843; Brisbane, 1874), COS brought rationality into the problem-solving mission of charity and philanthropy. This process began the emergence of social work as a recognised means of integrating those with special needs, and from that process emerged the philosophy that those in even the most oppressive of circumstances were and could be capable of helping themselves towards the stabilisation of their lives and their re-integration into the mainstream of society. The *science of prevention* was now being addressed (Chadwick, 1843, pp. 180–3). Chadwick saw early on that it was down to communities to take up the cause of public health and public well-being if the scourges of disease and social degradation were to be overcome (p. 180). This set the scene for the emergence of *community development* or *community organization* (USA) for local problem-solving activities, later to be recognised as a structured mechanism for planned intervention. At this early stage, professionalism was recognised as being the key element of purposeful social intervention for beneficial change (Chadwick, 1885; Woods, 1891).

Two distinct routes led to this path. The first, originating from COS, was the Settlement Movement in Britain and the USA, where a break with both the punitive framework of the Poor Laws and the philosophy of 'outside relief', or charity, was sought. The first idea, in a big break with the Poor Law and its Guardians' formal approach to relief, was the introduction of a personal dimension to the support of the poor. Volunteer *Visitors* were deployed by the charity organisations to visit the

51

poor in their own homes and to make a supportive analysis of their needs. Whereas charities had some funds of their own, in many cases, they became the agents for Parish relief as well (Carpenter, 1861; Greenwood, 1869; Bosanquet, 1874; Hill, 1877; Hopkins, 1878; Lowell, 1884). The principle of *outdoor relief* was to be extended and developed by these *Visitors* and their 'employing' agencies into a form of close-knit support. Nevertheless, the basic principle of poverty being a symbol of 'otherness' in society, was strictly maintained (Hopkins, 1878). Greenwood gives us an insight into the plight of an unemployed worker trying to prove his eligibility from the Parish Poor fund: 'I have witnessed instances in which the "labor test," instead of proving a man's willingness to work for what he receives, rather takes the form of a barbarous tyranny, seemingly calculated as nothing else than as a test of a poor fellow's control of his temper' (Greenwood, 1869, p. 321).

Humiliation faced the charity petitioner before he/she was forced to work on back-breaking work for the sake of scant rations and physical exhaustion, 'working' for the Parish (Greenwood, 1869, pp. 319–20). Considering the extent of the social gulf that existed between the early charity workers who 'visited' the poor in their homes, and, later, the advent of the Settlement 'resident' in these poorest of districts, considerable personal fortitude must have been necessary (Kellogg, 1894; Richmond, 1907). And so, in their drive to make the service more effective and efficient, handbooks and advice pamphlets for the newcomers to 'visiting' were produced across a wide array of settings and circumstances (Lady of Boston, 1832; Hill, 1877; Sears, 1918).

Although COS became a major and continuing force in the implementation and regulation of *outdoor relief* in support of the Poor Laws, they were not above criticism, either: 'there's no mercy, no charity, for a helpless woman in this big and wealthy city,' as 'They are such very fancy ladies'... 'I hate them all' (Devine, 1904, p. 262). Barnett reflected on the situation, as he sought a fresh approach to the enduring conditions of poverty in the cities of Britain. University people wanted hard evidence about the nature of poverty and the poor society. They also distrusted the established methods for doing good as a panacea for society's ills: 'A generation which had breathed something of the modern scientific spirit was not content with hearsay knowledge and with sentimental references; it required facts and figures—critical investigation into the causes of poverty and personal knowledge of the poor' (Barnett, 1898, p. 13).

Sharing the experience of better living practices, sharing the burden of life under taxing conditions, and sharing the benefits of collective outcome thus gained became the principles of the Settlement Movement.

The Settlement movement

In 1884, the first University Settlement, Toynbee Hall, was established in the East End of London (Barnett, 1888). The general philosophy of this, and its numerous copiers and derivatives (Bailward, 1885; Gorst, 1895; Addams, 1902; Residents and Associates, 1898a), was to *lead by example*. Barnett (1898, p. 13) distrusted philanthropists with 'long arms', who never engaged directly in the issues that confronted the poor. Instead, the new Settlement: 'is very suitable for men or women, who are anxious to devote some time to their poorer neighbours ... The University Settler has come to live among his poorer neighbours to share their life as far as is possible and learn their thoughts' (Jackson, 1895, p. 90).

Another powerful reasoning behind taking up residential status in the neighbourhoods being that some 'have poverty thrust upon them,' (Bailward, 1895, p. 157) and that the restoration of social and economic stability was achievable through direct association with good examples, and personal support. People from privileged and established circumstances would come to live alongside those in more straitened circumstances, and engage and assist/support these less well-off people with everyday tasks and activities. Using the pattern of behaviour specially designed to suit this process, those in the lead would contrive that the essential qualities rub off onto those in need of change, stability and fresh outlooks on the world. They would widen the boundaries of the possible, and increase confidence and personal skill levels. This was social engineering on a pretty transparent level (Residents and Associates, 1898b). This area 'is the most "charitied" region in Christendom, ... come about in the space of two decades [rapid social change and mobility] ... has called out such unparalleled [charitable] activity ... causing a great deal of confusion and lost force' (p. 245). '[Conversely...] The most searching charity is that which, ... aims to build a better life for the district out of its own material and by means of its own reserve of vitality' (p. 248).

Nevertheless, their mission was neither 'teaching nor conversion' (Barnett, 1898, p. 16). The first work projects involved the drawing together of local people, and the formation of activity-based formations and clubs of mutual interest. These were led by the '*residents*' of the Settlement, and, to a large extent, this activity pattern persisted for many years into the future in some Settlements (Fraggos, 1968; Blackfriars Settlement, 1973).

In America, once the idea of purposeful intervention in this way gained some publicity and interest, they went about it in a more forceful way, and with less class-bias than in Britain. Bruno records that, in 1863, Massachusetts began the first Charities Board in the USA, and in 1874, that Board called together Connecticut, New York and Wisconsin to join them in a common approach (Bruno, 1957, p. 6). Buffalo began the work of consolidating the work of its charities in 1875, and in the same year, 'the Co-operative Society of Visitors among the Poor was formed in Boston' (Kellogg, 1894, p. 6). From that time, the idea and movement towards co-ordination of local philanthropy and charitable work spread rapidly. At the same time, however, it was seen that even the '*New Charity Work*' of the Charity Organization societies, set up in major cities in the USA on the COS model of the UK, to co-ordinate charity activities, failed to meet some of the fundamental objections that arose from those in close contact with the poor and their predicament. Co-ordination, it was felt, distanced these associations from the fieldwork on the ground (Bruno, 1957, p. 193 *et seq.*). In 1884, Lowell called for more creative responses to the situation. He formed a *Friendly Society* to work for the good of the whole town. The society would target all the symptoms of social dislocation, and stimulate positive activities. In this way: 'it could give the wisest advice to private almsgivers were any almsgivers necessary, and it should make itself and its influence so prominent that all who wished to help others would come to it first for information and advice' (Lowell, 1884, pp. 98–9).

The answer was, in part, the Settlement movement. This was developing in London, and would soon, thereafter, in the USA, come under the enthusiastic guidance of Jane Addams, who threw herself without constraint into this cause. Addams, on a visit to Oxford University in 1888, paid a visit, also, to Toynbee Hall where she was converted to the Settlement idea. Addams writes (1912, pp. 88–9):

> In June, 1888, five years after my first visit in East London, I found myself at Toynbee Hall equipped not only with a letter of introduction ..., but with high expectations and a certain belief that whatever perplexities and dis-couragement concerning the life of the poor were in store for me, I should at least know something at first hand ... The next January found Miss Starr and myself in Chicago, searching for a neighborhood in which we might put our plans into execution.

The same year (18 September 1889) she, together with Ellen Gates Starr, opened Hull House Settlement in Chicago, and they immediately threw themselves, and their colleagues, into challenging not only the social situation of the poor district which they had selected, but also the industrial and organisational situation of the workers and residents of the area (Addams, 1912, pp. 46; and 136 *et seq.*).

The initial spirit of this more organised voluntary effort began to identify some significant issues: whereas strong motivation was essential for effective work in a new and alien environment, for the 'residents' (Potter, 1929), considerable training and preparation were needed if they were to be effective: 'to grasp the true principles of relief, learn what the needs of the poor are, what agencies there are to supply them, get to know the neighbourhood and the people, and to discover personal leanings in this regard' (Sewell, M. in MacAdam, 1925, p. 26).

The training programmes for 'residents' in the Settlements began almost immediately. It began as lectures in topical issues, and then developed steadily into focused training with insight being provided into 'preventive' work as well as how to deal with presenting issues (MacAdam, 1925, p. 28). Soon this was formalised through special training programmes in London (LSE) and Liverpool, where the work of Eleanor Rathbone and Elizabeth MacAdam did much to raise the profile of social work (MacAdam, 1925; Pederson, 2004a, b; Simey, 2005).

From the work in Hull House, Chicago, Addams recognised that a comprehensive understanding of the political, economic and social environment was essential if the work was to target most effectively the critical issues facing the population (Addams, 1930). The role of the Settlement lay in two directions – providing direct contact with and support for the poor, and being at the front line in promoting change at the level of local and central government. Jane Addams, herself a tireless campaigner and lobbyist on behalf of her causes, goes to great lengths to identify and affirm the work of others in this direction. In her 'Introduction' to her colleague, and Settlement founder, Rev Graham Taylor's work of 1913, *Religion in Social Action*, she praised the value of this work, which introduced the need for Health and Safety legislation, and also Worker's Compensation schemes. These schemes drew workers together in co-operative financial arrangements, and raised the public's commitment to this kind of activity (Addams in Taylor, 1913, p. xxiv; see also Davis, 1967, p. 13).

Taylor concerned himself with the spiritual side of life, the value of interpersonal relationships, and the intrusion of the State and the economy into this sanctum. Pulling public policy and human practice together was his cause:

> These deliberate and definite efforts for the revival of neighbourhood relationships chiefly centre about the public school, the public playground and recreation centre, the public library, churches of an institutional type, and social settlements. No more hopeful movement to unify and advance local communities, and no more inspiring prospect of doing so, is to be noted in America than that which seeks to use public school buildings as neighbourhood centres' (Taylor, 1913, p. 151).

Many others followed the same path, and it is important to emphasise these people's roles, as it was the direct forerunner of the *Social Planning* strand of community development, which was to consolidate itself in the latter years of the twentieth century.

Addams, in Chapter 2 of her *Democracy and Social Ethics* (1902, pp. 13–70) presents us with the three-way divide that confronted her Settlement (Hull House) workers: the values prevalent in charity and alms giving vs. the essential capabilities of the poor themselves vs. the professionalism of the Settlement Workers. Nevertheless, Bremner (1956) informs us that in the United States, no serious attempt was made before the end of the nineteenth century to measure the extent of poverty in that country. Social reformers, instead, used a combination of moral arguments backed up with anecdotal information (e.g. Riis, 1902). The Settlements became centres for support of the poor (Taylor, 1913), for research (Chaplin, 1920) and investigation of social ills (Woods and Kennedy, 1913), and for activism for social change (Hill, 1875; Darley, 2007). Because 'it helps the people to realize that law is the most powerful instrument for helping them against invisible enemies of health and life' (Henderson, 1899, p. 164), the settlement movement became a potential force in the political arena.

Whereas in the UK the State made no major effort to break out of the essential mould of 'provider of the first resort', as manifested in the Poor Laws and subsequent reform legislation in the early twentieth century, in the United States the lobbyists and other social factors began to influence the State to follow a different pathway. In Boston, the City Hall was able to discover first hand just how beneficial co-operation between charities and community groups (often ethnically focused and 'separate' from other communities) could be (Residents and Associates, 1903). As the new century progressed, radical political ideologies began to condition the mind-set of the nation. Characters like Theodore Roosevelt began to command widespread support politically because they gave the notion that change was possible (de Witt, 1915; Thayer, 1919).

The problem for the emergent professional of social work was that, as it became more organised in theory and in its practice methods, so it became more structured and integrated in the system of 'management' of the social conditions it had originally sought to eliminate. In 1907, Mary Richmond had written: 'There is a need for charity and support ... [nevertheless] ... [t]here are many things that the good neighbor cannot safely leave to any agency' (Richmond, 1907, p. 19). 'But things that can never be accomplished outside the family by measures the kindest and best intentioned, can be accomplished inside the family by contact, by persuasion, by neighborly help and by sympathy' (Richmond, 1907, pp. 33–4). She suggested the need for the active co-operation between agency and the surrounding neighbourhood. By 1908, her attitude had hardened to: 'There are sham families, and unstable families, and broken families, and families (so-called) that are mere breeding places of vice and crime. The trained worker, instead of juggling with words, will deal clearly with facts and conditions ...' (Richmond, 1908, p. 80).

National solidarity and engagement were central issues for many. For example, Lillian Wald, who began as a pacifist and civil rights campaigner like Jane Addams, then, eventually, headed up the US Government Commission on Housing, and became a close adviser to President Franklin D. Roosevelt as he launched his *New Deal* in the 1930s (Ware, 1938; Chambers, 1963; Davis, 1967). Like Jane Addams, Wald was a founder member of the National Association for the Advancement of Colored People (NAACP). Davis (1967, pp. 101–3) describes how the radical leaders of the settlement movement in Chicago and New York (William Walling, Anna Strunsky-Walling, Mary Ovington, Henry Moskowitz, Charles Russell, Florence Kelley) worked with Black Americans (led notably by figures such as Ida B. Wells and W.E.B. du Bois) over a period of years, 1908–9, to ensure that the civil rights movement began formally with Black people at the helm, in partnership with their White colleagues (Schechter, 2001). Addams used her powerful presence to join the struggle for equality for the Afro-American Black population, joining forces with Ida B. Wells and du Bois, amongst others, to push for the self-promotion of the '*Negro*' population. Addams promoted *Negro* self-help and organizational coherence towards their goals of equality and enfranchisement (Aptheker, 1977, pp. 6–10). Whilst Wells was a militant organizer in the Black community against the evils of lynching, she and Addams did not always see eye to eye on the full enormity of this phenomenon. In any event, the momentum for their work in the minority communities received a considerable setback with the election of President Woodrow Wilson (see below), who had priorities other than racial harmony and integration (Aptheker, 1977, pp. 16–20). Reliance on the assistance of outsiders (e.g. Whites) was no substitute for preparedness, self-reliance and self-help (Wells-Barnett, 1892). Du Bois describes how the small Black communities in the South had been held together through self-help in educational and religious associations and how the *Freemason Movement*, through their Lodges, had provided the structural example for many of these organisations to flourish (du Bois, 1907).

The growing professionalism within the welfare movement was beginning to throw up anomalies. Richmond's seminal work, *Social Diagnosis* (1917), had created a sea change in the way the new profession thought about itself, and this led to a narrowing of focus onto intensive work with the individual, which, conveniently, mirrored the State's general concerns with the fortunes and behaviour of the nation's poor (Colcord, 1919). Case work would become too localised, introspective, and individualised. By 1922, Devine was warning that the new professional front being adopted by social work was leading to: 'the neglect of a historical background [which then obscured an] explanation of much that is superficial – even if pseudo-professional and pseudo-scientific – in the social work of the present generation' (Devine, 1922, p. 306).

New forms of social organising

As the COS movement matured, criticisms began to creep in. Canon Barnett himself is recorded in saying that COS had: 'lost touch with the poor, and its methods of work were outmoded' (Bosanquet, 1914, p. 142), and the move began to secularise and diversify to make choices available to people in the community and to help them to initiative their own activities. In America, neighbourhood centres were identified as a necessary investment for communities to make on their own behalf, and formal community organization should become a stabilising factor in local life (Ward, 1915, p. 2). Ward continued to explore the ramifications of formally organising the community through the employment of a full-time community organising secretary, saying: 'This amounts practically to the establishment of a new profession' (Ward, 1915, p. 29). Gradually, after initially being glossed over as an informal role in communal organising (Perry, 1913; 1914; 1916), the professional role became centrally recognised – see below (Devine and van Kleek, 1916; Carbaugh, 1917; US Congress, 1916; Richie, 1917). The potential of the local school had long been identified as the source of community cohesion and generation. Perry, in two studies (1914; 1916) describes the potential thus:

> Neighborhood Development Dependent Upon Organization: ... It would seem that there are two fairly distinct types of social center development: The first, ..., is characterized by the fact that there is no special effort to organize the neighborhood into a co-operative responsible element in the government of the center. The second type of development is that which is illustrated in [creating social centres in public schools]. Here there is in the part of the promoters a conscious purpose to develop neighborhood organization. ... In differing degrees the neighborhoods are called upon to support and participate in the management of their centers (Perry, 1914, p. 9).

Two years later, he went on:

> The school as the focal point of certain phases of life which the people of a neighborhood have in common is much more accurately named when it is called a 'community center.' [This] marks the adoption, on the part of the Board, of an active and constructive policy in an important field of education and establishes the nucleus of what is destined to be a development of greater and greater magnitude. (Perry, 1916, p. 96)

Whereas in the city, charitable and philanthropic activity was becoming highly organised and effectual, there were other areas in American life which were now beginning to stir into raised awareness and collective activity. These were the rural and farming communities, who began to sense a social, economic and moral decline in many urban areas, and wanted to do something about their own situation before it became too late (Butterfield, 1909). In particular, the rural church and schools were seen by the local communities as the natural foci for most of their activities and interests (Richie, 1917; Hanifan, 1920; Burr, 1921; Steiner, 1925). There were those, however, who argued for a more secular approach. Hemenway (1916, p. v) calls for the unlocking of the church funds in the face of a public health crisis. Further, in reinforcing the idea of community-based professionals, answerable to the people, he states: 'Where the same cause is liable to produce illness in an entire community, and that cause is external to those made ill, protection is a community problem, and should be handled by the agent of those interested' (p. 3). He believed that the ongoing vulnerability of communities to illness and unsanitary conditions could best be served through the infusion of public health principles and knowledge in professional training programmes (p. 267).

Burr (1921, p. 193) highlights the 'hidden agenda' behind much of this work:

Often community workers are inclined to develop programs that seem to indicate their belief that all community activity which needs direction is in the region of recreation. This has been especially true in the attempt to apply city ideas to country life. It has been assumed that something must be done to 'keep them on the farm'. This is a put-down for the rural community.

These sentiments are echoed by Butterfield:

> The work of the farm and of the household, the life of the family, the amusements of the neighborhood, the interests of all in school, Grange [the Farmers' Union organisation], and church are closely intertwined. In social life, even if there be several churches in the neighborhood, a given church is quite dependent upon the general social resources of the community (Butterfield, 1909, pp. 69–70).

McMechen recognised that the potential for success in supporting individual families in the small community was increased greatly if a wider spectrum of support could be identified and developed for a purpose: 'that will meet the needs of the community as a whole and not alone those of the disadvantaged family, the community will learn to interpret the field of family case work in its true sense as something more than a relief program' (McMechen, 1920, p. 40).

Butterfield continues this theme:

> But for the most part farm life is broken up into little neighborhoods, without exact boundaries, without very much coherence, and, in fact, without much to tie people into a real group. Consequently ideals for the development of a community or a given area are difficult of crystallization [sic], because there is not much to crystallize about. Some device should be found, however, by which a nucleus of community pride may be developed, and around which may be gathered those forces of rural progress that will tend to give group unity, group ambition (Butterfield, 1909, pp. 45–6).

These examinations of the ideal components of community life and the best way to achieve it resulted in insights being obtained that would well serve, unchanged, community organization/community development across the decades: viz. 'Social Capital: [meanings:] ... goodwill, fellowship, sympathy, and social intercourse between families and individuals' (Hanifan, 1920, p. 78; Field, 2003). Hayes describes a great number of organised rural communities, which responded to the World War I momentum for change. Nevertheless, despite the level of sophistication that was emerging through the discussion of ways and means in the literature about 'organization', he does not record any roles filled by the paid organisers, who are considered essential by other commentators (Hayes, 1921;

Clarke, 1918; Follett, 1918; State Council of Defense, 1918; Norton, 1920; Hart, 1920). Hayes does, however, allude to the National Conference of Social Work and their work to identify a model for professional intervention (Hayes, 1921, p. 99).

It is worth noting that in the Black communities across America, the level of social organisation had fallen into disarray. A call for this movement to be resurrected came from Rucker Smith, in 1916, who pleaded: 'Five people can start an organization that can be made to do some very effective work. All of the big monied men have an organization for every separate branch of their business, no matter what obstacle may confront them, they usually overcome it' (Smith, 1916, p. 9). The church organisations, and the neighbourhood schooling structures, having emerged as strong foci for the community strengthening movement that was beginning to consolidate, made an impact on the State at the very top (Wisconsin State, 1913; Woods and Kennedy, 1913; Devine and van Kleek, 1916; Richie, 1917). In 1918, Ida Clarke published the first handbook describing the role and structure of a paid community organising worker (Clarke, 1918). She asserts: 'A Community may be organized with equal promise of success in city or village, or countryside' (p. 18); and 'The function of the secretary is nothing less than to organize and to keep organised all the Community activities herein described; to assist the people to learn the science and to practice the art of living together; and to show them how they may put into effective operation the spirit and method of cooperation (p. 37).

This structure had already served good purpose in the expansion of the role of the community organiser in the United States, where President Woodrow Wilson saw the *'Community Center Movement'* as an essential ingredient in the establishment of the supportive community at a time of national crisis. Each centre was to become the 'capitol of the little local democracy' (Dr Philander P. Claxton – US Dir. of Education – cited by Clarke, 1918, p. 10).

Formal structuring of community development/organization

In Britain, the training activities for social work were left very much in the hands of the Universities and other training organisations – mostly Charities (Rathbone, 1905; MacAdam, 1925; Payne, 2005; Simey, 2005). In the United States, however, a dynamic relationship emerged between the National Conference of Social Work, the Settlement Movement, the COS-style Charities, the University-based training programmes, and the agencies of the state (Brandt, 1907; Lee, 1937; Bruno, 1957; Chambers, 1963). This was given a big boost when, in 1916, the United States Congress passed the Army Appropriation Act (US Congress, 1916), which sought focus for the National effort towards greater rural productivity and social cohesion during World War II. President Woodrow Wilson (1913–21) was directly responsible for the impetus behind the community dimension of the

War effort. He required his officials to draw up and consolidate the structure of a *Community Center Movement* (sic) across the rural areas of the United States (Clarke, 1918). Butterfield (1919, p. 314) sets out the scenario:

> The National Council of Defense recently issued a nationwide appeal for the organization of school districts which are virtually neighborhoods of farmers. Much good will come from this effort. But it is a very grave question as to whether so small a group as live in a school district or farming neighborhood can be organized effectively, although there is no reason why such neighborhoods should not cooperate in every way possible for their common interests.

This was then taken up across a number of US Administration Departments: Austin and Betten (1990, p. 95) describe this process, citing the organisational work of one John D. Hervey from the University of Ohio, who is credited with the creation of rural community organizational techniques in response to the Department of Agriculture funding and directive policies following the Army Appropriation Act. Within the State administration, the War effort at community level was taken seriously to the extent that co-ordinated policy steps were undertaken:

> [This gives] a general outline of the work that should be undertaken by community councils. ... we believe, fully sufficient to justify every special effort toward community organization. The later usefulness and advantage of such organization to each community itself also is ample reason for this state-wide movement, urged by the national government and now undertaken in California (State Council of Defense (California), 1918, p. i).

Furthermore, the co-operation achieved during this period in inter-Departmental work led to the administrative unit of the County being recognised as the most effective in producing community development for Government policy implementation (Colby, 1933).

Responsibility for co-ordinating the relief to be given to Army veterans and their (often bereaved) families, was given to the American Red Cross – this work was led by Mary Richmond – which ensured that the impact of the work was felt in the immediacy of the local community, and not directed from a distant office or from above. Woodrow Wilson tapped into a thriving community-based social welfare consciousness in just about all settings in American society. In 1913, Amelia Sears had written the 1st Edition of her: *The Charity Visitor: a handbook for beginners* (Sears, 1918). She called upon all 'Charity Visitors' to take a holistic view of the client and the surrounding family and environment so that the agency and the Visitor might be better informed about the best way forward in supporting the client and to deal with the issues concerned. Of particular importance was the condition of housing, and the relationship with the landlord (pp. 12–34). Above all, the Visitor had to get beyond the image and attitude of the '*Lady Bountiful*' which, up until then, had acted as a barrier to tackling underlying causes of a client's situation (p. v). She also stressed the need to work across agency boundaries, and to utilise the expertise of those knowledgeable in ethnically sensitive matters, and others who might be more amenable to the client system involved (pp. 46 *et seq*.). There was a definite bridge between the 'caseworker' as practised in most COS-style agencies, and the emergent community-focused worker (Charity Organization Society, 1883).

Sears was following on from the example of other pioneer women community-based workers, such as Caroline Barnett Crane in Kalamazoo, who built up a *Civic Improvement League* as a means of reviving a failing Church community (Bennett, 1919). Crane also instituted a ground-breaking approach to what is now called *community profiling*, compiling comprehensive surveys of small towns, and city districts, in order that community governance and facilitators for charitable and municipal services could better plan their interventions (pp. 24–35). In the setting of the small rural community, Butterfield demonstrated how the local community, particularly small neighbourhoods, provided the ideal base for a US Presidential community initiative (Butterfield, 1919, pp. 134–43). He admonished the rural Church for adopting a one-dimensional, inward-looking and soul-seeking/saving approach to religion.

> But when it becomes a ministering agency of friendliness and neighborliness and good will to the entire community, then it lives and grows and vitalizes the spirits of men. It is not putting the matter too strongly to say that the country church will regain its leadership in rural affairs only when it applies the community idea to its motives and methods (p. 160).

For others, it was a civic duty to organise the community in order to safeguard the future: '... clear-minded men are coming to a fundamental philosophy of community action that will steer cities free from blundering in their future civic-commercial endeavors and lead to achievements worthy of Americans in 1930' (Wilson, 1919, p. 10). The local Chamber of Commerce must become the powerhouse for dynamic community leadership, and become the natural counter to '*Bolsheviki*' betrayal (p. 130). Harrison describes how charitable effort had to be carefully co-ordinated, under strong leadership. The centrality to local democracy this served was summed up as: 'Something that is fundamental in the fabric of our public affairs ... a process of peaceful civic renewal, through the scrutinizing of conditions surrounding our daily living, with a view not only to correcting those that are unwholesome but to quickening any that show promise' (Harrison, 1920, p. 19).

Directing and capitalising on the combined efforts of all like-minded organisations was essential for this purpose (Wilson, 1919, pp. 25–6): '[The] Chamber of

Commerce Secretary who finds himself the executive manager of an organization of citizens that is seeking ... community prosperity undertakes concerted action and does not resort to "public bombast"' (p. 26). Strong community leadership was the critical factor, but not all communities were so endowed (Hayes, 1921). Ida Clarke had seen the local community centre secretary as the inspiration and guiding force behind the social cohesion and development that was a necessary component of local (and national) progress (Clarke, 1918). This 'secretary' was the: 'servant of the whole community' (p. 37). The local school house was to become: a *'Community Center'* and 'an enterprise for mutual aid in self-development' (p. 44), and the secretary had to be skilled in the promotion of any activity from recreation for youth (p. 182), to 'community buying and banking' (p. 82), 'community gardening' (p. 99), and 'co-operative canning and catering' (p. 142). The secretary was to be equally at home nurturing the urban and the rural community, but it was in the latter situation that the really creative and entrepreneurial skills of the (community development) worker came into their own (pp. 161–81), being responsive to all the manifest inclinations, as well as the objective needs of the entire community. This was a positive legacy of the Woodrow Wilson community generation initiative during the First World War, albeit he did not see community building to include the integration of the Black population. President Wilson's stance on community integration might be summed up as outlined in the St. Louis Argus, on 14 May 1915: 'Who first sought, under the present administration, "to divide man from man, group from group"? Who first divided colored Americans from white Americans in the Federal departments at Washington? Who first instituted separate wash rooms, lunch rooms and work rooms in the great American administrative offices?' (It goes on ...)

In parallel with this National push for the development of community centres, the YMCA developed a similar approach, but theirs was a spiritual mission, as well: 'To supplement and strengthen the Home, the Church, the School, and the Municipality in their relations to the social, recreational, educational, moral, and spiritual life of the community' (Ritchie, 1917, p. 11). Mary Follett strengthened this analysis by tying in the local development process with a national movement. She was no populist, but saw the development of the character of the individual citizen as the bedrock for neighbourhood advancement through collective action and problem-solving (Follett, 1920, p. 11 *et seq.*; Chaplin, 1920). Even Mary Richmond was drawn into the discussion: 'Group thinking is superior to individual thinking', she declared, when referring to the co-ordinated work of America's 'great national charities' (Richmond, 1920, p. 2).

This is of particular relevance when the complex nature of early-twentieth-century American society is taken into account. Mass immigration from Europe posed considerable difficulties for welfare services. There was some discussion of eugenics in intellectual circles, including Mary Richmond (1920), but she was not completely convinced by these (Richmond, 1930, pp. 608–9). Nevertheless, subjective prejudices of the qualitative differences between ethnic groups were beginning to creep into the literature, and in national politics at the very top (Abbott, 1921; Link, 1954; Peterson, 1965). In an earlier period, when the mixed ethnic settlement of the major cities in America was at its height through mass migration and immigration, and despite the turmoil that this created until the mid-1920s, community activists like Addams, Taylor, Josephine Lowell, etc., just took it in their stride and organised 'their' communities accordingly (Woods, 1923; Stewart, 1911; Addams, 1912).

In 1921, Devine expounded a broad field for the conduct of social work. What is now called *Social Planning* (Rothman, 2001), Devine saw as: 'Top-down mechanism for policy and co-ordination — a clearing house for information and screening of agencies' (Devine and Brandt, 1921, p. 257). The State and the Voluntary Sector should seek to work together, employing the flexibility and creativity shown by the Settlements, and allowing social welfare for the poor and needy to escape the 'dead hand' of bureaucracy and routine practice models (p. 230). The pioneering lead able to be offered by social work because of its insight into local conditions, and its wider, campaigning role in society at large, would allow it to imbed itself into: 'the "organized social movements" which are characteristic of contemporary American philanthropy' (p. 19). Their emergent community organization techniques would gain much quicker and effective headway over common social issues, through the propagation of democracy and social engagement at the community level (Dinwiddie, 1921, p. 60).

In Cincinnati, arising out of the First World War drive for community organisation, the *Civic Council* had created a *Social Unit* to formulate and implant an interventionist model for: 'an intensive experiment in district health work' (pp. 2–3). This programme ran for five years and entailed the recruitment and engagement of the maximum possible number of the 15,000 residents in the project's catchment area. It enabled the local population, and its associated professionals, to implement organisational activities: 'in community organization in the following ways (a) As an effective educational force; (b) As a coordinating factor; (c) As a policy-making body in local affairs; (d) As a representative body; (e) As a direct cause of increasing materially the effectiveness of public and semi-public services, through adapting them to the needs and wishes of the people' (p. 36).

What is especially interesting about this early experiment in co-ordinated social organisation and social change involving participation to a high degree is the vitriolic attack from the city's Mayor. He claimed that the Unit was: 'a government within a government — a step away from Bolshevism, with dangerous radical tendencies' (p.128). This kind of charge would dog President Johnson's *War on Poverty*, and the British Community Development Project fifty years later!

Because of the special difficulties facing Black American soldiers in World War I, many black women were recruited to the American Red Cross and the YWCA. No records were kept of the respective races of the participants, but it is known (Scott, 1919, Chapter XXVIII) that a social planning exercise was undertaken in Europe by at least two prominent Black 'Y' Organising Secretaries. This was to ensure that the reception centres for Black American troops on furlough, or for the recovery and rehabilitation of the injured behind the front lines, were successfully run with ethnic sensitivity. These were to be run on a voluntary basis. The crisis-born *War Camp Community Service* embraced the (segregated) Black recruits, servicemen, and returning veterans. Local organisers and volunteers worked tirelessly toward boosting community morale and *esprit de corps* amongst the troops, etc. Many Black workers were involved in this process (Rogers, 1921). Rogers ascribes the success of this process to the Christian virtues of brotherly love, buttressed by the 'American Way' of 'by and for the people' (p. 49). As Ovington (1911) points out, social organization in the Black community was having to compete with a White-dominated legislature and social attitudes. This made cross-ethnic social contact and, thus, welfare co-operation, even in New York, more difficult to sustain. If Ovington is to be believed, also, the Black community was itself divided by class, political allegiance, and by skin colour (p. 184). On the level of class, Ida B. Wells, for example, had no difficulty in organising community and national activities with the like of Jane Addams and Susan B. Anthony, but after the First World War, the social climate had changed.

In 1920, Hart described how the newly emerging *social sciences* could be enlisted to serve solve the questions of social division and failing democratic forces (Hart, 1920). Social workers could, and should, be at the fore in this process: 'Social workers in increasing numbers are at work, and for the most part they can be counted upon to support the larger developments of this community work' (p. 180), and they could be called upon to provide leadership because: 'The fate of democracy and community is not with extrinsic powers and agencies; but with the calm, scientific deliberation, the serene yet serious aspiration, and the whole-souled democratic administration that are determined from within the community itself' (pp. 216–17).

Social workers were especially well placed to fulfil the function of assisting in the discovery of all the 'lost talent', and in the selection and support of community leadership in pursuit of their democratic purpose (p. 210). To this end, Lindeman saw the reconstruction of the local community as a mission for the civically minded. He saw that there were three types of community organisation: '1. Including the total citizenship. 2. Including those who "join" a community club (voluntary). 3. Including those who "join" a neighborhood club, which is related to the community organization organically' (Lindeman, 1921, p. 143). Driven by the spirit of Christianity and a civic imperative: 'The wise leader will retain his theory and his idealism, while he makes practical use of the tools at hand' (p. 150), Lindeman imposes a severe and mammoth responsibility upon these local leaders. With the breadth of the task before them, ranging from economic revival, social mobilization and engagement, to the spiritual upliftment of the entire community, the task must surely be beyond the potential for the voluntary community leadership. There is a glossing over of just how these tasks and changes are to be brought about without full-time and paid assistance.

Raymond (1921) saw a holistic responsibility for social workers to take up this approach to solving the social and personal ills of their clientele, and then both Rogers (1921) and Devine (1922) outlined how social workers might take a programmatic approach to their work that required a strategic appraisal of the entire community and its problems as a blueprint for intervention and action. Both Devine and Rogers included *social planning approaches*:

> Social work, then, is the sum of all the efforts made by society to 'take up its own slack,' to provide for individuals when its established institutions fail them, to supplement those established institutions and to modify them at those points at which they have proved to be badly adapted to social needs (Devine, 1922, p. 22).

> There is no single agency that can settle all of the community problems. The bringing together of all groups and interests that pertain to caring for the third community motive, namely, for individual and community welfare, at a round table, with good-will, a common program, a recognition of each one's part in the program, a mutual respect and understanding is the beginning for real community service (Rogers, 1921, p. 47).

Professional skill and application would be essential to the diagnosis of and the development and/or bringing together of all these forces. Watson put the challenge thus: 'To one with training and imagination, the social forces in any community capable of organization are legion. They include "personal forces," "neighborhood forces," "civic forces," "private charitable forces," "public relief forces," and above all, the "forces" within the particular family to be helped' (Watson, 1922, p. 136). This captures the range of opportunities for intervention within the *Community Organizing* movement.

There was emerging a strong sense of purpose and the desire to formalise the processes and methods of *Community Organization* in America. The scope and range of the methods covered the desire, also, to set a formal rationale for intervention, as well as standards, guidelines for intervention processes: 'to establish standards of technique in relieving distress as to relieve the distress itself' (Watson, 1922, p. 100). For the first time, the professional role and practice skills of the *community organizer* were set out in 1922 (McClenahan, 1922). This work presumes that community organization was embedded in social work, and that the professional worker needed to learn the philosophy and the skills necessary to intervene at both the local level and from a strategic and overall planning level (see McClenahan, 1922, pp. xiv, 70, 100, 112). This work differentiates between the needs of urban, small town and rural settings, and provides a template for insight and constructive development to take place within the profession. She sets out: 'The principles of community organization.' These grow out of the need to accomplish the task of creating strong community spirit and of fostering genuine co-operation, the community itself must see its needs and work out the solution of its problems. The community secretary or organizer becomes a non-directive orchestrator of this process, but is not in overall control (p. 208). McClenahan's descriptions firmly describe, for the first time in clarity, that this is a *professional*, and not a voluntary role. This work demonstrates, also, how far McClenahan had moved in her thinking since 1918, when she published the *Iowa Plan*, a State-sponsored blueprint for local community-based systems of relief, where the people of the local community were kept firmly out of the planning and delivery loop (McClenahan, 1918).

Steiner adds more substance to this description in 1925. He goes into more depth than McClenahan, by addressing the complexities of public response to intervention, to paternalism by the worker, nevertheless stressing that the professional had to show professional judgment in deploying scarce resources on unpredictable community personalities (Steiner, 1925, p. 7). Steiner places great emphasis on the over-sight and over-view, which the professional worker must develop in post: 'Community Organization is the increase in participating in groups, organisations, and inter-group activity — continuous and crucial to adjustment of social forces' (p. 323), and the success of the (community organising) social worker depends: 'upon his ability to start in motion forces capable of bringing about the need adjustments in all spheres of community life'. Communities that appear to be well organised are just one step along the road to this (and the community is a diverse entity) (p. 324).

By 1928, Pettit had accumulated enough material for longitudinal studies of small communities that had been subjects of community organisational interventions (Pettit, 1928). His study (compiled by students and staff of the New York School of Social Work) covers four completely different types of community: middle-class/ethnically restricted; rural/small town; inner-city/ethnically diverse; and church-based community, and they are presented purely in an objective way, without comment or conclusions, and they are commended to the Schools of Social Work as training instruments.

By 1937, the revered and much quoted, Porter R. Lee, for twenty-five years a lecturer at the New York School of Social Work (and President of the National Conference of Social Work in 1928), was able to publish an in-depth discussion on the question most needful of an answer: was social work a profession driven by 'vocation' — an idealistic *'cause'* — or was it a *'function'* carried out by those in need of practical outcomes to social questions? Where did *community organiza-tion* fit into the scheme of things? (Lee, 1937). The *'cause'* element is essential to the core of a democratic society, whereas, the *'function'* element is essential to the progress of public health, efficiency and prevention (pp. 3–24). Lee stresses the dilemmas oft-times found in community organization: 'Participation and advocacy are central to this mode of social work. The continuous need for social action is probably a phase of the process growth in any society. It sometimes leads to irrational and sometimes fantastic proposals, and sometimes to statesman-like planning' (p. 259).

In another, nationwide study, Lee and his collaborators discovered that in many communities there was a lack of vision and common purpose, especially when broader issues relevant to the development of a profession were concerned (Lee, et al., 1922). Commentators and exponents such as Helen Bennett (1919), Amelia Sears (1918) and Jane Addams ('We see idealistic endeavor on the one hand lost in ugly friction' – Addams, 1930, p. 139), always exhorting the virtues of idealism, and moral rectitude, often coloured with outrage at the social circumstances within which these pioneers of social work found their 'calling' had led them. On occasion, and in a more cynical vein where the *function* is less venial: 'a worker [might be] appointed because of his political service rather than for his ability for this particular position' (Colby, 1933, p. 4).

In the UK, and from an unlikely source, social work was being described as a generic profession that, to be authentic, must have a direct input into the political process as well as covering all other avenues for social intervention. The commentator was the future Prime Minister, Clement Attlee (Attlee, 1920), who saw a bright future for social welfare in the broadest sense at both the level of local government and in a burgeoning Voluntary Sector. Of most importance were the training requirements such that professionals must be conversant with the roles of governance, management and face-to-face welfare intervention (p. 126 *et seq.*).

In the 1930s, when economic recession was endemic, and resources for public services, along with philanthropic donations, were at a low ebb, social workers found themselves up against considerable pressures. As Lee put it in 1933, social work faced a crisis where: America faced an indefinite continuation of greatly reduced resources for social work outside the field of relief, which may itself be at risk; secondly, economic insecurity was set to continue for some time; thirdly, government was still driving expectations that there would be more provision for health, welfare and social services; and, lastly, the role of private philanthropy and wealth held an uncertain role in the scheme of things (Lee, 1937, p. 180). He goes on to say that, because of these pressures, and because of professionalisation, the more social work grows in 'efficiency', and the more it becomes bureaucratised, the more the *vested interests* become tied to partiality, rigidity of function, and loss of creative scope and imagination (p. 180). Social workers must banish this vested interest, and take on the holistic picture (pp. 185–6), and economic security for our clients must be the objective because poverty and its attendant degradations are 'abhorrent not only to an exalted sense of justice but to a sense of common decency' (p. 189). He concludes by stressing that when social conditions become intolerable for the client, then *social action* is the creditable way forward, with social work support and leadership (pp. 259–61).

A study of this pre-Second World War literature reveals that the main proponents of community organization (Addams; Devine; Steiner; Pettit; McClenahan (and even Mary Richmond, 1917; 1922) and other forms of welfare work, carried out their tasks in a virtually colour-blind fashion, omitting to reference the growing Black-American philanthropic movement, and the role of the Black churches in holding their communities together (Carson, 1993; Chang, et al., 1994; Burwell, 1996). It is no wonder that, with so many social and economic imponderables, and with so much active discussion in the ranks of the profession, some clarity was urgently needed.

Thus, in 1938, US National Conference of Social Work set up a working party to evaluate *community organization* and appointed a prestigious team to consider the matter. It is worth quoting quite extensively from their Report (Lane, 1940, pp. 1–2):

> 1. That the term community organization is used to refer to a process, and, as is often the case in other professions, to refer also to a field. 2. That the process of organizing a community, or some parts of it, goes on outside, as well as inside, the general area of social work — it is practiced by diverse organizations and for varied purposes. It is the social welfare nature of its objectives when carried on within the area of social work, as opposed to other arenas. 3. That within the area of social work the process of community organization is carried on by some organizations as a primary [function] ... 4. That within the area of social work the process of community organization is carried on not only in communities or neighborhoods, or on the local level, but also on a state-wide basis and on a nationwide basis, or on the state and national levels. 5. That organizations whose primary function is the practice of community organization do not, as a rule, offer help directly to clients.

These formal statements have set the normal boundaries for community organization within social work ever since, **but**, as the Report goes on to state, as some *community organization* is carried out in non-social work agencies, then there is room for considerable variation in the values, practice methods and objectives. Therefore (p. 4):

> We suggest that the general aim of community organization is to bring about and maintain a progressively more effective adjustment between social welfare resources and social welfare needs. This implies that community organization is concerned with (a) the discovery and definition of needs; (b) the elimination and prevention of social needs and disabilities, so far as possible; and

(c) the articulation of resources and needs, and the constant readjustment of resources in order better to meet changing needs.

The consequences of the Lane Committee for American social workers were that, henceforth, *community organization* was to become an equal partner in the syllabus for social work education in the United States. This vindicated the persistence of the early reformers to discover a community-related solution to solving the often structural problems of urban life. It acted as a counter-weight to the tendency towards creating a social work mystique around 'relationships' and individualisation promoted by Richmond. Richmond loomed large over the profession, but a lively debate had been started as early as 1922 about the range of social work engagement over social issues (van Kleeck and Taylor, 1922). Obviously, the record of the social reformers within the emergent profession of social work, such as Addams, Devine, Clarke, and, certainly, Richmond, had not always been without friction within the economic and social fabric. For the most part, however, they had all been driven by the ideal of consensus and common cause. Lurking in the wings of American community organization, and, for the British, 'community work', lay the spectre of the *conflict model* within social work.

Conclusion

A number of issues emerge from this part of the study:

1. Urgent remedies were needed for the endemic social problems that followed industrialisation and urbanisation and for the residual difficulties experienced by rural communities. The Poor Laws essentially failed to provide anything but a punitive and stigmatising remedy for unemployment, homelessness, and general indigence. Charitable organisations grappled with the problem of moving from an essentially moralistic appraisal of the people who were the victims of this situation, to adopting a more professional, non-judgemental, and problem-solving approach. Persistent economic fluctuations, poor social/civic planning and war created the conditions for the continuance of this broad problem. Nevertheless, there was a reservoir of publicly spirited people who were prepared to come to grips with the issues in the form of philanthropic and charitable effort.

2. The application of scientific and rational analysis to these problems saw the gradual abandonment of prejudicial and superstitious ideas about cases and their remedies. Some of the social activists that joined this struggle applied themselves directly to the work-face of engagement with the poor, within their impoverished communities. It was from this group that a pioneering cadre of professionals emerged – the corps of *'home visitors'*, the settlement *'residents'*, and the managers and funders of social experiments, such as social centres and community-based institutions. The gathering of data, information, insight and a body of experience proved invaluable to the progress of this activity.

3. The application of rationality found the emergence of a model that could serve to solve the problems of the society, at the level of the community, by applying the efforts of the people themselves, with or without the assistance of the community's institutions. This mechanism became known as *community organisation* in the United States. Sociological data on the social milieu was emerging, and it was the application of this to identify intervention targets, plus, most significantly, the application of experiential knowledge that led to the clarification of models for intervention strategies. It was this combination that enabled the models of intervention, championed and lobbied for by Greenwood, Octavia Hill, Samuel Barnett, Jane Addams, and the American settlement movement that appealed to influential people like President Woodrow Wilson.

4. The State can play an active role in supporting and even harnessing community development. Official recognition and patronage allowed the State to buy into this process. As it became officially engaged in promoting this form of intervention strategy, its involvement promoted a national dimension to strategic planning in this area. This laid the groundwork for the development of a comprehensive theoretical analysis and practical modelling framework for community organisation/community organization/social planning.

5. Despite an early start, social activists in the UK failed to capitalise on this approach to social intervention. The UK was not much concerned with the consolidation of the theory and practice of its own Settlement movement's experience. Social work curricula involved some applications (Liverpool, for example) from the start in the early 1900s, but elsewhere it was the dictums of Richmond and Freud that absorbed the energies of the British theorists. Attlee tried to bridge the gap between Class and welfare intervention, but he failed to grasp that the work of the '*Working* Class', with their ideals of mutuality and in their many self-help activities, could be harnessed by the new '*social work*', which he saw as a Middle Class activity (Attlee, 1920, pp. 251 *et seq.*). In the UK, the Lane Committee made scant impact, despite its influence on the National Association of Social Workers in the USA (see Chapter 5, below). The academic divide between what happened at home, and what was good practice overseas was ignored due to the failure of UK social workers and academics to absorb the lessons being provided by the Colonial Office.

The Women's Institute

As a footnote to this chapter, which has been more or less exclusively about the drive towards coherence in community development in the United States, must be added an unrecognised but fairly self-contained and parallel development in Canada and the United Kingdom.

The Women's Institute (WI) presents an excellent role model and case study for the achievement of community development goals and methods. The WI was founded in Ontario, Canada in 1896 as an off-shoot of the local Farmers' Institute. This new women's organisation soon caught the Provincial Government's eye and start-up grants were forthcoming. Thus began a long association with government that was to assist it greatly in its formative years and the new 'WI' became a conduit for public health messages to the women of Canada (Fenner, 2000). Soon Provincial Governments were paying local organisers to spread the vision of the Women's Institute. Like many of these innovative organisations, the WI was launched by a few charismatic personalities. In this case, it was Adelaide Hoodless who carried the message across Canada and then to the United Kingdom in 1899. Meanwhile, the movement spawned its own brand of mobile trainer-development organisers, which allowed it to expand right across the country, producing a national Federation of WIs by 1919 (Federated Women's Institutes of Canada, 2015). The purpose of these paid organisers was to build local organisations to strengthen community cohesion and personal capabilities. In this way, the Women's Institute in Canada became the first agency to recognise community organization as a professional, paid activity, implementing both neighbourhood development interventions and social planning objectives. As the WI spread across Canada, the opportunity for a far wider enlistment to the cause of women's self-help arose. One founder member, Margaret Rose Robertson Watt, a recently widowed editor and writer from Vancouver, emigrated to London in 1913. 'Madge' Watt had been a driving force in the WI at home, in British Columbia, but she had difficulty in enlisting British women to the cause. One reason she gave was that they were 'slavishly bound to the class system' (Robinson, 2011, p. 30). It seemed that too many social norms would be violated if universal membership were to be afforded across the local community.

On 14 July 1915, the UK Ministry of Agriculture was beset with worries about food production in time of War. It was interested in the notion of local organisations to meet these needs and Madge Watt was hired, as *'Outside Organiser'*, to organise a new network of women's organisations to assist their cause (Scott, 1925, p. 30). Seeking a more sympathetic audience than she had found in the class-bound, South-East of England, Madge Watt moved North. And so it was that the first WI in Britain was established in Wales, in *Llanfairpwllgwyngyll*, in Anglesey (Anglesey FWIs, 2013).

The Agricultural Organisation Association (offshoot of the UK government's Board of Agriculture) provided funding for Watt to work spreading the message of women's self-help across a wider audience. This proved to be a successful gambit to rally community focus on the food and social needs of a nation at war. Each new, local branch 'signed up' to the War effort, producing craft goods and food products for the national cause. Following the ensuing success of the initiative, the Ministry extended the grant to fund assistant organisers for Madge Watt and by the early 1920s there were five in post (Scott, 1925, p. 125). Over the eight years, 1917–26, the government grant-aided the WI to the extent of £55,000 (p. 267).

The WI also began to realise its potential as an agency for social planning. As it developed over the years, it formed a national Federation of WIs and established a training and education centre at Denman House in Oxfordshire in 1948 (Cohen, 2011). The WI thrived on its educational work, introducing topics such as sexually transmitted diseases, women police, humane slaughtering of animals and peri-natal mortality into its enquiries and campaign issues (Robinson, 2011, p. 77). Madge Watt grasped the essentials of good community development practice: training for organisers; creating sustainable structures for local organisations; a strategic, yet common-themed, approach for social impact; good communications (house magazine *Home and Country*); and goal-focused activities such as social enterprises in food production and marketing. These women development workers and their Branch members were no *feminists* in the modern sense of the word, but they severely challenged the gender norms of their day (Ambrose and Hall, 2007). Along with the *Suffragettes*, the WI became an unstoppable force in the development of women's rights and capabilities. By 2011, this organisational method had realised over 200,000 members across 6,500 groups in the UK alone (Cohen, 2011).

Summary

1. Charity work augmented the attempts by the local state to manage pauperism in the nineteenth century.
2. Consolidation of these efforts gave rise to the Charitable Organization Society and the Settlement movement. In turn this led to the professionalisation of social intervention practices and to formal social work. Jane Addams exported this approach to the USA.
3. In the USA, professionalisation was given State backing during World War I and the impact of the Settlements and other charities produced a practice model for professional community intervention – called *community organization* in the USA.
4. As social work became established as an academic and institutional force in the emergent field of social welfare practice, so community organization work became recognised as a distinct model for planning and achieving positive social change.
5. In 1940, the Lane Committee of the US National Conference of Social Work produced the first recognised definition and training curriculum for community organization.

3

Community development in the modern era – an international perspective

Community development in the modern era is divided into two sections – Chapter 3 and Chapter 4 in this study. Chapter 3 is concerned with bringing up to date the history of community development in developing countries, as a feature of the deployment of international AID for development, and then, as *community organization*, in the United States. This is done before exploring the same period in the UK because, first, it will be shown that there are considerable divergences between international practice-as-development and that found in the United States. These two areas of deployment of community development have been far more productive and intensive than that found in the UK Secondly, this study will show that the development of these distinct models of community development, from the USA and in the developing world, have a great deal to inform theory, practice and policy in the United Kingdom. These models will be clearly defined and compared, and this will allow a strong basis for analysis of the UK approach to the subject. From this study, a model for application in the UK will be developed for the sustainable support of older people in the community (Chapter 5).

Introduction

Is community development what it appears to say on the tin – a mechanism that provides a framework for community problem-solving? In this chapter, I shall isolate the main themes around this topic that have developed since 1940. As we have already seen, and which will now be further elaborated, this term has many variants of meaning: the most useful generic term is *community practice* which encompasses *community organisation, community organizing, community development, extension work, social action, social planning*, and *social development* (McMillen, 1945; Hardcastle, et al., 2004; Weil, et al. (eds) 2013), but most of these terms have no currency in the UK as yet. Many of the dominant terms for these activities originate in the USA:

Perry, 1916; Ritchie, 1917 – community work;

Clarke, 1918 – community organization;

State Council for Defense, California, 1918 – Government-led community organization;

Hart, 1920 – community organizing;

Lane, 1940 – professionally codified community organization;

Lane, 1940 – social planning;

Ross, 1955 – (Canada) theoretical community organization;

Alinsky, 1957 – conflict as community organization;

Rothman, 1970 – formal modelling of community organization.

The previous chapter identified and analysed these themes in some detail up to the threshold of the Lane Committee in 1940, where community organization was formally recognised by the (American) National Association of Social Work. From that date onwards, community organisation became incorporated in the training curricula of the American Schools of Social Work, alongside case work (Richmond, 1917), and group work (Perry, 1913; Ward, 1915; Devine and van Kleek, 1916). Because of the association of the term *community development* with colonial exploitation (Batten, 1957), or the national economic development of emergent nations (UN Bureau of Social Affairs, 1955; Brager and Specht, 1973), or even the paternalistic consideration of indigenous American communities, such as Black communities (Eugster, 1970; Mayo, 1975), there has always been a reluctance in the USA to use this term. Khindulka (1975) makes the case that the term *community development* is employed where those planning a local intervention wish to create some social change without *structural change* in the wider context. That is perhaps why *community organization* emerged as the generic term over there.

There are strong themes in community development arising from the efforts of the international community to 'develop' emergent economies and to strengthen local communities as a part of that process. In the international development scene, there is a remarkable agreement about terminology, but not everywhere is there agreement as to how to prioritise objectives and value systems that go into the work. As we have seen, the UK Colonial Office began its interest in this activity as a State-led service to the Empire as *Mass Education* (Colonial Office Advisory Committee, 1925). We shall follow the development of the terminology, noting that the level of inclusivity required in the process of instituting social or economic change leads to variations in the terms being used. One of the broadest in use sums up the process as *social development* (Midgley, 1995).

The difficulty is that within the UK literature, there are a number of terms in use, as well. It is my opinion that some of this is due to a lassitude in definition. There is a prevalence of the term *community work*, which pervades much of the literature as a sort of shorthand for the general field of community intervention.

The reader, however, is going to need to interpret the context within which each variation the term is used in order to discover its local significance. This chapter's purpose is to discover, analyse and discuss the emergent models of community development as they develop, diverge and merge across the many work settings of the United States of America (with some inclusions from Canada). The development of this model for social intervention in the United Kingdom will be explored in the next chapter.

The major exclusions from this study include India, which has comprehensive coverage in terms of development policies, but a myriad of models and agency types implementing them. A separate study of India is needed to do justice to them. Australia, New Zealand and South Africa, are more or less strict observers of the models followed in the 'North', and it was also deemed to be divisionary not to get a deep study of these practices for a reduced pay-off for our particular needs. Three 'Northern' nations have also been excluded – France, Netherlands and Ireland. British/English language literature carries little information on continental practices, so this was not pursued. In the case of Ireland, although, nationally, the government and community development institutions did adopt a structural approach to the causes of social ills quite early on into their current context of economic decline (Lee, 2003). National policies then somewhat followed their British counterparts into a contentious hiatus with their *'partner'* sectors in development – particularly the Community Workers Co-operative (Taoiseach, 2000; Broaderick, 2002; O'Carroll, 2002). The current political tangle, and unresolved ideological differences there is too complex to be able to disentangle here (Gaynor, 2011).

1. Community development from an international perspective

It is hoped to examine four points of focus for the discussion in this section.

In community development as found in the developing World, the following arise as significant study areas:

a. Development planners, funders, administrators, and professional operatives adopt both a structural and structured approach to social planning. They are able to agree a vocabulary and framework for analysis of their work, which centres on the adoption of the term *social development*. This is an over-arching term – from the project up to the regional/national strategy for development.

b. Participation is now a planned element of all project work – at the grassroots, community development, and an essential ingredient of all social planning.

c. Evaluation is a given from the outset.

d. Social planning is an essential ingredient of all project/programme design. This situation has not always been the case, and we will show how these ideas and approaches gained currency.

A structural approach to community development

In the 'developing world', under the auspices of 'development AID' or sovereign, national development policies, a wealth of experience has been obtained on the efficacy and necessity for policies that might produce sustainable economic and social change. Investment at the level of the human, community level proved to be essential. The United Nations led the way on this with a Report on the economic state (poverty) of 80% of the populations of the World's developing nations. The UN saw community development as a powerful tool to assist communities to adjust to rapid social and economic change, and at the same time, harnessing the resources of a wider constituency than national governments and international co-operation (UN Bureau of Social Affairs, 1955). Because of the culture of the international community at the time, these development drives were directed from above or outwith the particular local setting. These initiatives were to be conducted by: local governments; international donors; international organisations; and non-governmental organisations (NGOs) – both local and international, often funded by the international community in their entirety. These all combine, in various ways, to 'develop' communities, economies and representative organisations according to criteria that are established (in the main) by outside *experts*, and not by those living in the localities targeted for this development (Perez-Guerrero, 1950; UN Bureau, 1955; du Sautoy, 1962; Dasgupta, 1967; Myrdal, 1968; Conyers, 1982; Cornia, 1987; Midgley, 1995; Das Gupta, et al., 2003; Mikkelsen, 2005; Whitehead and Dahlgren, 2006; WHO and Litsios, S., 2008; Shah, 2012; Mansuri and Rao, 2013).

The first really significant grant of international AID was the 1947 Marshall Plan, where the US Government made available $13 billion for the reconstruction of Europe, and for the suppression of Communism (OECD, 2012). These moneys were made available for the purchase of American goods, and provided virtually the only form of foreign exchange available to the war-exhausted European nations. This was in addition to another $13 billion made available in bilateral AID to several European countries (OECD, 2008; 2012). This demonstrates that, since these earliest days of intervention into local affairs, the motives behind AID have often been coloured with 'political' objectives beyond the presenting needs of the populations. For example, the work of the United Nations, and the United States, in post-Second World War Europe was ostensibly to aid reconstruction and stability (Mayo, 1975), but, in the case of Greece, to directly combat the rise of communism (Haralambides, 1966; Doutopoulos, 1991; OECD, 2008). Nevertheless, it can be clearly seen that it is the practical and evaluative work done 'in the field' in these settings that have yielded a wealth of theoretical as well as practical insight into the development process. The value of this approach can be seen in evaluations provided for Ministerial briefing documents at British Government level. State security, community fragility, and strategic priorities are all weighed up in deciding 'investment' possibilities (Chapman and Vaillant, 2010). This point is made to emphasise, generally, the lack of political neutrality about the social and community development process. Midgley analyses how the United Kingdom hardened its approach to *social development* in the process of relinquishing its Empire in the 1950s, but, at least, some systematic framework was produced to enable local administrators to structure their investments in social change at the community level (Colonial Office, 1954; Colonial Office, 1958; Midgley, 1981; 1995; 1997).

The post-Second World War years saw the rapid growth in investment AID to developing economies (the *Third World*). In 1990, the rich nations of the World promised US$170 billion, which represented 0.3% of the donor nations' Gross National Income (at 2009 prices), but they only delivered US$84 billion. This figure declined for ten years, before rising again to reach US$120 billion in 2010 (promised: US$270 billion – OECD, 2012). This led to a shortfall of over US$600 million in 2011 (OECD, April, 2012 – cited in Shah, 2012). Despite these disappointing delivery figures, AID still represents a massive investment potential for the developing nations. But it also gives 'donor' states considerable influence in the affairs of those nations drawn into AID 'partnerships'. Since 2003, the UK Government has invested £2.3 billion in 'fragile states' (Chapman and Vaillant, 2010, p. 12). Shah (2012, p. 30) shows how even large charitable injections from the West to the developing World (such as the Bill and Melinda Gates Foundation) can also have considerable political impact.

Achieving sustainable development is an elusive goal (Harrison, 2000). The required adaptiveness of the development process is fraught with risk and uncertainty in the face of the complexity of economic and social forces at work when this form of investment and social intervention is made (Harrison, 2000, p. 103 *et seq.*). Kingsbury points out that the conflict between the market forces of globalism, and the directive nature of top-down planning and implementation, leads many projects to failure or unsatisfactory outcomes (Kingsbury, 2004). The politics and population trauma of rapid development in some countries, e.g. Taiwan, India, Singapore, Malaysia, saw the adoption of a 'Western model of development', which produced severe dislocation of the culture and social relations in these countries. The introduction of a palliative and yet positive mechanism for introducing social measures that might accommodate these changes (for example, contraception) was seen to require an additional administrative/facilitative element. Community development was seen as an appropriate and successful vehicle for this purpose (Myrdal, 1968, especially, p. 2158 *et seq.*).

The oil price crisis of the 1970s brought in dramatic changes in inter-governmental lending and support mechanisms. The International Monetary Fund, in 1980, brought in strict restructuring conditions on indebted nations – *Structural Adjustment* (Broughton, 2010; Storey, 2001). These steps were mirrored by the World Bank, after the departure of Robert McNamara as President, in 1981 (Toye, 1993). These new financial conditions forced a withdrawal of the state from many developmental projects and activities (structural adjustment), including funding the non-governmental sector, leaving it reliant on foreign AID (Cornia, 1987; Clark, 1991). The influence of the (Western) World Bank, and International Monetary Fund, that policed the economies and political stability of the *Free World* and *Non-Aligned Nations* rose significantly (*Comecon*, and the Soviet political bloc had its own system of controls). This, then, enabled the foreign policy of the United States, through the UN and its associated bodies, to strive for an international adoption of the market economy *'ideal'* for all nations engaged in this process. It would follow that financial and political stability would go with it. International AID by the major Powers was linked to this agenda (Hulme, 1994; OECD, 2008; 2012). The social consequences of this powerful stream of influence has been considerable (Chambers, 1998a, b; Mansuri and Rao, 2004; 2013).

Participation

With this as a background scenario to international AID, over the years, a radical shift in local institutional thinking was needed if its objectives, principally *social stability* were to be realised. To this end, intervention was pioneered by UNICEF, through its economic analysts (Cornia, et al., 1987). A change of approach had to be made, chiefly the alleviation of poverty, the engagement of the community, and the revitalisation of economic growth (Cornia, et al., 1987; Shepherd, 1998). This shift was a significant move away from the belief that development could be imposed upon a community from without. The scarcity of outside resources required fresh, and immediate, adjustments to the methods of bringing change to the people. To be successful in any sustainable sense, a top-down approach, based upon the identification of *'objective need'*, required that grassroots participation be enlisted, and this resource had then to be permanently embedded in the fabric of the intervention (Conyers, 1982; Chambers, 1983; Cernea, 1985; Oakley, et al., 1991; Midgley, 1995; Chambers, 1994; 1997; Hulme, 1997a, b; Mansuri and Rao, 2004). (Work in the UK regarding the Empire, and how to get rid of it, was quite highly advanced in this thinking – Colonial Office, 1943, see below.)

In its first Annual Report, in 1990, the United Nations *Human Development Programme* described how this process had gained, and then lost, support in the application of development AID. Since the earliest days of local and international development initiatives, the community, and its organisations at grassroots level, had always been the poor relation in the process of policy selection and implementation (United Nations Human Development, 1990). A good case example of this is in Zimbabwe, where the government had, in 1991, arbitrarily imposed a notorious *'adjustment'* policy on the nation, ten years after independence (Zimbabwe, 1991). The result was over twenty years of economic decline, mass unemployment, and monetary inflation, leaving international donors and NGOs in disarray as how best to intervene (Cornia, et al., 1987; United Nations Human Development Programme, 1990; Wintour, 2009; Kramarenko, et al., 2010). All outside intervention was deemed to be subversive, although, even in a post-coalition governmental environment, some developmental co-operation is now possible (Wintour, 2009).

Chambers (at IDS at the University of Sussex) in the 1980s, began to change the culture of social and economic development into a participatory and co-operative process for the 'beneficiaries' – the local people (Chambers, 1980; 1986; 1989). This school drew heavily on the works of a widely diverse community of scholars: the Brazilian, Paulo Freire, Ivan Illich, an American institutional analyst, Saul Alinsky, an American social activist, and Franz Fanon, an Algerian nationalist and revolutionary. Freire described how, from his extensive fieldwork experience among the cane cutters of Brazil, sustainable progress in human development depended crucially on how deep an understanding of the culture and mores of the ordinary people could be obtained and how many of them could be engaged in the change process. A person's awareness of being '*in*' the world (a subjective experience), and also being '*with*' the world (an objective experience) enabled integration of experience that empowered a person to act meaningfully upon external circumstances (Freire, 1972a, b). Freire introduced the term '*conscientization*' to describe this process (Freire, 1972b, pp. 49–50). Illich provided professionals in the field with a framework of thinking that enabled them to re-define the nature of the '*expert*' in the development situation (Illich, 1973, 1977; Chambers, 1993), and Alinsky asserted why and how people at the bottom of the economic and social order might combine to assert their power (Alinsky, 1969). Fanon identified how colonised people (the poor in a development context) have nothing to lose by casting off their chains, but that they needed to be well organised to accomplish it (Fanon, 1970; 2001).

After twenty years of field work experience, Oakley described the way in which the theory and realisation of '*participation*' worked out in practice in development programmes (Oakley, et al., 1991). Only through building in the principle of '*participation first*' could highly valued social objectives be realised – e.g. health objectives (Oakley and Kahssay, 1999). Midgley had developed an analysis based on the themes of Illich (above). This demonstrated how centralised power structures, representative of the State and large corporations with interests in overseas development, might ensure that their design and timeframe for development over-ruled or ignored any local circumstances that might impede or contradict them (Midgley, 1987). Oakley produced an analysis of how structural factors impeded participation (institutional, administrative, tradition, gender politics, elite interest groups, etc.), and suggested a concrete framework for the strategic and tactical methods required of a development agent in achieving the objectives of an '*inclusive*' programme (Oakley, et al., 1991, pp. 5–13 and 182).

There is still an active debate about how community-level intervention must be implemented if it is to be successful – sustainability is still an elusive goal (Harrison, 2000; Labonne and Chase, 2008). Following on from the lead established by Chambers in the pioneering of *Rapid Rural Appraisal* (RRA) then *Participatory Rural Appraisal* (PRA) through the work of the IDS (Chambers, 1980; 1992), international development initiatives sought to get behind and beyond the political and institutional motives, which, traditionally, had inspired the formal investment in social, technical and economic development. The priorities of government agencies, international NGOs operating as agents for Donor funds, etc., were governed by the *social engineering* insight of these agents of change. They believed that they, really, had the answer to the community's needs/problems (Cernea, 1991, p. 29). The officially recognised ends justified the means, and any social costs were a necessary price to pay for progress. This approach was inspired by the analysis provided by Rostow, where a linear view of economic (and, thus, social) development held sway in many political power circles (Rostow, 1960).

Hulme and Edwards identified this further as a form of *private sector* approach to social and economic development, where somehow a *market* was operating, and the dependent community was identified as *customers* – i.e. the development process imposed from outside was in some way a voluntary contracted relationship between the provider and the recipients (Hulme and Edwards, 1997a, b). Edwards and Egbert-Edwards disagree, in some part, claiming that the precipitous rush into participation at the expense of centralised planning has corrupted the long-term mission of developers (Edwards and Egbert-Edwards, 1998). But State-designed plans generally lacked the flexibility required for local applications, and they also proved to be politically sensitive or contentious. Hashemi (1995) shows how the State can react violently to challenges to its authority from below, and CDF (1995b) calls on the professionals in the field to re-define their roles, and to challenge the State in this process (Popple and Redmond, 2000).

In the thirty years that have passed since the introduction of structural adjustment policies, this aspect has not changed dramatically. Nevertheless, in their wake, the role of the international non-governmental organisation (NGO) has been strengthened considerably. Likewise, the local NGOs have consolidated their position as necessary agents for development and continuity in working with the poor and other vulnerable groups. Michael Edwards and David Hulme (2000) describe how the antagonism between the State and NGOs continued, but that the NGOs had begun to learn from their experiences.

A major concept to emerge is that of '*scaling up*', the replication of projects and programmes, producing bigger and more effective investment and outcomes in fresh areas (Clark, 1991; Edwards and Hulme, 2000). Clark presents choices that can be made over the structure, direction and objectives of a scaled-up project. The 'participation' element can be focused upon to create extensions into other communities – a social movement. This is a contentious choice, politically.

Alternatively, simple replication of good practice models can enhance the impact of a development programme, generally. The third direction for escalating the impact of a successful model is to use the political leverage that this may produce to lobby for policy change and the redirection of public or other investment resources into this field (Clark, 1991, p. 83 *et seq.*). Shepherd cautions us, assuming that the social context of a development process is far too complex for there to be much chance of being able to reproduce these structures, processes and outcomes somewhere else (Shepherd, 1998, pp. 161–70; Lahiri-Dutt, 2004). Midgley (1995, p. 75) advises that there is little agreement in development circles about the way in which outcomes can or should be assessed. Additionally, Remenyi suggests that, despite the lofty goals of development professionals and theorists, the self-interest considerations of the governing elites decide, ultimately, which programmes go ahead, and how they are received (Remenyi, 2004). Lahiri-Dutt presents case-study material to suggest that there are so many contradictions involved in complex development strategies that no effective mechanism can be developed for the satisfactory accommodation of the public's participation (Lahiri-Dutt, 2004, p. 23).

Klinmahorm and Ireland, and Parry-Williams, separately, believe that on the one hand, demonstration and active partnership with government can yield positive results (Klinmahorm and Ireland, 1992) and Parry-Williams (1992) describes how active lobbying by NGOs can produce structural change (statute changes) (Parry-Williams, 1992). Governments should be instrumental in creating delivery systems and institutions, which are suited to the tasks of development and cohesion-building (Midgley, 1995, p. 141). Wils is convinced that, as the greatest good for the greatest number is the goal sought by the NGO community generally, then the NGO should grasp the opportunity to scale-up its activities, and to combine with government, provided that it keeps its *raison d'être* under constant review, and that it takes all reasonable steps to sustain its virtue (Wils, 1995).

There are obviously several agendas on the table in all development programmes, and the realities of political manoeuvring are a constant reminder of their vulnerabilities and frailties (Karim, 1995). Some of the difficulties in analysing these can be found in the efforts of Maru and Woodford (2007), when a model assessing *Resources and Shaping Forces* has to be applied to a society facing an unsettled political outlook, and beset with environmental upheavals as well (pp. 8–11). In essence, however, this approach boils down to the use of focus groups in setting priorities for project interventions. In the end, this participation affects little in the arena of prior planning and investment decisions, which are made in a centralised system. The cultural 'set' of the prevailing system of governance permeates the decision-adjudication process as well (Lahiri-Dutt, 2004, pp. 36–7). Ultimately, so much depends on the ability of the professional workers on the ground, and the institutional receptivity of their employers to the work they are doing, and the preparation they have to do it (Lekoko, 2013). Unless the preparatory work is done, and the frames of reference are presented and agreed, then the process of engagement will lack depth and conviction (Cernea, 1991; Marfo, 2008).

At different ends of the scale, therefore, we find contending and contradictory principles behind the intervention models. At the most extreme end are those who believe that the starting point is the people in their own locality, with their own culture values, and self-defined objectives (Kelly and Sewell, 1988). This model is predicated to the Freirean school of consciousness-raising (*conscientization*) as embodied in the *Transformation* approach to locality development (Hope, et al., 1984; Wallerstein, 1993). Here, the people's engagement is solely around the locally perceived issue, and the process of engagement binds the community into commonality, and new levels of achievement. Conversely, the model promoted by the World Health Organization (and the World Bank), is one where the issue, the '*diagnosis*' and prognosis are defined externally, and the preferred method of intervention is prescribed by central government planning and structural perspectives (Dahlgren and Whitehead, 1991; Rifkin, 1996; Dahlgren and Whitehead, 2006; Whitehead and Dahlgren, 2006). At the same time, this model insists that the highest levels of '*grassroots participation*' are engaged. The State, NGOs, private sector and, perhaps, the 'beneficiary communities' are all in the market place together.

Evaluation

There are difficulties addressing the question of evaluation of development work/ investment programmes/projects, and the like (Casley and Kumar, 1987; Uphoff, 1995; Wallace, 2000). The State is often the main delivery vehicle for these policies, but limitations on the State's ability to function at the local level means that the responsibility for this is either delegated on a statutory basis to local government, or it is hived off to NGOs (Panet-Raymond, 1992; Edwards, 1994; Hulme, 1994; Hulme et al., 1997b; Klitgaard, 1998, p. 72 *et seq.*; Mansuri and Rao, 2013), or, even, the private sector (Tõrnquist, 1999). Because of this, the question of evaluation is inextricably bound up with the nature, purpose and structure of funding and management (Cusworth, and Franks, 1993; Rossi, et al., 1999; Tõrnquist, 1999; Paton, 2003).

Relations between the hierarchy of the powerful agencies in development work and their employees can become divergent in many ways, but relations between the employees of development agencies and the 'beneficial' community can become even more so (Oakley, 1990). Expectations of loyalty, confidentiality and reciprocity can soon become convoluted as political pressures between the interests of these interest groups become entwined (Mikkelsen, 2005). The relations with the State can be an ongoing and changing factor in the effectiveness of NGO activity. Clark (1991) and Blair (1997) emphasise how difficult it is for NGOs to negotiate with the State on issues that have a direct bearing on the government's reputation or image. Mowbray reports that the State has now entered into the 'market economy' and, as such, operates as a competitive element, conscious of its own 'brand' and its image (Mowbray, 2005, pp. 261–2). Shaw suggests that within this all-embracing, global, 'neo-liberal' culture, community development's practitioners are caught in the middle, as hapless spectators, who have to carry the tensions of marketing 'social change' to its clients, whilst being trapped as employees of the prevailing 'system' (Shaw, 2011, pp. 130, 137). Because of the neo-liberal financial policies of the current time, and the subsequent contractions of the State's public services in most developed and developing nations, we are concerned here mainly with the position and the role of the NGO in this process.

Therefore, for these different parties to a, supposedly, common purpose, evaluation can have a markedly different significance.

As an international commentator on development, the World Bank keeps a critical eye on progress and issues such as government–NGO relations (Shah, 1998, p. 103 *et seq.*; Tõrnquist, 1997; Storey, 2001). Helleiner and Stewart describe how, after considerable pressure from international NGOs, the World Bank was now considering the impact of national social policies on poverty, and was to suggest mechanisms for alleviating it (Helleiner and Stewart, 1987). The alleviation of poverty, the expansion of opportunity and education within a nation, etc., in line with the *Millennium Development Goals* of the United Nations (United Nations, 2000), were adopted by the World Bank as the basis for their evaluation process (World Bank, 2004). The evaluation of development operations now counts this indicator as significant for determining the Bank's relationship with nation states (Stiglitz, 1998, p. 283 *et seq.*; Wallerstein, 2006; Jolly, et al., 2012). Recent research on this issue (Mansuri and Rao, 2013) suggests that this is now a substantial element in the Bank's appraisal of a country's credibility as an agent of development. Nevertheless, the Bank still retains its neo-liberal philosophy on finance and development, and those in development work must retain their own critical filters to ensure that they are not seduced by the Bank's attempt to rebrand itself as an agent of progressive change (Kane, 2008).

Attempts by the Bank to come to grips with the issues presented by an ageing population produced some disquiet for developers. In developed economies, financial support schemes for older people (pensions and social security) were considered to be unsustainable if they relied on State support and not market forces. In developing economies, there was no encouragement for any kind of scheme until a firm economic model for each nation emerged (International Bank for Reconstruction and Development, 1994). Measuring and reconciling the differences may take some time.

Programme and project evaluation has been part of the formal language of community development since the earliest days of recognition of the technique. The Lane Committee in the United States (Lane, 1940) stipulated that evaluation be conducted in the context of the best practice procedures (Lane, 1940, p. 8), and Trecker (1959) saw it as the basis of all credible social planning. Nevertheless, despite the growing amount of national resources that was being put into international AID, it was not until 1985 that the Thatcher Government in Britain insisted that a proper, systematic evaluation approach be adopted for British overseas AID (Cracknell, 2000). The adoption of the 'logic framework' by the Overseas Development Administration (ODA) ensured that a transferable and more reliable framework could be applied to all projects. This framework had been employed by the United States since the 1970s (Harding, 1991; ODA, 1995; Picciotto and Wiesner, 1998; Roche, 2001) and it had been under serious discussion in British Overseas Development circles since 1979 (Oakley, 1990). Wiesner stresses that all development processes are best when confined within the boundaries established by those with political oversight, and that the real task is to seek out the most appropriate means of attaining the objectives required within these (Wiesner, 1998, p. xiii). In cases of weak, or corrupt, government, however, this relationship can rapidly break down (Pradhan, 1998, p. 57 *et seq.*).

The earliest formulation of the parameters of the 'logic framework' was rather rigid – these parameters were: goals; purpose; results; activities; inputs (Harding, 1991; Cracknell, 2000, p. 115), or: wider objectives; immediate objectives; outputs; inputs (ODA, 1995, p. 80). These limitations became apparent as the focus for development projects became less centred on material outputs, *per se*. They developed from a quantitative analysis towards a more qualitative assessment, to where the nature of the 'outputs' became dependent on more a fluid, less material definition – process outcomes. Gradually over the years, the call grew for the 'beneficiaries' of development to be included in the planning and execution of development proposals (Chambers, 1980; 1983; *et seq.*; Hope, et al., 1984; United Nations, 1984; Cernea, 1985). An area of contention developed between 'value-for-money' ideologies (usually external, governmental donors), and those responsible for the delivery of 'results' in the field (and including academic theorists) (Cornia, et al., 1987; Midgley, 1987; Marsden, 1990).

In 1990, the United Nations published a report into the *Concept and Measurement of Human Development*. Central to this was the philosophy that human development depended on constantly widening choice for those experiencing poverty, suppression, oppression or reduced life chances (United Nations, 1990, p. 10). From then on, the literature on development and evaluation became studded with the imperative for community participation, engagement and direct benefit of social and economic investment (Clark, 1991; Dahlgren and Whitehead, 1991; Uphoff, 1991; Hulme, 1994). These culminated in the UN Declaration of the *Millennium Development Goals*, in 2000 – see above. The extent of the World Bank, the International Monetary Fund and the United Nations' combined influence in real terms on the World's economic affairs can be extrapolated from the fact that, with only three years to go to the 2015 target date, only three of the eight Millennium goals had been reached (United Nations, 2012). There has been sustained pressure, however, to raise and consolidate the level of citizen participation in the planning and implementation of development programmes (UN Secretariat, 2014; 2015).

Impact assessment

One of the difficulties of the evaluation process arrives when a flexible approach to programme/project delivery is required, as the process itself can have immediate (or delayed) negative effects on the 'beneficiary community'. These could be such that modifications to the delivery process have to be made. The so-called *'virtuous circle'* of development, which takes these factors into account, has to be applied (Roche, 2001). Mikkelsen shows how the only way learning can be abstracted from change is if the process is being thoroughly monitored and evaluated (Mikkelsen, 2005, pp. 267–300). The potential correctly to gauge the impact of any scheme is to ensure transparency, and the participation of the *'beneficiaries'* throughout the planning, monitoring, and delivery stages. Additionally, the 'stakeholders' at all levels in the delivery of a programme must also be included in the evaluation processes, and they may have different criteria for assessing 'benefit'. Influential funders, such as the IMF, or World Bank, have set their own criteria (Bourguignon, et al., 2002; World Bank, 2004). The ODA (UK Government's Overseas Development Administration) employs the 'logic framework' approach to assess whether or not it is getting value for money from its Foreign AID budget (ODA, 1995). Oakley, in his study of participation for the International Labour Organization, considers how evaluation might be addressed depending on what parameters for success are in the frame of reference of the project/programme. Macro-level economic outcomes might produce completely different measurements than might *'capacity-building'*, grassroots projects (Oakley et al., 1991).

There is definitely a considerable difference between evaluators who seek qualitative measurements as opposed to quantitative analysts. Traditionally, cost, scale and time-bounded outcome expectations dominated the thinking of funders and government administrators and their political masters (Rondinelli, 1993; Rubin, 1995; Patton, 1997; Leurs, 1998). The problem was, and still is, that there is little scope to conduct controlled experiments in the development field (Patton, 1997). The best that donors, political policy-makers, planners, and field workers can expect is to search out the way to create a 'virtuous spiral' (Fowler, 2000), or a 'virtuous circle' (Roche, 1999). Patton suggests three approaches: *inductive* – the use of field work to produce theory, based upon the testing of indicators; *deductive* – the use of theory to produce models; and *user-focused* – building theory from interactive circumstances (Patton, 1997, pp. 220–2). The objective of developmental intervention is, obviously, beneficial change, to be measured against criteria hitherto, mainly, decided from outside the area (Fowler, 2000, pp. 17–19)).

Considering the emergent need now to take into account the feelings and more personally felt needs of the 'consumer' or 'beneficiary', then another form of risk assessment and outcome measurement is required.

From this dimension of evaluation has emerged '*Impact Assessment*'. This is a predictive investigation of how the planned intervention might impact on the society/community across a wide spectrum, of areas, beyond the immediate, planned objective of the intervention (Barrow, 2000). Focusing agencies, in advance, on the consequences of their activities should draw them away from writing laudatory descriptions about their efforts in interventions, and towards documenting their progress towards programme objectives across a wider spectrum (Fowler, 1997, pp. 164–6).

As Oakley describes (Oakley, 1991, pp. 241–5), it is very difficult to predict how the social impact of participation, for example, might change a culture or material circumstances of a community. How are *cost-benefit analysis*, for example, or *impact assessment* techniques to be applied to something which itself is a qualitative phenomenon? Mikkelsen reminds us that the monitoring and evaluative mechanisms cannot control the actual dynamics of the development process, once under way (Mikkelsen, 2005, pp. 304–6). Eade stresses that the intervention should, where possible, start with the institutions and organisations that are already developed in the community in order to minimise the dislocation that intervention will inevitably bring (Eade and Williams, 1995, pp. 334–5). Roche explains how assessing the costs (in material terms) to the funders, agents of change and beneficiaries of change in advance is one thing, but trying to evaluate, assess and communicate the impact of change on social, economic and environmental dimensions of society is a much more difficult task (Roche, 1999).

Patton's *Utilization-focused Evaluation* model (Patton, 1997) now covers most of the aspects required by both quantitative and qualitative approaches. Clarke provides us with a matrix of this approach (Clarke, 2000, p. 263), where interventions at different levels can be assessed using independent criteria, but where they can be integrated into a common analytic analysis. The continuum of change, as projected by the 'logic framework' can be seriously augmented through the collection of qualitative insight. This will produce the necessary level of understanding required for developers, so that they may come to grips with the significance of change to the indigenous culture and knowledge that they have encountered (Marsden, 1994). This will provide considerable extra dimensions to their understanding of the targets of their work (Mikkelsen, 2005). Patton recognises the contradictions involved in attempting to reconcile the quantitative with the qualitative focus in data collection, yet seeks to address the dilemma through seeking balance itself. He recognises that there are significant ideological issues involved, but that evaluation is a framework for assessing the validity of relative values and definitions (Patton, 1997, p. 280).

Patton further acknowledges that there are likely to be considerable differences of opinion between the 'experts' about ways and means, even before the indigenous community are brought into the equation (Patton, 1997, pp. 260–2). Rubin asserts that, in the end, each result has to be judged on its own merits, and this applies particularly to agencies and agents who presume to intervene in the lives of people who are not able successfully to resist this intervention (Rubin, 1995). One might ask: In the end, who will bear the costs of all this investment and activity? The International Labour Organization insists that *impact assessment* be built into all evaluation processes in order to provide an incremental balance sheet of how this process is progressing (International Labour Organization, 2012, p. 13).

Social Planning

The other major contribution to the theoretical and modelling framework of international community development is in the field of social planning. As we shall see in the following sections on American (below) and British (Chapter 4) community development, it is by default that the community development institutions have paid so little attention to this vital element of providing a sustainability dimension to social development programmes and initiatives. Myrdal set the scene in 1968, for the need for sustainable development at all levels in society if the endemic problems of poverty and disease were to be overcome (Myrdal, 1968). This theme was greatly expanded upon and the whole issue clarified in the cumulative international initiatives, culminating in the Millennium goals being set in 2000 (WHO (Alma Ata Declaration), 1978; (The) Brandt (Commission), 1980; Brundtland (Commission), 1987; UN Human Development Programme, 1990; United Nations, 2000).

Most of the 'developing world' commentators who concern themselves with the relations between State and NGO agencies (North and South) find the need to include some form of explanation of how, in practice, at least, the two crucial engines of development interact and explain their actions to each other (Conyers, 1982; Booth, 1994; Midgley, 1995; Hulme and Edwards, 1997a; Edwards and Hulme, 2000; Ziglio, et al., 2000; OECD, 2008; Chapman and Vaillant, 2010; Mansuri and Rao, 2013).

In 1983, the Swedish sociologist and development researcher, Harold Swedner, described the conditions that were required before a successful development intervention could be made. This embraced the focusing of all the institutions on the collective endeavour that they were preparing to undertake, and for the establishment of the appropriate mechanisms that would ensure their ongoing collaboration and co-operation (Swedner, 1983a, pp. 65–70). Thake reminds us, if the community are in ownership also, in concert with local government, then the progress of any initiative may be better ensured. Nevertheless, this may be a considerable challenge for powerful agencies (Thake, 1995). The crucial factor in this process must rest with local government, which affects the essential linkage between the local community, central policy-makers, and any other intervening agencies/institutions. Local government may consider itself to be central to this change, but the literature contains scant reference to the mechanism that local government might go with to prepare itself for the challenge.

Murphy (2002) reports on how the Irish Government failed to take advantage of the opportunity offered by the Irish Prime Ministerial initiative to establish a *'New National Agreement'* on community development partnerships across the nation as part of their *Programme for Prosperity and Fairness* (Taoiseach (Office of), 2000). This *Agreement* covered nine areas of social and economic importance – including poverty, gender and race relations (pp. 2–9). The Irish Voluntary Sector failed to find a satisfactory way in, within which they could establish some form of equality, and obtain a status position for the communities at the grassroots (Murphy, 2002, p. 84; see also Laughry, 2002). Walker and Shannon reported that in New Zealand, after a decade of good intentions, the Government had failed to make any advances along a line similar to the Irish Government: towards a pluralist structure for the administration of local development (Walker and Shannon, 2011, pp. ii, 63). In less developed structures of governance, there is even less potential for movement. Karagkounis reports, in Greece, on the absence of a really positive input by the 'weak' local government structure, retarded interventions and progress towards development goals (Karagkounis, 2009).

How then might the situation be modified to accommodate the necessary mechanisms for good governance? How can the resources, informed and well-prepared agents of change from within local government be assembled for the task? Rothman presents us with a model of 'social planning', which outlines the methods through which a community organizer intervenes at the level of the agency to produce vehicles for planned social change (Rothman, 2001, p. 31). As with the Rothman model for intervention at the level of the community, in social planning the agents of change 'manipulate' formal organisations and data (p. 44), with their eyes firmly on the outside forces requiring adaptation and change. The presumption here is that the agencies engaged in the exercise are aware of, and are willing partners in, the change processes they are planning, and have the internal capacities to accomplish the task. Sanders had described the inevitability of the institutional change process, by insisting that managed social change was just a matter of government agencies taking a firm lead, and instituting the appropriate systems of communication (Sanders, 1970). Lauffer, however, emphasised just how unready, and how far from this objective, government agencies were. He stressed that many officials were completely unaware of the complexities of community life, dynamics, and social mores (Lauffer, 1978, p. 239 *et seq.*). Perlman, and Guirin, saw a public service function of specialised 'planning organizations', which worked outside the agencies that would bring about the changes in society planned by policy-makers or when social problems arose that needed collective solutions

(Perlman and Guirin, 1972, p. 80). Midgley (1995) explained how development was a process of *managed pluralism*, and that all levels had to be prepared for the experience (Midgley, 1995, p. 175). Midgley gave no insights as to how this was to be achieved, however.

Janelle Plummer has published two guides into the processes required to present the agencies of governance – *'municipalities'* is the term Plummer uses to describe local government entities – at the required level of readiness for the challenges that engagement with the community presents. In the first (Plummer, 1999) she presents a schema that identifies the issues at stake at every level in municipal structures, and outlines a process through which the agency as a whole can be re-oriented towards the social planning (p. 8 *et seq.*). The central element of this process depends on there being a management structure sufficiently empowered to carry out the process, and being sufficiently committed to the process. This means that the municipal agencies have to have adopted a principled framework for social planning and social developmental change that permeates all municipal policy, training, and operational planning and engagement (pp. 95 *et seq.*; 119 *et seq.*). Whereas this policy has to be implemented from the very top down, Plummer recognises that *bureaucratic inertia*, and the hierarchical nature of municipal structures are antagonistic to participatory action systems (p. 125).

Additionally, as we have been pointing out, the essence of *participation* is that it should stem from the grassroots upwards. Where Cornwall (2008), Kemp, et al. (2008), Shaw (2011) and Jolly, et al. (2012) find this approach to policy implementation totally unacceptable as it violates the principle of *power to the people* (Cornwall, 2008, p. 281), and retards progress towards democratic organisation of society, Kane (2008) and Mansuri and Rao (Mansuri and Rao, 2013), while recognising the pitfalls, accept that policy must be implemented by someone, and that international and national scrutiny of government and donor motives is much more critical and severe than ever before.

Plummer is one who accepts this point of view (she is a consultant to the World Bank, and to DfID on development matters). In her second major publication (2002) she outlines how the municipal function can better be fulfilled if democratic government sees its role as co-operative and in partnership with the citizens. Having overcome the barriers to mobilising for social planning and the active implementation of social policy (Plummer, 1999, above), the municipality must now restructure itself for active engagement within specially constructed vehicles for this task – partnerships. From the inward-looking, self-appraisal of the first guide (Plummer, 1999), Plummer now calls on this now-reinforced and prepared agency to pursue its objectives with firm structures and leadership. This will not be without pain, as political and bureaucratic resistance will be high (Plummer 2002, p. 290). Notwithstanding this, if government is to be serious about implementing its policies, then this pain will have to be confronted. Across the UK, national administrations have sought actively to centre their policies for Health and Development upon the principle of partnership (Dept for Communities and Local Government, 2008e; Scottish Government, 2007) and, as has been described above, within Welsh Government policy, partnerships are the central plank of government policy (Hutt, 1999; Welsh Assembly Government, 2003a, 2003d; WG, 2011d; etc.). None of these administrations appear to have a workable vehicle for achieving their objectives in this regard across their nations. We have seen in this section how investment in developmental programmes has produced rationally bound structural approaches to planned social change. A clear model has appeared, based upon institutional restructuring and forward planning. Nevertheless, this is contested by those who seek 'bottom-up' approaches to development.

2. Community organization in the United States and Canada

The United States gave the impetus to the whole World for community organization (CO). The US Government recognised CO as early as 1913 (Lever/U.S. Committee for Agriculture, 1913), when it appreciated the value of community-building even before the nation's rural communities were put under strain during World War I. Congress also saw the need to provide training for field workers so that standards could be established and it linked this initiative to Colleges responsible for apportioning grants for the extension development (p. 2). In the 1920s, urban area-based experiments took place to see if they could be regenerated and rehabilitated following social and economic decline. The most famous of these was the Cincinnati Social Unit experiment (Dinwiddie with Bennett, 1921; Betten and Austin, 1990, pp. 35–49). This experiment was mounted by the National Social Unit Organization in 1916, and the Cincinnati Project ran for three years, during which time, valuable data was collected to establish CO as a legitimate application in situations such as this. Additionally, at that time, a number of books on CO appeared which formulated a body of theory and model frameworks (Hart, 1920; Burr, 1921; Rogers, 1921; McClenahan, 1922; Steiner, 1925; Pettit, 1928). These books were mainly aimed at the 'self-help' market in community relations, but the role of an 'organizer' was clearly spelled out, be it for a paid worker, or for an organisation leader figure.

From the beginning of the twentieth century, welfare provision for the needy and indigent had, traditionally, been provided by philanthropic organisations (see the narrative above on the Settlement movement), but the lessons learned from providing paid organisers for welfare and recreational activity in this sector were taken up in the general context of community-building at large (Bremner, 1956; Cox, et al., 1970; Brueggemann, 2013). By the 1930s, social work was becoming a thoroughly organised, salaried profession in the United States, and the National Conference of Social Work had been institutionalised since 1917. Bruno records the changes in those subject strands in the officially recognised curriculum for Social Work College programmes – reduced from twelve in 1926 to four in 1934, retaining '*Community Organization*' as a permanent strand in training (Bruno, 1948, p. 359). The National Conference dates back to 1873, but now it began to take seriously that community organization was a significant part of the social welfare intervention structure. Because of this, the Conference established a sub-Committee to set out the parameters for this form of activity within social work (MacMillan, 1945). The Lane Committee reported in 1939 (Lane, 1940), and his Report was adopted by the National Conference. Having established its professional credentials, therefore, community organisation became a factor within social work training curricula.

After the Lane Committee Report, Community Organization in the United States began to divide into a number of 'schools' of thought. During the Great Depression of the 1930s, some social workers and other community activists (e.g. Trade Union organisers) sought more radical outcomes and tactics than the integrative and palliative model presented by organised welfare agencies and the social work profession, generally. One iconic figure bridges all those descriptions – Saul Alinsky. While CO within social work was heading off towards the respectability of the mainstream social work curriculum, Alinsky was preaching a radically different creed (Chambers, 2004). The Alinsky model is based upon the term 'community organizing', whereas the term 'community organisation' compares with the British/ International terms of community development, or social development. Some background information is necessary. *Community organizing* describes a model of intervention based upon *conflict*, and not *consensus*. The latter term describes the *raison d'être* of most community organization and community development.

Alinsky and the post-Alinsky model

In his vivid history of the making of the *Back of the Yards*, the area around the meat-packing industry and its community in Chicago, Robert Slayton (1986) related how the community was already well established as an urban 'jungle' well before Upton Sinclair made it notorious with his novel, *The Jungle*, in 1908. As Trade Union organisers for the Congress of Industrial Organizations (the CIO), Joseph Meegan and Saul Alinsky were drawn into the area because of the very low impact that union membership made on the working and living conditions of the workers in the meat industry (Fisher, 1994; Warren, 2001). *The Back of the Yards* was a neighbourhood of tenants, and immigrants, usually associated separately in associations of 'nationalities' – Poles, Czechs, Afro-Americans, Slovaks, Germans, Ukrainians, etc., most of whom were Roman Catholics, which gave the organisers a target for leverage (Alinsky, 1941). The best way forward, according to Alinsky, was to organise the neighbourhood along social lines, non-employment-related, and to form a powerful, cross-cultural, inter-faith social organisation, which would become firmly embedded in the aspirational needs of the residents. This came into being in 1939 (Fisher, 1994), and this all-embracing structure became known as the *'broad-based organization'* (Staples, 1984; Davies, 1988; Fisher, 1993; Rubin, 2000; Warren, 2001, pp. 65–7).

The broad-based organization aimed to embrace, engage, organise, and then represent all interests in the community – be they ethnic, economic, geographic, gender, social, or demographic. This organisation could then confront the City and the meat-packing industry across a wide spectrum of issues (Staples, 1984, pp. 80–2; Alinsky, 1969). It was from the earliest days of community organizing that Alinsky recognised the necessity (a) to strive for real power for the organisations he was facilitating, but also, (b) to seek alliances with outside power groupings that might be allies to the cause. In the case of *The Back of the Yards Council*, Alinsky sought out (even within a generally hostile hierarchy) the active support of the local Roman Catholic Bishop (capitalising on Meegan's Irish pedigree), which was good both for the community, but also for the standing of a Church that had hitherto sided with the meat-packing companies' management (Alinsky, 1969). Alinsky saw himself, and all those committed to social change that benefited the principles of a civilised society, as radicals. He saw the forces of oppression in all those who opposed this thesis (Alinsky, 1969, p. 134). Additionally, he saw the path to casting aside the oppression of these forces as justifiable by virtually any means at the disposal of the oppressed. His mission was to establish a path towards the *American Dream* of equal opportunity to success for all those whom he was able to help (Spergel, 1969, pp. 8–9; Alinsky, 1972, p. 3; Greenberg, 1999).

To achieve this, his organisation adopted the following framework for action: *Community organizing is an exercise in power; it uses the broad-based organisation; The dynamic is mobilisation, organisation, conflict, movement, momentum; the ethos is pragmatism; citizen evaluation produces the justification; the process is constantly accountable to the participants, who are the direct beneficiaries; the process relies on a paid organizer* (Alinsky, 1972; Pitt and Keane, 1984; Chambers, 2004; Thompson, 2005). Alinsky's new community organisation, *The Back of the Yards Council*, was successful in attaining its objectives of bringing the meat-packing industry and the housing situation in the area under some form of public accountability. Alinsky had broken with the CIO in 1939, to form his own business – the *Industrial Areas Foundation* (IAF) through which he was to work for the rest of his life – as a consultancy.

Alinsky moved out of Chicago to promote IAF and consultancy in this field of social intervention, and, in the process, recruited some of the most significant community organisers that would emerge from that sector. His personal assistant (and successor in IAF after Alinsky's death in 1972) was Ed Chambers (Chambers, 2004). In the South-Central US, Alinsky recruited Ernesto Cortes in Texas (Rogers, 1990); Fred Ross in California – who in turn recruited Cesar Chavez, the Chicano farm workers organiser (Ross, 1989; see also Howard, in Howard (ed.), 1970, p. 89 *et seq.*); and Gary Delgado, who became the mainstay of the ACORN organisation (Delgado, 1986). Each local development of IAF's work began to take on its own distinctive characteristics. Nevertheless, the essential model remained constant, and what was significant about IAF was that, in selling itself to local organisations, it insisted, and obtained, agreement on the ongoing engagement of the professional organiser, from the consulting firm. This not only guaranteed financial stability for IAF, but also underwrote the stability of the local broad-based organisation (and essential of the Alinsky model – Alinsky, 1972).

Bailey deplores the lack of analytical study of the '*Alinsky phenomenon*', and claims that the Alinsky model has spread so far throughout the American urban complex that it is now impossible to assess the full significance of his work (Bailey, 1974, p. 2 *et seq.*). In Chicago alone, there are four major communities organised to the point where they can dominate local politics if provoked/motivated (Fish, 1973; Bailey, 1974).

One such development with a distinctive personality was in the South of the USA – ACORN – the *Arkansas Community Organization for Reform Now* eventually became a nationwide membership organisation (re-named <u>Association of Community Organizations for Reform Now</u>, in the 1970s). It concentrated on poor communities, and set itself up as a 'trade union' for householders (Delgado, 1986; Atlas, 2010). ACORN, founded in 1970, was inspired by and persisted until 2010 as the brainchild and fiefdom of Wade Rathke (Atlas, 2010). Minority voter registration in the still, *de facto*, segregationist States was its first mission and the politics of democracy remained forever high on its agenda. Housing tenure and landlord–tenant relations was the other prominent feature of its work. Working on the basis that: 'if you pay taxes, then you are involved in politics', Rathke promoted direct political intervention by ACORN chapters. For example, ACORN (unsuccessfully) challenged the Mayor of Detroit's campaign for re-election on the issue of city tax rates (Staples, 1984). ACORN was based in Little Rock, Arkansas, and it often became involved in '*turf wars*' with other CO organisations. The *Local Initiatives Support Corporation* (LISC), a National civil rights organisation, pitted itself against ACORN for the engagement of the local Black community in Little Rock. LISC had a patchy track record, but, as it concentrated on building local *community development corporations* (CDCs – community-owned trading companies), it was possible to negotiate an uneasy peace between them (Gittell and Vidal,1998). Having been successful in New York State earlier, in 1996, ACORN successfully challenged the Los Angeles County *WORKFARE* programme, through signing up both the 'clients' of the system, and also the programme workers (Brooks, 2002; CDJustice, 2010). They then challenged the scheme on a number of levels simultaneously, using alliances with other organisations to swell their ranks. After thirty direct '*actions*', they forced a showdown, and won many concessions (Brooks, 2002).

ACORN (nationally) was officially disbanded in 2010, after a scandal involving Rathke's family, and some $5 million of irregular payments and money transfers. According to the California Department of Justice (2010), ACORN, at its peak, had over 400,000 signed-up members in over 1,000 chapters, across 110 US cities. As none of the affiliated Chapters of ACORN were implicated in the scandal, they continue to this day as independent charitable organisations (Harshbarger and Crafts, 2009). The 'ACORN model' of community organizing has proved to be very successful, and the viability of the organisations is not in doubt (Delgado, 1986; Feagin and Shettan, 1985; CDJustice, 2010).

Another offshoot of IAF was *Communities Organized for Public Services* – COPS (Rogers, 1990). It all began in 1966, when Ernesto Cortes Jr. was engaged as a volunteer by a coalition of Democratic Party activists and community leaders to help them organise Mexican-American voters to oust a Judge in the next election in San Antonio, Texas. This they did decisively, prompting Cortes to seek training from IAF in Chicago. Cortes then returned to San Antonio to begin community organizing, paid this time, as an IAF consultant to the local Catholic/ Mexican-American organisation, which became known as COPS. Over the next thirty years, Cortes organised communities across Texas to the point that the new organisation, COPS, began to dominate the whole political landscape (Vazquez, 2005). Eschewing formal political allegiance, COPS chose whom and when it would support electorally, and yet it could not escape the net completely (Rogers, 1990; Putnam, et al., 2004).

Vazquez notes that the combined forces of the united Churches of the major cities in Texas, combined with a vigorous fundraising capability (including State grants), has made COPS an exceedingly powerful influence across the State (Vazquez, 2005). Cortes's own theological background (post-grad theology) equipped him well to influence the Catholic Church hierarchy to support the community movement, and he then moved on to unite the Churches of Texas – outside the conservative, Southern Baptist Conference, that is (Warren, 2001; Chambers, 2004). Montiel, et al., criticise Cortes for his hypocrisy – raising money from the institutions and corporations of society, whilst claiming that the focus of his endeavour is the individual in the local community (Montiel, et al., 1998). In California, Cesar Chavez and co-organiser Dolores Huerta (Garcia, 2009), earned an international reputation for leading the grape-pickers in a local, and then a World boycott of California grapes and wine. Ross documents Chavez's rise as a local organiser, but it was his training and deployment by IAF that gave him the impetus to adopt confrontational tactics for his powerful organisational movement (Ross, 1989). This boycott found tactics such as adding pesticide to consignments of grapes meant for market in Washington as an example of the use of Alinsky's 'does this particular end justify these particular means?' (Alinsky, 1972, p. 47; Shaw, 2008). Chavez was the inspiration for Ernesto Cortes (above) to seek IAF training before he launched his San Antonio career as an organiser (Rogers, 1990). Chavez applied Gandhian tactics of passive resistance to confront the farm owners' violence against the striking workers (Ferriss and Sandoval, 1997).

Alinsky returned to Chicago himself to take up the cause of the Black community in the *Woodlawn* district, an area just to the East of *Back of the Yards*. Swedner, an action researcher in the area in the early 1960s, provides us with a full description of the economic and social circumstances of the district (Swedner, 1983a, pp. 8–42). As a sociologist, and an outsider (Swedish), Swedner hoped to provide an objective view of what became a very controversial confrontation between poor people and the City of Chicago's Establishment. The University of Chicago (UofC) employed tactics such as 'Block Busting', importing Black householders, and spreading racialised rumours to weaken the housing tenure of White residents (Swedner, 1983b, p. 8).

In 1960, four community clergymen, one Catholic, three Protestant, invited IAF to do a survey of Woodlawn. This was in an attempt to obtain for the community some objective information/data about Woodlawn in the face of a University of Chicago ultimatum of total redevelopment (the UofC was the major landlord in the area) (Rodham, 1969; Fish, 1973; Fisher, 1994). IAF's study produced *The Woodlawn Organisation* – TWO (Fish, 1973). Rogers (1990) describes how, in a 'safe' re-election for Mayor, a threat from TWO to congest the men's toilets at O'Hare Airport with hundreds of well-dressed Woodlawn residents unless concessions were made to TWO's demands for change in the planning legislation (redevelopment) led to a political climb-down (Rogers, 1990, p. 79 *et seq.*).

Silberman (1964) describes how Mayor Daley was forced out of denial of the '*Negro problem*'. Cary (1970) finds in the now predominately Black population of Woodlawn, and the rise of TWO, an assertive step towards Black people taking control of many aspects of their lives. This was a '*rejection of welfare colonialism*' (Silberman, 1964, p. 308 *et seq.*). In 2006, according to Gibson, of the Chicago University Magazine (Vol. 98, No. 3, 2006), TWO was still thriving: representing the community, building housing complexes, running community businesses, and demonstrating that, with the right support (IAF organizers), community organisations can be sustainable and viable. In 2012, it signed up as a partner with LISC (see above) for the *New Communities Program* of the Woodlawn District (LISC website, accessed 25 January 2013).

This analysis of how the Alinsky model breeds creativity and improvisation stems from the basic beliefs/'Iron Rules' of Alinsky that 'I start where the world is, not where I want it to be' (Alinsky, 1972, p. xix) and 'broad-based organisations, winnable actions' (Pitt and Keane, 1984, p. 2); and 'never do anything for people that they can do for themselves' (Putnam, et al., 2004, p. 23). The IAF went from strength to strength, despite having had a lot of pressure from the United States' Government during the Cold War/McCarthy era – 1950–4, and thereafter, despite McCarthy being disciplined by the Senate (Fisher, 1994, p. 73; Garvin and Cox, 2001). It may be that the sheer size and pluralistic complexity of the United States enabled the Administration to out-manoeuvre its opponents (Spergel, 1969). On the one hand, neighbourhood democracy was seen as an essential component of the American self-image (see Poston, in Harper, E. and Dunham, A., 1959, p. 28 *et seq.*), but at the same time it was thought to be a manifestation of primitive *communism* (Fisher, 1994, p. 75 *et seq.*). Pruger and Specht (1969) try and make the case that Alinsky's mission to convert the poor into active, empowered citizens should be down to their own leadership to accomplish and that its claims of success were, in any case, greatly exaggerated. This accusation about the inappropriate use of outside experts smacks of political bias and sour grapes by those who hold firm positions of power within the academic Establishment.

Community organization is all about creating local, accountable structures (*People's Organizations*), and, within the model of the *American Dream*, for these people to achieve social change through 'democratic' methods with *indigenous leadership* (Alinsky, 1969 —Vintage Edition of Alinsky, 1946). Power cannot be exercised in an orderly way by the masses, but it has to be channelled into formal structures for maximum effect (Zald, 1975). During the 1960s, and 1970s, ethnic tensions were widespread (Fisher, 1994), and the Black (Negro) community was often blamed for the decline in urban living standards and community relations (Moynihan, 1969; Glazer and Moynihan, 1970; Burghardt and Fabricant, 1982).

The contest for power, according to Alinsky (1957, p. 5 *et seq.*), is designed to bring out all the tension and real issues of the community. As he showed in Rochester, New York, when he confronted the Eastman-Kodax Corporation, racism and racial oppression were the tensions brought to the fore before a solution was forced on the Corporation (Horwitt, 1989, p. 452 *et seq.*; Fisher, 1994, pp. 16–18). Alinsky demonstrated that psychological factors can also play a part in the contest of power relations. In his fabled interview with *Playboy* Magazine in 1972, Alinsky outlined how his tactical threat to confront the high-status performance of the *Rochester Philharmonic Orchestra* with an 'orchestrated' *fart-in* by the Black population precipitated a cave-in by Eastman-Kodak management over wage and hiring practices (Alinsky, 1972).

Very often, the very poor, or those incapable of responding to the interventions of community organizers, find that they are left out of the loop of social regeneration. Whereas Alinsky always worked in communities, where there was an animated response at some level to his model, he did not advocate working within the *Underclass* (Murray, 1994), as they had few means to use as a resource base for their action plans. Nevertheless, Burghardt and Fabricant shift the Alinsky model somewhat to incorporate the poor themselves through empowered advocacy interventions and the building of coalitions and broad-based organisational alliances out of those agencies working on the breadline welfare circuit. The poor themselves are to be built into the structures of the agencies to support them and to empower them through exposure to tactical activities on their own behalf (Burghardt and Fabricant, 1987). The work of *Butterflies* (a street children support organisation in Delhi) used confrontational Alinsky tactics to gain recognition from the authorities for the street children's organisation – and it worked (O'Kane, 2011; see also: http://butterflieschildrights.org/home.php).

Eclectic community organization

A second strand of CO in the United States relates to a number of activists for whom theoretical modelling and public records carry little interest. Theirs is a desire to carry out the work, achieve the goals of the community through organising, and to do everything that they can to pass on the messages of their experience, many with Trade Union organising experience. Kahn (1982) fits this category, who, despite claiming College training for his task, cites not a single reference point for his contribution to the body of knowledge in his published contribution to this discipline. Kretzmann and McKnight have also produced a training manual that, *inter alia*, considers the situation of 'Seniors' in a fast-changing World (Kretzmann and McKnight, 1993, p. 51 *et seq.*). The difficulty that arises out of this sort of work, particularly with this sort of target group in mind, is that the 'ethics', the 'why?' etc., are all subsumed in the 'how'. Stoecker (1997, pp. 219–25) does point to the pitfalls of attempting collaborative research in the face of organised neighbourhood oppositions, but claims no allegiance to theoretical models nor reference points in the work. Bobo (et al., 1996), Mondros and Wilson (1994) and Morse (2004) describe, completely anecdotally, how community activists might work with well-established institutions without appearing to have any structured thinking behind the initiatives. The message from all the above works appears to be that: community organizing gets a good press in certain quarters, and the potential market for these books is for those activists who want to feel good about their work without considering the ethics, value framework or theoretical model that might bring long-term stability to their work.

Cummings (1998) tells a classic tale of the badly planned, structureless approach to top-down community planning: the sad case of *Rosedale*, Texas. Up until the 1970s, Rosedale was a racially segregated district of Fort Worth, Texas. Faced with a de-restriction in the Housing market (end of racial zoning), the district began a steady decline into a Black ghetto status. Racial hatred spread, White residents fled the area, and, in 1982, a series of violent racial incidents (Black on White) precipitated a critical situation. The decline in social and economic fortunes accelerated, and the area became crime-ridden and semi-derelict in a very short time span. In 1986, the Fort Worth administration decided to stimulate the local economy with an injection of funding for economic renewal: the *Texas Main Street Program*. This depended on there being positive community morale, self-help, and an active and engaged business community. *Rosedale* had none of these. By 1991, this had failed utterly, and the scheme was withdrawn. For the potentially viable and dynamic community, the Texas Main Street programme has obvious benefits. As an agency for combating social disorganisation, it has little to offer. It was histories such as that of *Rosedale* that gave rise to the identification of a new *underclass* in urban America (Wilson, 1987; Murray, 1994; Moynihan, 1969).

This situation and its symptoms have now been addressed to some extent. Commercial interests and local government concerns with public health issues could be combined with community interests. In 1993, Greenberg, et al., identified the problem of TOADS (Temporarily Obsolete Abandoned Derelict Sites), and the potential that they had towards dragging down a neighbourhood, with their propensity to attract itinerants, juvenile crime and other marginal activities. Community organising was the solution – to forge alliances between the organised community, local government and the private sector in bringing the sites under community control for improvement as social benefit (recreational activities, etc.). Negotiating a role for community organisations within a quasi-commercial initiative, whilst still retaining the right and the means to protest over the non-compliance of either partner with planning, health and hygiene regulations was seen as a delicate and potentially weakening characteristic for independent community groups (Greenberg, et al., 1993). Setterfield did not see this as a difficulty, however, as in times of strained economic circumstances, government and site owners were actively seeking economic solutions to vexatious politico-economic problems (Setterfield, 1997; Greenberg, 1999).

A classic example of formless top-down community intervention was the (Kennedy/Johnson) *President's Committee on Juvenile Delinquency*, the *Mobilization for Youth Program* (centred on New York City), and the *War on Poverty* and *Model Cities* programmes (Brager and Purcell, 1967). There were prototype projects in Boston, too, where the Ford Foundation ventured into collaboration with local government to tackle urban renewal and community regeneration. The scheme, Action for Boston Community Development (ABCD), from 1961 to the present, initially attracted widespread interest as a pioneer at combining multi-sources of finance for this kind of work, and also for applying *social planning* models to social issues of this kind (Cloward and Ohlin, 1960; Perlman, 1999). Although there was to be *behind-sight* criticisms of these schemes (Marris and Rein), these collaborative ventures between the Federal Government and the Ford Foundation pumped millions of dollars into the problem of acute poverty and unemployment, particularly in the Black, urban population of the USA. It also opened up a fresh trend in strategic thinking (Perlman, 1999). Millions of dollars were pumped into local government, local charities and local outreach organisations. The slogan was 'maximum feasible participation' (Marris and Rein, 1967, p. 216; Moynihan, 1969, pp. 90–1). (There is striking evidence that this scheme was 'set up for failure' (Blaustein and Faux, 1972; Rivera and Erlich, 1998, p. 17).)

Marris and Rein (1967, above) describe how the collaboration at the top (US Office of Economic Opportunity and the Ford Foundation) planned the exercise, but also how they made no effort to consider how the poor, on the one hand, and how local government on the other, might respond (Chavis, et al., 1993). The Kennedy initiative evolved greatly under President Johnson, and the *Community Action Programme* (CAP) grew out of the Economic Opportunities Act 1964 (Naples, 1998a). Over 900, Federally funded CAP projects were created in order to enlist local communities in activities for the elimination of poverty (Bailey, 1974, pp. 45–6). These were community self-help projects (Fisher, 1994) and it is estimated that over 125,000 people were funded to take part (Naples, 1998a). There was no satisfactory control system in place to activate or evaluate schemes, which were administered by City Hall. Political in-fighting was often the outcome, instead of economic planning and investment (Grosser, 1976; Naples, 1998a).

The outcome was uncertainty (Perlman and Guirin, 1972), corruption, disaffection by communities and local government alike (Grosser, 1975), and the branding of the community organizers in New York of being communist infiltrators (Marris, and Rein, 1967, p. 178; Brager, 2001). In fact, Marris and Rein (1967) point out that the main thrust of local interventions and investment was led by unrepresentative community organizers, who led from their own priorities, rather than involve and engage the local communities (p. 186). Moynihan accuses this new breed of professional community-change planners and project directors of hypocrisy – of actually hating the local, unresponsive government administrators of the programmes they implemented, but still pleased to earn the rich salaries they got for this publicly acclaimed activity (Moynihan, 1969, p. 111 *et seq.*).

The *Model Cities* programme was funded by the US Department of Housing and Urban Development (HUD). Part of their thinking was derived from the *Chicago Area Project* of 1933, which was the attempt by sociologist Clifford R. Shaw to grapple with the issue of juvenile delinquency in the poor areas of Chicago (Shaw and McKay, 1969). HUD's *Community Area Programmes* followed from these (Naples, 1998a). Unfortunately, there was clear evidence that, from the very beginning, this programme had not been planned on real information about community needs, and it rapidly became associated with the stigmatisation of the Black poor in the USA (Mogulof, 1969). Although some schemes ran until the late 1980s, and it started off quite well, the new Nixon Administration had no real interest in its success, and the initiative faltered (Naples, 1998a). Naples reports that women had a hard time sustaining their position within the *War on Poverty* programmes (Naples, 1998c). What this government initiative did produce was the community development corporation model for economic self-help, particularly in Latino and Afro-American communities (Peirce and Steinbach, 1985; Gittell and Vidal, 1998; Pardo, 1998; Feehan, et al., 2013).

Fifty years on, the *War on Poverty* effects are still being felt. Boteach, et al., record how the *community development corporation* movement (see below) began and thrives today as a result of Bobby Kennedy's initiatives in this sphere. It is the failure of the economy, they claim, that has undermined the government's desire to overcome the (now widening) gap in prosperity (Boteach, et al., 2014). The Ford Foundation, too, is still grant-aiding community development projects in America and around the world that places a high priority on local asset-based community development (Kretzmann and McKnight, 1993; Ford Foundation, 2002; Ellsworth and White, 2004). As the President of the Ford Foundation, Darren Walker, himself an ex-community development worker, put it in 2014: 'Neighborhoods are the unit of analysis, ultimately, because at the end of the day, that's the way people live their lives. And so you've got to have mechanisms that allow you to look across the neighborhood and across the region' (Shelterforce, 2014 – http://www.shelterforce.org/article/3683/darren_walker_interview/, accessed 5 August 2015).

The 'unfinished'

The Norwegian sociologist, Thomas Mathiesen advocated 'to be unfinished' is the only way in which those seeking social change can avoid being sucked into the ruling system and absorbed by it, or to be stigmatised and cut off by it (Rice, 2010; Mathiesen, 1970 – personal correspondence from author). Either way, the outcomes for any organisation, in serious competition with the established interests of society, are crushed (Mathiesen, 1974). This might give credence to Rubin and Rubin who provide a complex guide to CO, whilst acknowledging an Alinsky pedigree, but do not provide a full analytical guide to the consolidation of community and agency sustainable structures (Rubin, H. and Rubin, I., 2001). They claim that local government does not have the legal capacity to co-operate with campaign and community institutions, so that, at best, collaboration will be confined to consultative processes (pp. 263–4). In some US states, there is a thriving community self-build co-operative house-building movement (Rubin and Rubin, 2001; White, 2010).

The US Department of Housing and Urban Development (HUD) provides grants and technical support for such efforts, but much of the initiative for these localised projects comes from the Private Sector (Chapin, 2011). Greenberg documents how pressure on HUD has brought about a more favourable climate by the Federal Government towards supporting local house-building and neighbourhood control of the housing stock (Greenberg, 1999). In New York, the not-for-profit, Bed-Stuy community development corporation (*Bedford-Stuyvesant Restoration*), in addition to providing for a myriad of community-based activities, provides affordable housing for hundreds of citizens and makes good thousands of other houses in partnership with landlords and property owners (Bed-Stuy, 2010).

Another 'unfinished' agenda is the history and role of the '*Women's Movement*' in CO. Women, both feminists and non-feminists, have been in community organizing right from the earliest days. The *Women's Suffrage Movement* employed full-time community organizers from as early as 1857, and Carrie Chapman Catt put the structure of organizing on a methodological footing (Beck, et al., 2003). Jane Addams made a huge impact on the Settlement Movement in the USA, and many of the first academic commentators on CO were women. As a neighbourhood worker, Helen Hall was an early advocate of the *'confrontational'* style of social action on welfare issues, and taught many social work students in this vein (Chambers, 1963, p. 145 *et seq.*). Hyde (Hyde, 2001) points to some of the difficulties of women operating in the *'masculine'* ethos of CO as practised in many quarters. She calls for a better balance, and a more *'wholistic'* (sic) approach to modelling CO in practice (p. 77). Marston and Towers (in Fisher and Kling, 1993, pp. 75–102) describe the costs to women who have to overcome many structural barriers should they wish to get fully involved, even at the neighbourhood level. Bays (1998, pp. 301–25) describes how women have had to radicalise themselves and join the struggle against gender oppression in order to balance these forces in their own lives.

One such person was Madeline Talbott, who rose rapidly through the ranks of the ACORN establishment to become Rathke's National Field Director until its demise (Delgado, 1986; Talbott, 1997; 2012). It was claimed by many in the Press around the Obama election campaign in 2008 that she had been Barack Obama's boss in Michigan when he was a community organizer for ACORN (see Elliott, 2012, for example). She denies it, but it remains an open question for those interested in Right-Wing US politics (Atlas, 2010; Talbott, 2012). Virginia Ramirez rose from the ranks of the volunteer workers for COPS in San Antonio, Texas, to become a significant community leader, then co-Chair of the State-wide organisation. She reported that the IAF model was of particular appeal to women because of the way the supportive and domestic sides of the activities produced integrated practice framework (Warren, 2001, pp. 216–18).

The role of the American churches

Well before Alinsky, community organizers always saw the importance of starting where the people were, and one of the centres of their lives in American communities was the local Church. From his initial alliance with the Roman Catholic Church, Alinsky saw the benefit of targeting the Church (in all its forms and denominations) for future development initiatives (Alinsky, 1941; Rubin and Rubin, 2001). From the very beginning of CO as an interventionist agent, faith has been a logical focus of action (Taylor, 1913; Plater, 1914). Donahue and Robinson (2001) point out how very small groupings of people with a common cause (in this case their faith) can produce wide-ranging community building impacts. Putnam (et al., 2004, p. 120) rues the fact that the 'mainstream churches' of America have lost much of their following. Nevertheless, the collection of case material provided by Bane (et al., 2000) demonstrates that not only can a religious institution strengthen itself through collective capacity-building, but these strengthened communities can then diversify into social welfare activities across the whole spectrum of social concern.

Rubin (2000) shows how church membership, once it becomes focused upon social change issues, can be a powerful lever in influencing local political decision-making. This dimension was taken up by the University of Kentucky in their study of community responses to drugs and alcohol issues. The *Creating Lasting Connections* project was one such counter-drug scheme. This actively engaged forty-two Church congregations across the City of Louisville. A very high retention and engagement rate was sustained mainly because of the strong capacity-building energy put into the congregations by the project team (Johnson, et al., 2000, pp. 1–27). This scheme saw the capacity-building as a preventive agency in the fight against drugs, and the experiment produced a Rothman-based model for Church congregation mobilization (pp. 8 and 22–3; see also Chaskin, 2001, pp. 41–2).

Cnaan, et al., studied the levels of congregational involvement in social service provision, and support the findings of the project's work (Cnaan, et al., 2006). When the State withdraws from the provision of health and welfare services, it was down to the faith and other NGOs to step in and pick up shattered, migrant *colonias* (shanty towns) in the four-border States between the US and Mexico. These agencies had to start from scratch – basic service-provision, and community capacity-building, as well as to work out how best to co-ordinate their own diverse resources to bring stability to the new system they were implementing (Donelson, 2004). In situations where confidence cannot be established between the planners/change agents and the community, progress is not possible. This may well point to defective intervention techniques, mutual distrust, or other, off-scene agendas (Kotval, 2006). Arches analyses the limitations of some social work settings in the USA that limit the boundaries of intervention with 'difficult' communities (Arches, 1999).

In many of the poorest American communities, Church organisations provide material as well as spiritual leadership and support (Rivera and Erlich, 2001). A good example of this is the Abyssinian Baptist Church in Harlem, New York. In 1989, the Church founded the Abyssinian Development Corporation, which vowed to re-build Harlem 'brick by brick and block by block' until its former glory was re-established. This involved building affordable and mixed housing developments, recreation, educational and commercial premises. It also provides leadership training and input into citizen support systems in the community (Abyssinian Development Corporation, 2015 – http://www.adcorp.org/our-history, accessed 5 August 2015; *New York Times*, 17 August 2008, p. B1, NY Edition).

In co-founding the Southern Christian Leadership Conference (SCLC), Dr Martin Luther King Jr provided himself and others with a potent platform through which to lead the Civil Rights Movement during the 1950s and 1960s. SCLC demonstrated the need for comprehensive planning and delivery of forceful citizen activity and so leadership training became an important component of its repertoire. It provided role models in community organization through the examples of Andrew Young and Dorothy Cotton who developed organisational competence from the grass roots up to mass organisations (Carson, 1998; Brueggemann, 2013). In 1957, after some years as a grassroots organizer, Ella Baker was appointed to be Director of SCLC, who consolidated the organisation and then moved on to direct the Student Nonviolent Coordinating Committee in 1960 (Walker, 1974). SCLC also developed active alliances with other organisations, such as Albert Raby's *Coordinating Council of Community Organizations* in Chicago (Terry, 1988), to ensure that the national impact of the Civil Rights movement achieved the widest spread across America. The impact of the churches on the face of community organization in America has been considerable.

Academic community organization in the United States and Canada

As we shall find in our study of community development in the UK, most of the literature (outside Journals) on community organization is published by academics, and who, in the main, have only limited direct experience of prolonged exposure to fieldwork. This does not mean that this contribution is without merit. On the contrary, Jack Rothman (2001, see below) has made an indelible impression on the fieldwork of the majority of community organizers. There was also a burgeoning social research interest in these social tensions. Kurt Lewin had published his *Field Theory*, which aimed to explain why a balance between countervailing pressures sustained a tension in social roles and socio-politico-economic outcomes for the individual and class. The coping mechanisms of those under these pressures lose their stability if the forces change. This was the fate of many of the communities that became the focus for the *War on Poverty* interventions (Lewin, 1948; 1952; Brager and Holloway, 1978). This gave invaluable insights into the questions of group dynamics, action research methods and to basics of systems theory – all essential components of community development practice.

After the Lane Report (see Chapter 2 above), and several commentaries on the administrative functioning of Social Work education, etc., the first systematic texts on community organization emerged in the early 1950s. Hillman approached the subject from the vantage point of 'top-down' – social planning, whereas the Canadian, Murray Ross, saw community organization as a bottom-up approach to social change (Hillman, 1950; Ross, 1955). In 1947, Lynde (cited at length by Hillman, 1950, p. 194 *et seq.*) deliberately chose to ignore the community level of social change. He contended that local officials were the main impediment to the implementation of social change policy, and that a strategic approach to changing their behaviour was a priority. Therefore, he outlined in some detail how the community organizer might create a role and manipulate officialdom for the common good.

At that time, there was a great deal of international interest in planned social change and, at the United Nations, situated in New York, an outline of what community development should look like – 'bottom-up development' – was published (United Nations Bureau, 1955). Murray Ross, on the other hand, outlined a framework for professional community organizers to enter a community with the specific intention of mobilising them for a change process. In the process, it was the community organizer's specific responsibility to ensure that the targeting of issues and the mobilising around them were the self-identified and stated priorities of the community itself (Ross, 1955, p. 39 *et seq.*). The next prerequisite for Ross was that the community was to be 'organised', institutionally/formally, for the task of implementing social change itself (p. 154 *et seq.*). Ross published case studies to illustrate what he meant (Ross, 1958). From these two authors came many imitators and extenders, and two of these stand out – William Biddle and Arthur Dunham.

William Biddle, and his wife, Loureide, wrote three introductory texts, which fitted readily into the expanding number of College curricula on community organization in the USA (Biddle, W. and Biddle, L., 1965; Biddle, 1968; Biddle W. and Biddle, L., 1968) – one on the process, and the other as an introduction to training community organizers. The YMCA of America sponsored a collection of definitions and commentaries on community organization in 1959 (Harper and Dunham, 1959). This volume seeks, firmly, to place community organization within the bounds of intervention framed by a consensus model of social change. Co-editor of this work, Arthur Dunham, spelled out the scope for community organization work in an explanatory address to the National Conference on Social Work (Dunham, 1959), and he reinforced the connections with social work, and the need for support of the individual within the micro-system of community groups and organisations. In his book of the previous year, Dunham had provided a generic appraisal of the specialised role of community organization within social work, and also provided a social change dimension as the legitimising element that justified its inclusion within social work (Dunham, 1958). Pray (1959) supported this view, stating that if social action aimed at directing action away from the consensus, then it was no part of social work. The key distinction was whether or not '*welfare*', in the traditional, social support sense, was behind the action (Pray, 1959). By 1970, Dunham had changed his line of community organization, and on community organizing in particular. He devoted two chapters to the subject of *conflict*, and (political) *social action*, which he now saw as a legitimate component of a social work curriculum on community organization (Dunham, 1970). Dunham was not merely an academic. He had served as a community-based worker for a neighbourhood centre in St. Louis, and, after prison as a conscientious objector in World War I (Social Welfare History Project, 2013), he joined a religious charity as an administrator, before becoming an academic. His personal commitment to the causes he espoused (mainly Christian ones) was very strongly expressed in his work (Dunham, 1958; Social Welfare History Project, 2013).

Dunham's work prepared the ground for a number of more specialised explorations of the components of community organisation, and, at the end of the 1960s, and in the 1970s, a huge expansion in the American community organisation literature took place. A whole fresh market had been established, with the McCarthy witch-hunt era well behind them now. Perlman (cited in Garvin and Cox, 2001) records thousands of local groups that were receiving Federal or State aid, all supported by community organizers, and many local (or 'block') groups had been established to defend or represent their city block residential area (Garvin and Cox, 2001, pp. 96–7). Cox identifies the rise of Anti-Vietnam War protest with this rise in organised community-based activity. Additionally, the Kennedy/Johnson era saw the development of the (international) *Peace Corps* (1961), and the (domestic USA) *VISTA* (Volunteers in Service of America) programme – in 1965 (Cox, et al., 1970). In 1970, the Peace Corps, VISTA and the *National Senior Service* (1963) programmes merged under the umbrella of the Corporation for National and Community Service. Between 1965 and 2006, there had been over 140,000 VISTA community-based volunteer works, most of whom used community organization as their vehicle for stimulating community capacity-building and local social service support for vulnerable people (Corporation for National and Community Service, 2006).

In 1970, Cary published an anthology of community organization writings. Among them was one by Morris (Morris, 1970), who raises the question about whether or not a community organisation worker should be an expert in some specific field of social objective, or whether a generalist should be employed. Up to this time, this question has not been resolved. For many years, skills in any field might appear to have been a virtue. The United States' *'Corps'* programmes began with very little formal preparation, and they rapidly ran into difficulties. The *Infamous Peace Corps Postcard* incident highlighted this issue in 1961, when an ill-prepared volunteer reported home on the 'absolutely primitive living conditions' in her new (African) assignment, and how she had not been at all prepared for what 'underdevelopment meant' (Peace Corps Writers, 2008).

Midgley (1981; 1987), and Cornia, et al. (1987) make much of the impact that (well-intentioned?) volunteer programmes have on 'foreign' populations. The lessons learned in these fields have served the sponsoring-government's community organization structure at home, as much as they might have helped some foreign *'beneficiary'*. The practice competence of the returned workers (foreign and domestic) contributed greatly to domestic programmes and then fed into the academic profession directly. From thence, they helped in constructing the literature on the subject (George Brager, Ralph Kramer, Harry Specht, Martin Rein, etc.). Before the Alinsky influence on community organisation, the general ethos in American professional intervention was based upon an altruistic goal of 'community', or 'society', but Alinsky introduced 'self-interest', and the direct acquisition of power as the primary goals. To this end, in the new age of 'choice' of principle and method, community organization workers focused on the community and its individuals' needs. *'Participation'* became the key indicator of success (Cary, in Cary, 1970, p. 144 *et seq.*).

The post McCarthy era literature was a mixed collection. Many documents recorded historical events, and combined them with theoretical and philosophical analysis (Moynihan, 1969; Bailey, 1974). Other provided partial and segmented views of what they saw as the priority issue or approach to community organisation. Not that some of the writing was without content. In the First Edition of Cox, et al., 1970, of their (now, in its 7th Edition) iconic collection of readings from community organization, Lindblom (1970) describes the difficulties that professionals have in framing and planning their interventions. After McMillan (1945), these compendiums were popular (e.g. Harper and Dunham, 1959; Brager and Purcell, 1967; Cary, 1970; Gilbert and Specht, 1977b), particularly as community organization did not, at that time, have its own Journal. Communities and administration systems are too diverse, too determined to conform to their own set of values, traditions, structures and work methods that any attempt to marshal them all into a directions framework for development is fraught with difficulties (Lindblom, 1970).

Brager and Specht produced a generic text on *community organiz*ing that was inclusive (if critical) of the Alinsky model (Brager and Specht, 1973). Specht, elsewhere, seeks to ignore the 'organisational' aspects of *disruptive* campaigning altogether, attributing its sometimes successful outcomes to simple, formless, ideological commitment to spiritual leaders such as Gandhi, Guevara and Fanon (Specht, 1969; Grosser, 1976). Cloward and Piven stress that, as the organizers can exercise little influence over the context, much depends on their own organising ability to ensure coherence and success (Cloward and Piven, 1999; Bischoff and Reisch, 2001). Some very important issues were identified or re-discovered: e.g. social planning (Morris and Binstock, 1966; Perlman and Guirin, 1972).

Rothman

What is significant about the Cox, et al., 1970 compilation (above) is that this volume provides the first reprint of Rothman's *'Three Models of Community Organization Practice'* that has shaped the majority of American community organization writing since that date. In a mere sixteen pages, first published in a Journal in 1969, Rothman gives order and symmetry to the wanderings across philosophy, models, and ideological writing that preceded it. He separates three *'Modes'* of community organization practice – *Locality Development; Social Planning;* and *Social Action* (Rothman, 1970, pp. 20–36). The first, *Locality Development*, is directed to the generation of consensus at the local level, and cites communal anomie as the motivating cause. *Social Planning* is about manipulating established organisations, through the exercise of diplomacy, and the generating of joint-working structures – this is also a 'consensus' model. Mode C, *Social Action*, presents the engaged community organizer confronted with the necessity of taking extreme risks with the presentation of a conflict-generating approach to issue identification, and the contest for power. For this model of intervention to be successful, the locality-dependant organizer must be confident that they have both local autonomy (as a free-standing professional) and the unequivocal support of any funder or employer. Rothman breaks the conventional, social work taboo of always seeking consensus, and Saul Alinsky's model is made respectable (Rothman, 1970, pp. 24–5 *et seq.*).

In 1979, Rothman shared a re-edited version, of Cox, et al., with John Tropman, and then expanded the article under his own name in 1987. In 1995, Rothman made a major revision of the '*Modes*' to include a cross-discipline analysis, which greatly increased the complexity of the model. What he was doing was to increase the scope of analytical work that practitioners would have to do to satisfy the working of the *Models* in practice (Rothman, 1979; Rothman and Tropman, 1987; Rothman, 1995). In many respects, his model now reflects many of the complex organisational features of the '*Municipalisation*' model of social planning described by Plummer (1999, 2002, see above). This interest is taken forward by Checkoway (1995), who argues that experience within neighbourhoods, and official attempts at urban renewal (for example) can result in sophisticated local mechanisms for planning communities for their future needs. Unless the education of officials responsible for implementing planning functions of local authorities is brought into line with the realities of neighbourhood dynamics and politics, then policies that require the engagement of local communities cannot be realised without dysfunctional outcomes (Checkoway, 1995, pp. 323–4).

These ideas had been evolving over the years. First, Friedmann (1975), and Gilbert and Specht (Gilbert and Specht, 1979), then Checkoway (1995) had refined the argument in favour of the presentation of the economic and social situation of communities to the (organised?) members of that community, allowing them to engage on the issues and the implementation problems that might arise if change was sought. In 2001, Rothman provides us with an overview of this process, and highlights the tensions that arise out of the increasing capacity of officialdom to utilise data of formidable complexity (*metatheoretical*, as he puts it) (Rothman and Zalt, 2001, p. 309) in the face of the limitations of community members to either access, or even understand the modelling and multi-variable solutions that the technocratic process produces (pp. 298–311).

The consequences of this can be seen in the case material presented by Edwards and Egbert-Edwards, where whole communities are still being ignored by planners (Edwards and Egbert-Edwards, 1998). From 1995 to 2007, the Ford Foundation supported communities in New York City through the provision of community organizers and other logistical support, first to challenge, then to engage the City's Education planning programme. This initiative demonstrated the success of community organizing to underpin and support a community in an extremely complex, controversial and critical area of community life (Petrovitch, 2008).

Wells, et al., describe how a combined Rothman *Locality Development* and *Social Planning* model could best serve migrant communities in the Mid-West of the USA. Latino migrants, who have their own ethnic ties, are in need of integrative mechanisms, and local communities were receptive to accommodate them (Wells, et al., 1999). Similarly, but in contrast to the receptivity of the locals described above, the *Atlanta's Olympic Games legacy* of 1996 resulted in a negative impact on the poorest housing residents in the City due to a complete neglect of the social planning process (Newman, 1999). Bradshaw's study of Sacramento's complex planning regime shows that it is well up to the task of multi-tasking across a complex array of agencies and communities, to provide concrete and sustainable outcomes in community-controlled, low-income housing and economic development (Bradshaw, 2000).

In parallel with this formal consideration of the modelling of community organisation, Amatai Etzioni, in 1993, raised a considerable profile for a *communitarian* approach to community social regeneration. This gained the support of no less a figure than Tony Blair, who was aiming to gain power for the Labour Party in the UK (Driver and Martell, 1997, pp. 27–8; Hale, 2006). Etzioni's model required a totally rational approach to re-ordering democracy, from the bottom-up, but led by a cadre of intellectually prepared leaders (Etzioni, 1993). Stiles comments that this model is one that depends so much on 'rationality' that it cannot accommodate any conflict whatsoever, and is, as such, of no use for the tension required in power-contested social change (Stiles, 1998).

What is fascinating about the dissemination of ideas about theory and practice in community organization in the United States is the relative compartmentalisation of 'schools' of orthodoxy on the subject. Most of the different approaches recognise the 'Alinsky model' of confrontational intervention and organization – many with some disapproval (Pruger and Specht, 1969; Specht, 1979; Walton, 1979; Sites, 1998). Alinsky is not without substantial support, however, but very few writers have any class perspective in their writings (Burghardt, 1982). Some major writers do not recognise Rothman (Rubin, H. and Rubin, I., 2001), and some do not recognise anyone else but their own source of wisdom (Kretzmann and McKnight, 1993; Bobo, et al., 1996; Greenberg, 1999).

Canada

Canadian experimentation in community organization dates back to the 1930s (Brueggemann, 2013) and Alinsky made an early foray into Canada to work with

First Nations representatives over the question of land rights and inter-communal relations (video of training sessions owned by author). Absolon and Herbert trace the history of the Government, at Federal and Provincial level, to use community development to answer many of the *First Nations'* grievances and to meet their changing needs (Absolon and Herbert, 1997). In British Columbia, there has been a long-standing engagement with its First Nations population. In times of economic hardship, the Government has taken many steps to include this population in economic and social planning (Markey, et al., 2007), but in some localities, the difficulties presented by this community to community development facilitators has proved problematic (Partners of Learning, 2006).

Some intractable social issues (e.g. mental health, drug-related issues, alcohol dependence) remain, and there has been a lot of mistrust in this process (Ravensbergen and Van der Plaat, 2006). Despite great cultural differences, and completely different goals (e.g. child protection criteria), the official deployment of community development resources has had some successes (Absolon and Herbert, 1997). All the Provinces maintain a Department of State relating to community development – Alberta, which does not share many of the more industrialised economy/urban issues of the other Provinces, maintains a general community development interest in the cultivation of the localised Voluntary Sector and locality development (Alberta, 2007). In the Maritime Provinces, especially, community economic development is a priority due to the continuing state of depression of the economy (MacAulay, 2001; Prince Edward Island, 2009).

Women's health and poverty was the focus for direct, Province-sponsored, action in Quebec (*Action Sociale*), but gradually the movement that emerged was swallowed up by the central service Departments (Panet-Raymond, 1999; Herrick and Stuart, 2005). Centralised community development is most favoured across the nation (Bregha, 1970; Moffatt, et al., 1999), especially in areas like *First Nations* work, where there are acute sensitivities (Muller, 1995). Nevertheless, there have been some extremely adventurous projects at the local level – e.g. the Vancouver project creating economically viable businesses with '*bin divers*/homeless', itinerants (Dale and Newman, 2010).

One National programme that has attracted attention and deserves special mention is the *Company of Young Canadians* (CYC). This was modelled on the *VISTA* programme in the United States, and also replicated some of the characteristics of the British *Community Service Volunteers*. Later it overlapped with the UK *Young Volunteer Force Foundation* (now the Community Development Foundation – see below). CYC brought youth into an activity regime of community service with some community development projects built in. Initially, it was a 'hopelessly, liberal "do-gooder organization that would bring middle-class and paternalistic solutions to poverty and disenfranchisement' (Brushett, 2009, p. 248). From 1969 onwards, however, CYC rapidly radicalised itself under fresh leadership, and the scene was set for its demise. This radical period only lasted for five more years, because internal and political frictions brought the CYC into conflict with the Canadian public, who were anxious to get rid of these 'Government-funded hell-raisers' (p. 247).

CYC set a benchmark for government tolerance in terms of State-sponsored community intervention. It is claimed by Lotz (1998) that the Canadian Government did not 'discover' community development until 1993, by which time many other nations had decided that it was not the cure-all that it may have claimed to be. Hitherto, despite a robust approach to intervening with *First Nations* issues, the Federal Government saw community development as a palliative approach to some soft welfare issues (Mairs, 1992; Lotz, 1997). Nevertheless, once it started, the government was very wary of allowing too much participation, lest things got out of hand (Lotz, 1998).

The Canadian who has made the most significant contribution to community development, apart from Murray Ross (Ross, 1955), is Ronald Labonté, who has made his mark on community development as the foremost proponent of Health Promotion. Labonté's contribution to health promotion enabled practitioners in the field who wanted to effect meaningful social change, to apply Labonté's dictum as the most feasible and most cost-effective model for engagement on even the most intractable public health questions (Labonté, 1991a, b; 1998). Labonté is prepared to share some of the difficult truths about community development, such as it being a technique that calculates percentage, rather than universal, gains. It also is going to be in conflict always with a centralising and increasingly bureaucratic State as it has to be creative at all times and break free of boundaries, in the name of community and self-sufficiency (Labonté, 1998). Labonté's ideas are taken up by Chappell, et al. (2006), who analyse the All-Canada focus on community health and community development initiatives in their PATH programme (2001–6) within the National Comprehensive Community Initiatives (Promoting Action towards Health). PATH sought to steer a middle path between the Health Ministry's aims and the demands of the community for better health outcomes (Raeburn and Corbett, 2001), and this raised many contentious discussions on the effectiveness of community development in health matters, not least that the effectiveness of community development in Health Promotion is very difficult to quantify (pp. 21–2).

Analysis

The contributions to the development of community development theory and practice by the United Nations and the USA have been considered in detail. The role played by the economic system and the State's response to these uncovers the fact that the State can play a major role in instigating community development, and in shaping its direction. Within the context of the study, the value system is contained in a 'world view' of the State as the frame of reference for the community development activity. There is an acceptance of the ideology of the 'nation', and/ or that of the international bodies directing the economic development – this is one of OECD, free-market economics, with social democracy as the goal for the development process. Within this there are strict limitations placed on the extent to which boundaries of this context might be challenged. Community development is seen as a vehicle for improving the internal workings of the State, and a mechanism for achieving social mobility for (those organised) sections of the communities that make it up.

There are anomalies. The World Bank/IMF consortium, champions of the OECD's framework for successful nationhood, and most powerful challengers to national development programmes, have produced a potentially socially destructive model for 'progress'. This imposes the requirement for national governments in debt to adopt restructuring measures known as *structural adjustment*. These, for over two decades towards the end of the twentieth century, consigned millions around the World to unemployment, community decline and anomie. This restructuring was the penalty that national populations had to pay in response to the proclivities of their leaders (often 'elected' through the most undemocratic means). Community development programmes were often sent in to manage the reconstruction of communities under these circumstances. The lesson that we have to learn from this is, when the State decides to introduce community development programmes, what objectives do they have for the citizen communities? Are the motives conducive to democratic development, or is there something else afoot?

This caveat on 'development' is not to cast total aspersions on institutions such as the *Peace Corps*, or *Voluntary Service Overseas*, the UK forerunner to the *Peace Corps*. Rather it is to determine how the inputs and outcomes can be analysed and evaluated for the most beneficial outcomes, according to a pre-agreed system of value and impact assessment. It is within this framework that 'principles', which may sometimes be regarded as rhetorical slogans, such as *'participation'*, can be judged. At every stage in the change process, instituted by *'animateurs'*, aka community development workers, the tensions between these 'principles' and over-riding power pressure must be weighed up. This is also about the confrontation of *modernism* vs. *post-modernistic* goals: pre-determined objectives vs. process. Can, or must, a decision on this be made on either side without arbitrariness? What we learn from this is that *systems theory* lends itself to both sets of understanding. On the one hand, micro-management may well be the result. On the other hand, broad, sweeping conclusions can be constructed.

Evaluation shapes the individual project design and 'business model' (Cusworth and Franks, 1993). Depending on the agenda of the principal funders, so the process of evaluation extends. Consequently, it seems that the funding of evaluation is beyond most small, localised activities, and even broad strategic programmes have difficulty administering it (Adamson and Bromiley, 2008; Welsh Assembly Government, 2009c). If evaluation is to be successful, then the authority and determination of the agency requiring measurable outcomes must be sufficient to enforce it. But the purpose of evaluation is that its findings must be useful both to the funders, and to those active on the ground, including the beneficiaries as well (ODA, 1995; Patton, 1997). It is the determination to use the data, be it quantitative or qualitative that measures the ultimate outcome of evaluation.

Social planning is a modernist construction, with concrete, hard data, expectations. It entails the diagnosis of the problem, analysis of the choices, allocation of the means for achieving change, and establishment of the approved outcomes to be monitored, measured and evaluated. Plummer's (1999) framework for assessing the fitness to embark on change demands stringent tests and focus. Where Plummer's framework is deficient is that it lacks the process requirements for this to be implemented. Plummer's extension of the framework into a community-focused developmental approach falls short of building in partnership-to- the-point-of-joint-control, which may be a realistic appraisal of the extent to which those in authority may wish to go in sharing power with their constituents (Plummer, 2002). Nevertheless, it leaves the full potential for community responsibility unchallenged.

In the USA and Canada, whereas there are many instances of unstructured or open-ended change objectives, they are allowed to play a decreasing role in contemporary agency programmes. Perhaps it is because of the underlying competitive nature of this unrelenting model of free-market economies that leads even the most *'post-modernist'* of change seekers to, ultimately, resort to the pursuit of power, influence and plainly identifiable demands for change. The many apologists of consensus lose out to the essence of Alinsky's *'Ends and Means'* argument – to become goal-obsessed, rather than process-focused (Alinsky, 1972). The *'corporate structure'* (business model) is seen as the best mode for survival in this competitive age (Fabricant and Fisher, 2002). But the dynamism of the North American scene continues to awaken fresh visions, and greater challenges in the field, in the textbooks, and in the training programmes (Specht and Courtney, 1994; Weil and Ohmer, 2013). As the *'faith communities'* have demonstrated in the USA, small numbers of well-organised people can achieve great things, whether the structural boundaries in place 'plan' them or not.

Summary

1. America and Canada have a long history of theoretical understanding of community organizational practice. This is supported by a coherent professional training capability.
2. With a background of the American acceptance of a social democratic political structure and of the capitalist economic system, rival community organization practice models have emerged – consensus processes and/or conflict modelling.

3. Within the extensive body of literature on the subject, there is a marked inability of the various 'philosophical schools of thought' to recognise or communicate with each other.

4. Beyond the thinking of Jack Rothman, there is still not enough theoretical modelling to combine social planning and localised approaches to community organization.

5. There would be significant benefits all round should the distinctions between practice in developing and developed economies be eliminated.

4

Community development in the modern era – community development in the UK

The Colonial roots of British community development

The origins of British community development lie in the movement to bring education to the indigenous people throughout the British Empire, and to enable the Colonial administration to spread the responsibility of governance to the local populations – 'Mass Education' (Colonial Office, 1925). Whereas social and civic developments were to the fore, early priorities even included strengthening local people's traditional beliefs in the supernatural (Colonial Office, 1925, p. 5). From 1925 onwards, regular Colonial Office Conferences were held to refine the structure to administrative thinking on the matter. In 1943, and again in 1948, the question of 'extension' services – the provision of high-quality technical assistance, together with community-building mobilisation, was examined. The leadership of the United States' work in this area was acknowledged, but not built into any framework for future reference (Colonial Office, 1943). Additionally, the question of community development in urban areas was put forward as a priority, due to the rising political consciousness of the indigenous populations (Colonial Office, 1943; Colonial Office, 1948). The Colonial Office maintained these consultations with the field workers, administrators, and colonial leaders over the next decade. At and after the Conference of 1954, the term 'social development' came into vogue for a short time in British Colonial vocabulary, only to fade out again (Colonial Office, 1954). But this term was to rise to prominence four decades later as expertise in 'developing economies' work gained international currency (Midgley, 1995).

In 1960, a conference was held specifically to consider the administration and implementation of community development. At that time, community development was described as 'the most effective agency for raising the standard of living of communities', and a flexible approach to funding and control was considered essential. There was no conflict apparent between those local authorities responsible for development and the investment in national and/or local programmes of community development (Colonial Office, 1960, p. 30 *et seq.*).

The effect of this investment by the government was to establish a training programme at London University in 1949, under the Chairmanship of Professor 'Reg' Batten. Batten and his wife, Madge, embarked on a series of publications that defined the role and scope of community development for Colonial administrators, and which also set the framework for many practitioners in the UK, when the time arose (Batten, 1957; Batten, 1962; Batten R. and Batten, M., 1965; 1967). In 1951, they launched the 'Community Development Bulletin', which was succeeded in 1966 by the 'Community Development Journal'. From the Institute of Education, London University came many colonial administrators, and also a stream of ideas about how Britain might better use its educational and technological talents (Williams, 1979). Unfortunately, the *Bulletin* was more about case study material than it was about formulating a theoretical framework or a basis for evaluation of the fieldwork.

People like Peter du Sautoy (Obituary – *Community Development Journal*, 1968, No. 2, pp. 59–60) took some of these ideas forward to build a people-centred, consensus model of planned social change (du Sautoy, 1962). But du Sautoy bewails the failure of those responsible for fostering community development overseas to confront the need for community development practice in Britain. He uses the example of the USA, where the Biddles were defining the field (see above and below), but he saw his task, as the first Editor of the new *Community Development Journal*, as servicing the needs of overseas developers, rather than a UK market (du Sautoy, 1966). This work dove-tailed neatly into the work being done by the United Nations. Education, technical assistance, and community participation were the underpinnings of this work (Perez-Guerrero, 1950; UN Bureau of Social Affairs, 1955), and in the emergence of the Biddles' partnership as pioneer American theorists in the structure and methodology of community intervention in the United States (Biddle, W. and Biddle L., 1965; Biddle, 1966; Biddle, 1968; Biddle, W. and Biddle L., 1968).

The Colonial model developed by the British Government did provide future community development agencies and workers in the UK (and beyond) with a framework for development within communities, starting with and including a major role for the agencies of governance. As it was considered to be the 'colonial model', it was not immediately transferable into the UK context. Consequently, the detail of this was not codified in any systematic way, leaving much of the logistical and administrative (for example, training, evaluation) functions in the hands of local mechanisms and, more often, serendipity.

The beginnings of recognition in the UK

The late 1950s and early 1960s saw an increase in government interest in community development. Eileen Younghusband led the investigation into the future shape of social work, and she pressed her interest in community development at this point (Ministry of Health, 1959). This Report (the 'Younghusband Report') advocated training community development workers within and outside formal social work channels, but said that community development training would benefit all social workers because of the added dimensions it offered (p. 179). It also called for formalised training in community development as part of a restructuring of social work training, generally – which gave rise to the National Institute for Social Work (NISW) in 1961 (p. 252), and the establishment of a training programme for community workers (Henderson and Thomas, 1979). We will return to NISW below, but it was wound up in 2003 partly, it is believed, as its broad, community, problem-identifying and solving perspective was out of vogue with the new driving force within the social work training establishment – the Local Authorities (HM Government, 2000).

George Goetschius (1961), and, later, Hodge (1964), predicted that the American approach to *community organization* would come to Britain, due to the rise in social dysfunction within the inner-city areas, and the need to tackle these issues locally, rather than just through policy pronouncements. Kuenstler (1961) had linked community organization with social work, and Hodge (1964) strengthened this connection, calling for formalized training. The National Council for Social Service (NCSS) published two pamphlets on the subject of preventive intervention in the community. The first (NCSS, 1962) was an agenda guide for their National Conference (in 1964), and asked their membership (voluntary) organisations to consider how best their resources might be used in managing social change in both towns and rural areas. *Community organisation* could be a significant contributor to the arsenal of resources that Voluntary Organisations could possess in meeting this challenge. All the extant community organisation and community development writing was on their reading list for the edification of the Conference attendees (pp. 33–4). In their second pamphlet, the NCSS described how the idea had begun to spread across many Voluntary Organisations. Community Associations were forming co-ordinating bodies, and local groups were thriving (Twelvetrees, 1976). New Towns (three waves of which were to be built between 1947 and 1949 and 1968) were deploying 'Social Development Officers' to provide the social glue that would enable these large housing developments to consolidate socially (NCSS, 1965; Morley, 1968; Runnicles, 1970; Demers, 1972; Heraud, 1975). These, essentially establishment, steps to define a fresh intervention approach to social change trod a strictly consensus path. Elsewhere, other approaches were being tried.

One of these was an inspirational European figure in community organization in the Alinsky/American mould. This was Dalino Dolci, of Sicily. His confrontational approach and high-risk profile endeared him to many in Britain as he challenged both the conservatism of local communities and the direct violence of the Mafia. He rallied Sicilian peasant farmers in a civic revolt against them and galvanised the community to resist Mafia coercion (Dolci, 1959). Consequently, Dolci became known as the 'Sicilian Gandhi' for his non-violent methods (Booker, 1962; Ragoni, 2011). At a packed fund-raising meeting in Caxton Hall, London in 1970, Dolci called for support in his struggle against the violence of the Mafia. 'Only through non-violence can the tyrant be overthrown' he said (personal notes of meeting). However, his tactics of sustained direct action, coupled with passive resistance, were not the model of community organization that was going to be adopted in Britain. Nevertheless, there was a definite movement towards incorporating some of this newly discovered, structural approach to managed social change within the established order.

Momentous change in the 1960s and 1970s

The YWCA, and the London Council of Social Service, as agencies raising deep concerns about the situation of young people in British society, engaged an American expert on community development, George Goetschius, to provide a framework for interventionist strategies to tackle this issue. Following a five-year field study, Goetschius produced two significant publications (Goetschius and Tash, 1967; Goetschius, 1969), which called for the engagement of the local communities (inter alia) in the support and re-integration of local youth. Goetschius provides us with the first programmatic method for the engagement of local people (Goetschius, 1969), and this was to be the basic textbook for field workers for many years. The link was to be made to 'Group Work', then a standardised component in some forms of therapeutic social interventions (Klein, 1961), and Goetschius acknowledges his reliance on Klein, and also the Biddles (Goetschius, 1969, p. 227). He also tries to define community development as something different from community organisation (pp. 182–4). In so doing, he ventures into social planning, by suggesting that *community organisation* is about the manipulation of established organisations, and not aggregates of individuals in the community setting (community development).

On a similar tack, NISW launched a community development project in Southwark, London, in 1968, to provide some much-lacking fieldwork training for community development workers (Thomas, 1976). This project sought contact with local housing estates, and developed a network of support and empowerment strategies that enabled these communities to interact more forcefully with authority in pursuit of housing maintenance and community relations. The NISW project ran training seminars for the employees of the newly constituted Social Services Departments (Seebohm, 1968; and the Local Authority Social Services Act 1970) and an element of scientific enquiry and application emerged through the use of comprehensive community profiling and the measurement of stress factors in local communities (author was a participant in some of these in 1970/71).

Alongside this, the work of Philip Abrams gained some publicity. Abrams showed the positive and the negative sides of localised self-help schemes. Reliant on volunteers, with little formal training, and working unpaid, 'Good Neighbour' schemes ran successfully in some areas (Bulmer, 1986; Abrams, et al., 1986). Abrams's research and action programme demonstrated how people in neighbourhoods, despite utilising considerable social capital, nevertheless did not naturally gravitate towards, nor rely upon, neighbourhood schemes. Considerable promotion and professional support was needed to achieve a sustainable activity pattern and organisational consistency (Abrams, et al., 1986). Thus, there was a wide divergence in practice methods emerging between the well-resourced NISW scheme and the fledgling neighbourhood self-help movement.

The Calouste Gulbenkian Foundation had sponsored a study of 'community work' (Leaper, 1968), and then went on to sponsor two working parties into the philosophy behind community work, and the recruitment, practice and training of community workers (Calouste Gulbenkian, 1968; 1973). In the first Report, the call was for a professional input into the community with problem-solving skills, and strategic initiatives, and the major thrust of the thinking was towards introducing University-based training for these resources (Calouste Gulbenkian, 1968, p. 65 *et seq.*; p. 85 *et seq.*). Where the Gulbenkian panel differed from the message coming from the USA was that its 'models for intervention' did not contain any mention of conflict à *la* Alinsky. Like the USA, however, in Britain at the time, there was an intense interest in 'unattached youth' and the capacity of the State to engage with them (Albemarle, 1960; Morse, 1968). Significantly, in Scotland, training programmes in this area now included community development to impart the mechanism for problem-solving at the community level for issues that appeared intractable from the level of the State (Calouste Gulbenkian, 1968, pp. 52–3). Bryant describes the introduction of community work training to the Gorbals and Govanhill in the 1970s, where sectarianism and chronic housing conditions were the norm (Bryant, B. and Bryant R., 1982). Social circumstances, mainly housing conditions, and official disinterest in the community's plight gave rise to a series of campaigns involving civil disobedience. These protests led to short-term gains and raised the profile of community action. Nevertheless, these activities did not have a coherent model for action nor a structure that generated any real sustainability.

On another level, and at the same time, the Government was promoting its own-brand participation through the mechanism of the Town and Country Planning Act 1968. Here, Section 3 called for public consultation and representation as part of the process for local government's preparation of structure plans, and sections 7 and 8 required local consultation and representation in the formation of Local Plans. To amplify this, the Government's interpretation of the *community participation* elements of the Seebohm Report (see below) fitted neatly into the role it was setting in its Report 'People and Planning' (Skeffington, 1969).

Skeffington spelled out how this consultation must go. It included the power for local government to assist local communities prepare for participation in the planning processes. Modern critics of this permissive-only framework say that it was open to exploitation by authorities unwilling to really engage with communities. It failed to realise the necessary changes that would be needed for effective participation if a successful planning process was to be achieved (Shapely, 2013). This view is naïve.

The Report was never meant to be more than a smoke screen, and it was never more than a tokenistic nudge towards structural reform in local government. Local government was not prepared in any way to accommodate effective 'participation' in its affairs. In some areas of whole area redevelopment, public consultation took the form of a pictorial exhibition and that was it. The shallowness of the government's intent on this issue was borne out in the way in which the Home Office designed the (contemporaneous) Community Development Project (CDP – see detailed section below). The whole ethos for community development in the CDP was within a strictly reformist ideology. In this form it could never have changed the structural circumstances that confronted the projects. In some local authorities community development was blatantly used as a mechanism for social control (Benington, 1976; Cockburn, 1977; Mayo, 1979). *In extremis*, this has been stated thus: 'Throughout the western world, states are characterized by one of the two major symbols of control in capitalist society; the tank or the community worker' (Corrigan, 1975, p. 57). Additionally, Waddington (1979) and Barr (1991) pointed to the setback to professional confidence that cynical application of community development like this engendered. Gradually, a new mood developed, which sparked off a swing in ideological commitment from the old 'colonial' approach to managed change to a radicalised appraisal of the State and its mechanisms of control. This new, hostile view of the State was to be reinforced with what followed in the realm of social services.

Central government was looking towards more major changes in the way social services were provided. In 1965, Sir Frederic Seebohm had started an investigation into how social work services might be radically restructured (Seebohm, 1968, p. 11). The Seebohm Committee followed the path of the earlier study of Scotland's needs in Social Services (Secretary of State for Scotland, 1966), which had called for preventative community support and development for vulnerable people – older people, particularly (pp. 5–6; and 10). The Seebohm Report stressed the philosophy of the Beverage Report (1942), the National Health Service Act (1946), and the National Insurance Act (1949), whereby the British people might buy into insurance and service cover for their most critical needs, but that their basic needs might equally be borne by the family, the community and by self-help. Seebohm devoted a chapter of the Report to 'The Community', and to preventative support for the individual in society by the community and self-help (Seebohm, 1968, paras. 474–501). 'Participation' was to be encouraged, as was 'a sense of community' (paras. 481–2), and 'community development' was to be the mechanism for the State to support this process (para. 480 *et seq.*). Additionally, Seebohm called for the regulation of training for social workers, and his recommendations resulted in setting up the Central Council for Education and Training in Social Work (CCETSW) in 1971, through the Health Visiting and Social Work (Training) Act 1962 – as amended in 1970 (Hansard, HC Deb, 11 May 1970, vol. 801, cols. 972–7).

The first 'Seebohm' community development workers were employed by the London Borough of Lambeth in 1970, but their work was inhibited considerably by local elected representatives' suspicion and bureaucratic obsession with protocols and traditional administrative practices (personal observations by author). The model for local government was to be re-organised along corporatist lines and the community development workers were to be agents in this process (Cockburn, 1977). Thus, any actual contact with the citizens, participation in 'out-of-hours' activities and feedback into Council thinking was actively discouraged (author's experience at the workface). The primary role for these community liaison personnel was to be intelligence-gathering for the Council (Cockburn, 1977).

As Thomas described it (Thomas, 1983, pp. 21–2), the boundaries of what was accepted as being 'social work' were being profoundly stretched by the combination of the Plowden and Seebohm Reports, and the possibilities of exploring and evaluating the effectiveness of 'problem-solving' across a wider canvas than casework was enticing for some. Still reeling from the attack by Barbara Wootton (1959), who had called into question the validity of social intervention on any basis other than for advancing self-help (Wootton, 1959, pp. 292–3; Loney, 1983, p. 22), two more 'modernist' solutions presented themselves – systems theory-driven casework (Goldstein, 1973; Pincus and Minahan, 1973), and/or problem-solving community development, all the time building bridges between people and their communities (Younghusband, 1964).

In 1953, Younghusband had criticised British social work for not producing its own breakthroughs in professional thinking, but which, she claimed, had relied upon played out methods (charity), and half-digested ideas (Freud, for example) (Younghusband, 1973, pp. 20–1; Goldstein, 1973). Sinfield states that, in Seebohm's model for Social Services, there was no evidence to support the (he believes, justifiable) claims that generic social work can be an agent for community problem-solving and development (Sinfield, 1970).

The adoption of the 'Community' chapter in the Seebohm Report by many of the new Social Services Departments (Local Authority Social Services Act 1970), and by CCETSW, began social work's recognition of 'Community Work' as an established pathway to social work accreditation (CCETSW, 1974). By 1979, fifty such courses had been recognised (CCETSW, 1979, p. 2). Baldock expressed his encouragement at the experimentation that took place at the threshold of the new, *Seebohm*, era, but he also noted that there were going to be problems integrating community development into Departments that were still consolidating 'social casework' (Baldock, 1974). On the positive side, the possibility of adopting a systems theory approach in social work training programmes, via the works of Goldstein, and of Pincus and Minahan, provided the opportunity for social workers to apply more rigorous and objective methods to their work (Goldstein, 1973; Pincus and Minahan, 1973). This might give the profession a common, 'unitary' framework for analysis and planning, and a cross-over between the different applications within social work that would be intelligible and reinforcing for all concerned. But the 'rigorous use of theory ... required a high degree of systematic control ... to detailing theoretical propositions and empirical verification' (Specht, 1977a, p. 251). Even if this was going to be easy, which it was not (Specht, 1977b), a concerted effort would have to be made for any broad approach to be accepted (Vickery, 1977). Unfortunately, growing pains, preoccupation with professionalisation and status inhibited both social work and community work, each to come to grips with the needs of the other if they were to progress together. The 'verification' of their effectiveness was beyond both of them.

As freshly institutionalised methodologies for social intervention, each was looking steadily inwards towards its own interests (Baldock, 1974, p. 110 *et seq.*). A consequence of this was that the establishment of comparable evaluation method for community development interventions was never established on a systematic basis. CCETSW had issued two papers on the role and structure of community work within social work (CCETSW, 1974; 1979), but it never got over its original uneasy relationship with its community work component, such that they never called it community development. The profile of social work outlined in '*Paper 30*', the framework for the 1989 reform of qualifications for social work saw no mention of theory of organisations, measure of effectiveness, group settings, nor social change. There was an oblique mention of 'the community and organisational settings of practice' (CCETSW, 1989, p. 14). Nevertheless, it was not until 2001, when the General Care Council (the Care Council of Wales, in Wales) formally took over control of the regulation of social work training, that the community development component of the training curriculum was diluted so as to make it impossible to train as a competent community worker under the auspices of the social work profession (first student entry to BSc Social Work – 2005 (Care Council for Wales, 2012). No occupational 'client group' is listed under 'community' in the Care Council for Wales profile of registered social workers for 2012.

Outside the formal social work setting, however, community development methods had been explored in some depth and for some time. A pathfinder in the establishment of community development projects across the UK was the 'North Kensington Family Study', or the North Kensington Project, funded by the City Parochial Foundation from 1964–9, with three years' experimental work going before it. This 'Study' had emerged in the aftermath of the Notting Hill race riots of 1958, and it evolved from work with young mothers on play schemes into a community development project encompassing local action groups, and it acted as the forerunner for the Golborne Community Council, an experiment in local neighbourhood politics (O'Malley, 1970; Clark, 1976; O'Malley, 1977; see Hansard, HC Deb, 15 May 1969, vol. 783, cols. 1835–44). The Study's driving force initially was Ilys Brooker, who, with Muriel Smith, a seconded, senior Home Office Civil Servant, formed, and then worked for the Association of North London Housing Estates (Goetschius, 1969; Baldock, 1974). The Project had an elite Committee, comprised of academics (Batten, Jahoda, etc.), and worthies from Kensington. Relations between the community workers (Booker, for example) and the Committee over the community's say over social and material developments in the area began to deteriorate rapidly.

Had it studied this experiment carefully, and taken its own intelligence seriously (Higgins, 1980), the Home Office might have foreseen the difficulties that their future Community Development Project was going to have with local elected representatives. The conflict emerged out of differences of opinion about top-down, and bottom-up initiatives (Mitton and Morrison, 1972; Benington, 1974; see also, Thomas, 1976). At the same time, there emerged a form of grassroots radicalism, where direct action was the driving force – the Squatters Movement. This began in November 1968, as a client-based self-help organisation against their homeless situation, and led to (sometimes) violent confrontation between agents of Borough Councils whose property had been 'squatted' and the squatters and their supporters (Bailey, 1973). The 'squatters' had no formalised leadership nor trained professional organisers, but some celebrity leaders emerged (e.g. Jim Radford, later Director of Blackfriars Settlement) and they achieved a great deal of organisational coherence and made some spectacular gains for their homeless membership. Official channels, i.e. Housing Departments and social workers, had few resources, particularly homes for the homeless, to offer these people, and so, gradually, the State had, reluctantly, to come around to formalise recognise the organisations built up in this way (Bailey, 1973; Martin, 2005).

The Community Development Project (CDP)

There are many reports that there was considerable political wrangling behind the scenes over the publication of the Seebohm Report and the introduction of the Community Development Project – 1968–78 (CDP), sponsored by the Home Office (Benington, 1974; Thomas, 1983, pp. 24–5; Higgins, et al., 1983; Loney, 1983). Anxious to implement some of the central recommendations of the Plowden Report (Education Priority Areas, and special social support for communities (Plowden, 1967), and worried by increasing instances of family breakdown and juvenile crime, the Home Office had begun studies of the American urban intervention strategies – notably the President's Committee on Juvenile Delinquency, and the Model Cities programme under US Presidents

Kennedy and Johnson – 1961onwards (see Chapter 3, above). This initiative was led by a Senior Civil Servant, Derek Morrell (Higgins, et al., 1983; Loney, 1983).

Morrell made the introduction of state-sponsored community development a personal mission, but his untimely death in 1969 cast the scheme rudderless at the top (Higgins, et al., 1983). The CDP was launched under the umbrella of the Urban Programme (Hansard, HL Deb, 22 July 1968, vol. 295, cols 686–93) (Batley and Edwards, 1975). This was an attempt by Central Government to inject funding directly into grass-roots pressure points (inter-racial issues, poverty, housing), whilst sustaining a Local Government input to secure legitimacy. So, between 1968 and 1974, the Urban Programme provided a total of £31 million to local authorities and voluntary sector schemes (Batley and Edwards, 1975, p. 164). Local government was to pay 25% of the bill for these projects, which were designed to deal with 'residual' questions (such as deprivation, economic and social marginalisation) through engendering self-help, independence, and self-sufficiency (Lees and Smith, 1975; McKay and Cox, 1979; Loney, 1983; Higgins, et al., 1983).

The plan, executed over three years, was to establish twelve five-year projects, distributed across England, Wales, and Scotland, in receptive local authority areas. The first one, in Southwark, London, could draw immediately on the NISW experimental project (SCP), which ran in that Borough from 1968 to 1973 (above). The SCP had targeted community organizations as its vehicle for addressing social policy implementation, and the Borough Council was soon alarmed at the strident voices raised against its far-reaching redevelopment programme (Thomas, 1975; Thomas, 1976). CDP Southwark, although they did not target the Council's redevelopment programme, rapidly got drawn into it. An exhibition, in line with the Skeffington proposals, on the redevelopment of the Newington Ward, attracted large numbers of residents. This raised the profile of the question of consultation, and aroused the opposition of the County Planning Committee (Davis, et al., 1977; Rossetti, 1979; Loney, 1983), and relations never really recovered until the Project was re-focused, and restructured in 1972.

In some respects, SCP and Southwark CDP were working at cross-purposes, as the former was assisting residents to clear up planning blight situation, whilst the CDP was concerned with welfare situation, and human distress arising from the redevelopment. Under pressure from the Borough Council not to confront them with redevelopment issues or face a boycott, the CDP Team fragmented and had to be reconstituted. The new Team focused upon older people's welfare, and also on Children, and the (Plowden) Education Priority Area initiative.

Southwark CDP has been drawn upon here as an interesting case study of what was to come out of the CDP programme as a whole. All the remaining eleven local projects (Batley, Yorkshire; Benwell (Newcastle); Birmingham; Canning Town (Newham); Coventry; Cumbria; Glamorgan – Glyncorrwg; Liverpool; North Tyneside; Oldham; and Paisley) were mostly met with considerable suspicion, despite their host local authorities having volunteered to accept them. Paisley was the exception (Barr, 1991), but Batley and Cumbria Projects irretrievably broke down before the end of their contracted period due to the hostility of the local authorities.

Specht puts the blame for this on bad Central Government modelling, claiming that the expectation that small projects could influence National policy formation, or that (even) local authorities would be sympathetic to influence from outside agents were naïve (Specht, 1976). The CDP established an Information and Intelligence Unit (IIU) in 1973. This afforded Project staff and researchers to make a contribution to the debate on the causes of poverty, marginalisation, etc. The CDP IIU published a number of controversial Reports – most famously 'The Poverty of the Improvement Programme' (1975); 'Cutting the Welfare State' (Counter Intelligence Service/CDP IIU, 1975); 'Local Government becomes Big Business' (Benington, 1976); Whatever happened to Council Housing? (1976); 'Gilding the Ghetto' (1977).

Considering that, by this time, many CDP staff had abandoned all pretence at working through a reformist model, and that these papers demanded the structural reform of the way society's resources were distributed, and the way in which society was administered, it is no wonder that the vested interests in government (at all levels) became agitated (CDP IIU, 1974). Grassroots conflict with local administrations was spread evenly across the project network – except in Liverpool and Glamorgan, where these Projects set out deliberately to provide a consensual platform for managed social change (Penn and Alden, 1977, pp. 186–7; Topping and Smith, 1977). The Glamorgan Project set itself the task of negotiating with the County Council, and with the Regional authorities a procedural approach to exchanging information, and for negotiation. But the result was to establish a structure that allowed virtually no input for the people on the ground, except on the terms of the existing statutory structures (Penn and Alden, 1977, pp. 305–11). Liverpool 'stuck doggedly' to the consensus model at (mainly) the grassroots level. The team reported that this model exhausted the local residents, who then failed to sustain their inputs over the five-year cycle of the Project (Topping and Smith, 1977, pp. 6 and 35).

For their local, project, work, the majority of the CDP Projects selected a 'social planning' approach to community development (as had the SCP of NISW). In this manner, neighbourhood groups were developed, or strengthened, and brought into dialogue with local authority representatives on specific issues (Benington, 1975; Butcher, et al., 1979; Corina, et al., 1979). At the same time, the project's Research Team provided background analysis on the local situation with the intention of re-interpreting information in such a way that local authorities might re-appraise their own policies and action programmers (North Tyneside CDP, 1978; CDP, 1981). In most Team areas, the Project staff also joined in local council administrative and policy discussions in order to strengthen and co-ordinate the inter-service planning and delivery ability of the statutory services (Specht, 1976; Topping and Smith, 1977; Loney, 1983). Specht interviewed all of the Project Directors, and a majority stated that their real audience was policy-makers at the National level (Specht, 1976, p. 19). The Glamorgan and Liverpool Teams came closest to producing an evaluation framework that measured their own efforts against their Projects' aims (Davis, et al., 1977; Topping and Smith, 1977). In Oldham, the project Team reported that their efforts to develop a satisfactory structure for collaboration was frustrated by Council Officers and elected representatives (Corina, et al., 1979).

Specht criticises the main body of the CDP initiative of running projects on the one hand, doing research reports on the other. They failed, he states, to provide the evidence that their community development methods bore fruit in meeting the issues their research raises. Specht's research findings point to a serious mismatch between the aims of the overall CDP programme, and the objectives of the field teams on the ground (Specht, 1976, pp. 52–3). These disparities were often *irreconcilable* with the wishes of their host Councils (Kraushaar, 1982, p. 70). In the case of Coventry CDP, despite the disclaimer of their Research Director in their Final Report, and despite a prolonged, albeit usually tense, relationship being maintained at all levels, Project members strove to play a close part in discussions with the Council's Planning and other Departments (they were excluded from the Housing Planning Committee (Benington, et al., 1975, p. 35). They were forced to admit in the end that their efforts were: 'insufficient to bring about even relatively minor organisational changes' (p. 38). Benington (1975) describes how Coventry was rebuffed by a local Housing Estate over its plans to favour the local Football Club (Coventry FC) with the demolition of a blighted residential area. This did not enamour the CDP in the eyes of the Council, but it changed the Council's approach to its residents (p. 208).

Nevertheless, the CDP IIU reports raised many issues, and certainly raised the profile of many social questions in the field of employment, housing, welfare benefits, etc. that sparked off a prolonged debate (Lambert, 1981; Sharman, 1981), and they opened up and reframed the debate about the nature of community development in Britain (Craig, 1989; Hanmer, 1979; Kraushaar, 1982). Mayo suggests that, even after stimulating a debate in government over the welfare system, the government closed the CDP IIU as it did not want any more intrusions of this nature (Mayo, 1980). Hanmer admonishes the programme for not confronting the question of women in society, but blames this on an unreconstructed interpretation of Marxist theory (Hanmer, 1979; Smith, 1978; Smith, et al., 1978; Smith, 1981). In her Introduction to *Women in Community Work* (Mayo (ed.), 1977), Mayo highlights the barriers to women put up by male project leaders who share this interpretation of Marxism in community organising. This is the central theme of Gallagher in the same volume (Mayo (ed.), 1977, pp. 121–41). Gallagher then targets society's attempt at palliative treatment of women's issues (childcare, poverty, single parenthood, part-time employment, low pay, bad housing), of send-ing in social workers who, further, seek to control women's lives (Gallagher, 1977, p. 134; O'Malley, 1977).

One of the most striking features of the CDP programme was its failure in the area of Human Resources. Each Team comprised a Research and an Action component – recruited separately – the Research Team from a local/compliant University or College (Higgins, et al., 1983, pp. 12–13), the Action Teams from national recruitment advertising. Whereas the universities took responsibility for the research credentials of their field Research staff, the Action component relied on the recruitment of otherwise experienced field workers from outside the Civil Service – from agencies such as Voluntary Service Overseas (VSO), the Young Volunteer Force Foundation (YVFF, now Community Development Foundation – CDF), or local authority community development sections. Specht described the Project Directors as 'young, energetic, and resourceful', but completely untrained 'educationally and professionally' for the enormity of the task they faced (Specht, 1976, p. 44). While CDP had a national Research Intelligence Unit (under Professor John Greve, Southampton University – Higgins, et al., 1983), there was no national co-ordination agency for the preparation of local staff. The CDP Central Steering Group in the Home Office was distracted from the very begin-ning from the progress of the CDP's local projects by the conflict situations that arose (Specht, 1976, pp. 46–7; Davis, et al., 1977; Butcher, et al., 1979; Loney, 1980; Craig, 1989; Green and Chapman, 1992), and by the loss of Home Office jurisdiction over the Children's Department in 1968 (Loney, 1983). From 1970, the National Council of Social Service ran in-service community work training schemes at twelve Colleges across England. No CDP staff attended these courses, and there is no mention the literature of any community development training being offered elsewhere to CDP staff (Ward, 1975; Haines, 1980).

CDP was a well-publicised, large-scale programme – each Project had over £40,000 per annum to spend on pump-priming and project work (Davis, et al., 1977, p. 71). This contrasts with the budgets of other programmers – such as the Young Volunteer Force Foundation's twelve projects from 1970 – at +/–£10,000 p.a. (including two to three salaries – documentation in personal possession – see below). CDP was spread (thinly in all parts) across Britain, and, therefore, it might be supposed that it would have some sort of lasting effect. The winding up of the CDP released a large number of experienced staff for deployment/recruit-ment elsewhere. A significant omission by the whole CDP enterprise was never to study the field within which they were working. No attempt was made to analyse a model for implementation in the sort of situation within which these projects had been mounted – mainly economically marginalised, run-down, poor and socially demoralised. This can, perhaps, be attributed to the lack of formal training in com-munity development of the field workers and within the Intelligence Unit. Instead of addressing a 'business plan' approach, with some theoretical presumptions, the resultant documentation merely reflected a vague quasi-Marxist dissatisfaction with oppressive local government structures.

The transformation of British community development in the 1970s

Scotland

Scotland's long, positive association with community development began after the publication of the Albemarle Report in 1960, and the decision by Moray House College to begin training Youth and Community Workers (McConnell, 1983). This provided a base-line for fieldwork, and a supply of qualified workers. One of the most famous community projects in Scotland was the Craigmillar Community Festival Committee, which ran an extensive community self-help agenda between 1964 and 2002 (Crummy, 1992). CPF (see below) opened a neighbourhood scheme in Lorne, near Leith, in 1975, as part of the Lothian Regional Council's programme to regenerate neglected areas (CPF, 1982), and there were also many localised schemes scattered around the Scottish urban areas, often in the mould of community enterprises (Miller, 1981). When Scottish Regional Government was established in 1974, a fresh emphasis was placed upon regeneration and locality improvement (Local Government (Scotland) Act 1973). Scotland then began to move the profile of community development onto a grander scale through its policy for regional, economic development in the Highlands and Islands (Dickie, 1968; Highlands and Islands Development Board, 1982). Tangible and material outcomes were expected from community development workers in this setting – the creation of local businesses, and economically strengthened communities. This drew directly on the experience of the Paisley CDP, and also of the staff it recruited from CDP Cumbria (Paisley College of Technology – Local Government Unit, 1982; LEAP, 1984; McArthur, 1984; Andrews, 1985; Pearce, 1993). It was this sort of initiative that strengthened the community development movement in Scotland, as evaluation became a prerequisite for funding and project development (Kuenstler, 1986).

From 1975 onwards, the newly constituted Scottish Regional Authorities embraced community development with gusto. Barr (ex-CDP Oldham) documents the establishment of these initiatives, which survive strongly today (Barr, 1991). The Scottish Office of the Community Projects Foundation (now Community Development Foundation – CDF) established a partnership that was to become the Scottish Community Development Centre (SCDC). This agency took full advantage of the positive policy approach of the Scottish regional government towards community development following the publication of the *Alexander Report on Adult Learning* (1975). The Report specifically called upon educators to grasp the opportunity offered by community development to enrich lives and to strengthen communities for the challenges they faced (text reproduced in McConnell, 2002, pp. 52–5)

To further its objectives in this field, SCDC built a strong relationship with Glasgow University. In 1997, Strathclyde Regional Council established a strategic commitment to community development. In 1977, it commissioned a Review of its work in this direction, and, in 1978, the *Worthington Report* (text reproduced in McConnell, 2002, pp. 75–94) presented a strong reinforcement for the policy. Teams had been set up across the Region, and the central strategic Committee was functioning well to maximize their beneficial input locally and regionally (pp. 83–6). Despite the reorganisation of local government in Scotland in 1996, this strategy has been sustained in Glasgow, and in the old-Strathclyde Regional area authorities (e.g. Renfrewshire, 2009). This gave rise to the publication of two frameworks for community intervention: ABCD (Achieving Better Community Development) – a framework for evaluating community development (Barr and Hashagen, 2000); and LEAP – the Learning, Evaluation and Planning framework (Scottish Office, 1998). Community planning and active citizenship were to be the essence of this strategy (pp. 5–7).

In 2003, Health Scotland carried this philosophy and methodology of community engagement into the Health Sector (Health Scotland, 2003). The whole programme, to be applied across all Council areas, was renewed in the Scottish Government's strategic document: 'Working and learning together to build stronger communities' (Scottish Executive, 2004; and Scottish Executive, 2007). All sectors were included: e.g. local authorities, Health Boards, Partnerships, Colleges, ... (p. 5).

From The Young Volunteer Force Foundation (YVFF) to Community Development Foundation (CDF)

After the Gulbenkian Reports of the 1960s and the Seebohm Report, the many local institutions (Social Services Departments; Councils of Voluntary Service) mounted community initiatives on their own (Craig, 1974; Dungate, et al. (eds), 1979; Twelvetrees 1980; Knight and Hayes, 1981). Holman reported that some residents' organisations wanted more demonstrative responses to social issues than those that were being offered by institutional agencies (Holman, 1978).

In 1968, Parliament announced that YVFF was to start work as a National volunteering and community development charity, sponsored by Government (HL Deb, 11 June 1968, vol. 293, cols 3–4). The focus of its work rapidly changed from organising volunteer support for elderly people to community development, mounting a series of small-scale community projects across Britain (Dungate, 1980; Pitchford, M. with Henderson, P., 2008). A small, central resource unit supported up to twelve local projects, and these became very innovative. By 1976, two regional resource centres (Manchester, and Tyne and Wear) had been established to support community development on a more localised basis (Taylor, 1980). YVFF staff established the Federation of Community Work Training Groups (now the Federation of Community Development Learning), which developed the National Occupational Standards for Community Development in 2009, and also the Scottish Community Development Centre (1994), and the *Journal of Community Work and Development* (Scotland), in 2001. A YVFF team successfully relocated and settled 1,500 ex-Uganda Asian refugees, who were stranded in a camp in Staffordshire, by applying a community development model to resettlement, building mutually supportive, artificial families (1973 – unpublished Report in author's possession).

Considering its reduced resource base, and despite, also, being tied, since 1968, into the Home Office (as had CDP), then through the Home Office Voluntary Services Unit (from 1973), this agency flourished. Within limits, it had also proved to be extremely adaptable to shifts in government priorities. It changed its name in 1977 to 'Community Projects Foundation' (CPF), under which title it became a 'National Centre for Community Development' (Calouste Gulbenkian, 1984), and then again to Community Development Foundation. From 2012, it operated as CDF Ltd, a company limited by guarantee, following its formal separation from direct government funding in 2011 (CDF, 2012).

It was forced, for reasons of devolved governance, mainly, to close its resource operations in Scotland, and in Wales, where it had major establishments since the early 1990s, and it no longer operated its own field projects. It ran as a limited company as consultants to government, local government partnerships and programmes (pp. 14–17). Its major operation was then as an independent contractor/consultant in community development matters, administering the Government's 'Big Society' initiatives in 'Active at 60 Programme' for the Department of Work and Pensions, and the (Lottery-funded) 'Big Local' scheme. Between 2009 and 2011, CDF Ltd administered the 'Faiths in Action' for the Department of Communities and Local Government (Pearmain, 2011). From 2011, CDF had managed the £80-million 'Community First' – a small grant programme, and community endowment challenge for local social action and development (HM Government, 2011). CDF made a consistent contribution to community development literature over the past thirty years, but latterly its publications department became electronic-only publications. It had not, since its adoption of independent status, published anything of substance. CDF Ltd went into voluntary liquidation in March 2016.

In many respects, CDF's history reflects, and had acted as a leader to, the gradual adoption of a philosophy of realism by community development workers. Marris (1982) re-insisted that community workers should put rationality over ideology, and that the alternative is to banish themselves to 'clandestine activity' in spaces out of sight of the mainstream (Barr, 1991, p. 127). Getting to that position, however, had not been straightforward.

The neo-Marxist interlude and a more radical landscape

From 1973 onwards, with the publication of the first public papers from the CDP, an ideological debate arose within the ranks of community development workers across the country. There were calls for radical action: *Community Action* magazine was published describing alliances between professionals and working class communities. There was a national social work strike in response to *Case Con* magazine's 1970 *exposé* of social work's 'rationalisation' into a state-supporting agent of social control (Case Con, 1975). *Case Con* had identified community development, being a component of the Seebohm reforms, as an agency for social control, not reform. It described the new Social Services Departments as centres for professional elitism and Class divisiveness (pp. 145–6). Cox (Cox and Derricourt, 1975, p. 85) suggests that this view is not representative of the majority, anyway, and a trawl of its membership in 1978 by the Association of Community Workers (ACW) produced a wide array of values when the question of a definition of community work was attempted (ACW, 1978). The spread here was 'socialist', on the one hand, and 'instrumental' at the other extreme. Only the 'socialist' (Smith, 1978) had any overtly ideological content. This points to a suggestion that, outside the CDP, there was little formal adoption of the CDP's pronounced 'structuralist' position.

The discussion was carried into the literature by two publishers: Routledge and Kegan Paul (seven + two volumes); and Macmillan (seven volumes) between 1974 and 1983, with a mini-series by Arnold (two volumes). The Arnold publications dealt with 'radical social work', with contributions from many the most prominent Left-of-Centre names in community development – Leonard, Corrigan, Mayo, Ron Bailey, etc. The first volume (Arnold – Bailey, R. and Brake, M., 1975) posed many of the unresolved contradictions in inherent in social work, and set the scene for the argument on structural issues in social change. The second volume (Brake and Bailey, 1980) concerned itself more with the issues confronting practitioners in the field on a day-to-day basis. In the 1975 volume, Leonard (Leonard, 1975b, pp. 59–60) argued for a dialogical relationship between the professional and the client population, drawing on Freire and Mao Tse-tung. Mayo saw some potential for community work, but identified the focus on self-serving and safe options chosen by most social workers, and found the whole role between the needy and their governors untenable (Mayo, 1975). Ultimately, Mayo (Lees and Mayo, 1984) favoured a Labour Party-sponsored, radical community work, pushing for alternative forms of social organisation to capture the energies of ordinary people to satisfy their varied needs, such as the Greater London Council sponsoring 'alternative' groups (pp. 193–4).

The Routledge series covered a wide range of subjects, discrete volumes focusing on Employment, Race, Politics, Women, Poverty, the State, and two general Readers. Apart from providing a wider platform for many of the ideas rehearsed in the CDP writings, these edited compilations gave credibility to the breadth and variety of the community work of the time. Nevertheless, despite their values in this respect, it is not possible to glean any coherent underlying ideology from them, other than a veneer of left-leaning sympathies, and an opening up of the question of women in community work. The place that Race might command on the community development agenda was explored for the first time by Ohri (Ohri, et al., 1982). The question of whether or not, and how, perhaps, to seek '*separation*' for the Black community as the only viable opening for community organisers is discussed by Phillips (Phillips, 1982, pp. 107–12). Historical factors and the cultural derivatives of that history, set the scene for Black organisation. Unless control, across the variety of cultural differentiations of the Black community can be established, then the perception will be that, at best, the only gain through participation in the wider context will be further loss of control over their destiny. Community development workers have to proceed on the basis that gaining control over organisations, activities, facilities and the vocabulary of the public discourse is the best, if imperfect, way forward (Phillips, 1982, p. 119). No case is actually made for racially segregated areas or 'national autonomy, as was by Elijah Muhammad and the *Nation of Islam* in the United States (Nation of Islam website: www.noi.org, accessed 8 August 2015). Nevertheless, without understanding of the degree of exclusion that Black communities experience, little headway can be made to understand the tensions that are raised.

In a companion volume to the Routledge series (Butcher, et al., 1980, pp. 23–50), the prominence of 'senior citizens' in the Cumbria CDP project is explained. Whereas the community workers were under heavy, and direct, scrutiny from their political paymasters in this project, older people were able to play an increasingly important role in providing for the well-being, support and direct welfare of this sector of the population (pp. 25–35).

The Macmillan series, meanwhile, was of a different order to Routledge. Each volume conveys an internal consistency of message, all authors supporting a variant on the need for a radical appraisal of the structural nature of social issues, and the need for structural mechanisms to counter them. Jones (1983) provides a historical appraisal of how social work has been a fellow-traveller of capitalism since its inception, and Ginsberg follows the same route, but through a Marxist analysis of the structure of the welfare state, with social workers in a supportive role as agents of control (Ginsberg, 1979). Gough provides another Marxist analysis, and describes how social work has been specifically re-designed to serve the needs of a state that attempts to preserve stability for the poor in a society with ever-widening opportunities and reward systems (Gough, 1979, p. 139 *et seq.*). Whilst dismissing community groups as essentially useless in the struggle against capitalism, Corrigan and Leonard (Corrigan and Leonard, 1978, p. 141 *et seq.*) do reflect that they may be important enough to be considered alongside Trade Unions as objects for targeting by activist Marxist change agents. The local struggle is to be aimed at the Town Hall, and the mobilised community has a central role in this (p. 149). Bolger (Bolger, et al., 1981) considers that community work, and community workers, are only marginally useful in mobilising community activists, but are essentially unreliable when it comes to action on Class issues. Their position within the state apparatus renders them only tangential to the Class struggle; and/but any activity that they might undertake must be carried out outside the state machinery and influence (p. 144).

The theme of an antagonistic state that conspired to ensnare workers through controlling their social and human potential capabilities is taken up by Cockburn. Cockburn describes the services and structures of the local authority (the '*local state*') as encapsulating the workers so that they may provide for the social reproductive requirements of the labour pool for capital (Cockburn, 1977, p. 53 *et seq.*; Mowbray, 2011). Wilson, who had opened up the whole discussion about women's, and specifically feminist women's role in social intervention initiatives (Wilson, 1972 – reproduced in Cowley, et al. (eds), 1977, pp. 94–100), amplified her assertion that the principles of the *Women's Movement*, power over all civil and personal rights, must be vested in community work, and that, because all personal life is political, community action must be a political statement about unburdening women in society (Wilson, 1977, pp. 1–11; Gallagher, 1977). From America, in 1970, came a stern admonishment that women, if they wanted their power to be felt in social change processes, had to adopt the appropriate organisational structures and processes that would focus their power, give it identity, and enable the maximum leverage over the established system to be exercised (Freeman, 1995). As the 1980s dawned, women had overcome many of their original barriers within community work, at least, and gender had been raised, along with racism, as the main contention in community work (Hanmer, 1991; Dominelli, 1994).

In 1979, another strident voice was raised against the orthodoxies of the mainstream structuralists. The London Edinburgh Weekend Return Group's '*In and against the state*' repudiated the conventional Marxist analysis (1979; Craig and Mayo, 1995). They (Edinburgh-based workers for Community Projects Foundation, who travelled regularly to London for work-related consultations) claimed that there would never be a mass response to a call for 'defence of the welfare state', which was the conventional response of the institutional Left to Conservative encroachment on public services. Instead, they called for a fresh approach to '*socialism*' – directing community development and social activist energies to forging an alternative to the capitalist structures of the state (p. 106). So, as community development workers faced the 1980s, there was no shortage of discussion within the profession about the way forward. Cowley, et al., argued that community development has always been complementary to social movements, and that its work is not contradictory to progress of displaced classes. They argue that community organising has proved to be very successful at providing alternative methods, structures and values to the Class Struggle, and that its further development is an essential factor in the progress of their cause (Cowley, et al., 1977). (What is interesting here is that one of this group of authors is Marjorie Mayo, who has discounted community development in a number of articles to date – Mayo, 1972; 1975).

Community development and race

Since the opening of the Golborne Community Council (see above) and the North Kensington Project (Mitton and Morrison, 1972; Clark, 1976), race has been an integral factor in the allocation of funds for community development in Britain. The American experience of rioting in the 1960s prompted the creation of the CDP, and, thereafter, 'Race' became conflated with the urgent need for community development programmes also to confront 'Racism' (CDP C.D., 1974; Ohri, et al., (eds) 1982); Welsh Office, 1998a; Shah, 1989). Ledwith sees racism in practice as direct oppression (Ledwith, 2005), while Mayo describes it as the engraved legacy of practice development since the institution of social intervention in a racist society (Mayo and Robertson, 2003). Whereas Shah believes that community development across racial lines is not feasible for lasting change or for the strengthening of minority communities' bargaining position (Shah, 1989), the community development consortium, *Community Development Challenge*, saw inter-racial co-operation as an essential goal for programmes (CDF, et al., 2006). What is interesting about 'race' in community development in the UK.is that it appears not to have gone down the Alinsky-road, as demonstrated by Alinsky in many of his most successful projects (Fish, 1973). In the case of the Church Urban Fund initiative into broad-based organisation, coalitions across racial lines are the preferred option (Jameson and Gecan, 2013).

The coming of community care and community social work

Waddington (1979) summed up the position of many community workers as rejecting bureaucracy and the control mechanisms of the State. The intrusion of the Manpower Services Commission (MSC) after 1973, into the way short-term funding for much community work was geared, and the provision of temporary workers through this route, seriously constricted the autonomy of many projects (Benn and Fairley, 1986; National Audit Office, 1987). The voluntary sector was drawn into the *Community* Programme, and later the *Special Temporary Employment Scheme* (STEP) with financial inducement and some marketing (Community Business Ventures Unit, 1981; Short, 1986). Community development projects were diverted into becoming employers, rather than being innovators for social change (Salmon, 1982). This was, in many ways, symptomatic of the direction that community development activities in the community would be going.

Mundy (1980) described the process whereby community work was being subsumed into social work, and how the objectives of social work, palliation rather than social change, were exerting a strong influence over the working object- ives of community work. He goes on to suggest two things — that if community workers accept as their parameters of working the boundaries of the systems presented when they are in social services deployment, then they will lose sight of the objectives of social change. Additionally, Mundy explains that, because of the low numbers of community workers, relative to case workers, in social services departments, their influence over the practice methods of social workers is going to be limited. The resultant activity will better be called *'community work'*, rather than *'community development'* (pp. 183–5). Specht had shown how theory could be abused in practice, especially when ideology became the over-riding driver of action (Specht, 1977a, p. 32). A clear example of this is highlighted by Baldock, who was an early critic of the 'head-in-the-sand' view of the daily welfare needs of communities by community development workers. He called it 'snobbish and repugnant' that workers should neglect these mundane but essential human needs (Baldock, 1983, p. 232). Nevertheless, realities in the way that Social Services Departments were appraising the future of care for the vulnerable would have a profound effect on the way community workers behaved in future (Jones, et al., 1982). In 1980, Patrick Jenkin, the Secretary of State for Social Services, had asked NISW to conduct an enquiry into social work and community care. Their Working Party reported back in 1982 (Barclay, 1982).

The Barclay Report prescribed a radical overhaul of the way conventional social work was to be practised. Embedding the social workers in the community was the first call, to be called *'patch social work'*, or *'community social work'* (Barclay, 1982, p. xvii). In Appendix A to the Barclay Report, Brown, et al., point out that the State and social workers may each have different agenda in mind when they intervene. Social Services may not see that their priorities are to support commu- nities when they approach dysfunction and vulnerability at the community level. Community social workers, on the other hand, may focus more on the systems of social support rather than on the individual cases of vulnerability. Additionally, systems of informal care will require considerable support from the (responsible) social workers, and adaptability by them into this new role may not be possible due to other pressures and concerns. It was envisaged that the strengthening of complete neighbourhoods to support informal care systems could be another dimension to community social work (pp. 119–24). In a dissenting, minority Appendix B to the Report, Professor Robert Pinker suggested that social work, as traditionally practised in assessment and casework modes, was a more realistic, coherent and achievable target for the profession. Communities were too diverse and intangible to be the primary target of social workers, and their accountability would be diversified and fragmented under the circumstances described by the substantive Barclay Report (pp. 236–52).

Conflicts of interest, even if the experience of the CDP projects was not enough, had clearly been identified by Briscoe (1977), and Pinker highlighted these. Payne accepts that there is a need for change, particularly at the social casework level of intervention, but urges caution as none of the new models have been adequately tested (Payne, 1983). Croft (Croft and Beresford, 1989) discusses the realities of the 'new localism' created by Barclay, and the 'patch' system. Croft and Beresford claim that pluralism, token participative structures, and tightened central political and managerial control over social workers are the result (p. 117). Bennett (1980) demonstrated how the potential of local social work and creative engagement with local issues might work, but the new 'patch' system may have wasted an opportunity to capitalise on this. Frost and Stein heavily criticise Barclay and its claims, for not being forceful enough and that, since it began to be implemented, the Government abandoned its proposals, particularly in respect of the training that would be required for professionals in this more complex environment (Frost and Stein, 1989, p. 29).

The Secretary of State had, initially, approved Barclay's suggestions, and NISW, following up on their work on the 'Barclay Working Party', embarked on an exploratory study in order to establish the definitions and practice dimensions of community social work. The implications of this, for local authorities changing their Social Services Departments, were identified and traced back to established community development practices (Henderson, et al., 1984, pp. 1–5). NISW then responded with the creation of a team of action researches to produce guidelines for community social work practice. In 1979, the Department of Health and Social Security had funded a social care experiment in Normington, Wakefield, where the concepts of community care were to be tested (Hadley and McGrath, 1984). The team developed a *'community-centred strategy'* (p. 13), where in addition to providing support for individuals in the community (about 5,000 people), whole sections of that community were to be supported and strengthened, along with the local voluntary sector, using community development methods (pp. 14 and 16).

It was into this scenario that the Barclay Working Party fed its recommendations on community social work. The pursuit of a model for community care was moving apace, and £15 million was voted to the Personal Social Service Research Unit (PSSRU) in 1983 to promote, monitor and evaluate the *Care in the Community Programme* (Knapp, et al., 1992). Challis and Davies describe the detailed outcomes of case management in the early experiments (Challis and Davies, 1986). The model that they describe is rooted firmly in Social Service-driven systems of care, with no thought given to enlisting wider community support, save on an individualised, paid helper, basis (p. 116 *et seq.*).

Whereas the PSSRU provides a clear model for institutional and structural modelling, they are insistent that their model is dependent on the acceptance of its own defined boundaries (Challis and Davies, 1985). Cooper (1989) challenges this new model for social work. The CDP had forcefully claimed that they identified that social issues can best be addressed through a combination of social work and community action (p. 186 *et seq.*). Davies (1987) criticises the Audit Commission's own, top-down, critique of community care and case management (Audit Commission, 1986) by insisting that community care is about a bottom-up perspective on personal and social need. The difficulty is that the PSSRU model does not explore the bottom-up model to a sufficient extent. Parsons's description of 'patch social work', which preceded both the PSSRU and the Barclay report, points to a flexible and adaptable approach to local need that, historically, answered these questions (Parsons, 1986). The risk of just creating a newly constituted system of client-professional dependence is all too evident (Clarke, 1982). In any event, the outcomes of the case management initiative would not be fully understood or evaluated for many years (Davies, 1987).

The scene was now set for a serious debate into the nature of social work, the future of community work/development as a way of addressing structural issues, and the new management model of social care. NISW's team of community social work practice theorists began to produce their texts on how this might be developed (Hearn and Thomson, 1987; Smale, et al., 1988; Smale and Bennett, 1989; Smale and Tuson, 1990; Darville, et al., 1990). Smale (Smale, et al., 1988) tried to come to grips with the accusation made by Challis and Davies that the fundamental weakness of social work was that it had never developed 'clinically focused base of knowledge' that would allow for some predictability for its interventions (Challis and Davies, 1986, p. 286). Smale structured an explanatory book around the application of the 'creative learning spiral' to community social work – a 'paradigm for change' in social work (Smale, et al., 1988). At every stage in the spiral, where function changed for a new set of tasks and processes, measurement and evaluation mechanisms could now be applied over time and circumstances (pp. 37–52).

The difficulty for NISW, and for Smale (Darville and Smale, 1990), was that, despite making a plea for their model to be applied to the new structure of *community case and case management* that was proposed by Sir Roy Griffiths (Griffiths, 1988), and by the Government White Paper, *Caring for People* (Depts of Health, etc., 1989), the Government was about to produce a fresh formula for Social Services' structure, function, relationship with the Welfare State, the Voluntary Sector, and the community at large (see below). Croft and Beresford discuss the realities of the 'new localism' created by Barclay, and the 'patch' system (Croft and Beresford, 1989). Pluralism, token participative structures, and tightened central political and managerial control over social workers are the result, Croft claims (p. 117). Bennett demonstrated how the potential of local social work and creative engagement with local issues might work (Bennett, 1980), but the new 'patch' system may have wasted an opportunity. The Barclay reforms to social work were soon to come under attack from a government that was beginning to feel the strains of an inflated social services budget. The issue was mainly residential care, and the Government's responsibility to fund it from Social Security. Frost and Stein write that the Barclay reforms were doomed from the start because it was NISW (a Voluntary Organisation) and not the Government that wrote the Report (Frost and Stein, 1989). Additionally, there was no statutory basis for the reforms, and, also, the Report itself was flawed due to the dissent within the Committee that wrote it – minority reports, etc. (p. 29).

The impact of the Griffiths reforms

The Griffiths Report (1988) recommended the decentralisation of service provision in social care, and that coherence be brought to a wildly varied service in 'disarray' (Willmott, 1989, p. 60). Griffiths's main recommendation was the creation of a local mixed-economy of welfare to introduce competition and savings, and he also emphasised that there was a finite pot of resources from which all activities had to be funded (Griffiths, 1988, para. 3.2.12). The Government's White Paper, *Caring for People* (Depts. of Health, etc., 1989) and the subsequent legislation (HM Government, 1990) all reinforced this view. One issue that was significant was that Social Services were to be the lead agency in this process of creating and prioritising the new statutory Community Care (para. 3.1.3.). It also spelled out in a concrete manner the expectations that government had for the Voluntary Sector, that it was to play an expanded role in the mixed economy of welfare as a paid service provider (para. 3.4.14). Government funds for this work should not inhibit voluntary organisations' normal work (services, campaigning, etc.), nevertheless, this initiative changed dramatically the Voluntary Sector's relationship with government. Henceforth, the Government's funding of contracted activities in terms of the National Health Service and Community Care Act 1990 gave the Government greatly increased leverage over its relationship with the Voluntary Sector.

As their dependence on sustained government funding for services provided grew, the Voluntaries needed to sustain good relationships with Government. Within local government, and in light of the restructuring of Social Services activities in keeping with the NHS and Community Care Act 1990, the level of 'patch social work' and community social work began to decline. Social Services Departments began a process of restructuring towards one of supporting contracted formal Community Care (in addition to their responsibilities towards protecting children – Children's Act 1989, etc.), and their interests in their social work staff maintaining a 'relationship' with their clients shifted towards a much more instrumental connection, rather than a personal one (Wistow, et al., 1994). The structure of a routine social work input became one of initial assessment, and then transition and support until formal care service packages bedded in.

The management of the care package was hived off to specialists (Jack, 1995; Eastman, 1995). In 1992, the Audit Commission made two studies of Community

Care. In the first, it stated that user groups and the community at large would provide a welcome support for statutory services (Audit Commission, 1992a). In the second, the community only feature as a small window at the bottom of a full-page diagram of how community care works (Audit Commission, 1992b).

Nevertheless, in the large, high population-density, urban areas, such as the inner cities, where the general welfare conditions of housing, race relations and endemic poverty loomed large, local authorities saw in community development a potential vehicle for engaging communities and addressing problem-solving in new ways (Association of Metropolitan Authorities, 1989). These Authorities recognised that without the active involvement and input of communities, the Authorities would lack insight, and fail to find acceptable remedies for local issues (Association of Metropolitan Authorities, 1990). This shift in thinking witnessed the rise of local authorities' interest (re-awakened since the CDP days, and the post-Seebohm reforms) in sustainable regeneration, and the connection of communities with the local economy.

The Thatcher years in government showed a very mixed picture from the perspective of community development. Popular resistance to some government policies provoked a great deal of social movement activity and overt political activism, as the various movements against poverty and Conservative rule manifested themselves (see *Community Action* magazine, 1971–90). However, against a continuing rhetoric of high moral solidarity with the poor and a demand for radical social change (Waddington, 1994) or a return to Gramscian and/or Freirean principles (Popple, 1994), pragmatic community workers followed a different path. From within conventional community work training and practice circles, funding cuts produced a significant drop-off in activism and radical thinking. In practice, community workers directed their efforts towards instrumental and incremental changes, rather than towards organising militancy amongst the poor (Jacobs, 1994). This was a time for new learning, and a time to consider the role of working with, instead of being semi-detached from, the institutions of government (Taylor, 1992).

Diamond's analysis of the situation in Manchester during this period was that the 'local socialist Labour Council' capitulated to, and became complicit and incorporated in, the Thatcher Government's design for a market-led state. As Manchester's cadre of community development workers did not resist this process, they became ciphers for this policy (Diamond and Nelson, 1993). It is significant, perhaps, that, in 1990, the last issue of the radical, community activist magazine, *Community Action*, which had inspired many community development workers in the 1970s and 1980s, bemoaned the demise of a radical perspective within community work generally, and itself published an article on a Prince's Trust housing project (*Community Action*, No. 83, 1990).

At the same time, in the United States, one of the mainstays of the establishment of *community organization*, and an opponent of Alinsky's brand of *community action*, Harry Specht, castigated American social work with the accusation that it had abandoned its principles of seeking structural and problem-solving remedies to social ills. Instead, Specht accuses, social workers had been in denial of their original mission, and hidden behind a screen of an 'individual-centred psychotherapeutic approach'. They must now dispel the 'myth of intimacy' (the spurious 'social work relationship'), and stand up to *authoritarian and populist tendencies* in society in pursuit of building the community's own problem-solving capabilities (Specht and Courtney 1994, pp. 152–5).

Drakeford calls for the social work and administrative establishment to recognise how local problem-solving can create positive change, if supported by an enabling authority (Drakeford and Hudson, 1993). Drakeford's comments pertain to a social dimension to economic policy, and the Thatcher Government instituted changes in priority that impacted severely on the social sector, to the gain of the private sector. The outgoing Labour government of the late 1970s tackled local economic regeneration with an emphasis on local resident participation in the process. Fortuitously for community development, it was a condition of the European Structural Fund grants that public engagement be secured in the planning and implantation of any strategy funded in this way (EU Commission, 1999; EU Directorate, 2005; European Commission, 2007). The conditions surrounding setting up Partnerships (including social partners) were strengthened (European Commission: Council Regulation (EC) No. 1260/99 of 21 June 1999). Thus it was necessary for the UK that a mechanism be put in place to reflect these policy directives, or the moneys would not be forthcoming. At this point, it is very clear to see that the European Union and the European Region of the WHO are following parallel paths towards the population's engagement in their own futures (Gowman, 1999). For this process to be sustainable, however, ongoing community development input had to be ensured (Robson, 1988).

The Church of England and the Church in Wales

In the face of rising poverty (Townsend, 1979), the Church of England underwent a crisis of confidence in its mission as protector of the down-trodden: as 'the servant of the Kingdom in the World, for God's purpose is that all can live in peace, justice, hope and love' (Ballard, 1990). Somehow a meaningful route had to be found to get back to the basic workface for social change with engaged communities. The Archbishop of Canterbury commissioned and published his stark report on the state of poverty in England's inner cities in 1985 (Archbishop, 1985). In addition to attacking the fact that government had allowed the fabric of society to crumble under economic forces, this Report called for radical Church action, mobilising its resources, centrally and locally, to combat poverty. It set out a chapter on community work, and the need for this activity to rebuild society/communities around the needs of the vulnerable.

Every priest was to become a model for community change, and become a community development worker, and the Church of England should not confine its role and impact to the confines of its own membership. The resources of the Church should be deployed where they could do the most for the common good. Special considerations, too, must be made to support ethnic minorities in English society (pp. 272–92 and 361 *et seq.*). Additionally, the Church of England called for parish contributions to a central fund, the *Church Urban Fund*, to fund the training and deployment of community organizers in the poorest areas (Jameson, 1988).

In Wales, the Church in Wales, too, produced its own appraisal of the social and economic conditions – *Faith in Wales* (Church in Wales, 1991). This document was critical of government policies, and the divisions that it created, but its solution was not to launch a civic movement or to mobilise its parishioners to the cause of the poor. Rather, *Faith in Wales'* message was to Parish Priests to mobilise their flocks in service of the Parish and to revive religiosity and the spirituality of the Church's message. Interestingly, this message was similar to another initiative of the Archbishop of Canterbury, who wanted to obtain a rural perspective on poverty, in addition to the situation in the cities – *Faith in the Countryside* (Archbishops' Commission, 1990). As part of the *Faith in Wales* publication, the Church in Wales had produced graphic descriptions of the nature and the precise location of poverty in Wales, such that their study pre-empted the Welsh Government's annual publication *Welsh Index of Multiple Deprivation* (WAG, 2008d). Nevertheless, the Church in Wales's response, following this penetrating analysis, was parochial in the extreme. In theological terms, any reflective cycle of theological analysis was being ignored, and 'doubt' was left out of the equation (White and Tiongco, 1997, p. 11). Where *Faith in Wales* did call for social intervention, and where some community development did take place, the emphasis was towards providing welfare support rather than challenging the system that produced poverty (Davis, in Church in Wales, 1991, pp. 16–23; Church in Wales, 1992). The Archbishop of Canterbury's first Report (1985) went almost to the point of inviting its clergy to embrace the theology and action framework of *liberation theology* in its demands for action on behalf and with the poor. This would have entailed priests identifying completely with the poor, at the expense of the hierarchy of the Church itself (Boff, 1985; 1989; Gutierrez, 1988). In the case of *Faith in Wales*, and *Faith in the Countryside* (above) the plight of the poor was not addressed, except obliquely.

Government and city regeneration

As the 1980s progressed, a definite shift took place in government policies towards community and social objectives. There was less money for 'projects', but consultancies aimed at social issues were in demand. For example, CPF (to become

CDF in 1989, and CDF Ltd in 2011 (CDF, 2012)) shifted from locality-based project work (mainly), from the 1970s onwards, to become (mainly) an agency of consultation and scheme management (CPF, 1988). Thomas describes his shift as from *'oppositional'* to *'functional'*, whereby community development workers and agencies focused upon the task at hand, rather than on the political and ideological considerations that had defined them in the past (Thomas, 1995b, p. 6). The economy was being directed by a Government (Margaret Thatcher's) that was not interested in social cohesion so much as liberal market economic regeneration, with state assistance, if necessary (MacInnes, 1987; Thomas, 1995b).

Because of its prominence and high political profile, London was a specific focus of interest — a Labour-controlled Greater London Council, and Conservative Government, together, instituted a *Docklands Joint Committee* (DJC), which included a nominated community contingent to represent local interests (30%) (Klausner, 1987, p. 48; LDDC, 1992). There, the principles of joint working were instilled, but the development interests of the London Boroughs represented on the LDDC (Ginsberg, 1999) and those of the private sector soon overtook the original intentions. There was also the vexing interpretation of the term *'community'*, as the representatives chosen to promote community interests on the DJC did not necessarily represent the views of the community groups living within the regeneration area. In 1981, the fresh Thatcher Government abolished the LJC and created another format for urban regeneration, with unique planning powers — the London Docklands Development Corporation (LDDC). The new Board structure (twelve members, only) left no place for community representation, and so any community interests had to be negotiated or organised outside the LDDC's structure. There was, therefore, no role for community development within the boundaries of the Corporation's boundaries (LDDC, 1992). This economic model was then put to use elsewhere in the government's regeneration programme, as in Cardiff in 1987, with the Cardiff Bay Development Corporation (Auditor General, 2001).

De Groot describes the tensions that this evoked, which started in the Labour/Conservative regeneration strategies for the London Docklands, but which then spilled over into the Conservative Government's next regeneration strategy — *City Challenge*, in 1991 (de Groot, 1992). *City Challenge* was designed to elicit competition between deprived urban areas for the limited funds in the *Urban Programme* (enhanced by the passing of the Inner Urban Areas Act 1978). Cities bid for the funds, and this was expected to produce raised standards of achievement across physical regeneration, social and cultural arenas. Partnership was the key word, but there were tensions between the private sector, the public sector and the community interests. Whereas the interests of the 'community' had been restored in the general scheme of things, it was not until *New Labour* was elected in 1997 that the role of a state-sponsored community development strategy emerged (see below).

It was obvious that the Conservative Government did not want to encourage community control of services, or over public investment. But it did consider that the engagement of the community was a necessary component of its regeneration and public/private investment strategies. The Department of the Environment embarked on an initiative to harness investment in community renewal through structural investment. To do this, local 'Development Trusts' were formed (Warburton, 1988). These were smaller-scale structures than had been created through the New Towns and Development Corporations Act 1985, through which, for example, the Cardiff Bay Development Corporation had been established. Development Corporations made no pretence of their design to proceed without community participation at any level, whereas the Development Trust structures did include token references to this dimension. Nevertheless, the template described in the Warburton framework (1988) describes participation by opportunist or specially selected representatives of the community rather than providing a mechanism for ensuring and developing their potential for participation in an informed and structured manner. Thus, it can be seen that during the latter days of the Thatcher administration, 'urban regeneration' meant state-and-private capital-led development, and it was not until the election of a Labour Government in 1997 that the Department of the Environment opened the process of regeneration to the community with a concerted effort (Cabinet Office, 1998).

There was a lot of other advice around at this time: Etzioni (Etzioni, 1993) was calling for a renewal of community spirit and co-operation, which tied in well with the *'Third Way'* approach to economic and welfare building later to be expounded by Tony Blair, the *New Labour* Prime Minister after 1997. Giddens produced his text on the *Third Way*, a call for a capitalism-plus-welfare model of economic and social development (Giddens, 1998). Mayo too addressed the implications of the, now-strengthening, *mixed economy of welfare* and the position of community development in its relations with the State. She goads community development workers, many of whom are heavy critics of the State, to take some radical steps towards consolidating their own position as a body of opinion for change, to achieve something more positive. Further, she asserts that the communities, with which the government implementers of regeneration wish to co-operate, are too under-resourced to be able to sustain any activity for very long (Mayo, 1994). Conversely, Jacobs (1994) chides community workers for sustaining an outmoded class analysis of society, and suggests that the lack of appeal of community development workers to the poor is because they have little to offer outside slogans and outmoded Marxist theories (p. 167). Jack suggests that the transformation of the welfare state into the *mixed economy* has already gone too far, and that effective community participation would be a wasteful exercise (Jack, 1995). Checkoway describes how, if communities are engaged and resourced, they are well up to the task of planning and overseeing their own regeneration (Checkoway, 1995). Dominelli analyses the way in which women have been made to shoulder the burden of responsibility for the restructuring of the welfare and health services, and calls for a radical response (Dominelli, 1994).

By 1994, the *City Challenge* initiative had been further refined by the Conservative Government, with the *Single Regeneration Budget Challenge Fund* – SRB (Rhodes, et al., 2007a). The competitive bidding system was widened considerably, and the specific intention to engage the local communities in the process was underlined. Nevertheless, despite the issuance of explicit guidelines, which exhorted the full engagement and integration of the community in the planning and delivery of community regeneration, there is no real incentive to comply (CDF, 1995a; Thake, 2001). There was still no mandatory requirement for the generation of the community's engagement, and, the constraints placed upon local communities that wished to participate in the SRB were very restrictive. The time frame for engagement was very short, and there were no mechanisms for engaging them in the process (Nevin and Shiner, 1995). So, whereas there were structural vehicles for the engagement and development of communities within the regeneration framework in the 1980s, there were few meaningful opportunities for these to be taken up.

It was not until the 'New Labour' Government (1997) that the Social Exclusion Unit was established to carry forward the active integration of the community in regeneration processes (Social Exclusion Unit, 1998; Social Exclusion Unit (SEU), 2001). Various strategies were developed (*New Deal for Communities* (NDC); *Sure Start*, etc.) to enable people to participate and to consolidate this participation on a sustainable basis (Social Exclusion Unit, 1998 – Chapter 4; Dinham, 2005). The SRB was adopted and extended by *New Labour* after 1997. This drew in other government agencies to support the central themes of regeneration, community engagement and social planning (Home Office, 1999; and 2001; Larson, 2004). The Government sought to bring much of the regeneration and other Departments' work at the local government level under some sort of 'working together' framework, and so the Local Strategic Partnership structure was adopted (DETRs, 2000; 2001). This was an undefined concept, and as the implementation of these new policies began to take effect, it was seen that, although a great improvement on the previous government's approach, there were still improvements needed if citizen participation was to be realised (Cooke, 2008).

Despite the vision of *'joined-up working'* envisioned by the SEU (SEU, 2001, pp. 43–53; DETRs, 2001) a long-term action programme was required for the planning and effective integration of communities with the planning and delivery of local services (Fisher and Sarkar, 2006). In some cases, such as civil disturbances in deprived cities, there was an air of expectancy that community development was the only vehicle that could solve the problems (Home Office, 2001). Despite all these good intentions, however, no complementary scheme for the training of the enablers, community development workers, was instituted.

Localised community development
in Wales, Northern Ireland and England

Building on its own experiences in these areas, the Church of England had published a further Report in 1999, where it identified weaknesses in the State model for community development and community engagement. It reported that Government planning and implementation time-scales were too short for meaningful interventions and sustainable change, even in ten-year *New Deal for Communities* (NDC) projects (Musgrave, et al., 1999, pp. 2–5). These criticisms were to be borne out by the official evaluation study of the NDC schemes (Lawless, 2007; Morris, 2007), and by many of the Final Reports on local NDC schemes (e.g. Pearson, et al., 2012; Ekosgen, 2010). CEA, an independent evaluation agency, reported that a majority of the NDC programmers had reported a beneficial outcome of community development interventions. This intervention method (community development) received the highest rating given by the communities themselves to any of the evaluated categories – help into jobs, community safety, improved health, etc. (CEA, 2005, p. 18).

Within this picture of relative success, however, there appeared to be a number of planning faults, most of them emanating from the structure, expectations and processes of local government agencies. These, it seems, stemmed from local government not fully understanding the complexities of organizing a community-engaged regeneration programme. Similarly, in the SRB programme, the state's failure to grasp the complexities of community development, despite having its own 'exclusion unit', led to the under-resourcing of the community engagement aspect of the policy. This had a seriously deleterious effect. SRB, it is claimed in the official evaluation, also failed to engage the participation of the private sector (Rhodes, et al., 2007a, c), whereas this had been a specific design feature of the original package (Nevin and Shiner, 1995; Rhodes, et al., 2007b). The community sector was not engaged as a lead agency in many schemes (31 out of 1,028 across the six phases), and those that were, were generally underfunded (Rhodes, et al., 2007c, p. 266). There was great variation between schemes, regarding the level of community development used. In one scheme, less than £24,000, over five years, was spent on the engagement of the community, whereas the figure for most schemes was over £1 million on this factor – four times that figure in some areas (p. 238).

A renewed attempt by the government to bring some coherence to the salient points in their policies, including community engagement, was to institute another competitive element into local government – the Beacons Scheme, through its Department of the Environment, Transport and the Regions (DETRs, 1998). With its 'Local Innovative Awards' component, over 50% of local authorities took part over the first ten years of the scheme (Dixon, 2010). Originally, the Beacons scheme was aimed at engaging local Councillors (*the leaders of their*

147

communities – DETRs, 1998, p. 3) and at improving their awareness of the need to promote more local accountability of their authorities. After the enactment of the Local Government Act 2000, however, the DETRs began its pressure to convince Councils to engage actively with their constituents in an attempt to stimulate local citizen involvement in community and civic activities (DETRs, 2001). The award of Beacon status was a mark of excellence in a particular strategic area of local governance – housing, transport, environment, etc. A fresh list was produced each year, and bids from local authorities were invited. Once awarded, this status lasted three years. In 2007, for example, 239 applications for Beacon status were received, and 61 awards were made (IDA, 2007). In 2008, applications were invited for (inter alia) Police Authorities; Fire and Rescue Authorities; National Park Authorities; Waste Disposal Authorities; Best Value town councils. It can be seen that these service areas are discrete, and do not emphasise 'joined up governance', but in 2009, engagement of the community in governance, particularly the engagement of older people, was a separate sector for the awards (Local Government Group, 2009). This awards scheme, from the point of view of an integrated strategy, may have had the effect of focusing local government on raising its standards, but it failed to produce a national change in authorities' approach to governance.

Wales

In Wales, the mantel of the SRB and the other schemes aimed at regenerating urban areas had been taken over by the devolved authority, the National Assembly for Wales, in 1999. The creation in Wales, in 2000, of its own community and economic regeneration scheme, *Communities First* (NAforW, 2000), came with a massive injection of European Social Fund assistance. Up to 150 local projects were launched over the first decade, centrally funded but under local, day-to-day management. This provided a policy lead for the rest of the UK. All the other 'national' administrations did likewise, following an extensive (UK) pilot scheme, *Bringing Britain Together* (Social Exclusion Unit, 1998). In the first public report on this scheme, social exclusion and the renewal of deprived neighbourhoods were the priority, planned on a whole-community basis (DETRs, 2000, p. 49). UK-wide social experiments on issues such as community regeneration can be seen as indicators that, even after governmental devolution, considerable co-operation on UK-wide issues continues to be developed. Although predicated, nominally, on economic regeneration, *Communities First* was designed, in concept, to become an important prototype for integrated, inter-agency co-operation (WAG, 2003e). Tallon reported that there has been remarkable consistency between England and the devolved national administrations in this regard since devolution (Tallon, 2009), but Carley questioned the validity and coherence of a 'national' (i.e. regional) policy that has to be co-ordinated locally by a network of twenty-two unconnected, small-scale local authorities. Regional cohesion of the policy was being fragmented and allowed for too much local interpretation, he stressed (Carley, 2000, p. 29).

There was concerted action to try and standardise this process, and Adamson, with a team from the University of Glamorgan, was charged with producing a guidance document on good practice in the regeneration endeavour (Adamson et al., 2001). There is no real evidence that any of it was ever taken up. Later, Adamson, himself, produced a stinging rebuke to the policy, when he used the example of the Welsh Assembly Government's *Communities First* programme as a vehicle for assessing the viability of regeneration schemes (Adamson and Bromiley, 2008). They came out, generally, in favour of the thrust of policies in this sector, but stated that merely having a policy in place did not guarantee its suitability or its success potential. They claimed that the levels of intensive support provided under this umbrella would be unsustainable under 'normal' conditions. Adamson and Bromiley pointed out that there was a danger of competition and resentment against new, government policy initiatives from established local programmers and organizations. These, they claimed, had not been consulted over the scheme, and had been displaced in the process. In fact, many of the potential gains of developing a community-based regeneration scheme in Wales were not realised (see detailed description below).

Public health and personal health outcomes would also be a priority. The new strategy set new objectives for each of the new (fifty-two) schemes and declared that WAG would measure their outcomes. These regeneration initiatives would be planned together with Private Sector engagement in partnerships. This will dramatically change the nature of the programme (WAG, 2008d). WAG also declared its commitment to engage the formal Voluntary Sector in its plans for an integrated and institutionalised path towards planned social change across the board, harnessing their expertise and to help the Sector to make an ever more positive contribution to the quality of public services (WAG, 2008e, p. 6).

Northern Ireland

In Northern Ireland, militant sectarianism dominated the community development environment in its formative years. Griffiths relates how early efforts to introduce '*conciliation*' mechanisms into the irreconcilable communities through community development failed. Instead, money was thrown at both communities in appeasement (Griffiths, 1975). Lovett clams that the government then feared that communities were being radicalised (further) by community development workers, and tried to back off in its support. Nevertheless, community-building flourished, albeit on each side of the sectarian line (Lovett, et al., 1994). After this, the community sector weakened, and, as there were distinct polarised points of community loyalty during this period, some community development workers were exposed to considerable personal risk in suggesting conciliation, especially within their own communities (Oliver, 1990).

The needs of the State changed over the years. As peace, to some extent, had broken out with the 'Belfast Agreement' of 1998, the State could look wider towards adopting policies that might combine elements of both communities. Health and social care was one such area, and the Southern Health and Social Services Board, in 2000, presented a report compiled by the auditors Coopers Lybrand that suggested that community development be 'mainstreamed' throughout the provincial Health and Welfare system with the view to establishing self-help and strengthening community well-being (Southern Health and Social Services' Board, 2000). Community Relations were high on the agenda, and community development featured high on the priorities of the Northern Ireland Administration's *A Shared Future* policy of 2005. In the Action Plan that followed (OFMDFM, 2006), there was an interesting caveat to the general sweep of the policy introducing focused community development. It states that (p. 92) this support is contingent on good relations being sustained between the communities being supported by community development initiatives.

In anticipation of this, perhaps, Scotland's *Community Development Centre* had been commissioned to produce a framework and handbook for the evaluation of community development in Northern Ireland (Barr, et al., 1996). Apart from the significance of this for Northern Ireland, drawing on this material, Barr, Hashegan and Purcell then produced a format for the detailed analysis of community development (Barr, et al., 1996). This was to underpin the National Occupational Standards Framework for community development (PAULO, 2003). They entitled their framework 'ABCD' – Achieving Better Community Development. This document strengthened the most popular theme in British community development that community development was a practice activity done from the bottom-up. This placed a ceiling upon the worker's responsibility at the level of facilitating the working in partnerships with other bodies/organisations in pursuit of common goals. This is an important characteristic, to which we will be returning below.

Neighbourhood renewal – England

By 2004, it appeared to some that community development was becoming completely incorporated into the agenda of the State, in its (the State's) attempt to build cohesive communities and to consolidate the non-market aspirations of the *Third Way* (Diamond, 2004; Unwin and Molyneux, 2005; Paxton and Pearce, 2005). Objective data were hard to come by (Lupton and Power, 2004), but where there was commentary on its progress, the problems appeared to be that, the more it succeeded, the more the inherent tensions emerged (Diamond, 2004). The difficulty of marrying centrally planned initiatives, with expected outcomes, while opening up local aspirations within partnership vehicles, or self-help schemes, created stress and tensions for community residents, and, most particularly, for the community development workers, themselves. They were at the hub of the contradiction (Diamond, 2004; Mansuri and Rao, 2004; Dinham, 2005; Henderson and Glen, 2006).

In 2005, ODPM (the Office of the Deputy Prime Minister) produced a definitive framework for community development in England for the next five years – the *Neighborhood Renewal Unit,* and an *Action Plan* for implementing the neighbourhood renewal strategy (ODPM, 2005a and b). This Unit was to work closely with local government departments in order to ensure that partnerships for renewal targeted their goals as outlined in government policies (ODPM, 2005a), particularly the NDC schemes (above), which needed re-stimulating. A revamped Voluntary Sector was also making a bid to become a central player in the delivery of services on behalf of the government, in keeping with the *Third Way* philosophy originally expounded by *New Labour* (Unwin and Molyneux, 2005; Giddens, 1998).

Additionally, Health workers were exploring ways through which health promotion could become an agent for change at the community level with NHS resources behind them (Chappell, et al., 2006). This tied in with the Department of Health's *Sustainable Development Action Plan* (Department of Health, 2006). This focus of varied and resourceful agencies would be vital if the potential of deprived communities was to be realised. Green found that it was the cumulative acquisition and deployment of indigenous community assets that enabled communities to experience raised and sustainable well-being (Green, et al., 2005). It is the outcome of sustained investment in the fabric of the community that ensures a solid base for progressive development, and, thus, enhanced well-being (Morrisey, et al., 2005). This form of investment was the hallmark of the NDC (New Deal for Communities – above) (Neighbourhood Renewal Unit, 2005a), and positive progress began to show almost immediately (Neighbourhood Renewal Unit, 2005b; CEA, 2005). In 2006, the Ministry of Communities and Local Government published its blueprint (White Paper on Local Government) for a corporatist approach to community renewal, calling its own agenda 'radical' and requiring government agencies at all levels to build in community empowering and inclusive mechanisms for planning and service delivery (Dept of Communities and Local Government, 2006b).

In 2005, the Government's Civil Renewal Unit (then in the Home Office, but later moved to the Dept of Communities and Local Government – DCLG) had asked CDF to review community development so as to widen understanding of this mechanism. CDF invited other agencies to participate, and the resultant Report (*Together We Can*) highlighted many of the weaknesses of government expectations surrounding the engagement of citizens. In particular, the relative inflexibilities within local government and the disparity of expectations between central and local government over outcomes and processes provided barriers to progress on government policy priorities (CDF, et al., 2006). Following this, CDF produced three documents and one analytical statement about the state of community development in 2006 (DCLG, 2006b; Bowles, 2008; Longstaff, 2008;

Miller, 2008). The result of their analysis was a wish-list, based upon a vision that had emerged from over a year's discussion between senior community development practitioners and managers across the country (DCLG, 2006b). This vision envisioned community development as becoming fully recognised in Britain as a nationally recognised, professional competence, well-funded, with a guild-like control over training and standards.

The first two documents that followed it went some way towards describing the function of community development as a strategic mechanism for bringing about social change, using the enhanced democratic forces that community development released in the community and between agencies (Bowles, 2008; Longstaff, 2008). The third document (Miller, 2008) was more difficult to rationalise. Entitled '*Management*', it attempts to reconcile a modernist concept of objectives-driven process control with a post-modernist, localised, empowerment-styled system of social justice and self-determination (Miller, 2008). Longstaff's companion document, '*Strategy*' (2008) has less difficulty in adhering to the policy framework provided by the principal paymasters – the National Government. This dilemma is summed up by Georghegan (Georghegan and Powell, 2009) when a choice is posited between neo-liberal economic rationality being applied to community development intervention, or co-option within a corporate structure, or separatist activism in conflict with the neo-liberal doctrine.

Miller's dilemma about management of community development is amplified by Scott, who describes the steady movement of programme and project management towards a centralising format. Here, community development is merely a component of a wider, instrumental strategy, with the 'mission' removed in the interests of programme outcomes (Scott, 2010). This jars with Henderson and Glenn, who had challenged community development to attempt to regain its earlier cutting edge, to assume a critical and radical dialogue with the State in the interests of change and democracy (Henderson and Glen, 2006).

Community development in Wales – the broader picture

In 1927, the Quakers opened Maes-yr-haf Educational Settlement in the Rhondda Valley, as a response to the 'desperate plight' of the Rhondda community as the General Strike of 1926 paid its toll (Naylor, 1986). From small beginnings, it was to become the hub for a community enterprise and community welfare network that reached up and beyond the Valley. Two full-time 'workers' were recruited (a married couple from Swindon), and they set about organising the resources of the communities and making appeals beyond the Rhondda. The Quaker community investment in the Rhondda was sustained until 1986. Not many agencies today set themselves a sixty-year agenda for development. All in all, the Quakers' Unemployed Workers Clubs in the pre-Second World War period numbered thirty. They also created thirty-five women's clubs, boot repair factories, welfare and recreational facilities, a theatre, which could produce operas(!), a health and welfare service in crises, etc.

The Welsh language has been a spur to community organization in the rural areas. In 1979, *Antur Teifi*, a community co-operative was formed to support the Language, and local trade. In 1982, it was consolidated into the community development agency, and developed as a model for further developments in the field. Carmarthenshire County Council made a positive investment in *Mentrau* (initiatives/enterprises) with *Mentrau Iaith Myrddin* as the co-ordinating body. In the Gwendraeth Valley, a local doctor had started a Welsh Language self-help community scheme, and this expanded into a local community development agency with part-time development workers (Carmarthenshire County Council, 2001; also: student placement reports). Access to European Development funding played a large part in under-pinning these agencies, but eligibility to and the scope of these funds has been reduced considerably over the years (Adamson, et al., 2001; ECOTEC, 2006; WEFO, 2008).

The Aberfan coal mining disaster of 1966 drew another church organisation into South Wales – Tŷ Toronto. The Canadian-Welsh community's response to the disaster endowed the Merthyr Council of Churches to set up a Ministry in the Valley, and Dr Erastus Jones was appointed to lead. Jones rapidly developed into a community development organizer, working with the local communities to re-establish their stability after the disaster. He maintained his position and, when the economic fortunes of the Valley declined along with the coal-mining industry, Jones sought social planning alternatives to de-industrialisation. Between 1973 and 1975, Jones assembled a committee to consider alternative economic models for the regeneration of the Valleys, and this group pressurised government to re-draw the county boundaries so that the Valleys communities could be considered as having city status. This did not come to anything in the end, but it drew together many community groups, churches and community-based organisations across Wales (Ballard and Jones (eds), 1975).

Community development, as a professionally generated activity, came to Wales in 1968/69, when the Young Volunteer Force Foundation launched four field projects in South East Wales – two each in Cwmbran and Newport. Additionally, it undertook a consultancy study for Cardiff with the view to projects being established there, but not as part of YVFF's portfolio (CPF, 1982). This began a long association with various parts of Wales, from the Ogwr Valley, to Wrexham (CDF, 1995a; Bell, 1992; Thomas, 1996). The initial fieldwork projects were: two youth volunteering projects in Newport, Gwent; a youth coffee bar project and a community planning organisation project in Cwmbran. CDF finally wound up its Cardiff office in 2011, after a 'national UK-wide' community development agency became untenable in a devolved Wales (CDF, 2012). During this forty-plus-year period, YVFF-CPF-CDF adapted and changed from project work in small localities to county-wide resource centres – Ogwr Valley (CDF, 1995b), Newport, South

Wales (Dungate, 1980; CPF, 1988), Wrexham Maelor (Bell, 1992) – that offered economic regeneration consultancies, intensive community group development, and local social planning input to Councils (CDF, 2011).

In 1971, one YVFF scheme in Newport converted from youth work to community development in the Pillgwenlly district. Comprehensive redevelopment was the Borough Council's agenda for the district, but the residents (with a little prompting from the Team) thought otherwise. A prolonged campaign to reverse and/or modify the redevelopment plan took place, entailing a very high level of technical input – something that the Team did not possess in any depth. Outside assistance was sought in the form of a newly established (UK national) resource Team from Shelter – the *Shelter Community Action Team* (SCAT). SCAT seconded two planner/architect experts to work full-time in Pillgwenlly as part of the *Polypill* (YVFF) team, and thus began an ongoing relationship between SCAT and South Wales that lasted for over a decade. This technical input into *Polypill* enabled the community development strategy, and the residents' repertoire of know-how to increase exponentially. Public Inquiries were contested, and won by the residents, and significant technological expertise was acquired in the process (e.g. Ove Arup Consulting Engineers provided, at a 'socially responsible' fee, detailed reports on sub-soil structure and subsidence), and the Borough Council were forced to the consultation and negotiating table. The integrity of the comprehensive, redevelopment plan was undermined and had to be completely redrawn to be replaced by home and environmental improvement across large areas of the district (Clarke, et al., 2002a, b).

The arrival and deployment of SCAT raised the bar as far as social planning for community development projects was concerned. It placed to the fore the whole question of how far 'ordinary residents' could acquire and use highly technical information and data, and whether or not they could represent themselves once they had it. Was the missing ingredient in situations of urban decline, etc., one of residents lacking a technical resource of their own – one they could trust? SCAT team members moved on from Pillgwenlly to provide a powerful impetus to the South Wales Association of Tenants (SWAT), and their approach and input put pressure on Councils in Glamorgan to reconsider their consultation and planning processes (Bailey et al., 1980; Lees and Mayo, 1984).

The churches have always been active in community development, particularly the church-connected children's societies – Barnardos, The Children's Society. Barnardos established a long-running community development project in Ely, Cardiff (Drakeford and Hudson, 1993), and this project established a Credit Union, which has continued to provide much-needed financial support to a community at risk. The Children's Society ran community-centre-based projects in Bettws, Newport, Swansea, and St. Asaph (Davies and Evans 1992). From 1975, in Newport, the Presbyterians and Methodists combined to provide a community centre (Selby, 1990, pp. 60–3). This acted as a base for community development workers – initially funded by the *Urban Programme*, and then the MSC in the 1980s (see Fullick, 1986; Short, 1986). In 1984, the Wales Council of Churches was instrumental in establishing the Newport-based *People and Work Unit*. This agency combines research into employment and economics affairs, and enters into action, educational and support services to schools and communities (Bowen, et al., 2005).

In 1975, the European Economic Community launched its Anti-Poverty Strategy, and the Voluntary Services Unit of the Home Office made moneys available for six resource centres across England, Scotland and Wales (Taylor, 1980). The South Wales Action Resource Centre (SWAPAC) was established, following prolonged negotiations between David Smith (of the Adamsdown Law and Advice Centre, Cardiff) (Garth, 1980) and Erastus Jones of Ty Toronto (see above). Eventually, a team of seven specialist workers was appointed and Merthyr Tydfil was selected as the location for the Centre. SWAPAC provided active community resource input for community groups (such as the SWAT – above), work with trade unions promoting local employment initiatives, as well as direct, personal active support for income maintenance and employment tribunal advocacy. This was not always met with official support, but the funding was extended to a maximum of six years, to 1981 (Hansard, 30 June 1981). SWAPAC provided a model for future community development approaches – high-powered, qualified workers with multi-discipline skills, operating at a number of levels simultaneously – interceding with officials, and providing grassroots support to individuals and groups (SWAPAC, 1980; Clarke, et al., 2002a).

The major investment in community development in Wales since 2000 has been the local regeneration programme *Communities First*. This programme has now spread to over more than 130 local, deprived areas, and brought community development to most of them for the first time (WAG, 2002b; WAG, 2007c). Unfortunately, the scheme became fragmented, lost its objective coherence, and achieved few of its economic goals. In 2011, the Welsh Government launched a consultation process regarding restructuring the programme (WG, 2011b). There was widespread response to this, mostly favourable. Where dissent was voiced was where the Welsh Government wished to remove the status and power of the local partnership boards, which had managed the local projects until now. Centralising the control and monitoring of the programme was seen by many as a retrograde step. Notwithstanding these protests, the Welsh Government proceeded with the re-organisation in 2012 (WG, 2012b), as part of its sustainable development strategy (WG, 2012b, c and d).

In March, 2013, Huw Lewis, Minister for Communities and Tackling Poverty announced to the Welsh Assembly that *Communities First* would be regrouped into fifty-two management 'clusters', in line with the new policy, spending over £75 million over three years, providing over 900 jobs. A centralised training programme for workers was given to the Welsh Council for Voluntary Action (Lewis, statement to Assembly, 19 March 2013). *Communities First* is now a mature and experienced, albeit fragmented, community development strategy aimed at reducing poverty and community decline (Communities Directorate, 2001; NAforW, 2000). To some extent it has been successful, but it is still deficient in that there is still no co-ordinated vision for local development and evaluation. It is hoped that the new structure might produce these essential elements.

Another significant thrust for the new Welsh Administration into community-based support services was the creation of the *Sure Start* programme in 1999. This was established by the Welsh Office as a final act of policy-formation before the assumption of power of the new National Assembly for Wales. *Sure Start* was to focus on community development processes and strategies to provide support and opportunities to the very young children in Wales, and their families. Capacity-building in the most deprived communities would be the first priority (Welsh Office, 1999). *Sure Start* has had mixed fortunes. It was placed under an umbrella Fund, *Cymorth* (means 'support'), of the Welsh Assembly Government in 2003 (WAG, 2003a; WAG, 2008f). It has been evaluated a number of times (Broadhurst, et al., 2007; Kelly, 2008; York/WG, 2006; McCrindle, et al., 2006), and whereas it has been praised for its impact on children on a face-to-face basis, it has not satisfied its monitors on inter-agency working, evaluation, capacity-building, etc. Kelly found that the workers on these projects had no training whatsoever in community development, and appeared to have been appointed for criteria based upon traditional nursing qualifications. She found, further, that the qualified workers had no knowledge that they were supposed to engage in these developmental strategies (Kelly, 2008, p. 235 *et seq.*).

Although the evaluations point to a collaboration with the *Communities First* projects, which have been aligning with the new strategy *Flying Start* since 2005, in their areas (WAG, 2005c; York/WG, 2006; WAG, 2009b), there is no evidence that this has been possible. Whereas the anecdotal evidence of positive outcomes of *Sure Start'/Cymorth/Flying Start* are recorded as positive (WAG, 2008f; WAG, 2009b), there are also strong statements in the evaluation that there is little strategic awareness in the local schemes, little 'joined-up-thinking and action'. One of the reasons for this might be that the trained professional workers in *Sure Start* are the Health Visitors (now called Specialist Community Public Health Nurses) have little training opportunities in community development.

Outside the National (Wales) strategy orbit, a voluntary organization, *Communities that Care* (CtC) has set up a number of projects across the UK and one in Swansea, in a deprived neighbourhood (Fairnington, 2004). CtC is a formulaic approach to community development that promised '*prevention*' as its main outcome. It depends on a preliminary marketing exercise being accepted by a community, which is then analysed for its 'readiness' to undertake CtC's intervention. The aim is to prevent risk to young people through intervening in the community, changing its structural profile, and changing the social norms of the area into those that are suitable for a community challenge to lawlessness, and moral decline (CtC, 1997). CtC employs social planning (in the Rothman sense), organising community leaders, agencies concerned with youth-centred welfare, health, etc., and builds new social networks and organisations around its agenda for change. The Joseph Rowntree Foundation sponsors this scheme, and has had it evaluated. The findings, across three UK projects, were that there was a limited benefit from this intervention, with more promised than delivered (Crow, et al., 2004). These findings were confirmed in American studies, where CtC is an established operator (Feinberg, et al., 2010; Shapiro, et al., 2015), and both studies pointed up the weakness that being an 'interloper' into the local scene reduced its impact and set up, in some cases, tensions that were not fully overcome. Another evaluation across seven US States found more positive outcomes, but stressed that this was a long-haul programme and that results usually relied on anecdotal and/ or self-reported data (Hawkins, et al., 2008). Nevertheless, it is the employment of a sophisticated model of community development that sets it apart from its peers (competitors or rivals in some situations), which augers well for the general prospect of community development in Wales as a role model.

Another source of community co-operation has been developed in America, and has been adopted with apparent enthusiasm in Wales (Thomas, 2014). This is *'Co-production'* (Cahn, 2000; Poll, 2007; Brandsen and Pestoff, 2009). In this model, the needs of the community and of the public sector can be met through harnessing voluntary activity, and structuring the delivery vehicles for community services to exact the maximum of cross-sector co-operation and resource deploy-ment in a tightly focused way. Pestoff and Brandsen identify three models for this form of delivery institution: co-production, co-governance, and co-management (Pestoff and Brandsen, 2009, p. 5; Co-production Wales, 2014). Each of these approaches to inter-sectoral co-operation suggests variants on citizen control and engagement, which, they state, have been easily achieved in many settings across the USA.

Bode analyses the application of co-production structures in three European settings, and suggests that in 'England', with its high citizen commitment to the Welfare State service model, the acquisition of the appropriate co-operative culture may be more difficult to introduce than it was in the USA (Bode, 2009). In terms of the model described here, co-production, in theory, presents a very useful struc-ture for the application of social planning interventions. Co-production is based upon the principles of felt-need, administrative priority, and problem-solving. The early literature on the subject does not include any reference to catalytic, support-ive or managerial inputs from the State or elsewhere. The pervading philosophy is towards mutuality, voluntary endeavour, and self/mutual help, in order to make a break with the past: 'Co-production demands that public service staff shift from fixers who focus on problems to enablers who focus on abilities' (Stephens, et al., 2006, p. 13).

For those seeking guidance as to how and when intervention should or could be brought into this scenario, the literature and policy documents provide scant encouragement. In Wales, Thomas (2014) does not offer a firm framework for the positive implementation of the 2014 Social Services and Well-being Act (2014), which she promises will be implemented: 'through our broad-based, cross-party, cross-sector leadership Partnership Forum'. The legislative framework in Wales is strong on 'sustainability' (WAG, 2004b; 2010a; WG, 2012e), but Thomas does not include a community dimension in her statement, particularly a community development approach. This is in spite of an earlier statement of intent to extend service planning and delivery into the heart of the community (Thomas, 2012); something that features quite strongly in the Welsh Government's approach to sustainability. For example: 'do anything which they consider is likely to achieve the promotion or improvement of the economic, social or environmental well-being of their area' (WAG, 2004c, p. 19; NHS Wales, 2013). Unfortunately, a feeling of *déjà vu* is aroused as, when other Welsh Government community-based policies have been implemented, 'centralised', 'technocratic' and 'bureaucratic' are the terms that come more readily to mind. Apparently and from now on, co-production is to be the preferred method for implementation, but implementation is slow. Hitherto, co-production has been defined mainly to include only the institutions of state, rather than the supposed beneficiaries of these policies. It is hoped that 'Co-production Wales' can take advantage of the window that presents itself. Otherwise it would be a pity and a lost opportunity to finally ground community-based initiatives in the community itself. In 2016, the *Big Lottery* approved a grant of £400,000, over three years, for the creation of a Co-production network for Wales. The framework for this network is on the basis of voluntary association and mutual support (Cartrefi Cymru, 2015). There is no mention of professional, community development underpinning for this endeavour. The Welsh Government (via the *Big Lottery*) will get something on the cheap, for as long as it lasts. In principle, and with a few tweaks to the theoretical focus of the practice guidelines, for example, in Scotland: Loeffler, et al., 2013, community development could easily have become the bedrock on which co-production is based, but the insight appears to be lacking (Garven, 2013).

South Wales has a rich history of community activity, usually led by community development workers who manage to scrape together funding for short-term projects, or are reliant on dissident professionals who give their time on a voluntary basis. The *Hook Road* organization was one of the latter, uniting architects, town planners (often from the local authority), public health officers, academics, and the like. *Community Action Magazine* (1972–90), in London, acted as a conduit for disseminating information and appeals for professional assistance for the whole country.

Community development has also flourished from time to time in the Community Arts world. From the *Agitprop* days of the late 1960s, and early

1970s, when Cardiff Street Theatre engaged summer play and community festivals, enthusiast actors and entertainers gained their first experiences, literally, on the road. Street theatre gave way to the Chapter Arts Centre, Cardiff, in the mid-1970s, and this was a joint development project of a film club, street video workshop, and community activists in the Canton area. These groups grew out of the *Hook Road Action Group*, which whipped up huge resident resistance to a fast road development (see Dumbleton's, and Beard's articles in *Community Action* Magazine, No. 1, 1972, and No. 6, 1973). Similarly, on a small scale, *Dymamix* in Swansea started out as the organiser of summer play-schemes in the 1980s. It has now grown into a consultancy and development agency, providing innovative community enterprise development schemes across the UK (Clarke, 2004a) and working with the Welsh Government and its Young People strategy, etc.

A notable sustained success in the Community Arts sector is *Valley and Vale Community Arts* – Valley and Vale (Cope, 2002). Cope established Valley and Vale in 1979, at the top of a de-industrialised Valley, and revitalised the local Miners' Welfare Hall and Theatre with dance, theatre, photography, film, local writers' schemes, and local history programmes that spanned the generations – including re-connecting the South Wales Spanish Civil War veterans in a film, sound and reunion project. Working with people with disability, especially mental disability, is their forte. A visit to their website (http://www.valleyandvalecommunityarts.co.uk/) shows how Valley and Vale has thrived over the years.

Community Development Cymru (CDC) was established as a community workers network and representative organisation in 2000 (Clarke, et al., 2002b). It drew is membership mainly from the newly established pool of *Communities First* workers, academics, social enterprises (such as *Cymdeithas Tai Eryri* – a housing and social support agency in North Wales), and consultants. CDC was grant-aided by the Welsh Assembly Government, and was able to establish three outpost offices across Wales for the promotion of community development at the local level. CDC hoped, along with the Wales Council of Voluntary Action, to benefit considerably from the *Compact* signed by the National Assembly for Wales in 2000, which attested to the wish of the Assembly to support community development as a capacity-builder and force for prevention of social decline in Wales (NAforW, 2000). CDC was a major contributor to compiling the *National Occupational Standards for Community Development* (PAULO, 2003), the *National Strategic Framework for Community Development in Wales* (CDC, 2007), and supported the development for the Welsh Assembly Government's *Sustainable Action Plan* policy (WAG, 2004c). Unfortunately, CDC experienced financial restraints over the past years, with the major grant from the Welsh Government being withdrawn, and then being only partially restored. CDC had to close two of its offices, and this highlighted the problems for community development in Wales, as negotiating sustainable funding has always been a problem.

In an effort to widen the scope of regeneration expertise, in 2010, the Welsh Government established the Centre for Regeneration Excellence Wales (CREW) to provide research, information training, and exchange of experience across the field of physical and social regeneration. They have produced reports on aspects of the progress of the *Communities First* programme since it was re-organised, CREW has offered proposals for the comprehensive regeneration of the *Old Town Dock* in Newport, and provides feedback on Welsh Government policy implementation (CREW, 2012a, b; 2015). The Welsh Government's White Paper went out for consultation and the Regeneration Bill was presented to the Assembly in the autumn of 2013 (WG, 2012e). It drew heavily on the commissioned practice guide produced by the University of Glamorgan (Adamson, et al., 2001), and its intention is to embed sustainable regeneration at the heart of local and central government programmers, and this entails the full engagement of the community in this process. They then embarked on another consultation strategy to explore community engagement (WG, 2012g).

Wales still experiences a deficit in training for community development (Adamson and Lang, 2013). Since 1970, community development workers had been able to train at Swansea University, as a stand-alone, post-graduate, qualifying programme for social work: CQSW (CCETSW, 1974). Additionally, between 1989 and 2005, post-graduate students, who wished to specialise in *community organisation* received a two-year, full-time programme, which included a comprehensive skills package, and professionally supervised practice placements. This programme was discontinued after the re-structuring of Social Work education in 2006. Today there is only one designated Certificate/Degree programme in community development listed on the *Community Development Workforce Wales* website, in North Wales. There are a number of post-graduate degrees in '*regeneration*', but the part-time Bachelor degree has closed in Swansea University. A number of short courses exist at the local community level (Qwest – Tonyrefail, e.g. free training up to 'Foundation Degree' level over four stages). Some of these local training programmers are provided by the local *Communities First* Team. There are two 'Youth and Community Work' training certificate courses on offer in Wales (CDWW, 2012). Before the Albemarle Report, 1961, Swansea was the only British University offering a full-time Certificate in Youth and Community Work (Albemarle, 1960; Robertson, 2009), and this continued until community development became an academic subject in its own right.

To the greatest extent, the future of community development in Wales is tied to the future of the *Communities First* and regeneration agenda (CREW, 2015; Adamson, et al., 2013). The new structure was announced by the Welsh Government in November 2011 (WG, 2011b). In 2012, *Communities First* was re-structured into a directly controlled Government initiative, and local projects were 'clustered' under operationally managed district or regional control. The local management Trusts were side-lined to a consultative role (WG, 2011b). In 2012, the Welsh Government also published two policy documents that focused upon 'sustainable development' and 'poverty reduction' (WG, 2012c, e). Although the 'sustainable development' document (WG, 2012e) did not mention *Communities First* by name, the whole focus of this policy drew it into the need for concentrated community development in order to deliver the necessary 'community engagement' aspects of the policy. The second document (WG, 2012c) saw *Communities First* as an essential element in the fight against poverty in the community, as community resilience had to be restored as a matter of urgency (p. 24). These are now mature community projects, with wide networks of interest, and their function extends into training community leadership and providing technical expertise and motivation. This augers well, provided that some of the structural Fund weaknesses can be eliminated (Adamson, D. and Bromilly, R., 2008; CREW, 2015). Reductions in European input to *Communities First* since 2014 has meant that more stringent operational conditions had to be drawn up for the monitoring and control of the *Communities First* programme (CREW, 2012a). Funding now stands at £31 million for 2015–16 (Ministerial statement: 23 December 2014).

Community Organization in the UK

The UK has been very slow to take up the stridency and power-centredness of the Alinsky model of *community organisation* (*community organization* in the USA). For some reason, perhaps, because of the ex-colonial experience of the fieldworkers and early theorists, or the nature of the model handed down by the Home Office, the CDP projects did not resort to militant street action, nor confrontational power manoeuvres in their community settings. Alinsky had first published his *Reveille for Radicals* in 1946, and pioneers in British community development were eulogising about Alinsky in their reportage of Dalino Dolci's work against the Mafia in Sicily (Booker, 1962). Smith had placed Alinsky at the centre of his analysis, for British audiences, of the Black Power movement in America (Smith and Anderson, 1972), but, generally, American literature was not popular within British and Empire development circles.

Whereas Batten was seen as a source of inspiration to American writers (viz. Biddle, W. and Biddle, L., 1965; Dunham, 1970), the sentiment was not reciprocated in the UK. As the Home Office was anxious for the CDP to avoid the sort of confrontation between race groups in Britain as they had witnessed in the USA, it is not surprising that Alinsky was not at the top of their reference list. Nevertheless, as Loney points out, Alinsky was seen as the model for radical activism in Britain throughout the 1960s (Loney, 1983, p. 161). Some of those activists went on to work for the CDP (John O'Malley, who was prominent in the *Golborne Community Council* (above), and the London West Way protests of the late-1960s, directed the Newham CDP). The difficulty for British community workers with Alinsky was that Alinsky did not make a Class analysis of the issues his clients faced, but rather made collective action a matter of seeking corporate power over other corporate monopolies – the community versus the business corporation, or versus the political administration (Ross, 1955; Brokensha and Hodge, 1969; Mullaly, 1997). The only agency, eventually, to take *community organizing* seriously was the Church of England, which, after the publication of *Faith in the City* (above) in 1985, sent its future workforce to the Industrial Areas Foundation (Alinsky's corporate social action instrument) for training (Jameson, 1988).

The Alinsky message did make some impact, and broad-based organizations were set up in Bristol, in 1990, and in North Wales in 1995 (http://www.tcc-wales .org.uk/, accessed 2 May 2013; Henderson and Salmon, 1995). In 2010, however, it came as less of a surprise when the future Prime Minister, David Cameron, announced on 31 March that, if elected, he was going to implement his *Big Society* programme, which would tackle 'multiple disadvantage' (Cabinet Office, 2010) (http://www.conservatives.com , accessed 8 September 2012; Norman, 2010). In May, 2010, he restructured the 'Office for Civic Society' (OCS), and OCS established a competitive bid for a contract to train 5,000 community organizers over the first five years of the new government. This £15 million award went to the 'Freirean broad-based organisation: *Locality* (*Third Sector*, 18 February 2011), as opposed to the Alinsky-linked *Citizens UK* (*Third Sector*, 8 March 2011).

As we have seen above, Paulo Freire believed in an essentially non-abrasive approach to individual learning, whereas Alinsky organized with organisational power as its *raison d'être*. Four hundred local organizations were to be enlisted by *Locality* as 'hosts' for the new community organizers, and they would be funded for eleven months. After that, local organizations were expected to pick up the responsibility for funding them – something which caused disquiet in 2012, because the local, often small, faith-based organizations had been seen to lack the continuation funding (*Third Sector*, 8 March 2011). On 11 September 2102, the OCS reported that spending on placements had fallen quickly over the past twelve months, due to falling take-up. There must be some serious questions asked about the nature of the training offered to these community organizers. *Locality*'s training will be an 'experiential' placement of six months, after a 3.5-day residential orientation programme (Locality, 2012; Cabinet Office, 2013c). This compares favourably with the one-day training originally offered in community development as part of the Wales *Communities First* programme (personal consultancy arrangement, 2001–3). The first evaluation report on this scheme (Cameron, et al., 2015) claims that, whereas skill levels of workers have shown marked improvement, sustainability factors have not been addressed. In a pre-emptive intervention into his scheme, Fisher (Fisher, et al., 2013) analyses how this model is not going to achieve what it sets out to do due to the lack of sustainable funding, shortage of training and ill-conceived objectives.

Apart from the *Big Society* initiative, there are a number of broad-based organizations operating across England and Wales. These follow the Alinsky pattern of organising, but with a far lower public profile. The most prominent of these is *Citizens UK*, formed in 1996, which narrowly lost out to *Locality* in its bid for the above government training contract. *Citizens UK* comprises nine major local networks of citizen action, spread from London to Birmingham. It is led by Neil Jameson, who founded the Church of England-funded *Citizen Organising Foundation* in 1988, and *Citizens Organised for Greater Bristol*, in 1990 (Henderson and Salmon, 1995). In 2010, *Citizens UK* organised a mass rally to quiz the leaders of all major political parties over their Election Manifestos. This drew an audience of 2,500 community leaders, and enabled all the Party leaders to pledge their loyalty to the ideal of community organising, and to report back annually to the organisation on their achievement in this regard. *Citizens UK* are currently running campaigns on 'a living wage', community-led housing, community safety, and a 'better governed London' (www.citizensuk.org, accessed 12 March 2013).

Faith-based organizations make up the bulk of the membership of these institutions. In order to further this end, *Citizens UK* have produced a community organising manual following Muslim principles (Ali, et al., 2012), and Jameson has produced one for Christian Parishes under the same umbrella (Jameson and Gecan, 2013). In her study of comparative community organising across five countries, Kenny discovered that in the more pluralist, and settled countries of Northern Europe, including the UK, citizens had less inclination to adopt critical stances *vis-à-vis* the State, and to seek social change, than did citizens in less developed nations, such as Muslim Indonesia (Kenny, 2011). It will be interesting to observe the progress of Britain's broad-based organizations in light of this.

Analysis

The introduction of the Griffiths reforms to social care provision in 1990 (Depts of Health, etc., 1989), saw the collapse of community social work (Barclay, 1982). From now on, strictly individualised, formulaic interventions by professionals would be allowed in Social Services Departments. This changed, completely, the relationship between social workers and the communities from which they drew their cases. Regarding education and training, this meant that community development was no longer relevant, and so it was dropped. This created a vacuum in the training sphere for community development workers generally, most particularly because it removed them from the status level of earning a higher education degree. Instead, many part-time, vocational programmes were set up outside the degree curriculum.

This fed into the agenda of the Federation of Community Development Learning (FCDL), and the anti-elitist position of the (now-defunct) Association of Community Workers. FDCL has been the major force in promoting the recognition of the Community Development National Occupational Standards (PAULO,

2003, as amended), which is predicated on a hierarchy of distance-learning and non-academic credit acquisition (FCDL, 2008). It is an open-access gateway for community leadership engagement in the social change process. Nevertheless, this is more than just an issue of access to paid, community-based employment. It conceals a much larger ideological question: whether or not one can enter into a potentially life-changing process for third parties without the capacity to oversee the whole scenario from a position of pre-preparedness with some theoretical insight and professional boundaries. Grassroots and Class solidarity may be one thing, but it generally has limited horizons. Conceptualising a holistic model of Health in the community change context is something that usually defeats even trained professionals. At least, from their professional training, they are supposed to know what it might entail (Dahlgren and Whitehead, 1991). There was a time when Masters-level community development students in the UK aspired to that objective.

The need for multi-disciplined, professionally trained community development workers is underlined by the introduction of national regeneration strategies across England, Scotland and Wales. These produced a fairly uniform model of community development at the project level. In England, this was a localised component of each Council's regeneration strategy, which could vary greatly. In Scotland, there was considerable national co-ordination through the influence of the Scottish Executive (Muir, 2004; Scottish Executive, 2004; and 2007). This model comprised a top-down conceptualised planning objective, followed by localised, development-implementation activities (Barr, 2005). We will consider Wales in detail below. The impact of this model results in a gap between planners and implementers, and the introduction of the 'community' into a consultative/management structure provides formidable boundaries if serious, structural social change is required (Webster, 2003). The old Colonial model of paternalistic guidance for the dependant community (now abandoned, and replaced by the *Logic Framework* systems-based project – ODA, 1995) is carefully disguised in this approach. It can be found clearly in Northern Ireland's Health Boards' community-focused intervention. It demonstrates the efficacy of the ABCD model (Barr and Hashagen, 2000), and this has been adopted, usually without acknowledgement, in many settings. The ABCD model is, however, strong on anti-discriminatory practice, and consciousness-raising on ageism, racism, sexism, etc., and is a good instrument for engaging at the grassroots level and ensuring participation up to the level required by the planning perspective described above. (Note: ABCD: this acronym has currency in the USA, indicating 'asset-based community development, so-called by the ABCD Institute of Northwestern University at Evanston, IL. This will be described in Chapter 5, below).

Despite the gains made on the regeneration agenda by the introduction by *New Labour* after 1997, and the devolved administrations in the regional administrations, government has not fulfilled its own commitments to overcoming 'silo' restraints on inter-agency and inter-departmental co-operation and joint working. Some progress is reported but considering these policies for integrated, joint working systems have been legislated for across the regeneration evolution, little real progress has been made (National Audit Office, 2009; National Audit Office, 2013). The Blair Government was initially committed to implementing a vision for communitarianism and the *Third Way*, but this soon withered away. Today, a Conservative Government was promoting the idea that society should pull together as one *Big Society*, but this changed emphasis as the financial crisis hit home – e.g. the 20,000 community organisers heralded at the launch of the initiative now turn out to be mainly volunteer helpers instead of paid workers (Cabinet Office, 2010; Pearce, et al., 2012; Locality, 2012). Community development workers remain caught in the grip of not being institutionalised, and being constantly vulnerable to short-termism, and poor, inconsistent political leadership (Cameron, et al., 2015). It is for this reason that the progress of co-production initiatives will be watched with great interest.

Broad-based community organising is at the crossroads in Britain. The impact locally is still confined to micro-impact programmes, and their mass organising demonstrated by *Citizens UK* is still at the stage of the big, one-off event and image-making level. Despite the claims that they are based on the Alinsky, or Freirean, models, they seem to lack the cutting edge of impact-making that their American counterparts strive for. The key is **power**, and the UK organisations still appear to be coy about making power their objective, choosing localised, small-scale objectives over challenges to the overall system (Hopper/TCC, 2012). The main focus of the classical (US) broad-based organisation has been around the notion of the community organiser being the driving force behind strategy and action-planning. The Citizen Organising Foundation did not make much of an impact since its inception in 1988 (Jameson, 1988), with its founding endowment coming from the Church of England, with its 'call for action' in the mode of Christ the radical (Archbishop, 1985).

Since the Second World War, Britain has relied on special budgets to fund a large part of its community development work – the Marshall Aid package, the Government's Urban Programme; European Union's Social Fund; Church of England's *Urban Fund*; *The Big Society* and the *Community Organisers' Programme*. This has meant that it has been impossible for the model of community-based problem-solving to be built into regular, mainstream local policy development, and for the discipline of community development practice to become fully regularised. This subject will be discussed in full in the final chapter (5). Apart from the input by charitable trusts (Esmée Fairbairn Foundation; Woodward Charitable Trust (Sainsbury); The Big Lottery Fund; Allan Lane Foundation; Wates' Family Enterprise Trust; etc.), there is an another anomaly between UK and USA funding in that it is virtually unknown for the community to fund its own community development, as is found in Alinsky/ACORN-style organisations in the USA.

Self-help in funding is a prominent feature of most American projects, in addition to the work of the major Foundations, such as the Ford Foundation, Aspen Institute, etc. Of course, the American Foundations' contribution to sustainable social investment, covering human and institutional capital is immense by UK standards (Sabeti, 2009).

In Wales, the most consistent element in the realm of policy has been the determination of the Welsh Government, since 1999, to include, develop and then amplify the World Health Organization's principles as laid out in the *Jakarta Declaration* of 1995 – promotion of social responsibility; increased investment for development; consolidation and expansion of partnerships; increasing community capacity and individual empowerment – all of which were embodied in the Wanless Report of 2003 (WAG, 2003b). The only factor included in the *Jakarta Declaration* that has been omitted is the exhortation to governments to secure an infrastructure for the promotion of this framework, as has been discussed above. Within the temporary structures that the Welsh Government did provide for this activity (*Communities First; Sure Start; Healthy Living Centres*; SWAPAC – to name the most prominent), the output was varied in its success. All the programmes could be said to have failed in so far as they failed to become exemplars of good practice.

As the Welsh Government only has limited powers to influence directly the work of the Local Authorities, this failure over seventeen years of devolved government to influence local Councils to implement key features of Government policy provides an interesting insight into the limitations of central power in a social democracy. It may also mark out the failure of the State better to market and convince those lower down in the chain of implementation the efficacy of community development. Alternatively, this may reflect a failure of the bureaucracy fully to understand what it is about, or for them not to value it as highly as the wording of their own policies implies. Can a tendency towards centralisation be detected in the restructuring of *Communities First*, or is it a risk factor beyond which central government is not prepared to go – as in the SWAPAC situation? SWAPAC was an independent voluntary organisation, but on a State stipend. Like the CDP earlier, frictions generated by the local projects, within a loosely defined boundary of project independence, proved too much for the establishment to tolerate, whatever the beneficial outcomes might be.

The Community Development Foundation (CDF) was charged with implementing this strategy at the local government level. The process has seen it off. CDF had come through the many changes in political priority and policy with great resilience and CDF Ltd also managed to secure funding for a number of innovative programmes that stretch further the definition of community development consultancy: managing the *Big Local* – funding maximisation scheme; *Active at 60 Scheme* – pump-priming small grant scheme for older people; *Community First* – the *Big Society* local development scheme. CDF also demonstrated that a purposeful institution can push its message into government with sustainable effect. This has all come to nothing, mainly because central government does not have any stomach for longer-term processes, meaningful prevention strategies and funding commitments that extend beyond the Parliamentary funding cycle. Communities with long-term vested interests in sustainable social change planning processes appear to be one step too far for the social democratic system of governance.

The UK as a whole has produced a rich literature on community development, with the *Community Development Journal* being pre-eminent in its international field. Wales, too, has produced its quota of input into this genre: David Thomas and David Adamson being the most prominent. What is significant about the UK literature is the more or less total absence of reference to the American literature. A perusal of Irish, Australian and Indian literature produces a steady stream of references to Rothman, Rubin, Weil, Specht, etc. This may be because much of British literature has insistently been shot through with a thread of political ideological preference. British community development literature is characterised by use of one or other of two concepts: Class analysis, or Transformative/Freirean learning frameworks (Hope, et al., 1984; Hickey and Mohan, 2004; Gilchrist, 2009). Class is an aspect of community organization that is more or less absent in the American context. In Britain, often, the capitalist state is the object of criticism, and the target for action. Nevertheless, many of the practice guides and compilations of case-study material demonstrate a lack of ideological analysis and targeted practice (Duncan and Thomas, 2000; Clarke, et al., 2002a; Popple and Quinney, 2002; Twelvetrees, 2008). Probably the most influential practice guide in the UK, presently, is the non-ideological ABCD schema. This provides a straightforward analysis of the job to be done, and a systematic approach towards achieving all the objectives, including evaluation (Barr and Hashagen, 2000). Further, it conforms readily to the WHO approach to a holistic and environmental appraisal of the way to combat health and social inequalities (Whitehead and Dahlgren, 2006; Dahlgren and Whitehead, 2006).

This detailed study of community development has been conducted from a generic standpoint, with the view of establishing just what the format is when a community development approach to community problem-solving might be taken. Can the generic demands and structures of a community development approach to community problem-solving be applied to broader Public Health issues? Is the situation of older people adaptable within this framework?

Summary

1. The emergence of community development in the UK has been enabled by the fortuitous availability of short-term funding, mostly from government sources. This has not allowed for any systematic appraisal of how best to go about holistic problem-solving across society.

2. There is a confrontation between the values of the institutional desire for gradual and controlled change versus the ideology of class-based radical change solutions. This usually marks the divide between public sector administrators and elected representatives on the one hand, and field-based practitioners on the other.

3. The government-sponsored CDP programme demonstrated just how sensitive political systems in Britain are to the engagement of communities in social planning and service provision functions.

4. Government policies enabling community development practice have not been supported by a coherent training programme.

5. Scotland and Wales lead the field in terms of enabling policies and field experience of community development.

6. There has been little learning from American or British overseas experience and modelling in this field.

5

Conclusions and final analysis

In this study the major themes examined have been the history of community development in the USA and the UK and any salient connections that could be made with Public Health policy in the nations of the United Kingdom. Of particular interest in this regard is the progress that has been made in Wales, as governmental responsibility for Health has been a devolved function of the National Assembly for Wales since 1999. Because of the relatively small size of this nation, its example might be instructive for other regional administrative authorities seeking answers to pressing social issues. This is the hope of the present work.

Key findings from the focused research

Chapter 2

Here the path of community development was traced more or less exclusively in the United States, due, mainly, to the total absence of other literature on the subject. In the USA, we found the first systematic attempt to analyse in depth what was involved, and to discover its utility. This was successful in that the US Government was able to enlist its benefits as a strategic intervention initiative to focus (especially) rural communities on the agricultural and economic needs of the nation in the time of War, and in post-War reconstruction.

Alongside this, the theoreticians produced an extensive literature on the subject, which gave it sufficient, non-ideological, intellectual respectability to enable the National Conference on Social Work to establish the Lane Committee in 1938. The Lane Committee established that community development was a rational, systematic, application for the development of strategic objectives for planned social change, and that it should be included in the regular repertoire of all American social workers, and in their basic training (Lane, 1940; Harper and Dunham, 1959; Dunham, 1970).

Almost no notice was taken of this process in the United Kingdom, despite the fact that the UK had furnished the basics for community intervention from the end of the nineteenth century. In 1943, the UK Government acknowledged that the application of community development in the USA had brought about some positive, developmental improvements in the lives of poorer, rural and urban Americans (Colonial Office, 1943, p. 54), but it was not until 1954 that these issues were taken up in any systematic way. Even then, after being provided with the basic framework, colonial administrators were to use their own initiative in its implementation (Colonial Office, 1954).

Chapter 3

Community development progressed determinedly across a number of fronts after 1940. In the USA, two models competed for respectability – the conventional, consensus model of the Lane Committee, and the conflict-oriented Alinsky model. In the relatively *laissez-faire* climate of American community activism, charities adopting community-organizing approaches (as opposed to more therapeutic approaches) had to become business-oriented if they were to survive. The State, and some Foundations, to be sure, did offer some spectacular grant-aid programmes, such as the *War on Poverty* (Marris and Rein, 1967), but, mainly, community organisation was dependent on local subscriptions, *Community Chest* fund-raising initiatives, or established charities such as the Bank of America's community development grants programme (to promote community stability through house-building).

The Alinsky-based, 'membership organisations', however, could take a more aggressive stance in the face of intractable local issues, and thus the conflict model was always an option for all, depending on the levels of social need, frustration or wilfulness of the population. The notion of democratic choice and control is always at the back of the American community organization experience. In taking donations from powerful supporters (such as the Roman Catholic Church) Alinsky always insisted on autonomy and resisted pressure from his funding sources for control over the unfolding activity. The people on the ground, who held feedback sessions after every '*action*' (act of confrontation) decided for themselves on the next steps, and how the mission strategy was progressing (Fagan, 1979; Pitt and Keane, 1984; Delgado, 1986; Gittell and Vidal, 1998). Another significant feature of American community organizing is that it is mostly self-funded from the indigenous resources of the poor, or other groups in society. Alinsky used outside resources (very often the Roman Catholic Church), often to pump-prime the activities (in *Back of the Yards*, Chicago, for example), but Alinsky found that equity (ownership) is a vital component for underpinning motivation. Across Britain, outside the pretty parochial, Welsh Language sector, rural co-operatives, there is very little evidence of self-funding, even on a small scale. Even in this sector, many

Welsh projects, such as *Mentrau Iaith Cymru*, are directly funded by the Welsh Government, as well.

The Americans also invented the community development corporation – CDCs (Twelvetrees, 1989), after the collapse of the *War on Poverty* and when poor communities were seeking some means of regeneration and self-sufficiency. The community housing co-operative or community-owned supermarket are all institutions that are now readily recognisable in America. But it was the acquisition of corporate financial support through 'leveraging' that made the biggest contribution to the enhancement of the community business model (Blaustein and Faux, 1972; Fisher, 1999; Rothman, 2008; Feehan, et al., 2013). Borrowed money had to be paid back, and this fostered and focused the business acumen within communities. Since the 1960s, the CDC has entrenched the business ethic, and financial orientation of community organizing in the United States. The business model proves particularly effective in strengthening ethnic minorities in the USA (Blaustein and Faux, 1989; Twelvetrees, 1989; Gittell and Vidal, 1998; Atlas, 2010). CDCs and the conflict model present to minority Americans an alternative to food stamps, and the often exploitative, privately rented tenement housing. The CDCs embody the capitalist ethos that permeates community life, and they also extol the business ethic of society at large.

At the other end of the scale, and as another symptom of the vitality of the American approach to the subject, the question of the 'dying American community' was raised pointedly by the sociologist James Coleman. Coleman identified the need for reinforcement of a feeling of the 'collective' – a value of social networks. It 'inheres in the structure of relations between actors and among actors' (Coleman, 1988, p. 16). This resonated with aspects of the personality that suspended self-interest, to enjoy the knowledge that 'belonging' was important. This theme was then taken up by the political scientist, Robert Putnam. Putnam had been studying Italian village life, and he concluded that the loss of traditional, communal pastimes led to social decay, unless replaced or compensated for in some way (Putnam, 1993).

He then applied the same logic to the United States, and his research found that the decline of team bowling activity, which consumed a great deal of Americans' social networking time in the 1950s, had resulted in the loss of community spirit and personal, social identity. Bowling had now been totally displaced by television, and other, more individualistic activities. As such, the sense of *'community'* was now more a myth than a reality for many Americans. Societal failure, as already demonstrated in this decline, was so critical that it was making parts of America ungovernable, especially parts of the inner city (Putnam, 2002; Putnam et al., 2004). Putnam's work raised a lot of interest, and the World Bank considered it to be of enough importance to make a thorough analysis of its place in social assessment processes (Grootaert, 1998). The concept quickly grew beyond the original boundaries studied by Putnam, and it soon became interwoven into the framework for assessing the quality of public health (Lynch, et al., 2000; Farrington, 2002; Morrissey, et al., 2005).

The concept of *social capital* has now become confused, or conflated with another concept, *human capital*. As Coleman explained in 1988, *human capital* constitutes the skills that enable our culture to transform materials into useable artefacts (Coleman, 1988, p. 18). Some writers, who are claiming that *social capital* has the ability to orchestrate social change through its innate qualities, are stretching the concept beyond reason (Muntaner, et al., 2008). The measurement of social capital is still an imprecise science because *social capital* is an ethereal phenomenon (Field, 2003). This is because the concept, itself, carries some moral connotations about the quality of social networks and the density of cultural ties (Etzioni, 1993; Field, 2003). Nevertheless, it is now established as an indicator of significance with the WHO, and with the UK Government (Marmot, 2010). Putnam's last word on this matter is that society must reform itself towards participation, and any form of participation will do. The most positive activities for increasing *social capital* are found in faith organisations, and in social service of some kind. Even re-establishing the camaraderie of the workplace would go a long way to raise morale and well-being (Putnam, 2002, p. 404 *et seq.*).

Chapter 4

Community development in the UK has presented a completely different picture to that in the United States. First, there is the matter of ideology, and the permeation of the profession with a socialist dream of better places to be, and the (almost) antagonistic orientation towards business that that embodies (*pace* New Labour). The problem arose from the institution of the CDP in 1970, and the lack of administrative control over the fieldwork philosophy of the teams *in situ*. Instead of taking up the challenge of inner-city (and rural) deprivation, and attempting to restore some economic recovery in their communities, the CDP teams set about castigating the capitalist system, and motivating their respective communities into endless challenges of their local authorities, etc. The result was that none of these communities benefited anything save a few short-term gains (housing maintenance, for example).

There was only partial success in one CDP project (Oldham), in the face of Council opposition, where even an orthodox approach to social planning met with stern resistance (Corina, et al., 1979). Alan Barr emerged from this situation with a positive learning experience, which he was able to transfer with success, incorporating community development into the Scottish *Community Development Centre*, with a continuing national impact (Barr, 1991). From CDP IIU (1975), Bennington (1976) and Cockburn (1977) to Ledwith (2011), Shaw (2011) and Jolly, et al. (2012), the market and the capitalist system are attacked for their oppression and failure to respond to democratic principles. Unfortunately, this study is not about choosing a preferred economic system, but is about discovering an intervention model that can survive and thrive within current circumstances for the support of older people. Today's older generation is stuck with the system we have.

The CDP project as a whole was disbanded and forgotten (except in the literature – see above), and in England and Wales, at least, the Labour Party went into denial of community development, generally. It remained in the doldrums until the emergence of the 'enlightened' philosophy of the *Third Way*, under New Labour (1997–2010). This resurgence was mainly the brainchild of John Prescott as Deputy Prime Minister, and Minister for Communities and Local Government. It was on his watch that the profile began to rise again. The attempts by the Social Exclusion Unit between 1997 and 2006 to bring public officials into the frame for social regeneration alongside economic regeneration had some limited successes, particularly in the area of child poverty and exclusion (Hills and Stewart, 2005). Nevertheless, despite 'taking poverty and exclusion extremely seriously', the Labour Government of those years did not achieve much overall for older people living in deprived circumstances, as housing costs escalated in this period (pp. 5–6).

In the UK, institutions have been developed that might serve an important function in the dissemination of a holistic model for community development. When YVFF was formed in 1968, a feature of its staff was their idealism, drive, creativity and vision of what they were trying to achieve in society – mainly a more equal society. Since that time, despite its having the ear of government, and a Parliamentary representative as its Chair, it failed to act as a lever on government to alter policy towards the universal adoption of a community development, problem-solving approach to governance. In 2012, CDF was forced to sever its formal links with government due to a shift away from funding QUANGOs (CDF, 2012). Finally, in 2016, CDF announced that it is to close down completely, which means that this potential for influence may have gone forever. If the State was to decide that it needed a semi-autonomous vehicle from which to launch a campaign to change governance towards community re-vitalisation, the CDF model would still be valid. CDF, however, was never given the autonomy nor the authority that this function required to be effective. This ends nearly fifty years of providing a focus for community development interests in the UK.

In England, the achievements of community development since 1940 comprise a shrugging off of the 'colonial model', and the assumption of a collaborative role alongside the newly elected coalition Government between 2010 and 2016 and its *Big Society* programme. It has failed to produce any real concrete learning from the intervening years, and it has failed altogether in adopting any of the learning that has been accruing in other countries, especially the United States. One of the major differences between British and American approaches to community development is that Americans deal in material effects, and the British deal more in abstractions. The British are focused on difficult-to-measure *social capital* (see above – identity through social network awareness), whereas the Americans tend to measure advances in *human capital* (the acquisition of quantifiable skills). Shaw (UK) talks about 'community as possibility' and protecting 'creative spaces' for people (Shaw, 2008) whereas Minkler (USA) invokes aggressive empowering planning interventions for the 'elderly poor' of San Francisco (Minkler, 2008). Ledwith urges us to achieve *praxis* and the 'radical agenda' as the basis for a viable model for community development in economically recessional Britain (Ledwith, 2011; Turbett, 2014). In the UK the theme in the heyday of activist literature, *Class*, was the only medium for communication (Leonard, 1975b; Bolger, et al., 1981), whereas in the USA class is hardly ever raised. There appears to be a cultural blind spot when it comes to recognising the contribution the USA has made to community development thinking over the decades.

It is still an open debate whether or not '*participation*', *per se*, enhances social cohesion (Mohan, 2013). In fact, some see it as a mechanism for binding people into processes that are anything but liberating (Cooke, 2001; Cooke and Kothari, 2001; Henkel and Stirrat, 2001; Hickey and Mohan, 2004). But the World Bank, and others, are of the opinion that social organisation in formal endeavour, particularly focused on economic outcomes, is the most powerful force for social well-being (Mansuri and Rao, 2013; Sagar and Weil, 2013). Plummer (1999, p. 9) sees community participation as a mechanism for building the authority's capacity for problem-solving, provided that the authority, itself, has developed the capacity to manage it effectively.

Community development and the community in Wales

Wales provides a cameo in the search for a workable programme by government for the attainment of viable Public Health strategies. The development of consistent policy in Wales reveals a huge potential for integrated, sustainable investment in socially relevant service delivery. Similarly, as the yardstick for tracking the progress of the Welsh Government in achieving its Public Health and well-being objectives is consistent with those of the WHO's own progress on these matters, common criteria might emerge for measurement and analysis. This consistency of policy has, therefore, made Wales a useful example for consideration in this study.

In England, by contrast, there is no such cohesion between policy and local administrative effort. Part of this is due to the relative scale and administrative distance between local and central government, but it is also due to the fragmentation of local authority approaches towards issues and problem-solving which have arisen. In 2008, the Department of Communities and Local Government (DCLG) – focusing solely on England – published a number of studies and polices that highlighted the importance that well-being has in the creation of the balanced society (DCLG, 2008a–g). It published a 'cross-government strategy for housing and communities, connecting housing, health and care' (DCLG, 2008a), which outlined their plans for reform towards guaranteeing an active ageing population through opening up opportunities within housing choice, and providing social support in order to realise housing's full potential as an underpinning service for well-being (DCLG, 2008c, p. 39).

The mental health of ageing people must be of prime concern (Dewe and Kompier, 2008), and the environment has to be nurtured to support people in their needs (Edwards, et al., 2008). Part of the task of generating well-being is to create a sense of ownership and control over all aspects of their lives (Dixon, 2008). This might extend towards taking control of the processes that give them support for the essentials of their lives. Kendall complains that: 'Too often lip service is paid to these issues' (Kendall, 2008, p. 45). Since 1991, the introduction of 'choice' and 'access' to public services have cast a particular bias towards the construction of policy by government. This came in with Prime Minister John Major's *Citizens' Charter* (Office of the Prime Minister, 1991, p. 49), and expanded in scope and significance ever since. Elbourne, acting for the Department of Pensions, and citing the Audit Commission, for England, found that barely one-third of Local Authorities had any meaningful contact with their older people, but where they did have contact clear models of engagement emerged with beneficial effect (Elbourne, 2008, p. 4). This showed that there was a very mixed bag of performance between England's Local Authorities, despite the introduction of *Beacon Authority* incentive schemes, etc. Elbourne's specific role was to explore the effectiveness of the *Better Government for Older People* initiative that had started in 1998. Harvey's study for the *King's Fund* found that there was a wide diversity of collaborative service model being employed by different Authorities in compliance with Health and Social Care policies, but that some positive reshaping of commissioning, monitoring and the setting of outcomes was urgently needed (Harvey, 2008). The Government's response to Elbourne (Department of Work and Pensions, 2009) was accepting of all points made, but lacked any clear statement of direction other than to reinforce existing measures and processes of consultation with older people.

Up to the end of 2012, the cumulative effect of policy formation in Wales for the support of older people in the community hinged on the Government's ability to provide a consistency of message to local government, the NHS, Voluntary Sector, and the community at large, and to push for its implementation across the board. The Welsh Government had certainly provided the policy framework, since 1999, building on the priorities of the Welsh Office's *Better Health Better Wales* (Welsh Office, 1998a), and following on with the *Strategy for Older People in Wales* (WAG, 2003c). With the complementary policies on service delivery – *Making the Connections* (WAG, 2004a), and for joint-working with community input – the *Beecham Report – Beyond Boundaries* (WAG, 2006c), it would appear that all the necessary frameworks were in place. The appointment of the *Older People's Commissioner for Wales* (OPCforW) was the final piece in the network to ensure that all resources were focused and channelled to the appropriate targets.

There are a number of caveats to this scenario – whether or not the Welsh Government has the necessary ability to deliver its own policies on the ground; whether or not it has the will to do so; and what forces are aligned against it in achieving its objectives, and why. One positive feature of the literature (and certainly in practice in the devolved Wales scenario) is that there now seems to be a fresh spirit to co-operate with government, and, in partnerships, with business as well, across the whole approach to community development in Britain. It seems to have originated around the time that Barr and Hashagen (Barr and Hashagen, 2000) published their *ABCD* model of effective community development work. There was no talk of *'class'* or *'struggle'* in this model, and, within the literature, things all began to come into an acceptance mode. In Wales, this was very evident in the compilation of case studies of community development in south Wales (Clarke, et al., 2002b), where every example was of a project working in co-operation with the State schemes.

There is no doubting the Welsh Government's concern to create the necessary environment for the continuing support of its older citizens. The early introduction of the *'sustainability'* programme to span all Government Departments (WAG, 2004c) promised integrated government engagement, partnership, and community participation. This consolidated the *Local Health Alliances'* initiative taken in 1999 (NAforW, 1999). Unfortunately, despite the reinforcement given to the Welsh Government in its endeavours by the Local Government Act 2000, where the well-being of all citizens was to be actively promoted by local government, much of the Welsh Government's efforts to create a legislative framework for this process was slow to materialise (Audit Commission in Wales, 2004; Audit Committee, NAforW, 2008; Audit Committee WG, 2012).

The Audit Commission noted that local government was having ongoing difficulty in developing effective partnership arrangements that might produce material results for the benefit of its constituents. The Independent Commission on Social Services in Wales (ICSSW, 2010) confirmed that the economic recession was taking its toll on the gains that had been made over recent years in raising the profile of social care within government priorities. But the underlying message is still told of the urgent need to build into the system of social care some of the urgency that had been reported to the WAG in 2003, with the publication of the *Wanless Report* (WAG, 2003d). Public statistics still reflected the unfortunate facts that Wales was an unhealthy place to live for older people, and that unless restructuring of public services took place to reduce the burden on shrinking government finances, the system would become unsustainable (Kenway and Palmer, 2007; ICSSW, 2010; OPCforW, 2010b; WG, 2012f).

One of the clearest areas of social need arises out of the situation of older people in Wales. Here, the demography and disposition of older people necessitated the creation of a focused agency, the *Older People's Commissioner for Wales* (OPCforW). It is not yet clear whether or not this structural innovation will deliver preventive or palliative solutions to the challenges ahead. With a rising population of older people, the *Strategy for Older People in Wales* (WAG, 2003c) certainly provides a mechanism that, combined with the role of the Commissioner, could produce dynamic pressure for change. Any development of this scenario must also consider that the older population in Wales is spread across many differing landscapes – urban, and rural. Below, a model that incorporates a positive strategy for the Commissioner is outlined.

A great deal of potential exists in Wales for the realisation of the social policy objectives in this area. Much of the preparation for structural change within service delivery has already been accomplished. In addition to the creation of the Older People's Commission, the appointment of a dedicated Minister in government for older people and the regeneration programme, *Communities First*, there has been a great deal of modelling along the lines of the *Healthy Living Centres* (Welsh Office, 1998d; Clarke, et al., 2002a; WAG, 2005b; Bridge Consortium, 2003, 2007; WAG, 2007b) and many community development projects and community-based community enterprises (Carlisle, et al., 2004). The work done in exploring the subject at the University of Glamorgan (Adamson, et al., 2001) has also identified the essence of good practice in this field, and the Welsh Government has established good relations with the community development workers' organisation, *Community Development Cymru*, which it continues to fund, albeit on a reduced scale.

We are dealing with a very complex issue in presuming, as we shall, to want to change the way in which a Government approaches the implementation of its own policies. Approaching a complex issue is fraught with difficulties, but then the whole question of development at any level is complex. It must be tackled. Jones (2011) identifies some of the issues that have to be faced, and facilitating governance and cultural change features high on his list. One of the main difficulties that an agent faces when attempting such a task is the problem of being enabled by employers, etc. to be flexible and to call upon resources to act out of their normal comfort zone or protocol (pp. 1–2). When the varied needs and ambitions of an ageing population are incorporated into this, a clear framework is needed and a powerful vision needs to be adopted by all participants. Nevertheless, not all the rules may apply ..., and so an understandable framework for its implementation must be devised.

Social innovation

In the Introduction, it was observed that, once the significance of what was being suggested sunk in, barriers might emerge to the adoption of new forms of planned social change. This would then result in failure or force compromises upon programme managers. One such compromise is the abandonment of the term 'community development' and the adoption of the term 'social innovation' in its place (Simon, et al., 2014). The result is a dilution of control over the setting of boundaries and the subsequent measurement of effectiveness of outcome (Clarke, 2004b). This has happened across the European Union in its efforts to promote innovation and co-operation in the delivery of effective social welfare practices between and within its member states (EU Directorate-General, 2013).

There have been attempts to document the efforts that try to link in with national programmes and projects, nationally (Gilchrist, 2012) and internationally (Dahl, et al., 2014). These studies identify the considerable range, but the regrettably small-scale nature of these innovative activities. There is also 'little interest in working on theory, choosing instead to frame the project around the problem(s)' that present at the time (EU Directorate-General, 2013, p. 23). Howaldt and Schwarz cite Roberts, of the *Guardian* (2008), on the 'uncertainty in international discourse' and the apparent 'obsession with social innovation' that has emerged (Howaldt and Schwarz, 2010, p. 7). They also maintain that, in this field, theories and ideas in vogue appear to have a shelf-life that is only as long as the technology that is being used to implement it (p. 5). For any success to be possible, there must be sufficient sensitivity to discover if there is a local cultural awareness of the need for change in the first place (p. 31). In outcome, there is an inevitable sloppiness over the definition of terms such as (the seemingly mandatory) 'user-centredness' of all 'innovation'. This enables the avoidance of setting firm parameters for achievement, or setting any demand for firm outcome expectations. Lessons could be learned from the conditions set for international AID projects, as described above. It also allows for the role of the professional *animateurs* to be obscured throughout the processes of 'innovation'. Fraisse (2009) insists that neighbourhoods and communities must not be blamed for their failure to respond to innovation or other benign interventions (p. 32). Overall, the problem is that no real attempt is made to establish a theory behind these strategies, nor to justify actions in terms of any established theory of social change. Pragmatism is in control (EU Directorate-General, 2009, pp. 26 *et seq.*). In keeping with the force of technological innovation, there is now a drive to accomplish social change through the application of tech-system-driven initiatives. This is exemplified by the EU Commission Joint Research Centre ITC-enabled social innovation initiative for the inclusion of young people. It can already report significant progress, but it must be recognised that these interventions are focused upon targeting service innovation and not service substitution (Cullen, et al., 2015). The net gain in terms of cost may be significant, but they are not eliminating the need for public expenditure and institutional oversight. Had a community development approach, aimed at the development of community-based infrastructure, been at the nub of these initiatives, completely different outcomes could have been recorded.

TEPSIE (a research project funded under the European Commission's 7th Framework Programme) seeks to justify this lack of firmness by insisting that targets such as 'social development' and 'social innovation' are shibboleths anyway as they are 'quasi-concepts' and unworthy of serious definition or measurement (TEPSIE, 2014, pp. 10–11). In a later Report, TEPSIE suggests that governments are unready for the work that is entailed in motivating, obtaining and activating citizen involvement (TEPSIE, 2015, p. 19). INNOSERV, a short-term EU research consortium into social services innovation, highlights the tensions that emerge when user-centredness and bureaucratic establishments meet face to face (Dahl, et al., 2014, p. 30). The study that they made into best current fieldwork practice in social innovation showed a remarkable diversity and spread of activity across twenty 'innovative practices' (p. 22). This revealed a multiplicity of work practices but it did not result in a firm, abstracted model for defining and directing 'progress' in this field. It is the weakness of 'social innovation' that professional leadership is pretty much denied, and that holistic and strategic analysis is absent. Much work must still be done, in the face of the pressing social and economic needs of nations, to get this approach to social innovation adopted as a priority (Hochgerner, 2014). The denial of the role of the professional, the lack of a strategic plan, the absence of a coherent model or theory behind the action are all reminiscent of Britain's Prime Ministerial *Big Society*, where the vagaries of spontaneous, voluntary action were going to somehow plug the gaps in the Welfare State.

The development of a systemic model for community development

The primary instrumental task of a community development worker is the building and sustaining of organisations. At the local level, this entails implementing the framework described by Barr and Hashagen in their *ABCD* model (Barr, and Hashagen, 2000), or, similarly, the framework of Henderson and Thomas (Henderson and Thomas, 1981; Henderson and Thomas, 2001). Put simply, this entails: entering a community, identifying issues of local concern, targeting local people who share a desire to solve these issues, and assisting and supporting them in organising local resources to deal with the issue. Sustaining the new organisations is the ongoing task of the worker, and assisting them to seek out new goals, etc. This responsibility extends, also, to the assessment of existing organisations in the community and assisting them to strengthen their situation, including organisational competence, and then 'guiding' them to develop a wider, general community interest for their activities. Building community-wide representative organisations follows from that, and all this has to be sustained over a considerable time period (Clarke, 1996a; Clarke, 2000). For older people, any social structure upon which they may later become dependent has to be set up in such a way that its sustainability can be ensured, and underwritten by its own inherent resources and characteristics (Clarke, 2004b; Clarke, 2006; Blake, et al., 2008).

We will consider here two templates for the construction of the model that will be required – with modifications: Rothman's three-level '*Approaches to community intervention*' (Rothman, 2001), and Plummer's '*Strategic framework*' for municipal capacity-building (Plummer, 1999). We have already considered the importance of these theorists above (Chapters 3 and 4) and we will describe how their frameworks combine, with modification, for the purpose we have: to provide a community development framework for the support of older people in the community. Rothman presented a number of major statements about how community organisation might best be analysed – into three 'modes'. The original framework (Rothman, 1970) was modified in 1995 (Rothman, 1995), to include a wider, international perspective, but the basics – *locality development, social planning* and *social action*, remained unchanged. Most recently, in 2008, a third revision to the model was made (Rothman, 2008). This was a more radical departure from the first two – breaking down the dimensions into a matrix across nine segments, divided across three main integral characteristics – *planning, capacity development* and *advocacy*. For closer, analytical purposes, this later analytical framework introduces nuances of difference between methods and value that are not strictly relevant for our purposes here, and so we have adopted the second model – Rothman, 1995. Notwithstanding this, Rothman's latest exposition is useful as a reference point.

Rothman's model first required a professional worker, and/or those who make social policy, to consider planned social change from the perspective of the local community (Locality), and then from the standpoint of the planner, in top-down mode (Social Planning). Rothman's third mode – *social action* – is omitted here because it entails producing a 'conflict' model of inducing change; something that is not, generally, compatible with stable governance (see Alinsky, Chapter 3 above). In our model, the professional is required either to acquire the necessary skills to operate at two levels/modes simultaneously, or to ensure that there is a team of other workers available and engaged to take on the second level of intervention.

It is necessary that this whole process is driven by policy, management frameworks and monitoring from the top-downwards. Only in this way can the process be resourced appropriately, the recruitment and training of staff be accomplished to the necessary levels, and lessons learned at each level by each 'mode' of functioning be fed into a combined learning institutional framework. The model adopted by the Welsh Government for the future governance of the *Communities First* programme is an appropriate one for this purpose, without the limiting factor of being confined to the areas of greatest social and economic need in the nation (WG, 2012b, d). At the local level, strong linkages between this policy framework and a local government *strategic planning partnerships* has already been proposed, using the *Local Service Boards* as the platform (WG, 2012f). The adoption of the framework for strategic planning, and the issuance of guidelines for implementation by the Welsh Local Government Association in 2013, ensured that, at least, there is a concerted orientation towards the outcomes that are desired (WLGA, 2013a, b). What remains now is for the presentation of a model to fit within this framework for the co-ordinated support of older people.

Building a local social development structure

Harding (1991) cites commentators on the USAID's Handbook on the *logical framework* for evaluation (Harding, 1991, pp. 295–7). How is a model for intervention selected, and how is it determined whether or not it has been successful? For evaluation, the problem of deciding between qualitative and quantitative indicators should be down to whether or not they can elicit verifiable results for the investment made. Some lend themselves more easily to describing process, and other outputs, but, in the end, the data from the qualitative indicators are all quantified, in order to make the assessment (p. 299). In the end, it is the final outcome of the project that is important, but data must be assembled to assess the project's achievements. The adoption of an intervention framework may be more problematic.

Although community development presupposes that it, itself, is an intervention strategy envisaged and implemented from the top-down in society, it is necessary to prepare intellectually for a bottom-up structure, because it is the stakeholders in the community who are the most vital ingredient of the mechanism that will bring about lasting change. The writings of A. K. Rice and Eric Miller, of the Tavistock Institute put the social applications of *systems theory* on the agenda for community development. In their 1967 work, *Systems of Organisation* (Miller and Rice, 1967), they make it plain that it is the quality of boundaries around a task-oriented organisation that determines the capacity of that organisation to carry out its tasks.

They distinguish between *sentient* and *task* systems. *Sentient* systems are those that attract loyalty from its members/participants, and *task* systems are focused upon the goal or objective as an end in itself. The type of organisation created will reflect on the nature of the activity undertaken – *task-centred* systems will be more outcome-focused, but may suffer from internal frictions, and loss of momentum unless 'motivated' by some form of external control. *Sentient* systems, however, which may start off highly focused and motivated, may erode quickly, unless buoyed up by incentives (Miller and Rice, 1990). Some sort of compromise must be made if the system we will describe is to work. A task-oriented group, which demands the loyalty and creative input of its members on an ongoing basis, has to be motivated and guided. Methods for conceptualising these ideas can be expressed visually.

The micro-structure

The principles of assessing the community development process are built up progressively through the examination of each and every organisation with which the professional has contact. The process of developing such a structure, which will deliver planned social change, beginning at the grassroots of society, can be represented diagrammatically. The primary formation needed is the simple organisation, at the local level. McKnight and Block stress that the importance and strength of local communities, if organised around self-interest issues and pastimes, cannot only provide solutions to problems for their communities, but also contribute greatly to general well-being and community identity (McKnight and Block, 2012). Drawing on the framework presented by Miller and Rice, a diagrammatic representation of the task may readily be seen in Figure 2.

In the diagram, the crucial organisational boundaries are defended by the Management function, which also has the task of delegating tasks within the system. The control of inputs and outputs of the system completes the cycle. The quality of the system depends on the nature of the *participation* of its members, which are discussed below. Because all effective models of social intervention require that monitoring and evaluation systems be instituted, on this micro-scale of organisational development, just what is happening will rapidly become clear to the professionals engaged on the ground, the external administrators, managers, or funders. It is the task of the community development worker, at the level of the *'locality'* (Rothman, 1995, p. 37 *et seq.*), to build viable organisations at the grass-roots level. This may be done selectively, according to the worker's priority briefing, or on an any-organisation-is-a-good-organisation basis. This process would then be repeated across communities in a strategic intervention area, which would have been targeted in advance.

To get to this position, the community development worker has to target a specific aggregate of people within the chosen sector of the community (a geographical area, young mothers, people with specific disabilities, an age group, etc.). This is done from data gleaned from a community profile of the area of work, or from some earlier selection process (including self-selection) (Hawtin, et al., 1994). The objective is to move the perceptions, increase the motivation and develop a sense of achievement of a non-connected aggregate of people, through

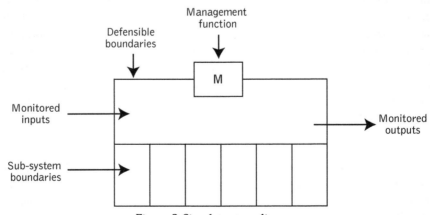

Figure 2 Simple system diagram

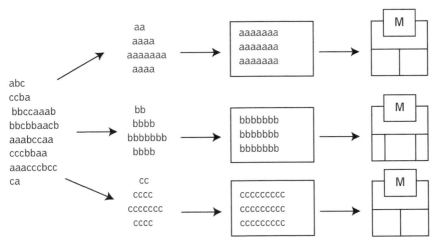

Figure 3: Creating a simple community organisation

a group-formation stage, and into a viable small organisation. This is demonstrated in Figure 3. The development task is to identify leadership within each interest group, 'a', 'b', 'c', etc., support them in instigating activity, assisting them to have successful experiences and fortify the resolve to recruit, expand and maintain activities. Setting up business-like structure for each and every one of these micro-organisations will reinforce their capacities and achievements (Henderson and Thomas, 2001; Clarke, 2000).

An essential component of the development process depends on the quality of the participation experienced by the people involved. The stable community is the well-organised community, and Rothman's Mode A model strives towards broadening the organisational base of a community as far as is possible. Much of the research centres on a narrow subject universe, for example: when the project target is a specific group, such as 'older people', meaning just working on/with the 'older people'. Evidence supports the need to cast the net wider, and to study the quality of interaction between the older segment of the population and the wider community.

Schmitz (et al., 2012) examined the attitudes of older people (using neighbourhood centres) towards neighbourhood, and found that it correlated very positively with reduced hypertension, and their interest in maintaining good health. This supports the findings of Reed, et al. (2004), who found that older people were much more likely to engage in spontaneous social activities the more they were engaged in other social activities. The Joseph Rowntree Foundation study of the same year examined most aspects of older people's social and residential lives. It found that older people valued their participation and also welcomed support and assistance in maintaining all their social connections. These connections covered a wide variety of outlet opportunities, and these were only restricted when the person's own individual capabilities failed, or when the support system failed them (Godfrey, et al., 2004). Osmond agrees, citing beneficial lifestyle changes, especially outward-going activities, but he states that official/governmental structures are especially bad at developing these options (Osmond, 2010).

Stevenson reflects on the powerful forces that assail older people who try and remain engaged in social and other activities. Ageism, sexism and increasing personal frailty are all factors that, if not recognised and countered, can result in a falling off of social interaction, thus increasing dependence and isolation. The diversion of people from oppressive situations is a powerful mechanism for raising well-being, but there is continuing pressure against it working (Stevenson, 1996; Taylor, 2012). Cooke, on the other hand, whilst recognising what can go wrong in groups, describes how easy it can be to sustain group focus and morale, if the task is properly managed (Cooke, 2001). Oakley (1990) opens up the discussion about *quality* vs. *quantity* in the debate about project outputs and evaluation requirements. Marsden (1994) poses the dilemma for the professional development agent. The closer that an outsider gets to understanding the local culture, the closer that person gets to being 'sucked in' as an 'insider', and loses objectivity. But the objective of getting close to the culture (and the population) is so that one can take full advantage of local resources, local knowledge and local leadership for the delivery of the project. 'This is a political step' (p. 52), but the ultimate reality of politics in this situation is that intervention, as a matter of policy, has to move ahead. Mosse asserts that professional workers are not passive agents of their employers, nor of the communities they serve. Instead, they should be careful not to confuse their 'mission' with the true needs of the community. Seeking out, and being sensitive to, local knowledge, *and participation, learning and planning* will ensure that the local culture is infused into a scheme for maximum benefit to all (Mosse, 2001, p. 17). Nevertheless, those running a project are acting at the behest of their sponsors, and participation might just be seen as window-dressing by the sponsors, in order to satisfy their desire to be *post-colonialist* (p. 33).

Richards accuses the advocates of *local knowledge* of being *anthropological romantics* (Richards, 1993, p. 62). This could be a limited, myopic approach to problem-solving, he claims. The donor/investor in project development strategies is seeking a practical, usually a material, outcome that will serve the long-term needs of the community and the administration together. Richards invokes Giddens (the inspiration of New Labour's *The Third Way* slogan of 1979), who advocated a combination of agency, structure and power orientations. This blends Marxist social science, structural functionalism and anthropology to assist in bringing in all the necessary ingredients for the social processes to work — people's action, administrative control and measurable outcome (p. 71). On one level, this would appear to be an opportunity for *'co-production'* ventures to be built up (Stephens, et al., 2006).

There are still challenges to be faced by those intent on implementing policies that require cultural change. The major barrier seems to be the reluctance of institutional power bases to relinquish their power and their freedom of self-determination. Cemlyn describes how, despite government support and investment inducements, local authority resistance to change and to outside intervention proved to be a significant barrier to real change (Cemlyn, et al., 2005). These findings have been reported continuously by the Welsh Audit Commission when commenting on the ability of local partnerships to overcome these barriers (Auditor General for Wales, 2005; Auditor General for Wales, 2009; Adamson and Bromiley, 2008). This study of community development will show that it is just that the correct model has not been applied to the process of ensuring sustainability in the development process.

Meso-structure

Having grasped the essentials of the micro-structure for organisational development, the professional will now extend the model into a wider context – into a locality development strategy of the local community. Once additional micro-systems (community groups, old or/and new) have been targeted by the worker, and they can be, or are already, engaged in working for their own specific objectives, the task of the worker is to widen the scope and interests of these groups to embrace wider issues of general community concern. Some of this can be done by extending the interests of each group – for example, to widen their capacities and to broaden their membership to embrace new segments of the population (e.g. vulnerable members of the community). This cannot always be achieved, or not to the extent that might meet the wider community's needs in any social issue (i.e. the support of older people), but this is an ongoing task. *Non-directive* leadership has been a constant component of community development (Biddle, W. and Biddle, L., 1965; Batten, T. and Batten, M., 1967).

There are many community interests or issues that individual groups either do not have the capacity for, or of which they are unaware of the need to address them. There are, for example, issues that concern the whole area, but are not the specific responsibility or direct interest of any group (e.g. the decline of the physical environment). The majority of these issues get referred to local authority, etc., on an individual basis, having no organised (read *powerful*) representative to ensure that the matter is considered formally by an authority empowered to react to it. A new kind of organisational structure is needed; one that is charged with making these issues its primary task. The community development task in this instance is to create the conditions within each (community) constituent group such that they see the relevance of this new kind of organisation. If enough groups are willing to establish a new problem-solving mechanism, a new organisation for this task, then this should be established, using representatives from the existing groups as its membership. The professional's task is to see it established, and then to 'manage' (non-directively) this new organisation to make itself representative of the wider community's wishes, needs and vision of itself. Each extant, constituent organisation, and the new, representative organisation must have a clear target responsibility, boundary integrity, proper management capability, its own resources, and a sustainable structure. The consolidation of all groups and the linking of them to this common agenda represents the community development task at this level. The key to success of any organisation is that it must have ownership, agency and resources. This is as much true for the higher-level organisations as it is for those at the grassroots workface of social interest.

The new organisation has a reciprocal relationship with the wider community, and with the constituent groups, all of which have representation on the new body. In the short term, the new body is likely to be financially dependent on the constituents, which will have to bankroll it from the start. What is likely to happen is that the new organisation is then poised to assume more power than was ever possible for the smaller constituent organisations, and become the arbiter of community outlook, policy-maker and driver of fresh activities within which the smaller organisations can participate (e.g. community festivals, campaigns, etc.). The community development worker can/will assist this organisation to assume this mantel on behalf of the whole community and to consolidate the reciprocal relationship upon which its credibility rests (see Figure 4).

A secondary function of the community development worker in this situation is to sustain (ensuring succession) the management quality at all levels, and to ensure that the constituent pool from which the new organisation gets its authority is fed by a widening number of new (or older, non-member) organisations from the community at large (Figure 4).

This process is discussed extensively in Clarke, 2000 (see also Miller and Rice, 1967; Miller, 2011). If this structure can be replicated across the whole

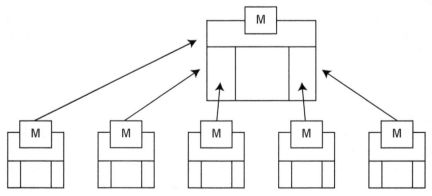

Figure 4: Representative community organisation: representational task delegated to new organisation

area for which an authority is the agency of governance, then it will constitute a *'Community Sector'*, with which it can work constructively for the solution of wider social issues.

The focus for community workers in this situation, for example, working under the auspices of a National strategy such as the *Strategy for Older People in Wales* (WAG, 2003c), would be to bring about the maximum support for older people in the community and to enhance their well-being. As a community becomes 'organised' in this way, their social capital will be enhanced, and their own life skills increased through their engagement in community life in the widest sense. This can be done through a combination of creating new organisations for older people out of their own sector-focused activities, or through integrating the older people into wider community resources. All participating individuals find that their interests are broadened and consolidated. By encouraging the older segment of the community to engage in wider social activities for themselves, and to join other organisations, inter-generational understanding is developed. Next, comes the focusing of all social groupings within the community at large on the needs of older people (and other vulnerable groups) in their particular community. The objective will be for the creation, eventually, of new organisations within the community that will act to provide direct support for older people, etc., on a sustainable, organised, reliable (thus semi-controlled) basis.

How this process fits into the wider strategy of the local authority is developed in the next stage of the model, below. Creating a network of older people's organisations will raise the whole profile of ageing, etc., across the wider community, and it will also strengthen the role of older people, for example, within other organisations of a more secular persuasion. The community at large thus becomes more self-aware and capable in dealing with issues across the board. The sense of purposeful structure across the whole community will permeate the lives of all citizens and further enhance the sense of identity and social capital. Focusing them on these tasks becomes the next phase of the community development worker's responsibility. We might call this new structural approach to community organisation: *community social planning.*

The macro-structure

As we discover every day, the problem for policy-makers is that the more that fiscal policies, brought on by the economic recession, undermine the tax base and public spending power, the more the spending capacity of government is restricted. The ability to provide services on a universal basis via the public purse is the first to suffer. Thus, this ideal becomes less and less viable. It then becomes all the more urgent to find an alternative way of doing things that does not place an escalating burden on public funds. There is also an open question as to whether or not the public provision of services is the best way to satisfy the wishes and needs of the population. Hitherto, we have had only a one-dimensional model to choose from – public services, or nothing (except for those able to pay for individual services). There has to be another way forward, so that the contraction of essential services in the NHS and welfare systems can continue to tackle critical need, without being forced out altogether (Wanless, 2002; WAG, 2003d; also WHO, 1997a).

The micro- and meso-structures (*community social* planning) outlined above will enable the community to begin to tackle the issues from a local perspective. This was usually the limit of most local government or voluntary sector community intervention vision – 'get the local community organised' sums it up – play schemes, activity groups, Health and Safety forums, etc. This can usefully be termed *'community work'* – palliative or therapeutic organisation, capable of little significant social change in itself (Arnstein, 1968). In the current economic and care crisis, local strategists are grappling with the issues raised by policy – how to effect the integration of the 'community' into planning and delivery of public services (WHO, 1997a, b, c; OPCforW, 2010a, c; Public Finance Committee, 2012; WG, 2012b). A more creative and far-reaching model is required, one which brings a measurable pay-back for the authority in terms of savings and more sensitive service delivery. This is evident from the mixed findings of the Local Government Association (England) when investigating the effects of recession on their capacity to deliver services. Austerity was a setback but they report that working together is still an issue to be perfected due to competition and uncertainty of jurisdiction (Local Government Association, 2015, pp. 38–41).

It must be borne in mind that the positive side of meso-structure development, with the adoption of this extended model of intervention, is that the community will have become empowered to handle many of the situations that confront it and the authority. Hitherto, the local authority would have been the first port of call for these minor, problem-solving activities. Small organisations will come to do things better for themselves, and members of these groups, with representatives on the meso-structure, representative organisations, will now have a reference point for social action, and engagement on wider issues. General members of the community will also have a point of reference, and will feel their community enhanced by that activity. The knock-on effect of this is enhanced *social capital*, or network awareness, within a community (Dasgupta and Serageldin, 2000; Field, 2003), and enhanced well-being (WAG, 2009d; WG, 2011d; Age Cymru, 2011; Thomas, 2012; WG, 2012e; WLGA, 2012). The next step is to get a new, focused strategic partnership constituted and up and working. This will enable the combined resources within an authority area to begin to solve problems on the part of the whole community, and to seek the most beneficial outcomes for local issues. In Wales, such a strategic partnership is the Local Service Board, which creates and administers the structure we are describing here – the *Single Integrated Plan* (SIP) (WG, 2012c; WG, 2015).

The model that will be described below will meet most of the criteria required to fulfil the needs of the SIP. For this, in the first instance, we need to call in the model presented by Plummer (Plummer, 1999), which is itself a modification of the *social planning* model presented by Rothman (2001). A detailed, holistic assessment has to be made of the field covered by a social issue. This is made by the administrative organisation – in Plummer's case, the *'Municipality'* or local authority. This assessment considers the capacity of the 'municipality', itself, to make the shift from service-delivery-style social administration to 'participatory' social planning, with 'people and communities at the heart of planning and delivery' (WG, 2011c). In Wales, the local authority is the lead authority in LSBs (WAG, 2008a).

Plummer describes the 'municipality's' task as making four separate appraisals in order to assess the issues before it. The first step is to acquire realistic knowledge of the forces at work in society, which may hamper or enhance the work to be done – the politics, the economic forces, the prevailing culture in the area, etc. The active engagement with political dynamics is not something that government officials do happily, but it has to be done. Advanced warning of possible hurdles and friction points are best anticipated before they become obstacles. The SWOT analysis is particularly useful here (Foo and Grinyer, 1995).

Plummer (Figure 5) seeks to make major changes in the capacity of the authority to come to grips with the process of engagement. This means that change has to start from within, and is not just foisting change and pressure by using outside force. If the internal capacities and the vehicles of change that could be brought out at the community level are not established, then the process will not work. Change does not, however, come about without leadership and will. The authority must wish to implement the policies of the Government on the vital issue of continuing and sustainable support for older people in the community, and it must be sure of its reasons for doing so. Selling it to a wider audience, an audience of stakeholders and contributing participants, is not going to be straightforward. The current expectations are still that the State will provide as a last resort. Plummer (Plummer, 2002) makes this point clearly when emphasising that the success and failure of this process starts and ends with the vision, management, internal structures, finances, and, above all, attitudes of the authority. To this must be added the skill, authority and motivation of the professional community development workers who must drive the process (p. 281).

Professional organisers within the authority have to be empowered to promote and monitor the necessary organisational changes. First, they will have to scrutinise Plummer's model (1999 – see Figure 5), and review the capabilities of the authority to adapt itself to the changes in service delivery that will have to take place. If it is to engage in community and other sector participation in the processes of local government, this will entail assessment, training, and experiments in extension of public service into the community. Internal management structures will have to be reshaped to accommodate these changes, and a strategy compatible with the authority's internal needs for addressing outside interests, culture and capabilities will have to be established. How does the authority wish to deal with outside agencies within its own structured procedures?

There will be many points of resistance (see CDP example in Chapter 4 above), as neither officials nor elected representatives will be anxious, in practice, to give up their authority, or to leave their established comfort zones (Parsons, 1947; Handy, 1988; 1990). In one case study, where there was a desire to focus the community on this process, the Chief Executive and the Executive team of the Council's Chief Officers fully accepted the concept of detailed agency planning, and full community involvement in its execution. They then found that the elected representatives threw the whole thing out without any discussion. The councillors claimed that the whole approach was hostile to their role as elected members (Clarke, 1996b). In this case there was no model in place, which would have ensured that the internal workings of the Council were prepared and receptive to the process. Additionally, there were no trained officials who had any competence in managing the changes that would have been required, and no prior warning had been given to the elected members, or their support solicited. The freshly instituted Cabinet system of Council leadership instituted in some authorities may provide a false illusion that highly centralised decision-making is all that is needed to change policy and direction.

Figure 5 contains tasks and abstractions, many of which have to be absorbed into the culture of the authority before work proper can begin. The professional, *social planner*, can assist directly by interpreting the implications of community participation, assisting the authority's divisions in establishing appropriate boundaries for the new circumstances, and assisting them to devise strategies for their own to feed into the new model for integrating the micro- and meso-structures into the partnership framework. Once the authority has come to grips with the necessary internal changes it has to make, it can concern itself with the way through which it is going to engage the wider community in its activities. The structure and the policy frameworks are already in place through the strategic partnership (LSB) mechanisms, but the authority has to decide how it is going to go about power-sharing with the new partnership structure.

For the professional worker, the *social planning* function (Rothman, 1995, p. 43 *et seq.*) within the municipality/authority is a continuous one in order that the strategic developments can be kept under scrutiny. Only in this way can the correct applications made by, first, the authority, and then by all the other institutional agencies. Communication, liaison, diplomatic intervention on behalf of all interests, and pressurising the leadership of participating agencies towards a common focus is the extension of the *social planning* role (see below).

In Wales, for example, it is the desire of the Government that the community-at-large play a full part in the planning and delivery of services — *mainstreaming*

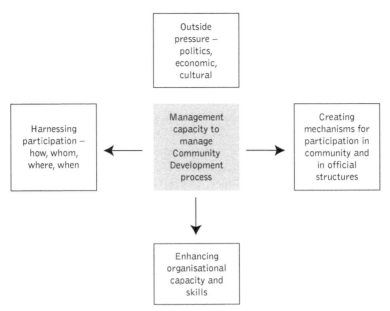

Figure 5: The capacity of the authority to implement community development strategies

the ageing agenda as outlined in the Older People's Strategy (WG, 2011a, p. 11). This means, at least, that costs of some of the process are going to have to be borne by the authority, in the first instance. Plummer shows that, for instance, the Private Sector is not experienced in engaging in joint activities, especially if it is expected to provide resources. The Public Sector has been a *milch cow* for the Private Sector in the normal run of events (Plummer, 2002, pp. 29 and 31). The same could be said of the Voluntary Sector, which, since the Thatcher reforms of the 2000s, had become a contracted provider of many services (Depts of Health, etc., 1989). The best way to establish this new way of working with all parties is for the existing strategic partnership organisation (LSB) to create a new organisation – a problem-solving, work accountable, cost centre for the LSB, with a specified plan of its own. It will comprise members of all the participating agencies, as deemed to be relevant, but this structure will also connect directly with local communities through their representation created through the meso-structures (above).

The next step for the authority is to begin linking these changes with outside sectors. Again, it is the task of the community worker (*social planner*), backed by the influence of senior officials, to effect this process. Much of the ground work at the community level has already been done, with a new, organised *Community Sector* having been prepared and rehearsed by community development workers in the community (see Figures 3 and 4). Bringing the voluntary sector on stream, in all its dimensions, and bringing in the private sector will become a focused task for a specialist worker – another *social planner* (Rothman, 2001). This will probably have to be done through forms of representational bodies. Miller warns that institutional change can bring about a greater level of centralist control, which is the last image that this process wished to introduce (Miller and Rice, 1967). The more there is differentiation between agencies in terms of power or resources, the more difficult it will be to off-set this tendency (Resnick and Patti, 1980). Nevertheless, the authority **is** going to want to control the nature and the direction in change in and outside the community, and so this is a sensitive and delicate path that must be followed (Ziglio, et al., 2000; Home Office, 2001; Barr, 2005; Mansuri and Rao, 2013). The extant model is for programmes and resource workers to be parachuted in without warning or consultation.

Patently, this will no longer suffice. The stakes are far too high, and the whole concept of sustainability has now been introduced and the basic formulas worked out in some detail.

In Figure 6, the diverse yet focused task of the community development process can be clearly seen. Micro-level, meso-level and macro-level workers combine to produce a problem-solving formula for tackling wider social issues of concern to both the community level of society, but also to the agencies responsible for managing them. A central, strategic organisation, organisation 'A' is going to assume considerable power within the wider community, and also become a reference point for the authority, and the co-operating sectors – Private, Voluntary and Community Sectors. The representation of each 'sector' will have to be negotiated, and a proliferation of '*representative organisations*' should be resisted. Levels of representivity can be worked out, as part of the work of the Strategic Partnership itself, with assistance from the professional support workers (*social planners*). The main task, overall, is the consolidation of effort and focus, over a long time-scale of the maximum amount of human, material and financial resource on the main issue – in this case, older people. Because of the potential for this model to involve community and institutional engagement across a wide spectrum, this effort and focus can be direct or indirect.

In this study, we are concerned with the outcome of the implementation of social policies on the fortunes of a specific group in society – older people. Once the lead Authority in the Local Service Board and the *Single Integrated Plan* become focused on the needs of older people, no resource that can contribute to their support, well-being and enhancement of their lives would be left out of the frame. The *social planner* would see to that. At the moment, public and contracted services are concentrated on the narrowest of interpretations of what constitutes 'a service', and what their purpose is – a problem-solving approach (Figure 6), with a full mandate to seek lasting solutions to the issues besetting our older community would choose a different route, and would require completely different work patterns and communications.

This is a model that worked well in Caerphilly, South Wales, for the short time that it was operational under the WHO *Verona Initiative* (Watson, 1999;

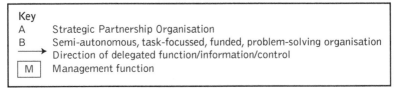

Key
A   Strategic Partnership Organisation
B   Semi-autonomous, task-focussed, funded, problem-solving organisation
———▶ Direction of delegated function/information/control
[M]   Management function

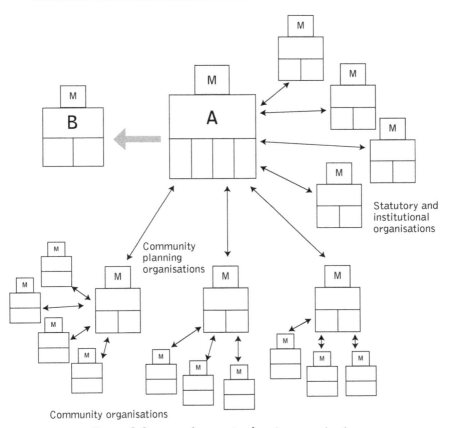

Figure 6: Integrated strategic planning organisation

Perry and Markwell, 2000; Watson, et al., 2001). However, the planning team within the lead authority was too shallow to survive changes in personnel, and the focus of the authority moved elsewhere. This highlights the necessity of in-depth preparation for such a sea change in outlook and practice by authorities. The failure occurred, partly, because the participating agencies were not prepared for failure – no 'Plan B'. Where responsibility for the sustainability of this organisational process is vested in individuals who, themselves, are not properly trained or strategically situated in the right roles within the administrative/managerial structure, then minor upsets of a diplomatic nature between participating agencies or indecision by the key players can bring the whole edifice down. In this instance, the WHO, itself, did not do enough to ensure that the *Verona Initiative* participating agencies were properly supported.

So far, we have worked along the lines that a consensus model is the only one that might be acceptable to work within a local authority. Is there a place for a *'conflict model'* to be introduced? Certainly, there is a very strong case for any professional worker to be fully aware of the theory and practice of the conflict approach. Conflict, modified according to the circumstances, can be a useful and powerful tool for the achievement of objectives. Alinsky was the past-master of managing brinkmanship, as community organisations and authorities were brought by him to the edge of communication breakdown before a final showdown (Alinsky, 1969). The exercise of naked power between unequal partners either has to be masked, or conventions agreed for its suspension. Often, as Alinsky showed, the underdog has the advantage as they are not inhibited by convention in the same way as legally bound institutions.

No authority can operate outwith its statutory powers, but often these are not explained fully to other participants and it takes a crisis to reveal how far these powers extend, or do not extend. In building an organisation whose function is to co-operate with an authority, advanced transparency would be a good practice model to follow. The authority will be aware that what it is planning through the implementation of this model will forever change its relations with the community (and other sectors), but it has no real option but to go ahead with it. Last minute (political – e.g. reneging on an agreement) manoeuvring would have to be ruled out. Uphoff examines Weber's analysis of power, and his concept of *'probability'* – that power will be exercised *'unless...'* (Uphoff, 2005, p. 221). He goes on to demonstrate through the presentation of case material, that the sharing of power – *empowerment* – can be beneficial for all parties in the social change context (pp. 239–42). Participants will exercise their power throughout any 'partnership' process and each participant will have their own priorities, which they will want to achieve. The community development social planner has to be able to ensure that the manipulation of power does not corrupt nor stifle this enterprise. Recognising *'brinkmanship'* and dealing with it diplomatically is a vital community development skill.

Interestingly, it is the notions of power and of 'conflict' that introduce the professional to the ethos of the 'business model'. Once 'problem-solving', cost-centre accountability, impact assessment, sustainability and regular evaluation are built into the formal structure of a project/programme, the new system cannot operate on unclear objectives, methods, expectations, or, even, sanctions if it fails. It is for these reasons that the spirit of the *New Public Health* model of participative, empowered, community delivered, social support systems has to adopt an entrepreneurial outlook and framework. Effective management will have to be grounded in financial reality, and the level of State resource input will necessarily be limited.

Wanless (WAG, 2003d) demonstrated how the State's finances cannot support peripheral services, particularly those in the community, as only the acute services demand priority for resourcing. Weaning the community off the State's *'welfare state'* stipend is a major and vital step to be taken. Community development is the art of garnering and mobilising resources outwith the State; to provide alternative resources, new resources, resources over which the State has only marginal control. The business model is the only one that might enable this development to aim to subscribe to self-sufficiency, sustainability and autonomy for this purpose.

Effective management is of the essence for the business model. The community development professional is going to be responsible for ensuring that the management of groups and organisations at all levels in the emergent structure is competent. Management will have to be versed in the vision of the enterprise, and have a firm grasp of the importance of the activity. The social planning community development worker must have this situation under constant monitoring, and this is as an ongoing, non-project, time-scale.

Accountancy texts, instead of Marx, or even Weber, will have to become the reference books for the *social planner*. Reading the *Financial Times* instead of *The Guardian* may re-orient the professional mind-set. The systems analysis approach is a great assistance in achieving this outlook (Pratt, et al., 1999). It must be remembered that the social planner is not going to be the instrumental 'manager' in this complex system of social change. The social planner role will be of being the constant 'adviser' to management. For this reason, the social planner has to be a better manager than the managers themselves, but they must not become aware of this. The Cabinet Office have sponsored a *Guide to the Social Return on Investment: an encouragement for regular business to invest in socially-beneficial projects as a part of their normal business strategy* (Nicholls, et al., 2012). This guide spells out the philosophy of the kind of entrepreneurial outlook our social planning partnerships might produce – a low social-cost enterprise, which is in surplus, but viable in the market place.

There is a complementarity between the model espoused by Alinsky and what is proposed here. Alinsky was under no illusions about what forces were up against the struggling, minority movements he supported. Nevertheless, he instilled in them the necessary resolution to overcome their opposition, and many of the 'enterprises' he assisted into being survived over many decades: e.g. ACORN (Brooks, 2002; Atlas, 2010); San Antonio (Warren, 2001; Vazquez, 2005); California – United Farm Workers (Ferriss and Sandoval, 1997; Thompson, 2005). This was social action in the market place of democracy. The parameters of the logical framework of evaluation stand up in this context, with the modifications we suggest. One great test for this model is whether or not 'social democracy' can stand the stress of power-sharing.

In acknowledgement of the role that the authority has to play in this process, it must be recognised that the bureaucracy will have a role as well. Nevertheless, this has to be reduced to the absolute minimum, and a semi-detached status for these new structures will have to be negotiated. Unless this new approach to community intervention, power-sharing, and results-dependent empowerment is recognised correctly, then it cannot work. It has to work for the reasons described as the conditions laid out by the WHO, the Wanless Report, and the Welsh Government. The professionals responsible for the execution of this policy need to be assured that their enterprise is grounded on a firm foundation. A business model would provide such a basis.

The final model that would meet all the needs of a preventive and supportive system for older people in the community would look like this:

Policy level

The WHO's (Regional) policy document *'Investment for Health'* (2000) puts it like this: 'Investment aimed at health and wellbeing also brings social and economic benefits for the whole community. A healthier population is a more productive population, and requires less support from the public services. [It] ... identifies investments that can improve health by attacking the causes of ill-health' (WHO Europe, 2000a, pp. 2–3). In the case of Wales, its Government could revise its policies regarding the *Older People's Strategy*, such that the Old People's Commission would have to adopt an interventionist role. This would be especially relevant at the level of Strategic Partnership in Local Service Board areas. This intervention and managerial oversight could provide oversight into the preparedness and capacity of local authorities and Public Health agencies to implement their own *Investment for Health* framework for the support of older people in the community. The Older People's Commissioner for Wales could be the consultative guide for all local authority and Health Board area to implement their own *Verona Initiative*. In other words, the Older People's Commissioner would translate itself into a social planning agency, in addition to its protective function for older people.

The Commission would also have a monitoring role regarding the implementation of local strategic initiatives and underwrite the Health aspects of social planning. *Investment for Health* is a sustainable community development model, embracing both social planning and locality community development (Ashish, 2000; Ziglio, et al., 2000; WHO Europe, 2000b). The Commissioner could be given the statutory authority to call in all the enabling policies already in place. The full range of proposals already exist in the 'Older People's Strategy' (WAG, 2003c), the sustainability agenda (WAG, 2003a; WAG, 2004b, c); well-being for the communities (Local Government Act 2000; WAG, 2003e); The *Beecham Report* – citizen engagement (WAG, 2006a, c); health alliances (NAforW, 1999); healthy ageing (WAG, 2005a); etc.

The creation of an enabling agency for public policy would be a necessity if a programme of this importance were to work. The Commissioner's target for implementation would be the Local Service Board, but working in liaison with the local authority and all the other participating sectors.

Implementation level: a policy framework for the Older People's Commission

The Commission would provide assistance to the Local Service Board, and local authorities, to prepare a strategic approach towards *Investment for Health* and the delivery of a *social planning* approach to service planning and delivery for older people. The local strategic objectives would be established for the prevention of older people becoming dependent on the services of the State, except as a last resort. Preventive work would entail: introducing the communities into the service planning process (Partnerships) as equity-holding stakeholders, and for the delivery of support services.

Within each Local Service Board Area Team:

- an older-people-centred, problem-solving organisation would be created (an organisation 'B' in Figure 6);
- this would have a delegated budget, an action plan, and developmental object-ives specified;
- planning and monitoring the deployment of social planning (community development) staff for the implementation of local development;

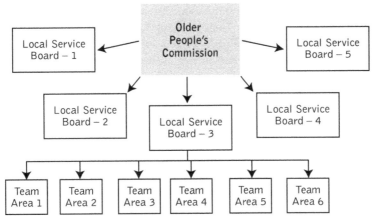

Figure 7: The Older People's Commission for Wales, and its relationship with Local Health Boards, etc.

- through this organisation, the LSB would be responsible for monitoring and evaluating localised development programmes;
- localised development would entail creating new and strengthening existing organisations for the community support of older people, and for increasing the profile of older people within existing networks;
- an establishment of trained and suitably deployed community development professionals would be made available to facilitate and support this process through tapping into local communities, and the local organisation and the institutions of the State at the local level.

Community development support work is required for all these function levels – at the social planning level, and at the community level. At the agency level, community development support and motivation is required to assist agencies to engage in cost-sharing, joint planning and staff re-orientation towards this process. At the community level, the community development task is the ongoing mobilisation of community organisations for locality problem-solving activities on a sustainable basis, and the engagement of these (and existing organisations) in representative participation as stakeholders in the social planning structures created for the purpose by the local authority. Enhancing the community's focus onto, and the integration of older people into, community life is the 'health' objective of the exercise.

The Welsh Government's Well-being of Future Generations (Wales) Act 2015 spells out the Government's commitment to the implementation of the Sustainability and Public Health aspirations of recent policy enactments. By sustainability it means that local government must seek 'to ensure that the needs of the present are met without compromising the ability of future generations to meet their own needs' (Part 2, Section 5). There will be come resistance to this as Local Government in Wales is hostile to the incursion of Central Government's consultation on its 'Sustainable Development Working Paper in 2012 (WG, 2012e; WG, 2013; WLGA, 2013b). The 'Well-being Act' contains no reference to community development, but pays great attention to collective planning, for which specialist skills of leadership and enablement will be required. It will be a test of resolve for all concerned whether or not their hopes for sustainability are to be realised.

Evaluation

One of the clearest of these evaluation processes is that described by the HM Government Overseas Development Administration (ODA) (now Department for International Development (DfID)). ODA/DfID has a long history of monitoring and evaluating overseas development programmes, and individual projects (Marsden and Oakley, 1990; Marsden and Oakley, 1991; ODA, 1995; Cracknell, 2000). ODA adopted the USAid model developed by Rosenberg in

1970 (Rosenberg, et al., 1970). This monitoring and evaluation framework won world-wide acceptance across the economic and social development arena, but mostly in the context of developing economies (Cracknell, 2000).

This method of measurement has some serious critics – namely because the parameters for measurement can often be set by powerful donors, or local political or administrative staff, who have their own sense of priority – political or financial, or both (Thomas, 2000). Nevertheless, with properly set objectives, secure boundaries and secure financial backing, this method of measurement has much to commend it (Clarke, 2000).

Critics aside, the intended outcomes of evaluation are laudable: to create a manageable evaluation method; to educate all the participants in the value of and in the processes of evaluation; and to produce recording of events that were relevant to all levels in the project hierarchy (funders, administrators, staff, and other stakeholders – citizens and agencies) (Rosenberg, et al., 1970, pp. 1–3). Any final project report should reflect not only what characteristics of the project were successful or not (indicators) but also provide linkages (using indicators again) between the different phases of the project/investment process – design, input, outputs, outcome (pp. 11–14). Within an organisation, process goals, such as communication processes, delegation suitability, etc., may have to follow different assessment and analysis, but they are subsidiary to the 'input/output' objectives set for the organisation (Clarke, 2000). The schema across which evaluation systems will have to be established are illustrated in the diagram below (Figure 8). Obviously, responsibility for establishing an evaluation regime across these wide perspectives would have to be accomplished strategically.

Generally speaking, community development funding in the UK has dictated that initiatives be set up on a *'project'* basis. In seeking an abstract framework for development, and ignoring the inherent weaknesses that this involves, Cusworth's project management design suggests the building in of monitoring and evaluation from the moment that a project is agreed upon, before the final design is implemented (Cusworth and Franks, 1993). In the model that is presented above and below, points for engaging in the evaluation process occur at every point of intersection of each function with another. This is one of the strengths of the logical framework of the ODA, but they, themselves, are slow to realise it.

If one is reliant on a long list of indicator values (qualitative analysis) then the correlation can become a statistical nightmare. Looking immediately for positive values, an 'on–off', 'plus–minus' set of criteria, from a pre-calculated set of objectives, will give the funders and the participants an immediate sense of success or failure. In an action framework, where change is ongoing, continuously, and where political and funding cycles are on short time-frames, it is this sort of 'result' that is desired. In Wales, the new, 'Cluster' configuration of the *Communities First* programme may find that a strategic, programme-wide perspective be adopted, rather than a localised one.

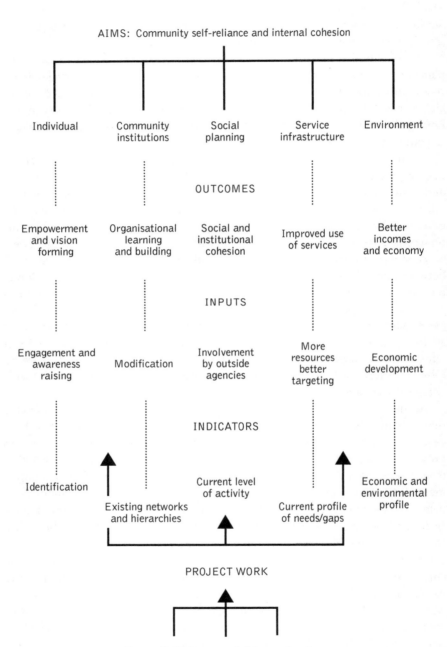

Figure 8: Holistic model for evaluation

There have been a number of attempts to evaluate *Communities First* and none of them have been completely satisfactory (Communities Directorate and Welsh Assembly Government, 2001; WAG, 2006a; Adamson and Bromiley, 2008). This is largely because the programme has been set a very difficult task, spread across two salient factors: first, the scope of the programme is too vague and broadly stated; and, secondly, the policy decision to abandon the development of the community dimension of the programme in favour of institutional and structural targets (numbers in work, taking up educational programmes, etc.). The scope of the programme is extensively described in the consultancy Report by Ipsos Mori in 2015 (Ipsos Mori and Wavehill, 2015). This describes a wide-ranging brief, which attempts to make the *Communities First* teams responsible for the economic regeneration of Wales. This is similar to the original CDP brief back in 1970, where unrealistic and poorly defined goals saw the fragmentation of the whole programme. In a second Report (Ipsos Mori and Wavehill Consulting, 2015), the conclusions were that despite a better management structure than in the previous programme (2000–12) and the consolidation of resources into 'clusters', the downgrading of the requirement fully to engage the local communities, poor recruitment frameworks and poor data-gathering capabilities made the task more difficult (Ipsos Mori and Wavehill Consulting, 2015, pp. 90–3). It would appear that merely to define the various objectives of *Communities First* as 'social planning' and 'locality development' would have cleared up a lot of confusion on the ground.

Community development is **not** a universal service, nor a panacea. It works on a percentage basis, benefiting those that are in the frame at the time, and those who are in a position or desire to take advantage of it. In our technological age, there may also be a tendency to seek the 'quick-fix' through the application of data analysis, particularly 'big data'. As Dávid-Barrett and Dunbar point out, there are considerable costs involved in seeking to enlarge the scope of 'social contact' through this means (Dávid-Barrett and Dunbar, 2013). It is a function of the professional worker to maximise this figure, but it all depends on the level of co-operation, the motivation and the morale of the participants to decide on the level of positive outcome that can be attained. Opportunistic approaches are not completely alien to official processes, as, originally, it was the WHO that introduced the concept of '*Rapid Needs Appraisal*' (Annet and Rifkin, 1988; Chambers, 1992; Lazenblatt, et al., 2001) – 'needs assessment on the back of a fag packet!' Many a project may have been established on these flimsy premises. Consultants on short-term contracts seldom remain anywhere long enough to count the costs of their failures.

It would be beneficial for a national programme if data were to become available across all dimensions of planned social change – individual citizen, local community organisation, agency planning and delivery level, agency infrastructure, and the environment (Clarke, 2000, p. 265 – see Figure 8). For some problem-solving activities, it would only be possible for this data to be gathered nationally — e.g. on infrastructure, the environment, etc., but the quality of the local social planning and locality community development processes, and the way in which these are recorded and measured, would be crucial for good programme evaluation. Currently (2016), there is no mechanism for doing this in Wales, even for *Communities First*. Kelly's study of *Sure Start/Cymorth* (Kelly, 2008) shows how far away this was for other targeted areas of social intervention.

Training and deployment requirements

The professional task of functioning competently as a *social planner* at all levels in communities, between communities and the local authority/Local Service Board requires highly trained, motivated professionals with an appropriate level of status. This can only come about if the present system of community development recruitment of taking on inexperienced, neophyte workers is scrapped, and a suitable mechanism for training and preparation of *social planners* is developed. Reinstituting something like the (now abandoned) post-graduate MSc/Diploma in Social Work (DipSW) level of community development training would be a suitable model for this. At Swansea University, the DipSW provided social workers to qualify with a complete repertoire of community development theory, skills and practice capabilities after a two-year programme.

Community development has been blighted to date by short-term funding cycles, and too little determination to see an agenda of sustained social change through under its auspices (Plummer, 2002). Somehow the potential for this model of social intervention has to be recognised and the opportunity grasped. Anecdotally, it has been said that those responsible for the changes which stripped community development out of the curriculum of social work education were motivated by the fact that community development was the only feature of professional practice that actually worked. The evidence points to endless tinkering with policies, the re-structuring of mechanisms, and redefining the linkages between Departments and agencies, without any firm hold being taken to confront the real issues. If prevention, anticipation, and focus on problem-solving are to be incorporated into the public health agenda, then community development has to be adopted.

Rural areas

The questions of geography and demography are especially relevant to the establishment of a viable intervention model. The uneven demographic spread of older people across society raises many issues for a Welfare State, as variation and flexibility have to be woven into the fabric of standardised policy frameworks. WAG, in 2009, produced its plan for Rural Health (WAG, 2009c), where it considered the priorities for rural health. Community cohesion, and the role of volunteering, were seen as highly valued components of the service delivery scenario (WAG, 2009c, p. 9 *et seq.*). In the consultative document over the role of Community Nursing (WAG, 2009e), community development was identified to be a basic component of the Community Nurse's repertoire (p. 22). The Welsh Nursing Confederation does not respond to this point in its feedback on the Consultation (Welsh NHS Confederation, 2009).

As the situation of older people in rural setting can become more critical, faster than their urban equivalents, social support is seen as a very important element in sustaining social relevance and an active engagement in personal good health (WAG, 2009d, pp. 10, 15). The application of this *social planning* model, therefore, in these circumstances is going to take more careful planning and execution. Special cultural features, such as the availability of the Welsh Language for people with incipient degenerative mental diseases is of great concern to planners. Social support connections have a central role to play here (pp. 14–15; WAG et al., 2009). Under these circumstances, and from a top-down perspective, social planning will have to provide sufficient resources for staff on the ground to make the more difficult connections. The delivery of *community social planning* for localised activities can probably draw upon traditional networks, which may have to be re-oriented to cope with these extra-ordinary needs (Edwards, et al., 2000).

The completed model

This model requires detailed testing in the field. It has been devised from a combination of historical research and analysis, and from extensive fieldwork experience. The uptake of this model is the only way in which extra resources, financial, material and human, can be drawn into the social care system without drawing on State funds. For that reason, there is no profit in it for the private sector. It is also the cheap option, requiring an investment of about forty staff, with suitable training, spread across the LSBs, to implement an imaginative and service-relieving community initiative. It will see the creation of a vibrant *Community Sector*, with equity (ownership) in social care, and a locally accountable structure. This model can also provide the necessary 'care', being community-based, which the public service, or for-profit sector cannot provide, outside residential units. Community development is an application of social intervention that can be replicated across the entire public service area. It elevates skilled personnel to positions with great social responsibility, but it does not remove from the people in community leadership positions the responsibility of local control. It is a culture-changing manipulation of people's orientation to the realities of their own circumstances, away from the dependency culture that is running out of financial and political steam at the present time.

This study has attempted to take the best from the past and integrate it into the needs of today and tomorrow. It is also an unashamed attempt to present the potential of community development, in its widest and complete sense, before a public that needs its insight and capabilities more than ever.

Summary

1. A system-based model is developed from theories and practices from around the world that would enable a localised public authority implement a strategic, holistic and sustainable Public Health agenda.
2. The employment of a systems-based model requires that a business orientation of all concerned in its implementation is maintained and assessed according to best business practice.
3. Examples are drawn from the Welsh policy structure and implementation experience to highlight how this might work on the ground.
4. The emphasis here has been to focus upon the need to support older people, in the community and at less expense than generalised 'care' policies. This is employed to project a model for localised development that could be employed across any care or development scenario.

Bibliography

Abbott, G. (1921) *The Immigrant and The Community*, New York.

Abrams, P., et al. (1986) *Creating Care in the Neighbourhood*, London.

Absolon, K. and Herbert, E. (1997) 'Community Action as a Practice of Freedom: a First Nations perspective', in B. Wharf and M. Clague (eds) *Community Organizing: Canadian experiences*, Oxford.

Acheson, S. (1998) *Independent Inquiry into Inequalities in Health*, London.

Adamson, D. and Bromiley, R. (2008) *Community empowerment in practice – Lessons from Communities First*, York.

Adamson, D. and Lang, M. (2013) *Regeneration Skills: a consideration of current and future requirements*, Merthyr Tydfil.

Adamson, D., et al. (2001) *Community Regeneration: Review of Best Practice*, Cardiff.

Addams, J. (1902) *Democracy and Social Ethics*, New York.

— (1912) *Twenty Years at Hull-House, with Autobiographical Notes*, New York.

— (1930) *The Spirit of Youth and the City Streets*, New York.

Age Cymru. (2011) *Opportunities and challenges: our ambition for public policy in Wales*, Cardiff.

AgeUK. (2013) *Later Life in Rural England*, London.

Albemarle, D. (1960) *The youth service in England and Wales: report of the committee appointed by the Minister of Education in November 1958*, London.

Alberta Community Development. (2007) *Working in Partnership: recipes for success*, Edmonton.

Ali, R., et al. (2012) *A New Covenant of Virtue: Islam and Community Organising*, London.

Alinsky, S. (1941) 'Community Analysis and Organization', *American Journal of Sociology*, 46, 797–808.

— (1957) *From Citizen Apathy to Participation*, Chicago.

— (1969) *Reveille for Radicals*, New York.

— (1972) *Rules for Radicals: A Programatic Primer for Realistic Radicals*, New York.

Alvesson, M. and Sköldberg, K. (2000) *Reflexive Methodology: new vistas for qualitative research*, London.

Ambrose, L. and Hall, K. (2007) 'A New Woman in Print and Practice: The Canadian literary career of Madge Robertson Watt 1890–1907', *History of Intellectual Culture*, 7, 1–20.

Andersson, G. and Karlberg, I. (2000) 'Integrated care for the elderly – The background and effects of the reform of Swedish care of the elderly', *International Journal of Integrated Care*.

Andrews, L. (1985) *Community Contracting – a feasibility study for a pilot programme in Scotland*, Edinburgh.

Anglesey Federation of WIs. (2013) *Llanfairpwllgwyngyll – the First WI in Britain 1915*, Llanfairpwllgwyngyll.

Annet, H. and Rifkin, S. (1988) *Improving Urban Health: guidelines for rapid appraisal to assess community health needs*, Geneva.

Aptheker, B. (ed.) (1977) *Lynching; Rape all Exchange of Views – Revised and with Additional Bibliography by Jane Addams and Ida B. Wells Occasional Paper No. 25 (1977)*, New York.

Archbishop of Canterbury's Commission on Urban Priority Areas. (1985) *Faith in the City – a call for action by Church and Nation – Report of the Archbishop of Canterbury's Commission on Urban Priority Areas*, London.

Archbishops' Commission on Rural Areas [Chair: Lord Prior]. (1990) *Faith in the Countryside: a Report presented to the Archbishops of Canterbury and York*, London.

Arches, J. (1999) 'Challenges and Dilemmas in Community Development', *Journal of Community Practice*, 6, 37–55.

Arnstein, S. (1968) 'A Ladder of Citizen Participation', *Journal of the American Institute of Planners*, 35, 4, 216–24.

Ashish, P. (2000) *Investing in Health*, Bangor.

Ashton, J. (1988) *Healthy Cities*, Liverpool.

— (1989) 'Liverpool: creating a Healthy City', in D. Seedhouse and A. Cribb (eds) *Changing Ideas in Health*, Chichester.

Ashton, J., et al. (1986) 'Healthy Cities: WHOs new public health initiative', *Health Promotion* 1, 319–24.

Ashton, T. (1962) *The Industrial Revolution 1760–1830*, London.

Association of Community Workers. (1978) *Towards a Definition of Community Work*, London.

Association of Metropolitan Authorities. (1989) *Community Development: The Local Authority Role*, London.

Association of Metropolitan Authorities and Federation of Community Work Training Groups. (1990) *Learning for Action: Community Work and Participative Training*, London.

Atlas, J. (2010) *Seeds of Change: the story of ACORN, America's most controversial antipoverty community organizing group*, Nashville.

Attlee, C. (1920) *The Social Worker*, London.

Audit Commission. (1986) *Making a Reality of Community Care*, London.
— (1992a) *The Community Revolution: Personal Social Services and Community Care*, London.
— (1992b) *Community Care: Managing the Cascade of Change*, London.
— (1998a) *Home Alone – the role of housing in community care*, London.
— (1998b) *Fruitful Partnership – effective partnership working*, London.
— (2002) *Integrated services for older people*, London.
— (2004a) *Older people – building a strategic approach – independence and well-being*, London.
— (2004b) *Older people – a changing approach – independence and well-being Part 2*, London.
— (2004c) *Older people – independence and well-being – the challenge for Public Services Part 1*, London.
— (2005) *Governing Local Partnerships – bridging the accountability gap*, London.
— (2009) *Working better together? Managing local strategic partnerships*, London.
Audit Commission in Wales. (2004) *Transforming health and social care in Wales: Aligning the levers of change*, Cardiff.
Audit Committee and National Assembly for Wales. (2008) *Report presented to the National Assembly for Wales on 20 February 2008 in accordance with section 143(1) of the Government of Wales Act 2006 Tackling Delayed Transfers of Care across the Whole System*, Cardiff.
Audit Committee and Welsh Government. (2012) *Tackling delayed transfers of care across the whole system*, Cardiff.
Auditor General for Wales. (2001) *Securing the Future of Cardiff Bay*, Cardiff .
— (2006) *Is the NHS in Wales managing within its available financial resources?*, Cardiff.
Auditor General for Wales, et al. (2005) *What Works: regeneration and improvement study*, Cardiff.
Austin, M. and Betten, N. (1990) 'Rural Organizing and the Agricultural Extension Service', in N. Betten and M. Austin (eds) *The Roots of Community Organizing, 1917–1939*, Philadelphia.
Bailey, J. (1974) *Radicals in Urban Politics: The Alinsky Approach*, Chicago.
Bailey, N., et al. (1980) *Resourcing Communities: Evaluating the experience of six Area Resource Centres*, London.
Bailey, R. (1973) *The Squatters*, London.
Bailey, R. and Brake, M. (eds) (1975) *Radical Social Work*, London.
Bailward, W. (1895) 'The Oxford House and The Organisation of Charity', in J. Knapp (ed.) *The Universities and the Social Problem*, London.
— (1920) 'The Slippery Slope' and Other Papers on Social Subjects*, London.
Baldock, P. (1974) *Community Work and Social Work*, London.

— (1982) 'Community work and social services departments', in G. Craig (ed.) *Community Work and the State: towards a radical practice*, London.

— (1983) 'Community Development and Community Care', *Community Development Journal*, 18, 231–7.

Ball, E. (2013) *African American Philanthropy*, New York.

Ballard, P. (1990) 'Community Work and Christian Witness', in P. Ballard (ed.) *Issues in Church Related Community Work*, Cardiff.

Ballard, P. and Jones, E. (eds) (1975) *The Valley Call: a self-examination by the people of the South Wales Valleys during the 'Year of the Valleys 1974'*, Rhondda.

Bane, M., et al. (eds) (2000) *Who Will Provide? The changing role of religion in American social welfare*, Rochester.

Barclay, P. (1982) *Social Workers: their role and their task*, London.

Barnett, S. (1888) 'University Settlements', in S. A. Barnett and M. Barnett (eds) *Practicable Socialism: essays on social reform*, London.

— (1898) 'Review of the possibilities of Settlement life', in W. Reason (ed.) *University and Social Settlements*, London.

Barr, A. (1977) *The Practice of Neighbourhood Community Work: experience from Oldham CDP*, York.

— (1991) *Practising Community Development*, London.

— (2005) *Outcome based community development practice – how did we get here and does it matter? Paper for Scottish Community Development Alliance Conference 3 June 05*, Glasgow.

Barr, A., et al. (1996) *Monitoring and Evaluation of Community Development in Northern Ireland*, Belfast.

Barr, A. and Hashagen, S. (2000) *ABCD Handbook: a framework for evaluating community development*, London.

Barrow, C. (2000) *Social Impact Assessment: an introduction*, London.

Batley, R. and Edwards, J. (1975) 'CDP and the Urban Programme', in R. Lees and G. Smith (eds) *Action-Research in Community Development*, London.

Batten, T. (1957) *Communities and their Development*, London.

— (1962) *Training for Community Development: A critical study of method*, London.

Batten, T. and Batten, M. (1967) *The Non-Directive Approach in Group and Community Work*, London.

— (1965) *The Human Factor in Community Work*, London.

Baum, F. (1990) 'The new public health: force for change or reaction?', *Health Promotion International*, 5, 145–50.

Bays, S. (1998) 'Work, Politics and Coalition Building', in N. Naples, (ed.) *Community Activism and Feminist Politics: organizing across race, class and gender*, Routledge, New York.

Beck, E., et al. (2003) 'The Women's Suffrage Movement: Lessons for Social Action', *Journal of Community Practice*, 11, 13–33.

Beck, U. (1994) 'The reinvention of politics: towards the a theory of reflexive modernization', in U. Beck, et al. (eds) *Reflexive Modernization: politics, tradition and aesthetics in the modern social order*, Stanford.

Bed-Stuy. (2010) *Programs and Calendar*, New York.

Bell, J. (1992) *Community Development Teamwork: measuring the impact*, London.

Benington, J. (1974) 'Strategies for change at the local level: some reflections', in D. Jones and M. Mayo (eds) *Community Work One*, London.

— (1975) 'Gosford Green Tenants' Association: a case study', in P. Leonard (ed.) *The Sociology of Community Action*, Keele.

— (1976) *Local Government becomes Big Business*, London.

Benington J., et al. (1975) *CDP: Coventry Final Report Part 1: Coventry and Hillfields – prosperity and the persistence of inequality*, Coventry.

Benn, C. and Fairley, J. (1986) *Challenging the MSC on Jobs, Education, and Training: enquiry into a National disaster*, London.

Bennett, B. (1980) 'The sub-office: a team approach to local authority fieldwork practice', in M. Brake and R. Bailey (eds) *Radical Social Work and Practice*, London.

Bennett, H. (ed.) (1919) *American Women in Civic Work*, New York.

Bentham, J. (1914) *Theory of Legislation – Being Principes De Legislation and Traites De Legislation, Civile Et Penale Vol. i. Principles Of Legislation; Principles Of The Civil Code*, London.

Betten, N. and Austin, M. (1990) 'The Cincinnati Unit Experiment, 1917–1920', in Betten, N. and Austin, M., *The Roots of Community Organization 1917–1939*, Temple University Press, Philadelphia.

Bibb, H. (1849) *Narrative of the Life and Adventures of Henry Bibb an American Slave written by himself*, New York.

Biddle, W. (1966) 'The "Fuzziness" of definition of Community Development', *Community Development Journal*, 1, 5–12.

— (1968) 'Deflating the Community Developer', *Community Development Journal*, 3, 191–4.

Biddle, W. and Biddle, L. (1965) *The Community Development Process: The Rediscovery of Local Initiative*, New York.

— (1968) *Encouraging Community Development: A Training Guide for Local Workers*, New York.

Bill and Melinda Gates Foundation. (2007) *Taproot Foundation's Awards to Local Nonprofits tops $600,000*, Seattle.

Bischoff, U. and Reisch, M. (2001) 'Welfare Reform and Community-Based Organizations', *Journal of Community Practice*, 8, 69–91.

Blackfriars Settlement, [with] Charing, G. (1973) *The Blackfriars Experiment: a look at how one voluntary organisation is trying to put principles into practice*, London.

Blair, H. (1997) 'Donors, democratisation and civil society: relating theory to practice', in D. Hulme and M. Edwards (eds) *NGOs, States and Donors: too close for comfort?*, Houndmills.

Blair, T. (1972) *Planning for Social Needs and Community Action in the Inner City*, London.

Blake, G., et al. (2008) *Community Engagement and Community Cohesion*, York.

Bland, R. (1999) 'Independence, privacy and risk: two contrasting approaches to residential care for older people', *Ageing and Society*, 19, 539–60.

Blaustein, A. and Faux, G. (1972) *The Star-Spangled Hustle: White Power and Black Capitalism*, New York.

Bobo, K., et al. (1996) *Organizing for Social Change: a manual for activists in the 1990s*, Santa Ana.

Bode, I. (2009) 'Co-governance within networks and the Non-profit-For Profit Divide – a cross-cultural perspective on the evolution of domiciliary elderly care', in V. Pestoff and T. Brandsen (eds) *Co-production: The Third Sector and the delivery of Public Services*, New York.

Boff, L. (1985) *Church, Charism and Power: Liberation Theology and the Institutional Church*, London.

— (1989) *Faith on the Edge: Religion and Marginalized Existence*, San Francisco.

Bolger, S., et al. (1981) *Towards Socialist Welfare Work*, London.

Booker, I. (1962) 'A Sicilian Experiment', *Community Development Bulletin*, XIII, 93–7.

Boonekamp, et al. (1999) 'Healthy Cities Evaluation: the co-ordinators perspective', *Health Promotion International* 14, 103–10.

Booth, C. (1902) *Life and Labour of the People in London*, New York.

Booth, D. (1994) 'How far beyond the impasse? A provisional summing-up', in D. Booth (ed.) *Rethinking Social Development: theory, research, practice*, Harlow.

Bosanquet, C. (1874) *A Handy-Book for Visitors of the Poor in London: Poor Law, Sanitary Law, and Charities*, London.

Bosanquet, H. (1914) *Social Work in London: A History of the Charity Organisation Society*, New York.

Boteach, M., et al. (2014) *The War on Poverty: Then and Now – Applying Lessons Learned to the Challenges and Opportunities Facing a 21st-Century America*, Washington.

Bourguignon, F., et al. (2002) *Evaluating the Poverty Impact of Economic Policies: Some Analytical Challenges*, Washington.

Bowen, R., et al. (2005) *What are the True Costs of Community Learning?*

Bowles, M. (2008) *The Community Development Challenge – Democracy: The contribution of community development to local governance and democracy*, London.

Bradshaw, T. (2000) 'Complex community development projects: collaboration, comprehensive programs and community coalitions in complex society', *Community Development Journal*, 35, 133–45.

Brager, G. (2001) 'Agency under attack: the risks, demands, and rewards of community activism', in J. Rothman, et al. (eds) *Strategies of Community Intervention*, Itasca.

Brager, G. and Holloway, S. (1978) *Changing Human Service Organizations: politics and practice*, New York.

Brager, G. and Purcell, F. (1967) *Community Action against Poverty: readings from the Mobilization experience*, New Haven.

Brager, G. and Specht, H. (1973) *Community Organizing*, New York

Brake, M. and Bailey, R. (eds) (1980) *Radical Social Work and Practice*, London.

Brandsen, T. and Pestoff, V. (2009) 'Co-production: The Third Sector and the delivery of Public Services – an Introduction', in V. Pestoff and T. Brandsen (eds) *Co-production: The Third Sector and the delivery of Public Services*, New York.

Brandt, L. (1907) *The Charity Organization Society of the City of New York 1882– 1907 History: Account of Present Activities Twenty-Fifth Annual Report for the Year Ending September Thirtieth, Nineteen Hundred and Seven*, New York.

Brandt, W. (1980) *North-South: a programme for survival: Report of the Independent Commission on International Development Issues under the Chairmanship of Willy Brandt*, London.

Bregha, F. (1970) 'Community Development in Canada: problems and strategies', *Community Development Journal*, 36, 30–6.

Bremner, R. (1956) *From the Depths: the discovery of poverty in the United States*, New York.

Bridge Consortium. (2003) *The Evaluation of the New Opportunities Fund Healthy Living Centres*, London.

Bridge Consortium, et al. (2007) *The Evaluation of the Big Lottery Fund Healthy Living Centres Programme FINAL REPORT*, London.

Brisbane, A. (ed.) (1874) *Part First: Introduction to Fourier's Theory of Social Organization: A. Brisbane; Part Second: Social Destinies – by Fournier*, New York.

Briscoe, C. (1977) 'Community Work and Social Work in the United Kingdom', in H. Specht and A. Vickery (eds) *Integrating Social Work Methods*, London.

Broaderick, S. (2002) 'Community Development in Ireland – a policy review', *Community Development Journal*, 37, 101–10.

Broadhurst, K., et al. (2007) 'Sure Start and the "re-authorisation" of Section 47 child protection practices', *Critical Social Policy*, 27, 443–61.

Brodie, I., et al. (2008) 'A tale of two Reports: Social Work in Scotland from *Social Work and the Community* (1966) to *Changing Lives* (2006), *British Journal of Social Work*, 38, 697–715.

Brokensha, D. and Hodge, P. (1969) *Community Development: an Interpretation*, San Francisco.

Bronfenbrenner, U. (1979) *The Ecology of Human Development: Experiments by Nature and Design*, Cambridge.

Brooks, F. (2002) 'Innovative Organizing Practices, ACORN's Campaign in Los Angeles Organizing Workfare Workers', *Journal of Community Practice*, 9, 65–85.

Broughton, J. (2010) *The Silent Revolution: The International Monetary Fund 1979–1989*, Washington.

Browne, P. (1887) *The World's Workers: Mrs. Somerville Mary Carpenter*, London.

Brueggemann, W. (2013) 'History and context of Community Practice in North America', in M. Weil, et al. (eds) *The Handbook of Community Practice*, Thousand Oaks.

Brundtland, G. [Chair] (1987) *Our Common Future: the World Commission on Environment and Development*, Oxford.

Bruno, F. (1948) *Trends in Social Work as reflected in the Proceedings of the National Conference of Social Work 1874–1946*, New York.

— (1957) *Trends in Social Work 1874–1956: a history based on the proceedings of the National Conference of Social Work*, New York.

Brushett, K. (2009) 'Making Shit Disturbers: the selection and training of the Company of Young Canadians' volunteers 1965–1970', in M. Palaeologu (ed.) *The 1960s in Canada: a turbulent and creative decade*, Montreal.

Bryant, B. and Bryant, R. (1982) *Change and Conflict: A study of Community Work in Glasgow*, Aberdeen.

Bryant, R. (1975) 'Social Work: new Departments old problems', in G. Brown (ed.) *The Red Paper on Scotland*, Edinburgh.

Bulmer, M. (1986) *Neighbours; the work of Philip Abrams*, Cambridge.

Burdick, J. (1992) 'Rethinking the Study of Social Movements: The Case of Christian Base Communities in Urban Brazil', in A.A.S.E. Escobar (ed.) *The Making of Social Movements in Latin America: Identity, Strategy and Democracy*, Boulder.

Burghardt, S. and Fabricant, M. (1987) *Working under the Safety Net: policy and practice with the New American Poor*, Newbury Park.

— (1982) *The Other Side of Organizing: resolving the personal dilemmas and political demands of daily practice*, Cambridge.

Burr, W. (1921) *Rural Organization*, New York.

Burwell, N. (1996) 'Lawrence Oxley and Locality Development: Black Self-Help in North Carolina 1925', *Journal of Community Practice*, 2, 18–29.

Bury, M. (2008) 'New Dimensions of Health Care Organisation', in D. Wainwright (ed.) *A Sociology of Health*, London.

Butcher, H., et al. (1979) *Community Participation and Poverty: the Final Report of Cumbria CDP*, Oxford.

Butcher, H., et al. (1980) *Community Groups in Action: Case Studies and Analysis*, London.

Butterfield, K. (1909) *The Country Church and the Rural Problem: The Carew Lectures at Hartford Theological Seminary*, Chicago.

— (1919) *The Farmer and the New Day*, New York.

Cabinet Office. (1998) 'Bringing Britain Together: a national strategy for neighbourhood renewal', London.

— (2010) *Office for Civil Society structure finalised*, London.

— (2013a) *Wellbeing Policy and Analysis – An Update of Wellbeing Work across Whitehall*, London.

— (2013b) *Big Society*, Policy and Analysis Team, London.

— (2013c) *Growing the social investment market: 2014 progress update*, London.

Cahn, E. (2000) *No More Throw-away People: the co-production imperative*, Washington.

Calouste Gulbenkian Foundation. (1968) *Community Work and Social Change: a Report on Training*, Longman, London.

— (1973) *Current Issues in Community Work*, Routledge Kegan Paul, London.

Calouste Gulbenkian Working Party. (1984) *A National Centre for Community Development*, London.

Cameron, D., et al. (2015) *Community Organisers' Programme; Evaluation Report*, London.

Campbell, A., et al. (2010) 'Social capital as a mechanism for building a sustainable society in Northern Ireland', *Community Development Journal*, 45, 22–38.

Cannan, C. and Warren, C. (1997) *Social Action with Children and Families: A Community Development Approach to Child and Family Welfare State*, London.

Carbaugh, H. (1917) *Human welfare work in Chicago*, Chicago.

Care Council for Wales (2012) *Profile of Registered Social Workers in Wales 2012*, Cardiff.

Carley, M. (2000) *Urban Regeneration through Partnership: A Study in the Nine Urban Regions in England, Scotland and Wales*, Bristol.

Carlisle, S., et al. (2004) *SHARP Overarching Evaluation Team: Phase 2 Report: (January 2003–July 2004) Case Studies, Comparisons and theories from SHARP*, Keele.

Carmarthenshire County Council. (2001) *Review of the activities of Mentrau Iaith Myrddin 1998–2001 Final Report*, Carmarthen.

Carpenter, M. (1861) *Reformatory School for the Children of the Perishing and Dangerous Classes, and for Juvenile Offenders*, London.

Carroll, L. (1939) *Alice's Adventures in Wonderland and Through the Looking-Glass*, London.

Carson, C. (ed.). (1998) *The Autobiography of Dr Martin Luther King Jr*, Stanford.

Carson, E. (1993) *A Hand Up: Black Philanthropy and Self-Help in America*, Washington.

Cartrefi Cymru. (2015) *Co-production network for Wales: an overview of the proposal submitted to the Big Lottery*, Cardiff.

Cary, L. (1970) 'The Role of the Citizen in the Community Development Process', in L. Cary (ed.) *Community Development as a Process*, Columbia.

Case Con Collective. (1975) 'The CaseCon Manifesto', in R. Bailey and M. Brake (eds) *Radical Social Work*, London.

Casley, D. and Kumar, K. (1987) *Project Monitoring and Evaluation in Agriculture*, Baltimore.

CCETSW. (1974) *The Teaching of Community Work*, London.

— (1979) *Council Policy for the Teaching of Community Work within the Personal Social Services*, London.

— (1989) *DipSW: Requirements and Regulations for the Diploma in Social Work*, London.

CDC – Community Development Cymru (2007) *Strategic Framework for Community Development*, Cardiff.

CDF. (1995a) *Community Development in Ogwr – foundations for the future*, London.

— (1995b) 'Regeneration and the Community in Wales: Guidelines to the community involvement aspects of the Welsh Office's Strategic Development Scheme', London.

— (2011) *Engaged, cohesive, strong communities: Community Development Foundation – Annual Report and Accounts 2009–10*, London.

— (2012) *Engaged, cohesive, strong communities: Community Development Foundation – Annual Report and Accounts 2010–11*, London.

CDF et al. (2006) *The Community Development Challenge 'CD2': Together We Can*, London.

CDJustice. – California Department of Justice Office of the Attorney General. (2010) *Report of the Attorney General on the Activities of ACORN in the State of California*, Sacramento.

CDP. (1981) *The Costs of Industrial Change*, Newcastle-Upon-Tyne.

CDP CD Working Group. (1974) 'The British National Community Development Project 1969–74', *Community Development Journal*, 9, 162–86.

CDP IIU. (1974) *Inter-Project Report–1973*, London.

— (1975) *The Poverty of the Improvement Programme*, London.

— (1976) *Whatever happened to Council Housing?*, London.

— (1977) *Gilding the Ghetto: the state and the poverty experiments*, London.

CDWW. (2012) *Schedule of Community Development Training opportunities in Wales*, Cardiff.

CEA – Cambridge Economic Associates. (2005) *National Evaluation of New Deal for Communities Key Findings from the Survey of Beneficiaries*, Cambridge.

Cemlyn, S., et al. (2005) 'Poverty, neighbourhood renewal and the voluntary and community sector in West Cornwall', *Community Development Journal*, 40, 76–85.

Centers for Disease Control and Prevention and The Merck Company Foundation. (2007) *The State of Aging and Health in America 2007*, Whitehouse Station.

Cernea, M. (1991) 'Knowledge from Social Science for Development Policies and Projects', *Putting People First: Sociological Variables in Rural Development*, New York.

Cernea, R. (1985) *Putting People First: sociological variables in Rural Development*, New York.

Chadwick, E. (1843) *Report on the Sanitary Condition of the Labouring Population of Great Britain. Supplementary Report on the Results of a Special Inquiry into the Practice of Interment in Towns. Made at the Request of Her Majesty's Principal Secretary of State for The Home Department*, London.

— (1885) *The evils of disunity in Central and Local Administration – especially with relation to the metropolis and also on the new centralisation for the people together with improvements in codification and in legislative procedure*, London.

Challis, D. and Davies, B. (1985) 'Long Term Care for the Elderly: the Community Care Scheme', *British Journal of Social Work*, 15, 579.

— (1986) *Case Management in Community Care*, Aldershot.

Chalmers, T. (1832) *Political Economy, in Connection with the Moral State and Moral Prospects of Society*, New York.

Chambers, C. (1963) *Seedtime of Reform: American social service and social action 1918–1933*, Westport.

Chambers, E. (2004) *Roots for Radicals: organizing for power, action and justice*, Continuum, New York.

Chambers, R. (1980) *Rapid Rural Appraisal: Rationale and Repertoire*, Brighton.

— (1983) *Rural Development: putting the last first*, Harlow.

— (1986) *Normal Professionalism, New Paradigms and Development*, Brighton.

— (1992) *Rural Appraisal: Rapid, Relaxed and Participatory*, Brighton.

— (1993) *Challenging the Professions: Frontiers for rural development*, London.

— (1994) 'The Origins and Practice of Participatory Rural Appraisal', *World Development*, 22, 953–969.

— (1997) *Whose Reality Counts? Putting the last first*, London.

— (1998a) 'Us and Them: finding a new paradigm for professionals in sustainable development', in D. Warburton (ed.) *Community and Sustainable Development: participation in the future*, London.

— (1998b) 'Forward', in J. Blackburn and J. Holland (eds) *Who changes? Institutionalising participation in development*, London.

Chambers, R., et al. (eds) (1989) *Farmer First: farmer innovation and agricultural research*, London.

Chang, P., et al. (1994) 'Church-Agency Relationships in the Black Community', *Non-Profit and Voluntary Sector Quarterly*, 23, 91–105.

Chapin, R. (2011) *Pocket Neighborhoods: Creating Small-Scale Community in a Large-Scale World*, Newtown.

Chaplin, F. (1920) *Fieldwork and Social Research*, New York.

Chapman, N. and Vaillant, C. (2010) *Synthesis of Country Programme Evaluations Conducted in Fragile States – Evaluation Report EV709*, London.

Chappell, N., et al. (2006) 'Multi-level community health promotion: How can we make it work?', *Community Development Journal*, 41, 352–66.

Charity Organization Society of the City of New York. (1883) *Hand-Book for 'Friendly Visitors' among the Poor*, New York.

Chaskin, Robert J. (2001) 'Perspectives on Neighborhood and Community: a review of the literature', in J. Tropman, et al. (2001) *Tactics; Techniques of Community Intervention*, F.E. Peacock, Itasca.

Chavis, D., et al. (1993) 'Nurturing Grassroots Initiatives for Community Development: the role of enabling systems', in T. Mizrahi and J. Morrison (eds) *Community Organization and Social Administration: advances, trends and emerging principles*, Binghampton.

Checkoway, B. (1995) 'Six strategies for community development', *Community Development Journal*, 30, 2–20.

Chief Medical Officer. (2004) *The Health Promotion Action Plan for Older People in Wales: a response to Health Challenge Wales*, Cardiff.

Church in Wales Board of Mission. (1991) *Faith in Wales*, Penarth.

Church in Wales Board of Mission: Rural Commission. (1992) *The Church in the Welsh Countryside: a Programme for Action by The Church in Wales*, Penarth.

Clark, G. (1976) 'Neighbourhood Self-Management', in P. Hain (ed.) *Community Politics*, London.

Clark, J. (1991) *Democratizing Development: The Role of Voluntary Organisations*, Earthscan, London.

Clarke, I. (1918) *The Little Democracy: a Text-Book on Community Organization*, New York.

Clarke, M. (1982) 'Where is the Community Which Cares?', *British Journal of Social Work*, 12, 453–69.

Clarke, S. (1996a) *Social Work as Community Development: A management model for social change*, Aldershot.

— (1996b) *Bon-y-maen: the community development options*, City and County of Swansea, Swansea.

— (2000) *Social Work as Community Development: a management model for planned social change*, 2nd edn, Aldershot.

— (2001) *Consultancy Report for CNO, WAG: Formal Review: Professor Dame J. Clark, et al: Report on Health Visiting: Recognising the Potential: the review of Health Visiting and School Health Services in Wales*, Swansea.

— (2002) *Community Health Development: A Study of Recent Field Appointments in South Wales*, unpublished consultancy paper, Cardiff.

— (2004a) *Co-operative and Social Enterprise in Educational Settings [CASE] Project 2003–2004 – Evaluation Report*, Swansea.

— (2004b) 'Community Leadership and Community Strategies: a pivotal issue', *Wales Law Journal*, 2004.

— (2006) *Health, Well-being and Community Development – a focus on policy and approaches to practice in Wales*, Swansea.

— (2014) *Can a suitable model for community development be developed for the sustainable support of older people in Wales?*, Ph.D. thesis, Swansea.

Clarke, S., et al. (2002a) 'Conclusions: the choices that have to be made', in S. Clarke, et al. (eds) *Community Development in South Wales*, Cardiff.

Clarke, S., et al. (2002b) *Community Development in South Wales*, Cardiff.

Cloward, R. and Ohlin, L. (1960) *Delinquency and Opportunity – A Theory of Delinquent Gangs*, New York.

Cloward, R. and Piven, F. (1999). 'Disruptive Dissensus: People and power in the industrial age', in J. Rothman (ed.), *Reflections on community organization: Enduring themes and critical issues*, Itasca.

Cnaan, R., et al. (2006) *The Other Philadelphia Story: how local congregations support quality of life in urban America*, Philadelphia.

Cockburn, C. (1977) *The Local State: Management of Cities and their People*, London.

Cohen, S. (2011) *The Women's Institute*, Oxford.

Colby, M. (1933) *The County as an Administrative Unit for Social Work*, Washington.

Colcord, J. (1919) *A Study Family Desertion and its Social Treatment*, New York.

Coleman, J. (1988) 'Social Capital in the creation of Human Capital', in P. Dasgupta and I. Serageldin (eds) *Social Capital: a multifaceted perspective*, Washington.

Colonial Office. (1948) *Colonial Office Summer Conference on African Administration, Second Session, 19th August–2nd September, 1948 at King's College, Cambridge: The Encouragement of Initiative in African Society*, London.

— (1954) *Social Development in the British Colonial Territories: a Report on the Ashridge Conference on social development*, London.

— (1958) *Community Development: a handbook*, London.

— (1960) *The Administrative Aspects of Community Development: Summer Conference on African Administration – eleventh Session, 5th September–17th September, 1960 at King's College, Cambridge*, London.

Colonial Office: Advisory Committee on Native Education in the British Tropical African Dependencies. (1925) *Education Policy in British Tropical Africa: Memorandum submitted to the Secretary of State for the Colonies by the Advisory Committee on Native Education in the British Tropical African Dependencies*, London.

Colonial Office: Advisory Committee on Education in the Colonies. (1943) *Mass Education in African Society*, London.

Communities Directorate and Welsh Assembly Government. (2001) *Communities First Guidance*, Cardiff.

Communities Scotland. (2005) *National Standards for Community Engagement*, Edinburgh.

Community Business Ventures Unit. (1981) *Whose Business is Business?*, London.

Conyers, D. (1982) *An Introduction to Social Planning in the Third World*, Chichester.

Cooke, B. (2001) 'The social psychological limits of participation', in B. Cooke and U. Kothari (eds) *Participation: the new tyranny?*, London.

Cooke, B. and Kothari, U. (eds) (2001) *Participation: the new tyranny?*, London.

Cooke, S. (2008) *The Future Role of the Voluntary and Community Sector in Bolton: Working Towards a Shared Vision Revised Background Paper: A Decade of Government Policy*, Bolton.

Cooper, J. (1989) 'From Casework to Community Care: "The End is Where We Start From"', (T.S. Eliot). *British Journal of Social Work*, 19, 177–89.

Cope, P. (2002) 'Beyond a Strong Voice', in S. Clarke, et al. (eds) *Community Development in South Wales*, Cardiff.

Co-production Wales (All in this Together). (2014) *Co-production strategies for success: briefing paper*, Cardiff

Corina, L., et al. (1979) *Oldham CDP: The Final Report*, York.

Cornia, G., et al. (1987) *Adjustment with a Human Face*, Oxford University Press, Oxford.

Cornwall, A. (2008) 'Unpacking "Participation": models, meanings and practices', *Community Development Journal*, 43, 269–83.

Cornwallis, C. (1851) *The Philosophy Of Ragged Schools*, London.

Corporation for National and Community Service. (2006) *VISTA – in Service of America: fighting poverty for 40 years*, Washington.

Corrigan, P. (1975) 'Community Work and Political Struggle: what are the possibilities of working with the contradictions?', in P. Leonard (ed.) *The Sociology of Community* Action, *Sociological Review No. 21*, Keele.

Corrigan, P. and Leonard, P. (1978) *Social Work Practice under Capitalism — a Marxist approach*, London.

Cowley, J., et al. (1977) 'Conclusion', in J. Cowley, et al. (eds) *Community or Class Struggle?*, London.

Cox, D. and Derricourt, N. (1975) 'The de-professionalisation of community work', in D. Jones and M. Mayo (eds) *Community Work Two*, London.

Cox, F., et al. (1970) *Strategies of Community Organization: a book of readings*, Itasca.

CPF. (1982) *Community Development — towards a National perspective: the work of the Community Projects Foundation 1978–1982*, London.

— (1988) *Ideas, Action, Change — CPF 1968–1988, 20 years of working with communities*, London.

Cracknell, B. (2000) *Evaluating Development Aid: issues, problems and solutions*, London.

Cracknell, R. (2007) *The ageing population*, London.

Craig, G. (1989) 'Community Work and the State', *Community Development Journal*, 24, 3–18

— (ed.) (1974) *Community Work Case Studies*, London.

— (ed.). (1980) *Community Work Case Studies*, London.

Craig, G. and Mayo, M. (1995) 'Rediscovering community development: some prerequisites for working in and against the state', *Community Development Journal*, 30, 105–9.

Craig, G. et al. (2004) *The Budapest Declaration — Building European civil society through community development*, Hull.

CREW. (2012b) *Glyncoch Community Partnership Programme Bending for Real (Euphemism for 'making a difference without dosh')*, Merthyr Tydfil.

— (2012a) *Regeneration in the UK An analysis of the evolution of regeneration policy — Review Evidence: Paper 1*, Merthyr Tydfil.

— (2015) *Response to the Communities First — The Future Consultation Document*, Merthyr Tydfil.

Croft, S. and Beresford, P. (1989) 'Decentralisation and the Personal Social Services', in M. Langan and P. Lee (eds) *Radical Social Work Today*, London.

Crow, I., et al. (2004) *Does 'Communities that Care' work? An evaluation of a community-based risk prevention programme in three neighbourhoods*, York.

Crummy, H. (1992) *Let the People Sing: The Story of Craigmillar*, Newcraighall.

CtC. (1997) *A new kind of prevention*, London.

Cullen, J., et al. (2015) *Exploring the Role of ICT-enabled Social Innovation for the Active Inclusion of Young People*, Luxembourg.

Cummings, S. (1998) *Left Behind in Rosedale: race relations and the collapse of community institutions*, Boulder.

Cusworth, J. and Franks, T. (1993) *Managing Projects in Developing Countries*, Harlow.

Dahl, H., et al. (2014) *Promoting Innovation in Social Services: an agenda for future research and development*, Heidelberg.

Dahlgren, G. and Whitehead, M. (1991) *Policies and Strategies to Promote Social Equity in Health*, Stockholm.

— (1992) *Policies and Strategies to Promote Equality in Health*, Copenhagen.

— (2006) *Levelling Up [Part II] — a discussion paper on European strategies for tackling social inequities in health*, Copenhagen.

Dale, A. and Newman, L. (2010) 'Social capital: a necessary and sufficient condition for sustainable community development?', *Community Development Journal*, 45, 5–21.

Darley, G. (2007) 'Octavia Hill', *Oxford Dictionary of National Biography*, Oxford.

Darville, G. and Smale, G. (1990) *Partners in Empowerment: Networks of Innovation in Social Work [Pictures of Practice Vol. II]*, London.

Das Gupta, M., et al. (2003) *Fostering Community-Driven Development: What Role for the State?*, Washington.

Dasgupta, P. and Serageldin, I. (2000) *Social Capital: a multifaceted perspective*, Washington.

Dasgupta, S. (ed.) (1967) *Towards a Philosophy of Social Work in India*, New Delhi.

Dávid-Barrett, T. and Dunbar, R. (2013) Processing power limits social group size: computational evidence for the cognitive costs of sociality, *Proceedings of the Royal Society B* 280, 1–23.

Davies, B. (1987) 'Review Article: Making a Reality of Community Care', *British Journal of Social Work*, 18, 173–87.

Davies, I. (1988) *'The IAF Training Programme and Philosophy of Organising'*, London.

Davies, I. and Evans, A. (1992) *Partners in Action: a partnership in community development between the Church in Wales and The Children's Society*, Penarth.

Davis, A., et al. (1977) *The Management of Deprivation: Final Report of the Southwark Community Development Project*, London.

Davis, A.F. (1967) *Spearheads for Reform: the social settlements and the Progressive Movement 1890–1914*, New York.

Davy, J. (ed.) (1888) *Elberfeld Poor Law System: Reports on the Elberfeld Poor Law System; German Workmen's Colonies, etc.*, London.

DCLG. (2006a) *Strong and prosperous communities The Local Government White Paper*, London.

— (2006b) *The Community Development Challenge*, London.
— (2008a) *Communities in control: Real people, real power – Improving local accountability: Consultation*, London.
— (2008b) *Evaluation of the take-up and use of the Well-being Power – Research Summary*, London.
— (2008c) *Lifetime Homes, Lifetime Neighbourhoods: A National Strategy for Housing in an Ageing Society*, London.
— (2008d) *Practical use of well-being power*, London.
— (2008e) *Sustainable Development Action Plan 2007–2008*, Wetherby.
— (2008f) *Sustainable Communities Act 2007: A Guide*, London.
— (2008g) *The Empowerment Fund: Consultation on proposals for funding third sector organisations to empower communities across England*, London.
— (2009) *Power to promote well-being of the area: Statutory guidance for local councils*, London.
de Groot, L. (1992) 'City challenge: Competing in the urban regeneration game', *Local Economy*, 7, 196–209.
de Witt, B. (1915) *The Progressive Movement: A Non-partisan Comprehensive Discussion of Current Tendencies in American Politics*, New York.
Delgado, G. (1986) *Organizing the Movement: the roots and growth of ACORN*, Philadelphia.
Demers, J. (1972) 'Community development in a British New Town', *Community Development Journal*, 7, 130–5.
Department of Economic and Social Affairs, UN Secretariat. (2014) *The Millennium Development Goals Report 2014*, New York.
DETRs. (1998) *Modern Local Government: In Touch with the People White Paper*, London.
— (2000) *National Strategy for Neighbourhood Renewal: Report of Policy Action Team 17: Joining it up locally*, London.
— (2001) *Local Strategic Partnerships Government Guidance Summary: Guidance 09 Wetherby*, Wetherby.
Department of Health. (2006) *Sustainable Development Action Plan 2006*, London.
— (2009) *Communities for Health: Unlocking the energy within communities to improve health*, London.
— (2011) *The New Public Health System*, London.
Department of Social Services. (1980) *Report of the Working Group on Inequalities in Health Chair: Sir Douglas Black*, London.
Department of Work and Pensions. (2009) *Empowering engagement: a stronger voice for older people. The Government response to John Elbourne's review*, London.
Depts of Health, SSWS (1989) 'Caring for People: Community care in the next decade and beyond', London.

Devine, E. (1904) *The Principles of Relief*, London.

— (1922) *Social Work*, New York.

Devine, E. and Brandt, L. (1921) *American Social Work in the Twentieth Century*, New York.

Devine, E. and van Kleek, M. (1916) *Positions in Social Work: A Study of The Number, Salaries, Experience And Qualifications of Professional Workers in Unofficial Social Agencies in New York City, based upon an investigation made by Florence Woolston for the New York School of Philanthropy and the Intercollegiate Bureau of Occupations*, New York.

Dewe, P. and Kompier, M. (2008) *Mental Capital and Wellbeing: Making the most of ourselves in the 21st century Wellbeing and work: Future challenges*, London.

Diamond, J. (2004) 'Local regeneration initiatives and capacity building: Whose "capacity" and "building for what?', *Community Development Journal*, 39, 177–92.

Diamond, J. and Nelson, A. (1993) 'Community work: post local socialism'. *Community Development Journal*, 27, 38–44.

Dickie, M. (1968) 'Community Development in Scotland', *Community Development Journal*, 3, 175–83.

Dinham, A. (2005) 'Empowered or over-powered? The real experiences of local participation in the UK's New Deal for Communities', *Community Development Journal*, 40, 301–12.

Dinwiddie, C. [with] Bennet, I. (1921) *Community Responsibility: a review of the Cincinnati Social Unit experiment*, New York.

Dixon, A. (ed.) (2008) *Engaging patients in their Health: How the NHS needs to change – Report from the Sir Roger Bannister Health Summit, Leeds Castle, 17–18 May 2007*, London.

Dixon, R. (2010) *Beyond Beacons: ten years of illumination*, London.

Dolci, D. (1959) *To Feed the Hungry: Enquiry in Palermo*, London.

Dominelli, L. (1994) 'Women, Community Work and the State in the 1990s', in S. Jacobs and K. Popple (eds) *Community Work in the 1990s*, Nottingham.

Donahue, B. and Robinson, R. (2001) *Building a Church of Small Groups: a place where nobody stands alone*, Grand Rapids.

Donelson, A. (2004) 'The role of NGOs and NGO networks in meeting the needs of US *colonias*', *Community Development Journal*, 39, 332–44.

Doutopoulos, G. (1991) 'Community Development in Greece'. *Community Development Journal*, 26, 131–8.

Drakeford, M. and Hudson, B. (1993) 'Social work, poverty and community economic development', *Local Economy*, 8, 22–32.

Driver, S. and Martell, L. (1997) 'New Labour's Communitarianisms', *Critical Social Policy*, 17, 27–46.

du Bois, W. (1907) *Economic Cooperation among Negro Americans – The Atlanta University Publications, No. 12*, Atlanta.

du Sautoy, P. (1962) *The Organization of a Community Development Programme*, London.

— (1966) 'Community Development in Britain?', *Community Development Journal*, 1, 54–6.

Duncan, P. and Thomas, S. (2000) *Neighbourhood Regeneration: resourcing community involvement*, Bristol.

Dungate, M. (ed.). (1980) *Community Works 1: aspects of three innovatory projects*, London.

Dungate, M., et al. (eds) (1979) *Collective Action, a selection of community work case studies*, London.

Dunham, A. (1958) *Community Welfare Organization: Principles and Practice*, New York.

— (1959) 'What is the Job of the Community Organization Worker?', in E. Harper and A. Dunham (eds) *Community Organizing in Action – basic literature and critical comments*, New York.

— (1970) *The New Community Organization*, New York.

Eade, D. and Williams, S. (1995) *The OXFAM Handbook of Development and Relief – Vols I–III*, Oxford.

Eastman, M. (1995) 'User First – implications for management', in R. Jack (ed.) *Empowerment in Community Care*, London.

ECOTEC. (2006) *Cross Cutting Themes Research Project (Objectives 1 and 3) Final Report*, Cardiff.

Edwards, B., et al. (2000) *Partnership working in rural regeneration. Governance and empowerment?*, Bristol.

Edwards, E. and Egbert-Edwards, M. (1998) 'Community Development with American Indians and Alaska Natives', in F. Rivera and J. Erlich (eds) *Community Organizing in a Diverse Society*, Boston.

Edwards, M. (1994) 'Rethinking social development: the search for "relevance"', in D. Booth (ed.) *Rethinking social development: theory, research and practice*, Harlow.

Edwards, M. and Hulme, D. (2000) 'Scaling up NGO impact on development: learning from experience', in J. Pearce (ed.) *Development, NGOs and Civil Society*, Oxford.

Edwards, P. and Tsouros, A. (2008) A Healthy City is an Active City: a physical activity planning guide, Copenhagen.

Eichler, M. (2007) *Consensus Organizing: Building Communities of Mutual Self Interest*, Thousand Oaks.

Ekosgen. (2010) *East Manchester New Deal for Communities: Final Evaluation. Executive Summary*, Manchester.

Elbourne, J. (2008) *Review of Older People's Engagement with Government – Report to Government*, London.

Elliott, B. (2012) 'Obama tied to architect of U.S. collapse – New Party leader planned to bring about "crisis" of overloaded welfare state', Washington.

Ellsworth, L. and White, A. (2004) *Deeper Roots: Strengthening Community Tenure Security and Community Livelihoods*, New York.

Engels, F. (1892) *The Condition of the Working-Class in England in 1844*, London.

English, J. (ed.) (1998) *Social Services in Scotland*, 4th edn, Edinburgh.

Etzioni, A. (1993) *The Spirit of Community: the reinvention of American society*, New York.

EU Directorate General on Regional Policy. (2005) *Partnership in the 2000–2006 programming period: analysis of the implementation of the partnership principle*, Brussels.

Eugster, C. (1970) 'Field Education in West heights: equipping a deprived community to help itself', in F. Cox, et al. (eds) *Strategies of Community Organization: a Book of Readings*, Itasca.

European Commission. (1999) *Council Regulation (EC) No. 1260/99*, Brussels.

— (2007) *European Social Fund: Investing in People*, Brussels.

Fabricant, M. and Fisher, R. (2002) *Settlement Houses under siege: the struggle to sustain community organizations in New York City*, New York.

Fagan, H. (1979) *Empowerment: skills for parish social action*, New York.

Fairnington, A. (2004) 'Communities that Care: a case study of regeneration from Wales', *Critical Public Health* 14, 27–36.

Fanon, F. (and Farrington, C. translator) (2001) *The Wretched of the Earth*, London.

— (1970) *A Dying Colonialism*, London.

Farrington, J. (2002) *Social Capital*, London.

FCDL. (2008) *Engaging and Influencing Decision-Makers: a guide for community groups*, Sheffield.

Feagin, J. and Shettan, B. (1985) 'Community Organizing in Houston: social problems and community response', *Community Development Journal*, 20, 99–105.

Federated Women's Institutes of Canada. (2015) *History of the Federated Women's Institutes of Canada*, St. George.

Feehan, D., et al. (2013) 'Community, Economic, and Social Development in a Changing World', in M. Weil, et al. (eds) *The Handbook of Community Practice*, Los Angeles.

Feinberg, M., et al. (2010) 'Effects of the Communities That Care Model in Pennsylvania on Change in Adolescent Risk and Problem Behaviours', *Preventive Science*, 11, 171.

Fenner, R. (2000) *A Canadian Woman of the 20th Century Who Has Made a Difference*, Vancouver.

Ferriss, S. and Sandoval, R. (ed.). (1997) *The Fight in the Fields: Cesar Chavez and the Farmworkers Movement*, Orlando.

Field, J. (2003) *Social Capital*, London.

Findlay, L. (2002) 'Negotiating the swamp: the opportunity and challenge of reflexivity in research practice', *Qualitative Research*, 2, 209–30.

Fish, J. (1973) *Black Power, White Control: The Struggle of the Woodlawn Organization in Chicago*, Princeton.

Fisher, J. and Sarkar, R. (2006) *The LSP Guide: a handy guide to getting involved for voluntary and community groups*, London.

Fisher, J., et al. (2013) *'Creative disruptors' or community development workers? – Community organising in the north of England*, Manchester.

Fisher, R. (1993) 'Grass-Roots Organizing Worldwide: Common Ground, Historical Roots, and the Tension between Democracy and the State', in R. Fisher and J. Kling (eds) *Mobilizing the Community: Local Politics in the Era of the Global City*, Newbury Park.

— (1994) *Let the People Decide: neighborhood organizing in America*, New York.

— (1999) 'The importance of history and context in community organization', in J. Rothman (ed.) *Reflections on Community organization: enduring themes; critical issues*, Itasca.

Fisher, R. and Kling, J. (eds) (1993) *Mobilizing the Community: Local Politics in the era of the Global City*, Newbury Park.

Follett, M. (1918) *The New State*, New York.

— (1919) 'Community is a Process', *Philosophical Review*, 28, 576–88.

— (1920) *The New State – Group Organization, The Solution Of Popular Government*, New York.

Foo, C. and Grinyer, P. (1995) *Sun Tzu on Management: the art of war in contemporary business strategy*, Singapore.

Ford Foundation. (2002) *Building Assets to Reduce Poverty and Injustice*, New York.

Foweraker, J. (1995) *Theorising Social Movements*, London.

Fowler, A. (1997) *Striking a Balance: a guide to enhancing the effectiveness on non-governmental organisation in international development*, London.

— (2000) *The Virtuous Spiral: a guide to sustainability for NGOs in International Development*, London.

Foxton, F. and Jones, R. (2011) *Social Capital Indicators Review*, London.

Fraggos, C. (1968) 'A Settlement's role in CD: a decade of experience', *Community Development Journal*, 3, 201–10.

Fraisse, L. (2009) *Potential and Ambivalent Effects of Grassroots Initiatives on Neighbourhood Development*, Paris

Freeman, J. (1995) *The Tyranny of Structurelessness*, Kingston.

Freire, P. (1972a) *Cultural Action for Freedom*, London.

— (1972b) *Pedagogy of the Oppressed*, London.

Friedmann, J. (1975) 'The Future of Comprehensive Urban Planning: a critique', in R. Kramer and H. Specht (eds) *Readings in Community Organization Practice*, Englewood Cliffs.

Frost, N. and Stein, M. (1989) 'What's happening in Social Services Departments?', in M. Langan and P. Lee (eds) *Radical Social Work Today*, London.

Fullick, L. (1986) The MSC and the local community, in C. Benn and J. Fairley (eds), *Challenging the MSC on Jobs, Education, and Training: enquiry into a National disaster*, London.

Gallagher, A. (1977) 'Women and Community Work', in M. Mayo (ed.) *Women in the Community*, London.

Ganz, M. and Hilton, K. (2010) *The New Generation of Organizers*, Boston.

Garcia, M. (2009) *A Dolores Huerta Reader*, Albuquerque.

Garth, B. (1980) *Neighborhood Law Firm for the Poor: A comparative Study of Recent Developments in Legal Aid; in the Legal Profession*, Alpena an den Rijn.

Garven, F. (2013) 'Co-producing with communities in Scotland – the potential and the challenges,' in E. Loeffler et al. (eds.) (2013) *Co-Production of Health and Wellbeing in Scotland*, Glasgow.

Garvin, C. and Cox, F. (2001) 'A History of Community Organizing since the Civil War with special reference to oppressed communities', in J. Rothman, et al. (eds) *Strategies in Community Intervention*, Itasca.

Gaynor, N. (2011) 'In-Active citizenship and the depoliticization of community development in Ireland', *Community Development Journal*, 46, 27–41.

Georghegan, M. and Powell, F. (2009) 'Community development and the contested politics of the late modern agora: of, alongside or against neo-liberalism?', *Community Development Journal*, 44, 430–47.

Giddens, A. (1998) *The Third Way: the renewal of Social Democracy*, Cambridge.

Gilbert, N. and Specht, H. (1977a) *Planning for Social Welfare: issues; models and task*, Englewood Cliffs.

— (1977b) 'The Incomplete Profession', in H. Specht and A. Vickery (eds) *Integrating Social Work Methods*, London.

— (1979) 'Who Plans?', in F. Cox, et al. (eds) *Strategies of Community Organization*, Itasca.

Gilchrist, A. (2009) *The Well-connected Community: A Networking Approach to Community Development*, Bristol.

— (2012) *Cross-country exchanges: a retrospective of SCCD's/CDX's achievements*, Glasgow.

Gilman, D., et al. (eds) (1905) 'Elberfeld', in D. Gilman, et al. (eds) *The New International Encyclopedia*, New York.

Ginsberg, N. (1979) *Class, Capital, and Social Policy*, Basingstoke.

— (1999) 'Putting the "social" into urban regeneration policy', *Local Economy*, 14, 55–77.

Gittell, R. and Vidal, A. (1998) *Community Organizing: building social capital as a development strategy*, Thousand Oaks.

Glazer, N. and Moynihan, D. (1970) *Beyond the Melting Pot: the Negroes, Puerto Ricans, Jews, Italians and Irish of New York City*, Cambridge.

Godfrey, M., et al. (2004) *Building a good life for older people in local communities*, York.

Goetschius, G. (1961) 'Conclusions', in P. Kuenstler (ed.) *Community Organization in Great Britain*, London.

— (1969) *Working with Community Groups*, London.

Goetschius, G. and Tash, M. (1967) *Working with Unattached Youth: problem, approach, method*, London

Goldstein, H. (1973) *Social Work Practice: a unitary approach*, Columbia.

Gorst, S. (1895) '"Settlements" in England and America', in J. Knapp (ed.) *The Universities and the Social Problem*, London.

Gough, I. (1979) *The Political Economy of the Welfare State*, Macmillan, London.

Gowman, N. (1999) *Healthy Neighbourhoods*, London.

Green, G. and Lakey, L. (2013) *Building dementia-friendly communities: A priority for everyone*, London.

Green, G., et al. (2005) *The Dynamics of Neighbourhood Sustainability*. Joseph Rowntree Foundation, York.

Green, J. and Chapman, A. (1992) 'The Community Development Project: Lessons for today', *Community Development Journal*, 27, 242–58.

Green, L., et al. (1996) 'Ecological Foundations of Health Promotion', *American Journal of Health Promotion*, 10, 270–81.

Greenberg, M. (1999) *Restoring America's Neighborhoods: how local people make a difference*, New Brunswick.

Greenberg, M., et al. (1993) 'Community Organizing to Prevent TOADS in the United States', *Community Development Journal*, 28, 55–65.

Greene, S. (2007) 'Including young mothers: community-based participation and the continuum of active citizenship', *Community Development Journal*, 42, 167–80.

Greenwood, J. (1869) *Seven Curses of London*, Boston.

Griffiths, Sir E.R. (1988) *Community Care: Agenda for Action*, London.

Griffiths, H. (1975) 'Community Development: Some more lessons from the recent past in Northern Ireland', *Community Development Journal*, 10, 2–13.

Grootaert, C. (1998) 'Social Capital: the missing link', Washington.

Grosser, C. (1975) 'Community Development Programs serving the Urban Poor', in R. Kramer and H. Specht (eds) *Readings in Community Organization Practice*, Englewood Cliffs.

— (1976) *New Directions in Community Organization: From Enabling to Advocacy*, New York.

Gutierrez, G. (1988) *A Theology of Liberation: History, Politics and Salvation*, London.

Hadley, R. and McGrath, M. (1984) *When Social Services are Local: the Normanton experience*, London.

Haines, J. (1980) 'In-Service Training for Community Work in the United Kingdom: A Review of Recent Experience', *Community Development Journal*, 15, 41–52.

Hale, S. (2006) *Blair's Community: communitarian thought and New Labour*, Manchester.

Handy, C. (1988) *Understanding Voluntary Organizations*, London.

— (1990) *Inside Organizations: Ideas for Managers*, London.

Hanifan, L. (1914) 'The rural school community center', *Annals of the American Academy of Political and Social Science*, 67, 130–8.

— (1920) *The Community Center*. Silver, Boston.

Hanmer, J. (1979) 'Theories and Ideologies in British Community Work', *Community Development Journal*, 14, 200–9.

— (1991) 'The Influence of Women on Community Development and Health', in J. Jones and J. Tilson (eds) *Roots and Branches*, Milton Keynes.

Haralambides, T. (1966) 'Community Development in Greece: the Royal National Foundation and the activities of its Central Committee for Community Development', *Community Development Journal*, 1, 19–22.

Hardcastle, D., et al. (2004) *Community Practice: Theories and Skills for Social Workers*, New York.

Harding, T. (1999) 'Enabling Older People to Live in their Own Homes', in S. Sutherland (ed.) *With Respect to Old Age: Long Term Care — Rights and Responsibilities Part II: Research*, London.

Harding, P. (1991) 'Qualitative Indicators and the Project Framework', *Community Development Journal*, 26, 294–305.

Harper, E. and Dunham, A. (1959) *Community Organization in Action: basic literature and critical comments*, Boston.

Harrison, N. (2000) *Constructing Sustainable Development*, New York.

Harrison, S. (1920) *Social Conditions in an American City: A Summary of the findings of The Springfield Survey*, New York.

Harshbarger, S. and Crafts A. (2009) *An Independent Governance Assessment of ACORN: The Path To Meaningful Reform*, Los Angeles.

Hart, J. (1920) *Community Organizing*, New York.

Harvey, S. (2008) *Shifting the Balance of Health Care to Local Settings: The See-Saw report*, London.

Hashemi, S. (1995) 'NGO accountability in Bangladesh: beneficiaries, donors and the State', in M. Edwards and D. Hulme (eds) *Non-Governmental Organisations – performance and accountability – beyond the magic bullet*, London.

Hawkins, J., et al. (2008) 'Early Effects of Communities That Care on Targeted Risks and Initiation of Delinquent Behavior and Substance Use', *Journal of Adolescent Health*, 43, 15–22.

Hawtin, M., et al. (1994) *Community Profiling: auditing social needs*, Buckingham.

Hayes, A. (1921) *Rural Community Organization*, Chicago.

Health Promotion. (1986) 'Strengthening Communities', *Health Promotion*, 1, 449–51.

Health Scotland. (2003) *LEAP for Health Learning, Evaluation and Planning*, Edinburgh.

Hearn, B. and Thomson, B. (1987) *Developing Community Social work in Teams: a manual for practice*, London.

Helleiner, G. and Stewart, F. (1987) 'The International System and the Protection of the Vulnerable', in Cornia, G., et al. (1987) *Adjustment with a Human Face*, Clarendon Press, Oxford.

Hemenway, H. (1916) *American Public Health Protection*, Indianapolis.

Henderson, C. (1899) *Social Settlements*, New York.

Henderson, P. and Glen, A. (2006) 'From recognition to support: Community development workers in the United Kingdom', *Community Development Journal*, 4, 277–92.

Henderson, P. and Salmon, H. (1995) *Community Organising: The UK Context*, London.

Henderson, P. and Thomas, D. (1979) 'Community Work Training at the National Institute of Social Work in the United Kingdom', *Community Development Journal*, 14, 115–21.

— (1981) 'Federations of Community Groups: benefits and dangers', *Community Development Journal*, 16, 98–104.

— (1987) *Skills in Neighbourhood Work*, London.

— (2000) *Skills in Neighbourhood Work*, 2nd edn, London.

— (2001) *Skills in Neighbourhood Work*, 3rd edn, London.

Henderson, P., et al. (1984) *Learning More About Community Social Work*, London.

Henkel, H. and Stirrat, R. (2001) 'Participation as spiritual duty, empowerment as secular subjection', in B. Cooke and U. Kothari (eds) *Participation: the new tyranny?*, London.

Heraud, B. (1975) 'The New Towns: the philosophy of community', in P.
    Leonard (ed.) *The Sociology of Community Action*, Keele.
Herrick, J. and Stuart, P. (eds) (2005) *Encyclopedia of Social Welfare in North
    America*, Thousand Oaks.
Hickey, S. and Mohan, G. (2004) *Participation: from tyranny to transformation*,
    London.
Higgins, J. (1980) 'Unlearnt Lessons from America', *Community Development
    Journal*, 15, 105–9.
Higgins, J., et al. (1983) *Government and Urban Policy: Inside the Policy Making
    Process*, Oxford.
Highlands and Islands Development Board. (1978) *An Outline of the Powers
    And Work of the Highlands and Islands Development Board*, Inverness.
— (1982) *The Highlands and Islands: a contemporary account*, Inverness.
Hill, O. (1875) *Homes of the London Poor*, New York.
— (1877) *Our Common Land (and Other Short Essays)*, London.
Hillman, A. (1950) *Community Organization and Planning*, New York.
Hills, J. and Stewart, K. (2005) *Policies towards poverty, inequality and exclusion
    since 1997*, York.
Hirsch, P. (1998) *Barbara Leigh Smith Bodichon 1827–1891: feminist and
    rebel*, London.
HM Government. (1990) *National Health Service and Community Care Act
    1990*, London
— (1999) *With Respect to Old Age: Long Term Care – Rights and
    Responsibilities: A Report by the Royal Commission on Long Term Care*,
    London.
— (2000) *Local Government Act 2000: Chapter 22 – Part I Promotion of
    Economic, Social or Environmental Well-Being Etc.*, London
— (2011) *Giving White Paper*, London.
Hochgerner, J. (2014) *The current state of social innovation in Europe*, keynote
    address: European Social Innovation Week, 15–19 September 2014,
    Tilburg/NL.
Hodge, P. (1964) 'Community Organisation and the Bristol Social Project',
    Community Development Bulletin, XV, 164–6.
— (1970) 'The Future of Community Development', in W. Robson and
    B. Crick (eds) *The Future of the Social Services*, London.
Hollie, D. (2012) 'Grand Fountain of the United Order of True Reformers',
    Encyclopedia Virginia, Charlottesville.
Holman, R. (1978) *Poverty: explanations of social deprivation*, Oxford.
Home Office. (1999) *Report of the Policy Action Team on Community Self-Help*,
    London.
— (2001) *Building Cohesive Communities: A Report by the Ministerial Group
    on Public Order and Community Cohesion*, London.

Hope, A., et al., (1984) *Training for Transformation: A Handbook for Community Workers* (4 vols), Gweru.

Hopkins, E. (1878) *Work in Brighton or, Woman's Mission to Women*, London.

Hopper, K./TCC – Wales (Together Creating Communities), *Community Organising*, Wrexham.

Horwitt, S. (1989) *Let them call me Rebel: Saul Alinsky – his life and legacy*, New York.

Howaldt, J. and Schwarz, M. (2010) *Social Innovation: Concepts, research fields and international trends*, Dortmund.

Howard, J. (ed.) (1970) *Awakening Minorities: American Indians; Mexican Americans; Puerto Ricans*, Piscataway.

Hughes, C. (2006) *Developing Reflexivity in Research*, Coventry.

Hulme, D. (1994) 'Social Development Research and the Third Sector: NGOs as users and subjects of social inquiry', in D. Booth (ed.) *Rethinking Social Development: theory, research and practice*, London.

Hulme, D. and Edwards, M. (1997a) 'NGOs, States and Donors: An Overview', in D. Hulme and M. Edwards (eds) *NGOs, States and Donors: too close for comfort*, New York.

— (1997b) 'Conclusion: too close to the powerful, too far from the powerless?', in D. Hulme and M. Edwards (eds) *NGOs, States and Donors: too close for comfort?*, Houndmills.

Hutt, J. (Secretary for Health). (1999) *Partnerships for Progress – Community Care in the 21st Century – Address to Developing Partnerships Congress*, Cardiff.

Hyde, C. (2001) 'Experiences of Women Activists: implications for community organizing', *Tactics and Techniques in Community Organizing*, Itasca.

IASSW, et al. (2010) *Global Agenda for Social Work and Social Development: Towards an Engagement Agenda: Mobilisation of Social Workers, Social Work Educators; Policy Practitioners and Developers for Global Social Change*, Geneva.

ICSSW. (2010) *From Vision to Action: The Report of the Independent Commission on Social Services in Wales*, Cardiff.

IDA (2007) *Impact 2007 Better and Brighter – The Annual Report of the Beacon Scheme*, London.

Illich, I. (1973) *Deschooling Society*, London.

— (1977) 'Disabling Professions', in I. Illich, et al. (eds) *Disabling Professions*, London.

Illsley, B. (2002) *Planning with communities: a good practice guide*, London.

ILO Evaluation Unit. (2012) *ILO policy guidelines for results-based evaluation: Principles, rationale, planning and managing for evaluations*, Geneva.

International Bank for Reconstruction and Development. (1994) *Averting the Old Age Crisis Policies to Protect the Old and Promote Growth*, Washington.

Inter-Project Editorial Team. (1977) *Gilding the Ghetto: the state and the poverty experiments*, London.

Ipsos MORI and Wavehill. (2015) *Communities First: a process of evaluation*, Cardiff

— (2015) *Process evaluation of Communities First Appendix 1: Communities First Theory of Change Report*, Cardiff.

Islam, N. (2015) *Towards a sustainable social model: Implications for the post-2015 agenda DESA Working Paper No. 136*, New York.

Jack, R. (1995) 'Empowerment in Community Care', in R. Jack (ed.) *Empowerment in Community Care*, London.

Jackson, C. (1895) 'The Children's Country Holidays Fund and the Settlements', in J. Knapp (ed.) *The Universities and the Social Problem*, London.

Jacobs, S. (1994) 'Community Work in a Changing World', in S. Jacobs and K. Popple (eds) *Community Work in the 1990's*, Nottingham.

Jameson, N. (1988) 'Organising for Change', *Christian Action Journal*, 4–5.

Jameson, N. and Gecan, M. (2013) *Effective Organising for Congregational Renewal*, London.

Jenks, J. (1910) *Governmental action for social welfare*, New York.

Jensen, H. (1958) 'Sociological Aspects of Aging', *Public Health Reports*, 73, 569–76.Johnson, K., et al. (2000) 'Mobilizing Church Communities to Prevent Alcohol and Other Drug Abuse: A Model Strategy and Its Evaluation', *Journal Community Practice*, 7, 1–27.

Johnson, L. (1964) *Proposal for 'A Nationwide War on the Sources of Poverty' – Lyndon B. Johnson's Special Message to Congress, March 16, 1964*, New York.

Jolly, R., et al. (2012) *Be Outraged: there are alternatives*, Oxford.

Jones, C. (1983) *State Social Work and the Working Class*, London.

— (2011) *Building strong, responsible communities is a priority*, Cardiff.

Jones, C., et al. (1982) 'Community work with the elderly', in G. Craig (ed.) *Community Work and the State: towards a radical practice*, London.

Kahn, S. (1982) *Organizing: a guide to grassroots leaders*, New York.

Kane, L. (2008) 'The World Bank, community development and education for social justice', *Community Development Journal*, 43, 194–209.

Karagkounis, V. (2009) 'Introducing a community work perspective in local policy – making a pilot community intervention in the Municipality of Aigeiros', Thrace, Greece, *Community Development Journal*, 45, 237–52.

Karim, M. (1995) 'NGOs in Bangladesh: issues of legitimacy and accountability', in M. Edwards and D. Hulme (eds) *Non-Governmental Organisations: performance and accountability – beyond the Magic Bullet*, London.

Kellogg, C. (1894) *History of Charity Organization in the United States. Report of Committee of National Conference of Charities and Correction*, Chicago.

Kelly, A. (2008) *Can Action Research Evaluate and Enhance Policy Implementation?*, unpublished Ph.D. thesis, Swansea University.

Kelly, A. and Sewell, S. (1988) *With Head, Heart and Hand: Dimensions of Community Building*, Brisbane.

Kemp, L., et al. (2008) 'What's in the Box? Issues in evaluating interventions to develop strong and open communities', *Community Development Journal*, 43, 459–69.

Kendall, L. (2008) 'What needs to change to meet the needs of future patients?', in A. Dixon (ed.) *Engaging patients in their Health: How the NHS needs to change – Report from the Sir Roger Bannister Health Summit, Leeds Castle, 17–18 May 2007*, London.

Kenny, S. (2011) 'Towards unsettling community development', *Community Development Journal*, 46, 7–19.

Kenway, P. and Palmer, G. (2007) *Monitoring poverty and social exclusion in Wales – Findings*, York.

Kenzer, M. (1999) 'Healthy cities: a guide to the literature', *Environment and Urbanization*, 11, 201–30.

Khindulka, K. (1975) 'Community Development: Potentials and Limitations', in R. Kramer and H. Specht (eds) *Readings in Community Organization Practice*, Englewood Cliffs.

Kickbusch, I. (1986) 'Introduction: Health Promotion', *Health Promotion*, 1, 3–4.

Kirckbusch, I., et al. (1988) *Healthy Public Policy: Report on the Adelaide Conference, April, 1988, 2nd International Conference on Health Promotion*, Adelaide.

Kingsbury, D. (2004) 'Community Development', in D. Kingsbury, et al. (eds) *Key Issues in Development*, Houndmills.

Kirkwood, C. (1975) 'Community Democracy', in G. Brown (ed.) *The Red Paper on Scotland*, Edinburgh.

Kjellstrom, T., et al. (2008) *Our cities, our health, our future: Report to the WHO Commission on Social Determinants of Health from the Knowledge Network on Urban Settings Acting on social determinants for health equity in urban setting*, Copenhagen.

Klausner, D. (1987) 'Infrastructure Investment and Political Ends: The Case of London's Docklands', *Local Economy*, 1, 47–59.

Klien, J. (1961) *Working with Groups*, London.

Klinmahorm, S. and Ireland, K. (1992) 'NGO-government collaboration in Bangladesh', in M. Edwards and D. Hulme (eds) *Making a Difference: NGOs and development in a changing World*, London.

Klitgaard, R. (1998) 'Comment', in R. Picciotto and E. Wiesner (eds) *Evaluation and Development: the institutional dimension*, New Brunswick.

Knapp, M., et al. (1992) *Care in the Community: challenge and demonstration*, Aldershot.

Knight, B. and Hayes, R. (1981) *Self-Help in the Inner City*, London.

Kotval, Z. (2006) 'The link between community development practice and theory: intuitive or irrelevant?', *Community Development Journal*, 41, 75–88.

Kramarenko, V., et al. (2010) *Zimbabwe: Challenges and Policy Options after Hyperinflation*, Washington.

Kraushaar, R. (1982) 'Review Article: Structural Problems and Local Responses: The Final Reports of the Local Community Development Projects', *Community Development Journal*, 17, 68–72.

Kretzmann, J. and McKnight, J. (1993) *Building Communities from the Inside Out*, Chicago.

Kuenstler, P. (1955) *Social Group Work*, London.

— (1961) 'Community Organisation', in P. Kuenstler (ed.) *Community Organisation in Great Britain*, London.

— (1986) 'Conclusions', in Calouste Gulbenkian Foundation (ed.) *Communities in Business – A report on the community enterprise monitoring project – 1983–1985*, London.

Labonne, J. and Chase, R. (2008) *Do Community-Driven Development Projects Enhance Social Capital? Evidence from the Philippines Policy Research Working Paper 4678*, Washington.

Labonté, R. (1991a) 'Econology: integrating health and sustainable development. Part I: theory and background', *Health Promotion International*, 6, 49–65.

— (1991b) 'Econology: integrating health and sustainable development. Part II guiding principles for decision-making', *Health Promotion International*, 6, 147–56.

— (1998) *A Community Development Approach to Health Promotion: a background paper on practice tensions, strategic models and accountability requirements for health authority work on the broad determinants of health*, Edinburgh.

— (1999) *Developing Community Health in Wales: a community development approach to health promotion*, Cardiff.

Lady of Boston. (1832) *The Visitor of the Poor*, Boston.

Lahiri-Dutt, K. (2004) '"I plan, you participate": A southern view of community participation in urban Australia', *Community Development Journal*, 39, 13–27.

Lalonde, M. (1974) *A New Perspective on the Health of Canadians: a working document* [Lalonde Report], Ottawa.

Lambert, J. (1981) 'Review Article: A Graveyard for Community Action? Housing Issues and the Community Development Projects in Britain 1968 to 1978', *Community Development Journal*, 16, 246–53.

Landon, F. (1920) 'Henry Bibb, "A Colonizer"', *Journal of Negro History*, 5, 437–46.

Lane, R. (1940) *'The Lane Committee Report': Report of Groups Studying the Community Organization Process*, New York.

Larsen, C. (2004) *Facilitating community involvement: practical guidance for practitioners and policy makers*, London.

Lauffer, A. (1978) *Social Planning at the Community Level*, Englewood Cliffs.

Laughry, R. (2002) 'Partnering the state at the local level: the experience of one community worker', *Community Development Journal*, 37, 60–8.

Lawless, P. (2007) *The New Deal for Communities programme in England: is area based urban regeneration possible?*, Sheffield.

Layard, R. (2011) *Happiness: lessons from a new science*, London.

Lazenblatt, A., et al. (2001) 'Revealing the hidden "troubles" in Northern Ireland: the role of participatory rapid appraisal', *Health Education Research*, 16, 567–78.

LDDC. (1992) *The Challenge of Urban Regeneration*, London.

LEAP. (1984) *The Last LEAP year Final Report of the Local Enterprise Advisory Project*, Paisley.

Leaper, R. (1968) *Community Work*, London

Ledwith, M. (2005) *Community Development: a critical approach*, Bristol.

— (2011) 'Reclaiming the radical agenda: a critical approach to community development', in G. Craig, et al. (eds) *The Community Development Reader: history, themes and issues*, Bristol.

Ledwith, M. and Springett, J. (2010) *Participatory Practice: community-based action for transformative change*, Bristol.

Lee, A. (2003) 'Community Development in Ireland', *Community Development Journal*, 39, 38–48.

Lee, P. (1937) *Social Work as Cause and Function; and other papers*, New York.

Lee, P., et al. (1922) *Report of a study of the interrelation of the work of national social agencies in fourteen American communities: This study was undertaken by a Conference of National Social Agencies*, New York.

Lees, R. and Mayo, M. (1984) *Community Action for Change*, London.

Lees, R. and Smith, G. (1975) *Action Research in Community Development*, London.

Lekoko, R. (2013) 'The perceived effects of field-based learning in building responsive partnerships of community development', *Community Development Journal*, 40, 313–28.

Leonard, P. (1975a) 'Introduction: The Sociology of Community Action', in P. Leonard (ed.) *The Sociology of Community Action No. 21*, Keele.

— (1975b) 'Towards a Paradigm for Radical Practice', in R. Bailey and M. Brake (eds) *Radical Social Work*, London.

— (1979) 'Restructuring the Welfare State', *Marxism Today*, December, 7–13.

Leurs, R. (1998) 'Current challenges facing Participatory Rural Appraisal', in J. Blackburn and J. Holland (eds) *Who changes? Institutionalising participation in development*, London.

Lever/US Committee on Agriculture (1913) *Establishment of Agricultural Extension Departments*, Washington.

Lewin, K. (1948) *Resolving social conflicts; selected papers on group dynamics*, New York.

— (1952) *Field Theory in Social Science*, London.

Lindblom, C. (1970) 'The Science of "Muddling Through"', in F. Cox, et al. (eds) *Strategies of Community Organization: a book of readings*, Itasca.

Lindeman, E. (1921) *The Community: An Introduction to the Study of Community Leadership and Organization*, New York.

Link, A. (1954) *Woodrow Wilson and the Progressive Era 1910–1917*, New York.

Littlejohn, E. and Hodge, P. (1965) *Community Organisation: Work in Progress*, London.

Lloyd, G. and Black, S. (1993) 'Highlands and Islands Enterprise: Strategies for economic and social development', *Local Economy*, 8, 69–81.

Lloyd, N., et al. (2014) 'Identity in the fourth age: perseverance, adaptation and maintaining dignity', *Ageing and Society*, 34, 1–19.

Local Government Association. (2015) *Ageing – the silver lining: The opportunities and challenges of an ageing society for local government*, London.

Local Government Group. (2009) *The Beacon Scheme Round 10. Annual Report of the Beacon Scheme 2009/2010*, London.

Locality. (2012) *Trainee Organiser's Pack*, London.

Loch, C. (1890) *Charity Organisation*, London.

Loeffler, E., et al. (eds.) (2013) *Co-Production of Health and Wellbeing in Scotland*, Glasgow.

London Congregational Union. (1883) *The Bitter Cry of Outcast London. An Inquiry into the Condition of the Abject Poor*, London.

London Edinburgh Weekend Return Group. (1979) *In and Against the State*, London.

Loney, M. (1980) 'Community Action and Anti-Poverty Strategies: Some Transatlantic Comparisons', *Community Development Journal*, 15, 91–103.

— (1983) *Community against Government: The British Community Development Project 1968–78*, London.

Longstaff, B. (2008) *The Community Development Challenge: Strategies – Local strategic approaches to community development*, London.

Lotz, J. (1997) 'The Beginnings of Community Development in English-speaking Canada', in B. Wharf and M. Clague (eds) *Community Organization: the Canadian experience*, Don Mills.

— (1998) *The Lichen Factor – the Quest for Community Development in Canada*, Sydney.

Lovett, T., et al. (1994) 'Education, Conflict and Community Development in Northern Ireland', *Community Development Journal*, 29, 177–86.

Lowe, K. (1992) 'Community-based service: what the consumers think', *British Journal Mental Subnormality*, XXXV[I], 6–14.

Lowell, J. (1884) *Public Relief and Private Charity*, New York.

— (1911) 'The True Aim of Charity Organization Societies', in W. Stewart (ed.) *The Philanthropic Work of Josephine Shaw Lowell Containing a Biographical Sketch of her Life together with a Selection of her Public Papers and Private Letters*, New York.

Lupton, R. and Power, A. (2004) *What we know about Neighbourhood Change: A literature review*, London.

Lynch, J., et al. (2000) 'Social Capital – is it a good investment strategy for public health?', *Journal Epidemiological Community Health*, 54, 404–8.

MacAdam, E. (1925) *Equipment of the Social Worker*, London.

McArthur, A. (1984) *The community business movement in Scotland: contributions, public sector responses and possibilities*, Glasgow.

MacAulay, S. (2001) 'The Community economic Development tradition in Eastern Nova Scotia, Canada: ideological continuities and discontinuities between the Antigonish Movement and the Family of community development corporations', *Community Development Journal*, 36, 111–21.

McClenahan, B. (1918) *The Iowa Plan for the Combination of Public and Private*, Iowa.

— (1922) *Organizing the community – a review of tactical principles*, New York.

McConnell, C. (1983) 'The development of community development in Scotland', in D. Thomas (ed.) *Community Work in the Eighties*, London.

— (ed.) (2002) *The Making of an Empowering Profession*, Edinburgh.

McCrindle, L., et al. (2006) *Evaluation of Cymorth – Final Report*, Cardiff.

MacInnes, J. (1987) *Thatcherism at Work*, Milton Keynes.

McKay, D. and Cox, A. (1979) *The Politics of Urban Change*, London.

MacKay, T. (1896) *Methods of Social Reform: Essays Critical and Constructive*, London.

McKnight, J. and Block, P. (2012) *The Abundant Community: awakening the power of families and communities*, Oakland.

McLean, F. (1910) *The Formation of Charity Organization Societies In Smaller Cities*, New York.

McMechen, V. (1920) 'The Field of Social Case Work in the Small Community', *The Family*, 1, 36–40.

McMillen, W. (1945) *Community Organization for Social Welfare*, Chicago.

Mairs, B. (1992) *Helping Seniors Mobilize: A Handbook on Community Organizing*, Toronto.

Mansuri, G. and Rao, V. (2004) *Community-Based and -Driven Development: A Critical Review – Policy Research Working Paper 3209*, Washington.

— (2013) *Localizing Development – does participation work? A World Bank Policy Research Report*, Washington.

Marfo, E. (2008) 'Institutionalizing citizen participation and community representation in natural resource management: lessons from the Social Responsibility Agreement negotiation in Ghana', *Community Development Journal*, 43, 398–412.

Markey, S., et al. (2007) 'Contradictions in hinterland development: challenging the local development ideal in Northern British Columbia', *Community Development Journal*, 44, 209–29.

Marmot, M. (2014) *Review of social determinants and the health divide in the WHO European Region: Final Report*, Copenhagen.

— (2010) *Fair Society, Healthy Lives – The Marmot Review: Strategic Review of Health Inequalities in England post-2010*, London.

Marris, P. (1974) 'Experimenting in social reform', in D. Jones and M. Mayo (eds) *Community Work One*, London.

— (1982) *Community Planning and Conceptions of Change*, London.

Marris, P. and Rein, M. (1967) *Dilemmas of Social Reform: Poverty and Community Action in the United States*, London.

Marsden, D. (1990) 'The Meaning of Social Development', in D. Marsden and P. Oakley (eds) *Evaluating social development projects*, London.

— (1994) 'Indigenous management and the management of indigenous knowledge', in S. Wright (ed.) *Anthropology of Organizations*, London.

Marsden, D. and Oakley, P. (eds) (1990) *Evaluating Social Development Projects*, London.

— (1991) 'Future Issues and Perspectives in the Evaluation of Social Development', *Community Development Journal*, 26, 315–28.

Martin, D. (2005) 'A squat of your own', *Inside Housing*, August, 20–3.

Maru, Y. and Woodfood, K. (2007) 'A resources and shaping forces model for community-based sustainable development', *Community Development Journal*, 42, 5–18.

Marx, K. and Engels, F. (1848) *The Communist Manifesto*, Peking.

Mathiesen, T. (1974) *The Politics of Abolition*, Oxford.

Mayo, M. (1972) 'Some fundamental problems of Community Work on Housing Estates in Britain', *Community Development Journal*, 7, 55–9.

— (1975) 'Community Development: A Radical Alternative?', in R. Bailey and M. Brake (eds) *Radical Social Work*, London.

— (1979) 'Radical Politics and Political Action', in M. Loney and M. Allen (eds) *The Crisis of the Inner City*, London.

— (1980) 'Beyond CDP: reaction and community action', in M. Brake and R. Bailey (eds) *Radical Social Work and Practice*, London.

— (1994) *Communities and Caring: The Mixed Economy of Welfare*, London.

Mayo, M. (ed.) (1977) *Women in the Community*, London.

Mayo, M. and Robertson, J. (2003) 'The historical and policy context: setting the scene for current debates', in S. Banks, et al. (eds) *Managing Community Practice: principles, policies, and programmes*, Bristol.

Michael, P. (2008) *Public Health in Wales (1800–2000): A brief history*, Cardiff.

Midgley, J. (1981) *Professional Imperialism: Social Work in the Third World*, London.

— (1987) 'Popular Participation, Statism and Development', *Journal of Social Development in Africa*, 2, 5–16.

— (1995) *Social Development: The Developmental Perspective in Social Welfare*, London.

— (1997) *Social Welfare in Global Context*, Thousand Oaks.

Mikkelsen, B. (2005) *Methods for Development Work and Research: a new guide for practitioners*, New Delhi.

Miller, C. (2008) *The Community Development Challenge Management: Towards high standards in community development*, London.

Miller, E. and Rice, A. (1967) *Systems of Organization: the control task and sentient boundaries*, London.

— (1990) 'Tasks and Sentient Systems and their Boundary Controls', in E. Trisk and H. Murray (eds) *The Social Engagement of Social Science: A Tavistock Anthology. Volume 1: The Socio-Psychological Perspective*, Philadelphia.

Miller, J. (1981) *Situation Vacant: the social consequences of unemployment in a Welsh Town*, London.

Miller, M. (2011) 'A Critique of John McKnight: John Kretzmann's "Community Organizing in the Eighties – Toward a Post-Alinsky Agenda"', *COMM-Org Papers, 15*, Madison.

Ministry of Education. (1960) *The Youth Service in England and Wales [the Albemarle Report]*, London.

Ministry of Health. (2014a) *Care Act 2014*, London.

— (2014b) *Care and Support Statutory Guidance Issued under the Care Act 2014*, London.

Ministry of Health and Department of Health for Scotland. (1959) *Report of the Working Party on Social Workers in the Local Authority, Health and Welfare Services* [the Younghusband Report], London.

Minkler, M. (2008) 'Community Organizing with the Elderly Poor in San Francisco's Tenderloin District', in J. Rothman, et al. (eds) *Strategies of Community Intervention*, Peosta.

Mitton, R. and Morrison, E. (1972) *A Community Project in Notting Dale*, London.

Moffatt, K., et al. (1999) 'Advancing citizenship: a study of social planning', *Community Development Journal*, 34, 308–17.

Mogulof, M. (1969) 'Community Development: the American Models Cities Programme', *Community Development Journal*, 4, 204–11.

Mohan, G. (2013) 'Beyond Participation: Strategies for deeper empowerment', in B. Cooke and U. Kothari (eds) *Participation: the new tyranny*, London.

Mondros, J. and Wilson, S. (1994) *Organizing for Power and Empowerment*, New York.

Montiel, M., et al. (1998) *Chicanos, Community and Chang*, Needham Heights.

Morley, K. (1968) 'Social participation and social enterprise in Redditch, England', *Community Development Journal*, 3, 4–9.

Morris, J. (2007) *Removing the Barriers to Community Participation*, London.

Morris, R. (1970) 'The Role of the Agent in the Community Development process', in L. Cary (ed.) *Community Development as a Process*, Columbia.

Morris, R. and Binstock, R. (1966) *Feasible Planning for Social Change*, New York.

Morrissey, M., et al. (2005) *Mapping Social Capital: A Model for Investment*, Belfast.

Morse, M. (1968) *The Unattached*, London.

Morse, S. (2004) *Smart Communities: how citizens and local leaders can use strategic thinking to build a brighter future*, San Francisco.

Mosse, D. (2001) 'People's Knowledge, participation and patronage', in B. Cooke and U. Kothari (eds) *Participation: the new tyranny*, London.

Mowbray, M. (2011) 'What became of the Local State? Neo-liberalism, community development and local government', *Community Development Journal*, 46, i132–i153.

— (2005) 'Community capacity building or state opportunism?', *Community Development Journal*, 40, 3, 255–64.

Moynihan, D. (1969) *Maximum Feasible Misunderstanding: community action in the War on Poverty*, New York.

Muir, J. (2004) 'Community Development in Health – a Scottish perspective', *Journal of Community Work and Development*, 5, 11–30.

Mullaly, B. (1997) *Structural Social Work: ideology, theory, and practice*, Toronto.

Muller, J. (1995) 'Management of Urban Neighborhoods through Alinsky-Style Organizing: An Illustration from Vancouver, Canada', *Community Development Journal*, 20, 106–13.

Mundy, B. (1980) 'The permeation of community work into other disciplines', in P. Henderson, et al. (eds) *The Boundaries of Change in Community Work*, London.

Muntaner, C., et al. (2008) 'Social Capital and the Third Way in Public Health', in J. Green and R. Labonté (eds) *Critical Perspectives in Public Health*, London.

Murphy, M. (2002) 'Social Partnership – is it "the only game in town"?', *Community Development Journal*, 37, 80–90.

Murray, C. (1994) *Underclass: The Crisis Deepens*, London.

Musgrave, P., et al. (1999) *Flourishing Communities: engaging Church communities with government in New Deal for Communities*, London.

Myrdal, G. (1968) *Asian Drama: an inquiry into the poverty of nations*, Harmondsworth.

Naples, N. (1998a) *Grassroots Warriors: activist mothering, community work, and the War on Poverty*, New York.

— (ed.) (1998b) *Community Activism and Feminist Politics: organizing across race, class and gender*, New York.

— (1998c) 'Women's Community activism: exploring the dynamics of politicisation and diversity', in N. Naples, (ed.) *Community Activism and Feminist Politics: organizing across race, class and gender*, New York.

National Assembly for Wales. (1999) *Better Health – Better Wales. Developing Local Health Alliances*, Cardiff.

— (2000) *Communities First: regenerating our most disadvantaged communities*, Cardiff.

— (2001) *Improving Health in Wales – A Plan for the NHS with its Partners*, Cardiff.

National Assembly for Wales/WCVA. (2000) *Compact between the Government and the Voluntary Sector in Wales: Community Development*, Cardiff.

National Audit Office. (1987) *Department of Employment and Manpower Services Commission Adult Training Strategy*, London.

— (2008) *A Review by the National Audit Office Performance of the Department for Communities and Local Government 2007–08*, London.

— (2009) *Innovation across Central Government*, London.

— (2013) *Department of Communities and Local Government: Case study on integration: Measuring the costs and benefits of Whole-Place Community Budgets – Report by the Comptroller and Auditor General*, London.

National Council of Social Service. (1962) *Communities and Social Change: a guide to studies*, London.

— (1965) *Community Organisation work in progress*, London.

National Health Service (2014) *Five Year Forward View*, London.

National Institute of Health and Clinical Excellence. (2015) *Top of Form, Bottom of Form Community engagement overview*, London.

National Public Health Service for Wales. (2009) *Press Release: Cardiff awarded Healthy Cities status*, Cardiff.

Naylor, B. (1986) *Quakers in the Rhondda: 1926–1986*, Chepstow.

Neighbourhood Renewal Unit. (2005a) *New Deal for Communities*, London.

— (2005b) *New Deal for Communities: Annual Review 2001–2002*, London.

Nevin, B. and Shiner, P. (1995) 'Community regeneration and empowerment: A new approach to partnership', *Local Economy*, 9, 308–22.

Newell, K. (ed.) (1975) *Health by the People*, Geneva.

Newman, H. (1999) 'Neighborhood impacts of Atlanta's Olympic Games', *Community Development Journal*, 34, 151–9.

NHS Wales (2013) *Co-producing services – Co-creating Health*, Cardiff.

Nicholls, J., et al. (2012) *A guide to Social Return on Investment*, London.

Norman, J. (2010) *The Big Society: the anatomy of the new politics*, Buckingham.

North Tyneside CDP (1978) *In and Out of Work: a study of unemployment, low pay and income maintenance services*, London.

Norton, W. (1920) 'Community Organisation', *Proceedings of the National Conference of Social Work 46th Annual Session at Atlantic City, June 15, 1919*, Chicago.

Oakley, P. (1990) 'The evaluation of social development', in D. Marsden and P. Oakley (eds) *Evaluating social development projects*, Oxford.

— (1998) 'Community Development in the Third World', *Community Development Journal*, 4, 365–76.

Oakley, P., et al. (1991) *Projects with People: The practice of participation in rural development*, Geneva.

Oakley, P. and Kahssay, H. (1999) 'Community Involvement in Health Development: an overview', in H. Kahssay and P. Oakley (eds) *Community Involvement in Health Development: a review of the concept and practice*, Geneva.

O'Carroll, J. (2002) 'Culture Lag and Democratic Deficit in Ireland: or "Dat's outside de terms of d'agreemnent"', *Community Development Journal*, 37, 10–19.

ODA. (1995) *A Guide to Social Analysis in Developing Countries*, London.

OECD. (2007) *Human Capital*, Paris.

— (2008) *The Marshall Plan: lessons learned for the 21st Century*, Paris.

— (2012) *50 Years of Official Development Assistance*, Paris.

Office for National Statistics. (2010) *Old People's Day 2010*, London.

— (2015a) *Persistent Poverty in the UK and EU, 2008–2013*, London.

— (2015b) *Guide to Social Capital*, London.

Office of the Deputy Prime Minister – Neighbourhood Renewal Unit. (2005a) *About the NRU: The Neighbourhood Renewal Unit*, London.

— (2005b) *National Strategy for Neighbourhood Renewal*, London.

Office of the Prime Minister. (1991) *The Citizen's Charter – raising the standard*, London.

OFMDFM (Office of the First Minister and the Deputy First Minister). (2006) *A Shared Future First Triennial Action Plan 2006–2009. Improving relations in Northern Ireland – Making it happen – Implementing the policy and strategic framework for good relations in Belfast*, Belfast.

Ohmer, M. and DeMasi, K. (2009) *Consensus Organizing: A Community Development Workbook: A Comprehensive Guide to Designing, Implementing, and Evaluating Community Change Initiatives*, Thousand Oaks.

Ohri, A., et al. (eds) (1982) *Community Work and Racism*, London.

O'Kane, C. (2011) *Children's agency and participation – its relevance for development, peace, and human rights: reflections on practice from diverse contexts*, Geneva.

Older People's Commission for Wales. (2010a) *Strategic Plan 2010–2013*, Cardiff.

— (2010b) *Impact, Effectiveness and Lessons Learnt: Establishing the Older People's Commission for Wales*, Cardiff.

— (2011a) *'Dignified Care?' The experiences of older people in hospital in Wales*, Cardiff.

— (2011b) *The Commissioner's Report 2010/11 – Helping make Wales a great place to grow older*, Cardiff.

— (2012a) *Voice, Choice and Control Recommendations relating to the provision of independent advocacy in Wales – An independent advocacy in Wales*, Cardiff.

— (2012b) *The Commissioner's Report 2011/12 – Making Wales a good place to grow older, not just for some but for everyone*, Cardiff.

— (2013) *An Independent Voice and champion for Older People: The work of the Older People's Commissioner for Wales 2012–2013*, Cardiff.

Oliver, Q. (1990) 'Community development in areas of political and social conflict – the Case of Northern Ireland', *Community Development Journal*, 25, 370–6.

O'Malley, J. (1970) 'Community Action in Notting Hill', in A. Lapping (ed.) *Community Action*, London.

— (1977) *The Politics of Community Action: a decade of struggle in Notting Hill*, Nottingham.

Orozco, G., et al. (2008) *A Brief History of a Pioneering Community Development and Service Organization*, San Francisco.

Osmond, J. (2010) *Adding life to years: Welsh approaches to ageing policy*, Cardiff.

Ovington, M. (1911) *A Half a Man: The Status of the Negro in New York*, New York.

Paisley College of Technology and Local Government Unit. (1982) *Flagstone Enterprises Limited: the setting up of a community business in a housing estate in the West of Scotland. Working paper No. 12*, Glasgow.

Panet-Raymond, J. (1992) 'Partnership: myth or reality?', *Community Development Journal*, 27, 156–65.

— (1999) 'A Postscript: Community Development in Quebec: between hope and doubt', *Community Development Journal*, 34, 340–5.

Pardo, M. (1998) 'Creating Community: Mexican-American Women in Eastside, Los Angeles', in N. Naples, (ed.) *Community Activism and Feminist Politics: organizing across race, class and gender*, New York.

243

Parry-Williams, J. (1992) 'Scaling-up via legal reforms in Uganda'. In M. Edwards and D. Hulme (eds) *Making a Difference: NGOs and development in a changing World*, London.

Parsons, R. (1986) 'Practice and Patch: Passivity versus Participation', *British Journal of Social Work*, 16, 125–48.

Parsons, T. (ed.) (1947) 'The Modern Western Institutional System', in *Max Weber: the theory of social and economic organization*, New York.

Partners of Learning Initiatives for Rural and Northern BC (LIRN). (2006) *Learning Together: A Dialogue on Community Health Presented by the Partners of Learning Initiatives for Rural and Northern BC (LIRN): Cortes Island*, Vancouver.

Paton, R. (2003) *Managing and Measuring Social Enterprises*, London.

Patton, M. (1997) *Utilization-Focused Evaluation: The New Century Text*, Thousand Oaks.

PAULO. (2003) *National Occupational Standards for Community Development Work*, Grantham.

Paxton, W. and Pearce, N. (2005) *The Voluntary Sector delivering Public Services: transfer or transformation?*, York.

Payne, M. (1983) 'Implementing Community Social Work from a Social Services Department: Some Issues', *British Journal Social Work*, 13, 435–42.

— (2005) *The Origins of Social Work: continuity and change*, Basingstoke.

— (2012) *Citizenship Social Work with Older People*, Bristol.

Peace Corps Writers. (2008) *The Infamous Peace Corps Postcard*, Washington.

Pearce, J. (1993) *At the Heart of the Local Community: Community enterprise in a changing world*, London.

Pearce, J., et al. (2012) *Locally Rooted: hosting community organisers*, London.

Pearmain, D. (2011) *Faiths in Action – Final Evaluation Report*, London.

Pearse, I. and Crocker, L. (1941) *The Peckham Experiment: a study of the living culture of society*, London.

Pearson, S., et al. (2012) *Burngreave New Deal for Communities: End of programme evaluation*, Sheffield.

Pedersen, S. (2004a) *Eleanor Rathbone and the politics of conscience*, New Haven.

— (2004b) *Macadam, Elizabeth (1871–1948)*, Oxford.

Peirce, N. and Steinbach, C. (1985) *Corrective Capitalism: the rise of America's community development corporations*, New York.

Penn, R. and Alden, J. (1977) *Upper Afan C.D.P. Final Report to Sponsors, Joint Report by Action Team and Research Team Directors*, Cardiff.

Peräkylä, A. (2005) 'Analysing Talk and Text', in N. Denzin and Y. Lincoln (eds) *The SAGE Handbook of Qualitative Research*, Thousand Oaks.

Perez-Guerrero, M. (1950) 'The expanded program of technical assistance', *Unisilva*, 4, 1–3.

Perlman, R. (1999) 'High Hopes, Hard Realities', in J. Rothman (ed.) *Reflections on Community Organization: enduring themes; critical issues*, Itasca.

Perlman, R. and Guirin, A. (1972) *Community Organization and Social Planning*, New York.

Perry, C. (1913) *The Social Centers of 1912–1913*, New York.

— (1914) *The School as a Factor in Neighborhood Development – Proceedings of The National Conference of Charities and Correction, Memphis, Tenn.*, New York.

— (1916) *Education Extension*, Cleveland.

Perry, G. and Markwell, S. (2000) *Promoting Health in Wales – strengthening partnerships for Investment for Health*, Caerphilly.

Pestoff, V. and Brandsen, T. (2009) *Co-production: The Third Sector and the delivery of Public Services*, New York.

Peterson, J. (1965) 'From Social Settlements to Social Agency: settlement work in Columbus, Ohio 1898–1958', *Social Service Review*, 39, 191–208.

Petrovich, J. (2008) *Strategies for Improving Public Education – a Foundation goes back to School*, New York.

Pettit, W. (1928) *Case Studies in Community Organization*, New York.

Phillips, M. (1982) 'Separatism or black control', in A. Ohri, et al. (eds) *Community Work and Racism*, London.

Picciotto R. and Wiesner, E. (1998) *Evaluation and Development: the institutional dimension*, New Brunswick.

Pike, J. (1874) *The Prostrate State: South Carolina Under Negro Government*, New York.

Pincus, A. and Minahan, A. (1973) *Social Work Practice: Model and Method*, Itasca.

Pitchford, M. [with Henderson, P.] (2008) *Making Spaces for Community Development*, Bristol.

Pitt, J. and Keane, M. (1984) *Community Organising? You've never really tried it! The Challenge to Britain from the USA*, Birmingham.

Plater, C. (1914) *The Priest and Social Action*, London.

Plowden, L. (1967) *Children and their Primary Schools: A Report of the Central Advisory Council for Education (England)*, London.

Plummer, J. (1999) *Municipalities and Community Participation: a sourcebook for capacity building*, London.

— (2002) *Focusing Partnerships: a sourcebook for municipal capacity-building in Public-Private Partnerships*, London.

Poll, C. (2007) 'Co-Production: Support for Self-Employment', in S. Hunter and P. Richie (eds) *Co-Production and Personalisation in Social Care; Changing Relationships in the Provision of Social Care*, London, 49–73.

Popple, K. (1994) 'Towards a Progressive Community Work Praxis', in S. Jacobs and K. Popple (eds) *Community Work in the 1990s*, Nottingham.

— (1995) *Analysing Community Work: its theory and practice*, Buckingham.

Popple, K. and Quinney, A. (2002) 'Theory and practice of community development: a case study from the United Kingdom', *Journal of the Community Development Society*, 1, 9–24.

Popple, K. and Redmond, M. (2000) 'Community development and the voluntary sector in the new Millennium: the implications of the Third Way in the U.K.', *Community Development Journal*, 35, 391–400.

Potter, W. (1929) *Thomas Jackson of Whitechapel: a record of fifty years of social and evangelistic enterprise*, Liverpool.

Pradhan, S. (1998) 'Reinvigorating state institutions', in Picciotto, R. and Wiesner, E. (eds) *Evaluation and Development: the institutional dimension*, New Brunswick.

Pratt, J., et al. (1999) *Working Whole Systems: putting theory into practice*, London.

Pray, K. (1959) 'When is Community Organization Social Work Practice?', in E. Harper and A. Dunham (eds) *Community Organizing in Action – basic literature and critical comments*, New York.

Price, C. and Tsouros, A. (1996) *Our Cities, Our Future: Policies and Action Plans for Health and Sustainable Development*, Copenhagen.

Prince Edward Island Dept of Fisheries et al. (2009) *Rural Action Plan: A Rural Economic Development Strategy for Prince Edward Island*, Montague.

Pruger, R. and Specht, H. (1969) 'Assessing Theoretical Models of Community Organization Practice: Alinsky as a Case in Point', *Social Service Review*, 43, 123.

Public Finance Committee. (2012) *A Picture of Public Services*, Cardiff.

Putnam, R. (1993) *Making Democracy Work: civic traditions in modern Italy*, Princeton.

— (2002) *Bowling Alone: the collapse and revival of American community*, New York.

Putnam, R., et al. (2004) *Better together: restoring the American community*, New York.

Raeburn, J. and Corbett, T. (2001) *Community development: How effective is it as an approach in health promotion?*, University of Auckland.

Ragone, M. (2011) *Le parole di Danilo Dolci*, Agropoli.

Randall, C. and Corp, A. (2014) *Measuring National Well-being: European Comparisons*, London.

Rathbone, E. (1905) *William Rathbone: A Memoir*, New York.

Ravensbergen, F. and Van der Plaat, M. (2006) 'Barriers to citizen participation: the missing voices of people living with low income', *Community Development Journal*, 45, 389–403.

Raymond, S. (1921) 'The Responsibility of a Family Agency at a Time of Industrial Readjustment', *The Family*, 2, 120–4.

Reed, J., et al. (2004) *Health, Well-being and Older People*, Bristol.

Rein, M. (1977) 'Social Planning: The Search for Legitimacy', in N. Gilbert and H. Specht (eds) *Planning for Social Welfare: Issues, Models and Tasks*, Englewood Cliffs.

Remenyi, J. (2004) 'What is development?', in D. Kingsbury, et al. (eds) *Key Issues in Development*, Houndmills.

Renfrewshire Council. (2009) *Paisley West End Area Development Framework*, Paisley.

Residents and Associates of the South End House. (1898a) 'Social Recovery', in R. Wood (ed.) *The City Wilderness: A Settlement Study*, Boston.

— (1898b) *The City Wilderness: A Settlement Study*, Boston.

— (1903) *Americans in Process*, Boston.

Resnick, H. and Patti, R. (1980) 'An Overview of Organizational Change', in H. Resnick and R. Patti (eds) *Change from Within: Humanizing Social Welfare Organizations*, Philadelphia.

Rhodes, J., et al. (2007a) *The Single Regeneration Budget: Final Evaluation Part I: The Single Regeneration Budget and the Evolution of Policy*, Cambridge.

— (2007b) *The Single Regeneration Budget: Final Evaluation Part II: Tackling Regeneration: The Key Issues*, Cambridge.

— (2007c) *The Single Regeneration Budget: Final Evaluation Part III: Turning Areas Around: The Impact of SRB on Final Outcomes*, Cambridge.

Rice, S. (2010) 'The challenge of remaining unfinished in the campaign for justice', *Proceedings of the National CLC Conference*, Melbourne.

Richards, P. (1993) 'Cultivation: knowledge or performance?', in M. Hobart (ed.) *An Anthropological Critique of Development: the growth of ignorance*, London.

Richmond, M. (1907) *The Good Neighbor in the Modern City*, Philadelphia.

— (1908) 'The Family and the Social Worker', *Proceedings of the National Conference of Charities and Correction Thirty-fifth Annual Session City of Richmond, VA, May 6th to 13th*, Fort Wayne.

— (1917) *Social Diagnosis*, New York.

— (1920) 'What Are You Thinking?', *The Family*, 1, 1–4.

— (1922) *What is Social Casework? An introductory description*, New York.

— (1930) *The Long View: Papers and Addresses By Mary E. Richmond New York, 1917–1928*, Philadelphia.

Rifkin, S. (1996) 'Paradigms Lost: toward a new understanding of community participation in health programmes', *Acta Tropica*, 61, 79–92.

Riis, J. (1902) *The Battle with the Slum*, London.

Ritchie, F. (1917) *Community Work of the Young Men's Christian Association*, New York.

Rivera, F. and Erlich, J. (1998) *Community Organizing in a Diverse Society*, Boston.

— (2001) 'An Option Assessment Framework for Organizing in Emerging Minority Communities', in J. Tropman, et al., *Tactics; Techniques of Community Intervention*, Itasca.

Robertson, S. (2009) *Leslie Button and developmental group work*, London.

Robinson, J. (2011) *A Force to be reckoned with: a history of the Women's Institute*, London.

Robson, B. (1988) *Those Inner Cities: Reconciling the Social and Economic Aims of Urban Policy*, Oxford.

Roche, C. (1999) *Impact Assessment for Development Agencies: learning to value change*, Oxford.

— (2001) 'Impact Assessment: seeing the wood and the trees', in D. Eade (ed.) *Debating Development: NGOs and the future*, Oxford.

Rodham, H. (1969) *There is only the Fight: an analysis of the Alinsky model*, Wellesley.

Rogers, J. (1921) 'Community organization for community service', in J. McCulloch (ed.) *'Distinguished Service citizenship' – Annual Report, Southern Sociological Congress, Knoxville, Tennessee*, Washington.

Rogers, M. (1990) *Cold Anger: a story of faith and power politics*, Denton.

Rondinelli, D. (1993) *Development Projects as Policy Experiments: an adaptive approach to development administration*, London.

Rosenberg, L., et al. (1970) *Final Report Project Evaluation and the Project Appraisal Reporting System, Volume One, Contract No. csd-2510, July 24, 1970 Summary*, Atlanta.

Ross, F. (1989) *Conquering Goliath: Cesar Chavez at the beginning*, Keene.

Ross, M. (1955) *Community Organization: Theory and Principles*, New York.

— (1958) *Case Histories in Community Organization*, New York.

Rossetti, F. (1979) 'Politics and Participation: a case study', in P. Curno (ed.) *Political Issues and Community Work*, London.

Rossi, P., et al. (1999) *Evaluation: a systematic approach*, Thousand Oaks.

Rostow, W. (1960) *The Stages of Economic Growth: A Non-Communist Manifesto*, Cambridge.

Rothman, J. (1970) 'Three Models of Community Organization Practice', in F. Cox, et al. (eds) *Strategies of Community Organization: a book of readings*, Itasca.

— (1979) 'Three Models of Community Organization Practice, Their Mixing and Phasing', in F. Cox, et al. (eds) *Strategies of Community Organization: A Book of Readings*, Itasca.

— (1995) 'Approaches to Community Intervention', in J. Rothman et al. (eds) *Strategies of Community Intervention: macro practice*, Itasca.

— (2001) 'Approaches to Community Intervention', in J. Rothman, et al. (eds) *Strategies of Community Intervention*, Itasca.

— (2008) 'Multi Modes of Community Intervention', in J. Rothman, et al. (eds) *Strategies of Community Organization*, Peostra.

Rothman, J. and Tropeman, J. (1987) 'Models of Community and Macro Practice Perspectives: their mixing and phasing', in F. Cox, et al. (eds) *Strategies of Community Organization: macro practice*, Itasca.

Rothman, J. and Zald, M. (2001) 'Planning and Policy Practice', in J. Rothman, et al. (eds) *Strategies of Community Organization*, Itasca.

Rowntree, B. (1901) *Poverty: A Study of Town Life*, New York.

Rowntree, B. and Lasker, B. (1911) *Unemployment – a social study*, London.

Rowntree, B. and Pigou, A.C. (1914) *Lectures on Housing: The Warburton Lectures for 1914*, Manchester.

Rowntree, J. and Sherwell, A. (1899) *Temperance Problem and Social Reform*, New York.

Rubin, F. (1995) *A Basic Guide to Evaluation for Development Workers*, Oxford.

Rubin, H. (2000) *Renewing Hope within Neighbourhoods of Despair: the community-based development model*, New York.

Rubin, H. and Rubin, I. (2001) *Community Organizing and Development*, Boston.

Runnicles, D. (1970) 'The social worker and community action', in A. Lapping (ed.) *Community Action*, London.

Sabeti, H. (2009) *The Emerging Fourth Sector Executive Summary*, Washington.

Sagar, J. and Weil, M. (2013) 'Larger-scale Social Planning', in M. Weil, et al. (eds) *The Handbook of Community Practice*, Thousand Oaks.

Salmon, H. (1982) *Unemployment: Government Alternatives and the MSC – a radical look at government policy*, Sheffield.

Sanders, I. (1970) 'The Concept of Community Development', in L. Cary (ed.) *Community Development as a Process*, Columbia.

— (1975) 'Professional Roles in Planned Change', in R. Kramer and H. Specht (eds) *Readings in Community Organization Practice*, Englewood Cliffs.

Schaeffer, C. (1914) *Our Home Mission Work: An Outline Study of the Home Mission Work of the Reformed Church in the United States*, Philadelphia.

Schafer, E. (2006) *Lilian Baylis: a biography*, Hatfield.

Schechter, P. (2001) *Ida B. Wells-Barnett and American Reform, 1880–1930*, Chapel Hill.

Schmitz, M., et al. (2012) 'The association between neighbourhood social cohesion and hypertension management strategies in older adults', *Age and Ageing*, 41, 388–92.

Scott, E. (1919) *Scott's Official History of the American Negro in the World War*, Chicago.

Scott, J. (1925) *The Story of the Women's Institute Movement in England; Wales and Scotland*, Kingham.

Scott, M. (2010) 'Managing democracy, localism in crisis: from dissent to incorporation, dilution and fragmentation', *Community Development Journal*, 46, i66–i82.

Scottish Education Department, et al. (1966) *Social Work and the Community: proposals for re-organising Local Authority Services in Scotland*, Edinburgh.

Scottish Executive. (2004) *Working and learning together to build stronger communities – Scottish Executive Guidance for Community Learning and Development*, Edinburgh.

Scottish Executive, et al. (2007) *Better Community Engagement – a framework for learning*, Edinburgh.

Scottish Government. (2007) *Better Health, Better Care: Action Plan*, Edinburgh.

Scottish Office. (1998) *Communities Change through Learning: Report of the Working Group on the future of Community Education*, Edinburgh.

Sears, A. (1918) *The Charity Visitor: a handbook for beginners*, Chicago.

Secretary of State for Scotland. (1966) *Social Work in the Community: proposals for reorganising local authority services in Scotland*, Edinburgh.

Seebohm, S., et al. (1968) *Report of the Committee on Local Authority and Allied Personal Social Services* (The Seebohm Report), London.

Seedhouse, D. and Cribb, A. (eds) (1989) *Changing Ideas in Health Care*, Chichester.

Selby, B. (1990) Congregation and Community Development Project, in P. Ballard (ed.) *Issues in Church Related Community Work*, Cardiff.

Setterfield, M. (1997) *Abandoned Buildings: Models for Legislative and Enforcement Reform*, Hartford.

Shah, A. (1998) 'Fostering fiscally responsive and accountable governance: lessons from decentralization', in R. Picciotto and E. Wiesner (eds) *Evaluation and Development: the institutional dimension*, New Brunswick.

— (2012) *Foreign Aid for Development Assistance*, London.

Shah, N. (1989) 'It's up to you sisters: black women and social work', in M. Langan and P. Lee (eds) *Radical Social Work Today*, London.

Shapely, P. (ed.) (2013) *People and Planning: Report of the Committee on Public Participation in Planning (The Skeffington Committee) – Introduction by Peter Shapely*, London.

Shapiro, V., et al., (2015) 'Building Local Infrastructure for Community Adoption of Science-Based Prevention: The Role of Coalition Functioning', *Preventive Science*, 16, 1136–46.

Sharman, N. (1981) 'Review Article: Community Work and the Local Economy: The Influence of the British Community Development Projects', *Community Development Journal*, 16, 142–7.

Shaw, C. (1964) *Children and Young Persons Scotland: Report by the Committee Appointed by the Secretary of State for Scotland* (The Kilbrandon Report), Edinburgh.

Shaw, C. and McKay, H. (1969) *Juvenile delinquency and urban areas: a study of rates of delinquency in relation to differential characteristics of local communities in American cities* (revised edn), Chicago.

Shaw, M. (2008) 'Community development and the politics of community', *Community Development Journal* 43, 24–36.

— (2011) 'Stuck in the middle? Community development, community engagement and the dangerous business of learning for democracy', *Community Development Journal*, 46, 128–46.

Shepherd, A. (1998) *Sustainable Rural Development*, Houndmills.

Short, C. (1986) 'The MSC and special measures for unemployment', in C. Benn and J. Fairley (eds) *Challenging the MSC on Jobs, Education and Training*, London.

Silberman, C. (1964) *Crisis in Black and White*, New York.

Simey, M. (2005) *From Rhetoric to Reality: study of the work of F.G. D'Aeth, Social Administrator*, Liverpool.

Simon, J., et al. (2014) *Doing Social Innovation: a Guide for Practitioners*, Heidelberg.

Sinfield, A. (1970) 'Which way for Social Work?', in P. Townsend, et al. (eds) *The Fifth Social Service: nine Fabian essays*, London.

Singer, B. and Manton, K. (1998) 'The effects of health changes on projections of health service needs for the elderly population of the United States', *Proceedings of the National Academy of Sciences*, 95, 15618–22.

Sites, W. (1998) 'Communitarian theory and community development in the United States', *Community Development Journal*, 33, 57–65.

Skeffington, A. (1969) *People and Planning*, London.

Slavin, S. (1975) 'Concepts of Social Conflict: use in social work curriculum', in R. Kramer, et al. (eds) *Readings in Community Organization*, Englewood Cliffs.

Slayton, R. (1986) *Back of the Yards: the making of a local democracy*, Chicago.

Smale, G. and Bennett, W. (1989) *Pictures of Practice Volume 1: Community Social Work in Scotland*, London.

Smale, G. and Tuson, G. (1990) 'Community Social Work: foundation for the 1990s and beyond', in G. Darville and G. Smale (eds) *Partners in Empowerment: networks of innovation in Social Work*, London.

Smale, G., et al. (1988) *Community Social Work: A Paradigm for Change*, London.

Smiles, S. (1873) *Self Help: with illustrations of Conduct and Perseverance*, London.

Smith, C. and Anderson, B. (1972) 'Political Participation through Community Action', in G. Parry (ed.) *Participation in Politics*, Manchester.

Smith, J. (1978) 'Hard Lines and Soft Options: a criticism of some Left attitudes to community work', in P. Curno (ed.) *Political Issues and Community Work*, London.

— (1981) 'Possibilities for a Socialist Community Work Practice', in P. Henderson and D. Thomas (eds) *Readings in Community Work*, London.

Smith, J., et al. (1978) *Towards a Definition of Community Work*, London.

Smith, R. (1916) *Organization and Cooperation are the Only Hopes for the Black Man in this Country*, Kansas City.

Social Exclusion Unit. (1998) *Bringing Britain Together: a national strategy for neighbourhood renewal*, London.

— (2001) *A New Commitment to Neighbourhood Renewal National Strategy Action Plan, Report by the Social Exclusion Unit*, London.

Social Welfare History Project. (2013) *Arthur Dunham*, Cincinnati.

Southern Health and Social Services Board. (2000) *Working in Partnership: Community Development and Health and Social Services — a strategy for public participation, equity and inclusion*, Newry.

Southgate, G. (1958) *English Economic History*, London.

Specht, H. (1969) 'Disruptive Tactics', in R. Kramer and H. Specht (eds) (1969) *Readings in Community Organization Practice*, Englewood Cliffs.

— (1976) *The Community Development Project: National and local strategies for improving the delivery of services*, London.

— (1977a) 'Theory as a guide to practice', in H. Specht and A. Vickery (eds) *Integrating Social Work Methods*, London.

— (1977b) 'Issues and Problems in Utilizing a Unitary Method', in H. Specht and A. Vickery (eds) *Integrating Social Work Methods*, London.

— (1979) 'Disruptive Tactics', in R. Kramer and H. Specht (eds) *Readings in Community Organization Practice*, Englewood Cliffs.

Specht, H. and Courtney, M. (1994) *Unfaithful Angels: how social work abandoned its mission*, New York.

Spergel, I. (1969) *Community Problem Solving: The Delinquency Example*, Chicago.

Staples, L. (1984) *Roots to Power: a manual for grassroots organizing*, New York.

State Council of Defense California. (1918) *Hand Book on Community Organization*, Sacramento.

Steiner, J. (1925) *Community Organization: a study of its theory and current practice*, New York.

Stephens, L., et al. (2006) *A Manifesto for growing the new economy*, London.

Stevenson, O. (1978) 'Some Educational Implications', in O. Stevenson and P. Parsloe (eds) *Social service teams: the practitioner's view*, London.

— (1996) 'Old People and Empowerment: the position of old people in contemporary British society', in P. Parsloe (ed.) *Pathways to Empowerment*, Birmingham.

Stewart, W. (1911) *The Philanthropic Work of Josephine Shaw Lowell: Containing a Biographical Sketch of her Life Together With a Selection of her Public Papers and Private Letters*, New York.

Stiglitz, J. (1998) 'Evaluatiion and an incentive instrument', in R. Picciotto and E. Wiesner, (eds) *Evaluation and Development: the institutional dimension*, New Brunswick.

Stiles, W. (1998) 'Communitarian theory and community development in the United States', *Community Development Journal*, 33, 57–65.

Stoecker, R. (1997) 'The imperfect practice of collaborative research: the "Working Group on Neighborhoods" in Toledo, Ohio', in P. Nyden et al. (eds) *Building Community: Social Science in Action*, Thousand Oaks.

Storey, A. (2001) 'The World Bank, neo-liberalism and power: discourse analysis and implications for campaigners', in D. Eade and E. Ligteringen (eds) *Debating Development*, Oxford.

Strauss, A. and Corbin, J. (1998) *Basics of Qualitative Research: techniques and procedures for developing grounded theory*, Thousand Oaks.

SWAPAC. (1980) *Final Report 1976–1980*, Merthyr Tydfil.

Swedner, H. (1983a) 'The Role of Sociologists in Community Planning', in H. Swedner (ed.) *Human Welfare and Action Research in Urban Settings*, Stockholm.

— (1983b) 'A White Island in a Black Sea', in H. Swedner (ed.) *Human Welfare and Action Research in Urban Settings*, Stockholm.

Talbott, M. (2012) *Madeline Talbott*, Chicago. On-line source.

— (1997) 'Chicago Association of Community Organizations for Reform Now [ACORN]', in P. Nyden, et al. (eds) (1997) *Building Community: Social Science in Action*, Thousand Oaks.

Tallon, A. (2009) *Urban Regeneration on the UK*, London.

Taoiseach (Office of). (2000) *Programme for Prosperity and Fairness*, Dublin.

Taylor, M. (1980) *Street Level: two resource centres and their users*, London.

— (1992) *Signposts to Community Development*, London.

Taylor, G. (1913) *Religion in Social Action*, New York.

Taylor, V. (2012) *Leading for Health and Wellbeing*, London.

TEPSIE. (2014) *Social Innovation Theory and Research: a Guide for Researchers*, Copenhagen.

Terry, D. (1988) *Albert Raby, Civil Rights Leader in Chicago with King, dies at 55*, New York.

Thake, Stephen. (1995) *The effect of community regeneration organisations on neighbourhood regeneration*, York.

— (2001) *Building communities, changing lives. The contribution of large, independent neighbourhood regeneration organisations*, York.

Thayer, W. (1919) *Theodore Roosevelt: an intimate biography*, Boston.

Thomas, A. (2000) 'What makes good development management?', in T. Wallace (ed.) *Development and Management*, Oxford.

Thomas, D. (1975) 'Chaucer House Tenants' Association: A case study', in P. Leonard (ed.) *The Sociology of Community Action, Monograph 21*, Keele.

— (1976) *Organising for Social Change: a study in the theory and practice of community work*, London.

— (1983) *The Making of Community Work*, London.
— (1995a) *Helping Communities to Better Health: the community development approach*, Cardiff.
— (1995b) *Community Development at Work*, London.
— (1996) *Uses and Abuses of Community Development: essays from the work of the Community Development Foundation*, London.
Thomas, G. (Departmental Minister for Social Services). (2012) *Speech to Age Alliance Wales Conference, 10th March 2011*, Cardiff.
— (2014) *Statement: Social Services and Well-being (Wales) Bill: Approach to Implementation*, Cardiff.
Thompson, E. (1968) *The making of the English Working Class*, London.
Thompson, P. (2005) 'Who's Afraid of Saul Alinsky? – Radical Traditions in Community Organising', *Forum*, 47, 199–206.
Topping, P. and Smith, G. (1977) *Government Against Poverty: Liverpool Community Development Project 1970–75*, Oxford.
Törnquist, O. (1999) *Politics and Development: a critical introduction*, London.
Townsend, P. (1979) *Poverty in the United Kingdom: A Survey of Household Resources and Standards of Living*, Harmondsworth.
— (1981) 'The Structured Dependency of the Elderly: A Creation of Social Policy in the Twentieth Century', *Ageing and Society*, 1, 28.
Townsend, P. (2001) *Targeting Poor Health: Report to the Health and Social Services Committee of the National Assembly for Wales: 4 July 2001*, Cardiff.
Toye, J. (1993) *Dilemmas of Development: Reflections on the Counter-Revolution in Development Economics*, Oxford.
Trecker, H. (1959) 'Planning', in E. Harper and A. Dunham (eds) *Community Organizing in Action – basic literature and critical comments*, New York.
Tsouros, A. (1990) 'Healthy cities means community action', *Health Promotion International*, 5, 117–18.
— (1995) 'The WHO Healthy Cities Project: state of the art and future plans', *Health Promotion International*, 10, 133–41.
— (ed.). (1992) *World Health Organisation Healthy Cities Project: A Project Becomes a Movement; Review of Progress 1987–1990*, Milan.
Turbett, C. (2014) *Doing Radical Social Work*, Basingstoke.
Twelvetrees, A. (1976) *Community Associations and Centres: a comparative study*, Oxford.
— (1980) North Braunstone Age Concern Group, in G. Craig (ed.) *Community Work Case Studies*, 2nd edn, London.
— (1989) *Organizing for Neighbourhood Development: a comparative study of community development corporations and citizen power organizations*, Aldershot.
— (1996) *Organizing for Neighbourhood Development: Comparative Study of Community Based Development Organizations*, Aldershot.

— (2008) *Community Work*, London.

Twigger, R. and House of Commons. (1998) *The Barnett Formula Research Paper 98/8*, London.

UN ACC Task Force on Rural Development – Panel on Monitoring and Evaluation. (1984) *Guiding Principles for the Design and use of M&E in rural development programmes and projects*, Rome.

UN Bureau of Social Affairs. (1955) *Social Progress through Community Development*, New York.

UN General Assembly. (2000) *Resolution adopted by the General Assembly 55/2. United Nations Millennium Declaration*, New York.

— (2014) *The road to dignity by 2030: ending poverty, transforming all lives and protecting the planet. Synthesis report of the Secretary-General on the post-2015 sustainable development agenda – Sixty-ninth session: Agenda items 13(a) and 115*, New York.

UN Human Development Programme. (1990) *Human Development Report 1990: Concept and measurement of human development*, New York.

UN Research Institute for Social Development. (2011) *Social Development in an Uncertain World UNRISD Research Agenda 2010–2014*, Geneva.

UN Secretariat: Department of Economic and Social Affairs (2014) *The Millennium Development Goals Report 2014*, New York.

— (2015) Mission Statement: Division for Sustainable Development, New York.

United Nations. (1983) *Vienna International Plan of Action on Aging*, New York.

— (1992) *Sustainable Development: Nations Conference on Environment; Development – Rio de Janeiro, Brazil, 3 to 14 June 1992 – AGENDA 21*, New York.

— (2002) *Report of the Second World Assembly on Ageing Madrid, 8–12 April 2002*, New York.

— (2012) *The Millennium Development Goals Report 2012*, New York.

— (2014) *Major Group Position Paper NGOs Major Group's vision and priorities for the Sustainable Development Goals*, New York.

United States Congress. (1916) 'Army Appropriation Act (39 Stat. 649), August 29, 1916. 39 Stat 649', Washington.

United Way, (2008) *Goals for the common good: the United Way challenge to America –What gets measured gets done*, United Way, Alexandria.

Unwin, J. and Molyneux, P. (2005) *The Voluntary Sector Delivering Public Services – Part II*, York.

Uphoff, N. (1991) 'A Field Methodology for Participatory Self-Evaluation', *Community Development Journal*, 26, 271–85.

— (1995) 'Why NGOs are not a Third Sector: a Sectorial Analysis with Some Thoughts on Accountability, Sustainability and Evaluation', in M. Edwards and D. Hulme (eds) *Non-Governmental Organisations: Performance and Accountability: Beyond the magic bullet*, London.

— (2005) 'Analytical Issues in Measuring Empowerment at the Community and Local Levels', in D. Narayan (ed.) *Measuring Empowerment Cross-disciplinary perspectives*, Washington.

van Kleeck, M. and Taylor, G. (1922) 'The Professional Organization of Social Work', *Annals of the American Academy of Political and Social Science*, 168, New York.

Vazquez, R. (2005) *The San Antonio COPS revolution*, Tucson.

Vickery, A. (1977) 'Social Work Practice: divisions and unifications', in H. Specht and A. Vickery (eds) *Integrating social work methods*, London.

Waddington, P. (1979) 'Looking Ahead – Community Work into the 1980s', *Community Development Journal*, 14, 224–34.

— (1994) 'The Values Base of Community Work', in S. Jacobs and K. Popple (eds) *Community Work in the 1990s*, Nottingham.

Wales Centre for Health (2007) *Doing it differently in Wales*, Cardiff.

Walker, E. (1974) *Interview with Ella Baker*, Durham.

Walker, P. and Shannon, P. (2011) 'Participatory governance: towards a strategic model', *Community Development Journal*, 46, ii63–ii82.

Wallace, T. (2000) 'Development management and the AID chain', in T. Wallace (ed.) *Development and Management*, Oxford.

Wallerstein, N. (1993) 'Empowerment and health: the theory and practice of community change', *Community Development Journal*, 28, 218–27.

— (2006) *What is the evidence on effectiveness of empowerment to improve health?*, Copenhagen.

Walls, D. (2014) *Community Organizing: fanning the flame of democracy*, Oxford.

Walton, R. (1979) 'Two Strategies of Social Change and their Dilemmas', in R. Kramer and H. Specht (eds) *Readings in Community Organization Practice*, Englewood Cliffs.

Wanless, D. (2002) *Securing Our Future Health: taking a long-term view – Final Report*, London.

Wanless, D., et al. (2006) *Securing Good Care for Older People: taking a long-term view*, London.

Warburton, D. (1988) 'A Passionate Dialogue: community and sustainable development', in D. Warburton (ed.) *Community and Sustainable Development: participation in the future*, London.

Warburton, J., et al. (2013) 'Social inclusion in an ageing world: introduction to the special issue', *Ageing and Society*, 33, 1–15.

Ward, E. (1915) *The Social Center*, New York.

Ward, J. (1975) 'In-Service Community Work Training: a job-centred approach', in D. Jones and M. Mayo (eds) *Community Work Two*, London.

Ward, S. (1855) *Autobiography: A Fugitive Negro. His Anti-Slavery Labours in United States, Canada; England*, London.

Ware, L. (1938) *Jacob A. Riis*, New York.

Warren, M. (2001) *Dry Bones Rattling: community building to revitalize American democracy*, Boston.

Watson, F. (1922) *The Charity Organization Movement in the United States: A Study in American Philanthropy*, New York.

Watson, J. (1999) *The Verona Initiative 1998–2000: update report*, Edinburgh.

— (2000) *Verona Benchmark: guide to the assessment of good practice within partnership working*, Edinburgh.

Watson, J., et al. (2001) 'The Verona Benchmark: applying evidence to improve the quality of partnership working', Geneva.

Webster, G. (2003) 'Sustaining community involvement in programme and project development', in S. Banks, et al. (eds) *Managing Community Practice: principles, policies, and programmes*, Bristol.

WEFO. (2008) *2000–2006 Programme Closure Guidance Note 1, and Note 2*, Cardiff.

Weil, M. (2013) 'Community-based Social Planning', in M. Weil, et al. (eds) *The Community Practice Handbook*, Thousand Oaks.

Weil, M. and Ohmer, M. (2013) 'Applying Practice Theories in Community Work', in M. Weil, et al. (eds) *The Handbook of Community Practice*, Thousand Oaks.

Weil, M., et al. (eds) (2014) *The Community Practice Handbook*, Thousand Oaks.

Wellbeing Wales Network. (2010) *Exploring Sustainable Wellbeing – or how to measure the real impact of a project or organisation – Facilitator's Manual*, Cardiff.

Wells, B., et al. (1999) 'Growing food, growing community: community-supported agriculture in rural Iowa', *Community Development Journal*, 34, 70–5.

Wells-Barnett, I. (1892) *Southern Horrors: Lynch Law in All Its Phases*, New York.

Welsh Assembly Government. (2000) *WEFO Takes Forward £100 Million Fast Track Package*, Cardiff.

— (2002a) *When I'm 64 ... and more: The report from the advisory group on a strategy for older people in Wales*, Cardiff.

— (2002b) *Communities First: Guidance for Co-ordinators*, Cardiff.

— (2002c) *Well-being in Wales – Consultation Document*, Cardiff.

— (2003a) *Wales: a better country*, Cardiff.

— (2003b) *Healthy and Active Lifestyles in Wales: a framework for action*, Cardiff.

— (2003c) *The Strategy for Older People in Wales: implementation project plan*, Cardiff.

— (2003d) *The Review of Health and Social Care in Wales: The Report of the Project Team advised by Derek Wanless*, Cardiff.

— (2003e) *Health, Social Care; Well-being Strategies: Preparing a Strategy*, Cardiff.

— (2004a) *Making the Connections: delivering better services for Wales*, Cardiff.

— (2004b) *Starting to Live Differently: The Sustainable Development Scheme of the National Assembly for Wales. Under Section 121 of the Government of Wales Act*, Cardiff.

— (2004c) *The Sustainable Development Action Plan 2004–2007*, Cardiff.

— (2005a) *A Report on the Second Year of the Strategy for Older People in Wales*, Cardiff.

— (2005b) *Healthy Ageing Action Plan for Wales – A response to Health Challenge Wales*, Cardiff.

— (2005c) *Flying Start – consultation document*, Cardiff.

— (2006a) *Interim evaluation of Communities First: Final Report*, Cardiff.

— 2006b) *People, Plans and Partnerships: A National Evaluation of Community Strategies in Wales.*

— (2006c) *Beyond Boundaries – Citizen-Centred Local Services for Wales: Review of Local Service Delivery – the 'Beecham Report'*, Cardiff.

— (2006d) *Making the connections: building better customer service – good practice guidance for public services. A consultation by the Welsh Assembly Government*, Cardiff.

— (2007a) *Fulfilled Lives, Supportive Communities: A summary – Improving social services in Wales from 2008–2018 – A summary*, Cardiff.

— (2007b) *One Wales: progressive agenda for the government of Wales – An agreement between the Labour and Plaid Cymru Groups in the National Assembly*, Cardiff.

— (2007c) *Communities First Guidance 2007*, Cardiff.

— (2008a) *Local Vision Statutory Guidance from the Welsh Assembly Government on developing and delivering community strategies*, Cardiff.

— (2008b) *One Wales: One Planet: Consultation on a new Sustainable Development Scheme for Wales*, Cardiff.

— (2008c) *Communities Next – Consultation on the future of the Communities First Programme*, Cardiff.

— (2008d) *Welsh Index of Multiple Deprivation*, Cardiff.

— (2008e) *'The third dimension' Strategic Action Plan for the Voluntary Sector Scheme*, Cardiff.

— (2008f) *Cymorth: Children and Youth Support Fund Guidance*, Cardiff.

— (2009a) *Our Healthy Future: technical working paper*, Cardiff.

— (2009b) *Flying Start and Cymorth: An Interim Evaluation Report*, Cardiff.

— (2009c) *Rural Health Plan – Improving integrated service delivery across Wales*, Cardiff.

— (2009d) *The All Wales Community Cohesion Strategy: Consultation Document*, Cardiff.

— (2009e) *A Community Nursing Strategy for Wales – Consultation Document*, Cardiff.

— (2009f) *Older People's Wellbeing Monitor for Wales 2009*, Cardiff.

— (2010a) *Sustainable Development Indicators for Wales*, Cardiff.

— (2010b) *Paying for Care in Wales: Written and On-Line Responses to the Green Paper Consultation: Consultation Report*, Cardiff.

— (2010c) *'Working with Communities': The Community Development Workforce Action Plan for Wales*, Cardiff.

— (2011) *What is Public Health?*, Cardiff.

Welsh Government. (2011a) *The Strategy for Older People in Wales Annual Report 2009–10 Living Longer Living Better*, Cardiff.

— (2011b) *Communities First – the future: consultation document*, Cardiff.

— (2011c) *Programme for Government – creating the Wales of the future is something that involves all of us*, Welsh Government, Cardiff.

— (2011d) *Hard to Engage!? A toolkit for engaging communities – Final Report*, Cardiff.

— (2012a) *Shared Purpose – Shared Delivery – Consultation Document*, Cardiff.

— (2012b) *Shared Purpose – Shared Delivery – Guidance on integrating Partnerships and Plans – Version 2 – December 2012*, Cardiff.

— (2012c) *Tackling Poverty Action Plan 2012–2016*, Cardiff.

— (2012d) *Communities First – the future: your short Consultation Guide*, Cardiff.

— (2012e) *White Paper: A Sustainable Wales Better Choices for a Better Future – Consultation on proposals for a Sustainable Development Bill*, Cardiff.

— (2012f) *Together for Health A Five Year Vision for the NHS in Wales*, Cardiff.

— (2012g) *Vibrant & Viable Places New Regeneration Framework – Consultation Document*, Cardiff.

— (2013) *The Sustainable Development Duty and Collaborative Working Discussion paper for Local Service Boards*, Cardiff.

— (2014) *Community Cohesion National Delivery Plan 2014–2016*. Welsh Government, Cardiff.

— (2015) *Well-being of Future Generations (Wales) Bill* [as passed], Cardiff.

Welsh Health Planning Forum. (1994) *Health; Social Care 2010: a report on Phase One*, Cardiff.

Welsh NHS Confederation. (2009) *A Community Nursing Strategy for Wales – Schedule of comments on the proposals contained within the consultative paper*, Cardiff.

Welsh Office. (1983) *All Wales Strategy for the Development of Services for Mentally Handicapped People*, Cardiff.

— (1985) *A Good Old Age: an initiative on care of the aged in Wales*, London.

— (1998a) *Better Health Better Wales*, London.

— (1998b) *Involving the Public*, Cardiff.

— (1998c) *Establishing Local Health Groups – Final Draft 2*, Cardiff.

— (1998d) *Better Health Better Wales: Strategic Planning Framework*, Cardiff.

— (1999) *Sure Start: A Programme to Increase Opportunity for very young children and their families in Wales, Welsh Office Circular 21/99*, Cardiff.

White, D. (2010) *HUD Awards Six Housing Authorities $113.6 Million To Revitalize Public Housing, Transform Surrounding Neighborhood*, Washington.

White, S. and Tiongco, R. (1997) *Doing Theology and Development: meeting the challenge of poverty*, Edinburgh.

Whitehead, M. and Dahlgren, G. (2006) *Levelling Up – Part I – a discussion paper on concepts and principles for tackling social inequalities in health*, Copenhagen.

WHO Regional Office for Europe. (1981) *Resolution WPR/RC32.R5 Strategies for Health for All by the Year 2000*, Copenhagen.

— (1985) *Targets for Health for All 2000: targets in support of the European Regional strategy for Health for All*, Copenhagen.

— (1986) *Evaluation of the Strategy for Health for All by the Year 2000 – Seventh Report on the World Health Situation, Volume 5*, Copenhagen.

— (1994) *Action for Health in Cities*, Copenhagen.

— (1996) *City Health Planning: the Framework*, Copenhagen.

— (1997) *Twenty steps for developing a Healthy Cities project*, Copenhagen.

— (1999) *Health21: The Health for All policy framework for the WHO European Region*, Copenhagen.

— (2000a) *Investment for Health: a briefing document on the concept and principles*, Copenhagen.

— (2000b) *The Verona Challenge – investing for health is investing for development*, Copenhagen.

— (2000c) *Verona Benchmark: facilitator guidance, partnership profile and audit templates*, Copenhagen.

— (2002) *Community participation in local health and sustainable development: approaches and techniques*, Copenhagen.

— (2008) *Approaching Mental Health Care Reform Regionally: The mental Health Project for South-eastern Europe*, Copenhagen.

— (2012) *European Action Plan for Strengthening Public Health Capacities and Services*, Copenhagen.

WHO Study Group. (1991) *Community Involvement in Health Development: challenging health services*, Geneva.

Wiesner, E. (1998) 'Transaction cost economics and public sector rent-seeking in developing countries: toward a theory of governance failure', in R. Picciotto and E. Wiesner, *Evaluation and Development: the institutional dimension*, New Brunswick.

Williams, G. (1979) 'Looking Back on British Community Work Practice', *Community Development Journal*, 14, 189–91.

Williamson, D. (2010) 'Ring-fencing NHS spending will "devastate health", Plaid claims', *Western Mail*, 9 November, Cardiff.

Willmott, P. (1989) *Community Initiatives: patterns and perspectives*, London.

Wils, F. (1995) 'Scaling-up, mainstreaming and accountability: the challenge for NGOs', in M. Edwards and D. Hulme (eds) *Non-Governmental Organisations – performance, and accountability: beyond the Magic Bullet*, London.

Wilson, E. (1977) 'Women in the community', in M. Mayo (ed.) *Women in the Community*, London.

Wilson, L. (1919) *Community Leadership: The new profession*, New York.

Wilson, W. (1987) *The Truly Disadvantaged: the inner city, the Underclass, and public policy*, Chicago.

Wintour, P. (2009) *Zimbabwe: rebuilding a nation*, Bexleyheath.

Wisconsin State Superintendent of Schools. (1913) *Social and Civic Work Country Communities: Bulletin No. 18: Report Of A Subcommittee of the Committee of Fifteen Appointed by the State Superintendent Of Schools to Investigate Conditions in the Rural Schools of Wisconsin*, Madison.

Wistow, G., et al. (1994) *Social Care in a Mixed Economy*, Buckingham.

WLGA. (2012) *Bringing generations together in Wales*, Cardiff.

— (2013a) *Equality and Integrated Planning: An advice note for local authorities in Wales*, Cardiff.

— (2013b) *WLGA Response: The Sustainable Development Duty and Collaborative Working: Discussion paper for Local Service Boards*, Cardiff.

Woods, R. (1891) *English Social Movements*, Charles Scribner's Sons, New York.

Woods, R. (1923) 'University settlements: their point and drift', in R. Woods (ed.) *The Neighborhood in Nation-Building. The running comment of thirty years at South End House*, Boston.

Woods, R. and Kennedy, A. (1911) *Handbook of Settlements*, New York.

— (1913) *Young Working Girls: A Summary of Evidence from Two Thousand Social Workers*, Boston.

— (1922) *The Settlement Horizon: A National Estimate*, New York.

Wooton, B. (1959) *Social Science and Social Pathology*, London.

World Bank. (2004) *2004 World Development Indicators*, Washington.

— (2011) *What is Social Capital?*, Washington.

World Health Organization. (1947) *Chronicle of the WHO*, Geneva.

— (1968) *The Second Ten Years of the World Health Organization 1958–1967*, Geneva.

— (1978) *Declaration of Alma-Ata: International Conference on Primary Health Care, Alma-Ata, USSR, 6–12 September 1978*, Geneva.

— (1981) *Global Strategy for Health for All by the Year 2000*, Geneva.

— (1985) *Community Involvement for Health Development: Report of the inter-regional meeting in Brioni, Yugoslavia, 9–14 June, 1985*, Geneva.

— (1986) *Ottawa Charter for Health Promotion*, Geneva.

— (1996) *The Ljubljana Charter on Reforming Health Care, 1996*, Geneva.

— (1997a) *Jakarta Declaration on Leading Health Promotion into the 21st Century*, Geneva.

— (1997b) *Jakarta Statement on Healthy Ageing*, Geneva.

— (1997c) *Brasilia Declaration on Ageing 1996*, Geneva.

— (2008) *Primary Health Care: Now More Than Ever – The World Health Report 2008: primary health care now more than ever*, Geneva.

World Health Organization and Litsios, S. (2008) *The Third Ten Years Of the World Health Organization 1968–1977*, Geneva.

York Consulting and Welsh Government. (2006) *Detailed Findings: First Stage Evaluation of Children and Young People's Frameworks, Early Entitlement and Cymorth*, Cardiff.

Younghusband, E. (1964) *Social Work and Social Change*, London.

Zald, M. (1975) 'Organizations as Polities: An Analysis of Community Organisation Agencies', in R. Kramer and H. Specht (eds) *Readings in Community Organization Practice*, Englewood Cliffs.

Ziglio, E., et al. (2000) *Increasing Investment for Health: progress so far – Report to the Fifth Global Conference on Health Promotion, Mexico, June 5–9, 2000*, Copenhagen.

Zimbabwe (Government of Zimbabwe) (1991) *Zimbabwe – A framework of Economic Reform (1991–95)*, Harare.

Index